Communications in Computer and Information Science 1116

Commenced Publication in 2007
Founding and Former Series Editors:
Phoebe Chen, Alfredo Cuzzocrea, Xiaoyong Du, Orhun Kara, Ting Liu,
Krishna M. Sivalingam, Dominik Ślęzak, Takashi Washio, Xiaokang Yang,
and Junsong Yuan

More information about this series at http://www.springer.com/series/7899

V. S. Shankar Sriram · V. Subramaniyaswamy ·
N. Sasikaladevi · Leo Zhang ·
Lynn Batten · Gang Li (Eds.)

Applications and Techniques in Information Security

10th International Conference, ATIS 2019
Thanjavur, India, November 22–24, 2019
Proceedings

 Springer

Editors
V. S. Shankar Sriram ⓘ
School of Computing
SASTRA University
Thanjavur, India

N. Sasikaladevi ⓘ
School of Computing
SASTRA University
Thanjavur, India

Lynn Batten ⓘ
School of Information Technology
Deakin University
Geelong, VIC, Australia

V. Subramaniyaswamy
School of Computing
SASTRA University
Thanjavur, India

Leo Zhang
School of Information Technology
Deakin University
Geelong, VIC, Australia

Gang Li ⓘ
School of Information Technology
Deakin University
Geelong, VIC, Australia

ISSN 1865-0929   ISSN 1865-0937 (electronic)
Communications in Computer and Information Science
ISBN 978-981-15-0870-7   ISBN 978-981-15-0871-4 (eBook)
https://doi.org/10.1007/978-981-15-0871-4

This Springer imprint is published by the registered company Springer Nature Singapore Pte Ltd.
The registered company address is: 152 Beach Road, #21-01/04 Gateway East, Singapore 189721, Singapore

Preface

The Applications and Techniques in Information Security (ATIS) conference series has been held annually since 2010 in various countries. The 10th ATIS conference was organized by the School of Computing, SASTRA Deemed University, Tamil Nadu, India, during November 22–24, 2019. ATIS 2019 focused on various techniques and applications in information security research. It included a global blend of participants from industry and academia. This volume includes all the accepted papers of this conference.

ATIS 2019 received 50 papers pertaining to the theme of the conference. Each paper was reviewed by three experts from the international Program Committee. As a result of a thorough review process, 24 papers were selected for publication in the current proceedings (an acceptance rate of 48%). The program of this conference included several outstanding keynote lectures presented by internationally renowned and distinguished researchers: Prof. V. Kamakoti (IIT Madras, India), Prof. Aditya P. Mathur, (Professor of Computer Science, Purdue University, West Lafayette, IN, USA; Professor and Center Director, iTrust, SUTD, Singapore), Prof. Kasi Periyasamy (Professor and MSE Program Director, University of Wisconsin-La Crosse, WI, USA), and Prof. Lejla Batina (Professor in Digital Security, Institute for Computing and Information Sciences, Radboud University, the Netherlands). Their keynote speeches contributed towards increasing the overall quality of the program and significance of the themes of the conference.

At this juncture, we would like to thank everyone involved in the successful completion of ATIS 2019. Especially, it is our immense pleasure to thank the Program Committee, for their diligence and concern towards the quality of the program. The conference also relies on the efforts of ATIS 2019 Organizing Committee. Specifically, we thank Prof. Lynn Batten, Dr. Gang Li, Prof. V. S. Shankar Sriram, Dr. V. Subramaniyaswamy, Ms. H. Anila Glory, and Mr. T. Santosh for dealing with the general administrative issues, the registration process, and the maintaining of the conference website. Finally, and most importantly, we thank all the authors, who are the primary reason for the success of ATIS 2019.

September 2019

N. Sasikaladevi
Leo Zhang

Organization

ATIS 2019 was organized by School of Computing, SASTRA Deemed University, Thanjavur, TamilNadu, India.

ATIS 2019 Organizing Committee

General Chair

Gang Li — Deakin University, Australia

Program Co-chairs

Leo Zhang — Deakin University, Australia
N. Sasikala Devi — SASTRA Deemed University, India

Local Organizing Committee

V. S. Shankar Sriram (Chair) — SASTRA Deemed University, India
V. Subramaniyaswamy — SASTRA Deemed University, India
Lynn Batten — Deakin University, Australia
H. Anila Glory (Secretary) — SASTRA Deemed University, India

Web Masters

Ziwei Hou — Deakin University, Australia
T. Santosh — SASTRA Deemed University, India

ATIS Steering Committee

Lynn Batten (Chair) — Deakin University, Australia
Heejo Lee — Korea University, South Korea
Jiqiang Liu — Beijing Jiaotong University, China
Tsutomu Matsumoto — Yokohama National University, Japan
Wenjia Niu — Institute of Information Engineering, Chinese Academy of Sciences, China
Yuliang Zheng — University of Alabama at Birmingham, USA
Gang Li (Secretary) — Deakin University, Australia

Program Committee

Heejo Lee — CCS Lab, Korea University, South Korea
John Yearwood — Deakin University, Australia
R. Muthaiah — SASTRA Deemed University, India

Kwangjo Kim	KAIST, South Korea
Rakesh Kumar Sehgal	Associate Director at CDAC Mohali, India
B. K. Murthy (Scientist G and Group Coordinator)	R&D in IT Group, MietY, India
Lei Pan	Deakin University, Australia
Leijla Batina	Radboud University, The Netherlands
Arvind Kumar (Scientist G and Group Coordinator)	MietY, India
Latit Garg	University of Malta, Malta
Qingyun Liu	Institute of Information Engineering, Chinese Academy of Sciences, China
Rafiqul Islam	Charles Sturt University, Australia
Morshed Choudhury	Deakin University, Australia
Matthew Warren	Deakin University, Australia
Ping Xiong	Zhongnan University of Economics and Law, China
Jinqiao Shi	Institute of Information Engineering, Chinese Academy of Sciences, China
K. R. Manjula	SASTRA Deemed University, India
Steve Versteeg	CA, Australia
Qiujun Lan	Hunan University, China
Gang Xiong	Institute of Information Engineering, Chinese Academy of Sciences, China
V. Venkatesh	SASTRA Deemed University, India
Ziqi Yan	Beijing Jiaotong University, China
Xun Yi	RMIT University, Australia
Leonie Simpson	Queensland University of Technology, Australia

Sponsoring Organizations

Contents

Intrusion Detection System

Authentication and Key Management System

Security Centric Applications

Information Security

A Memory-Efficient Multiple String Matching Algorithm Based on Charset Transformation

Yuhai Lu[1,2], Yanbing Liu[1(✉)], Gongxin Sun[1,2], and Jianlong Tan[1]

[1] Institute of Information Engineering, Chinese Academy of Sciences, Beijing, China
{luyuhai,liuyanbing,sungongxin,tanjianlong}@iie.ac.cn
[2] School of Cyber Security, University of Chinese Academy of Sciences,
Beijing, China

Abstract. Multiple string matching algorithm is a core technology in network intrusion detection system. Automata based matching algorithms such as AC and BOM are widely used in practical systems because of their excellent matching performance, but the huge memory usage of automata restricts them to be applied to large-scale pattern set. In this paper, we proposed a charset-transformation-based multiple string matching algorithm named CTM to reduce the memory usage of the automata. Based on the classical compression algorithm banded-row, CTM algorithm optimizes the compression method and increases the compression rate. The proposed CTM algorithm plays a charset transformation on the charset of the patterns to increase the continuity of distribution of non-empty elements in the automata, and then uses the banded-row method to compress the automata. Experiments on random ASCII charset show that the proposed algorithm significantly reduces memory usage and still holds a fast matching speed. Above all, CTM costs about 2.5% of the memory usage of AC, and compared with basic banded-row method, the compression rate of CTM can be increased by about 35%.

Keywords: Multiple string matching · Charset transformation · Automata compression · Network security · Intrusion detection

1 Introduction

Multiple string matching is one of the most classic problems in computer science, with the aim of finding all occurrences of a given set of patterns from input string. Multiple string matching is a core technology for network content detection, which is widely used in network and security fields, including intrusion detection and prevention, protocol identification, virus detection, web content filtering, etc.

Since the 1970s, many multiple string matching algorithms have been proposed. Among which the automata-based matching algorithms such as AC [1],

© Springer Nature Singapore Pte Ltd. 2019
V. S. Shankar Sriram et al. (Eds.): ATIS 2019, CCIS 1116, pp. 3–15, 2019.
https://doi.org/10.1007/978-981-15-0871-4_1

BOM [2], SBDM [3] have superior matching performance. But as the scale of the patterns increase, the memory consumption of the algorithm grows rapidly, requiring a large amount of memory to store the automata, this prevents them from being applied to large-scale pattern set.

In this paper, we proposed a charset-transformation-based multiple string matching algorithm named CTM, which is the optimization method based on the classical banded-row [4] method. Compression rate of the banded-row method depends on the distribution of non-empty elements in the automata, if the distribution is very discrete, the compression rate will be extremely low. Aiming at this problem, the proposed CTM algorithm plays a charset transformation on the charset of the patterns to increase the continuity of distribution of non-empty elements in the automata, and then uses the banded-row method to compress the automata. We evaluate the experiment on random ASCII charset with the AC automata and BOM automata. Experiment result shows that CTM can significantly reduce memory usage and the matching speed can be kept at the same level as both the original algorithms. Take AC as the example, CTM costs about 2.5% of the memory usage of AC, and compared with basic banded-row method, the compression rate of CTM can be increased by about 35%.

The rest of this article is organized as follows. Section 2 reviews the related work by analyzing representative works in multiple string matching. Section 3 introduces the key ideas and implementation of CTM. Experimental results and comparison are detailed and analyzed in Sect. 4. Section 5 concludes the article.

2   Related Work

2.1   Classical Multiple String Matching Algorithm

According to the characteristics of the multiple string matching algorithms, we divide the existing classical algorithms into three categories: automata based matching algorithm, hash based matching algorithm and bit parallel based matching algorithm. (1) Automata based matching algorithms compile the patterns into a whole automata, and then scan the data by the automata. AC [1] and BOM [2] are typical automata based matching algorithms. The performance of these algorithms is stable on different types of data sets and has linear scan speed in theory. But disadvantage is that automata need to consume so huge storage space that it cannot adapt to large-scale string matching. (2) Hash based matching algorithms calculate the hash value of the patterns and store the hash values in the hash table, KR [5] and WM [6] are typical hash based matching algorithms. The advantage of hash based matching algorithms is that they only need small storage space and get fast matching speed on random data with large character sets. But for data with small character sets or for patterns with short length, the matching speed of these algorithms drops rapidly. (3) Bit parallel based matching algorithms use bit vector to simulate the automata, the operation of the bit vector is used to represent the state transition of automata. Shift-AND/Shift-OR [7] and BNDM [8] are typical bit parallel based matching algorithms. These algorithms have the advantages of small storage space consuming and fast matching speed. But bit parallel based matching algorithms are only suitable for small-scale (only dozens of pattern strings) string matching.

Because of stable performance and linear scan speed, automata based algorithms, especially AC algorithm, is widely used in various fields. As mentioned above, automata need to consume huge memory, and this restricts its application on large-scale pattern set. In recent years, in order to solve the performance bottleneck caused by the storage space of the automata, researchers have proposed many compression algorithms to reduce the memory consumption of the automata-based algorithms. Until now, commonly used compression techniques mainly include row compression method [9], bit-split method [10, 11], double array method [12, 13], and banded-row method [4]. Row compression method only stores the input character and the next state of the non-empty transition for each state transition table row; bit-split method decomposes an AC automata into 8 binary automata to reduce memory usage; double array method uses a one-dimensional array to store all rows of the state transition table, and uses other two arrays to store the offset of each row and the exact row number of those elements stored in the one-dimensional array; banded-row method reduces automata storage space by eliminating empty transition at the head and the tail of each row.

We can conclude that the existing compression techniques of automata based algorithms can achieve good compression effect, but compression technology generally increases the time complexity of the original matching algorithm, reducing the matching speed of the algorithm and affects its real application. Among all the existing compression methods, the extra time overhead introduced by the banded-row [4] method is very small, and its matching speed is almost the same as the original AC algorithm. Because of the excellent performance of banded-row, it has been used in the Snort [15] project which is an open source intrusion detection system widely applied in network security filed.

2.2   Principle of the Banded-Row Algorithm and Its Insufficiency

As introduced in the former part, AC [1] and BOM [2] algorithms use automata as the matching data structure. Automata, also known as finite state automata (FSA), is an abstract machine used in the study of computation and languages that has only a finite, constant amount of memory (the states) [14]. There are a finite number of states, and each state has transitions to zero or more states. There is an input string that determines which transition is followed. Finite state machines are studied in automata theory, a subfield of theoretical computer science. FSA can be divided into deterministic finite automata (DFA) and non-deterministic finite automata (NFA). FSA used in AC [1] and BOM [2] is an DFA. Formally, a deterministic finite automata (DFA) consists of:

- an alphabet Σ
- a set of states S, one of which is chosen as a start state and zero or more as accepting states
- a transition function $\delta(S \times \Sigma)$

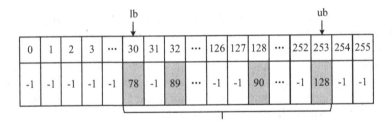

Fig. 1. Demonstration of banded-row method.

Automata can be generally represented as a two-dimensional matrix $A_{N \times |\Sigma|}$ with size of $N \times |\Sigma|$, where N is the number of states and $|\Sigma|$ is the size of the alphabet. For the current state s and the input character c, $A[s, c]$ represents the next transition state, represented by a non-negative integer or -1, $A[s, c] = -1$ indicates the current state s has no successor state for the input character c. In AC [1] and BOM [2] algorithms, most states usually only have a few successor states, that means most of the elements in the transition table are meaningless. It is a waste of storage space to store $|\Sigma|$ elements for each state table row in the transition table.

Norton [4] proposed a banded-row method to compress the AC automata. For row $A[s]$ of the transition table, banded-row uses an integer lb to record the character c of the first successor state, and uses ub to record the character c of the last successor state. Figure 1 demonstrates the value of lb and ub of one state row, in the Fig. 1, lb equals to 30, ub equals to 253, and 224 elements between interval $[lb, ub]$ needed to be stored.

$$lb = min\left\{0 \le c < |\Sigma|\,\Big|\,A[s, c] \neq -1\right\} \tag{1}$$

$$ub = max\left\{0 \le c < |\Sigma|\,\Big|\,A[s, c] \neq -1\right\} \tag{2}$$

By eliminating empty transition at the head and the tail of each row, and just storing the elements between lb and ub, the number of elements to be stored for each row of the transition table is $ub - lb + 1$, compared to original number of elements with $|\Sigma|$. We can know that the banded-row method can reduce the storage space of AC automata, and also the access speed of transition table is still $O(1)$. But obviously, the compression rate of the banded-row method depends on the size of interval $[lb, ub]$. For the state transition table with scattered distribution of non-empty elements, that means the size of interval $[lb, ub]$ may be very large, then the compression rate will be extremely low. The most extreme example is that lb equals 0 and ub equals to $|\Sigma|-1$, for this situation, the banded-row method will has no compression effect even if the current state row has only two successor states. Aiming at this deficiency of the banded-row method, we propose a mechanism based on bijective charset transformation in this paper. After the bijective transformation for the pattern charset, the continuity of non-empty elements of the state transition table can be increased, thereby greatly increasing the compression effect of banded-row.

Algorithm 1. State transition procedure of banded-row method

1: **procedure** NEXTSTATE(state_table= T, current_state=s, input_char=c)
2:     **if** $c \geq T[s].lb$ **and** $c \leq T[s].ub$ **then**
3:         **return** $T[s].next[c - lb]$
4:     **else**
5:         **return** -1
6:     **end if**
7: **end procedure**

---

3   CTM: Multiple String Matching Algorithm Based on Charset Transformation

3.1   Charset Transformation Mechanism

As previously described, banded-row is a competitive compression method for its good compression effect and without matching performance decline. But also we know that compression rate of the banded-row method strongly depends on the size of interval $[lb, ub]$. So our motivation in this paper is that we can increase the compression rate by decreasing the size of interval $[lb, ub]$. Aiming at this goal, we proposed a Charset-Transformation-Based Matching Mechanism (named CTM) in this paper, which will play bijective charset transformation on the charset of the patterns. The purpose of the bijective character transformation is to increase the continuity of the distribution of non-empty elements in the state transition table, and that means size of the interval $[lb, ub]$ can be reduced accordingly.

The CTM is independent of the specific string matching algorithm and can be applied to all automata based string matching algorithms, such as AC and BOM, etc. For the CTM method, the core point is the charset transformation function $f(c) : \Sigma \rightarrow \Sigma$. When designing the charset transformation function, three key aspects must be considered.

(1) The correctness of the matching algorithm after charset transformation must be ensured, must avoid false positives and false negatives, this means $f(c)$ must be a bijective function. The bijective function can make sure that any two unequal characters c_1 and c_2, $f(c_1)$ can not be equal to $f(c_2)$, and for any character c, it can only be mapped to a unique $f(c)$.

(2) The transformation process of $f(c)$ can not be too complicated. During the string matching procedure, the input original character needs to be transformed by the transformation function $f(c)$, and then do the matching procedure on the transformed character. If the transformation operation is too complicated, it will bring in excessive extra time overhead, and finally decreasing the matching speed.

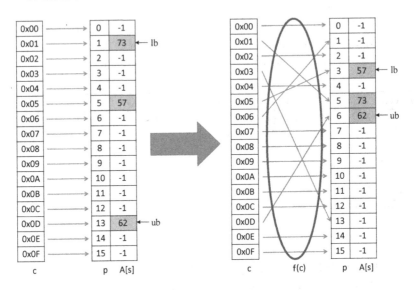

Fig. 2. Demonstration of charset transformation method.

(3) Transformation function should not bring in excessive extra space overhead. Excessive extra space overhead means reducing the compression rate, even maybe increase the storage space.

The example of charset transformation is shown in Fig. 2, $A[s]$ is a state row of the state transition table, p is the offset of each successor state in the state row, c is the corresponding input character. The left side of Fig. 2 demonstrates the banded-row method, in which input character c and offset p are the same. We can see that although there are only three valid successor states, but in order to store all of the valid successor states starting from the first valid successor state and to the last valid successor state, it needs to store 13 successor states 10 invalid successor states. The right side of Fig. 2 demonstrates the CTM method, in which the input character c is mapped to the offset p by the charset transformation function $f(c)$. After the charset transformation, all valid successor states are stored in a more continuous region, so the successor states those need to be stored has been reduced from 13 to 4.

3.2   Construction of Transformation Function

In our paper, we constructed two charset transformation functions, one is the XOR transformation $f(c) = a \ xor \ c$, and the other is the linear congruence transformation(LCT for short) $f(c) = (a \times c + b) \ mod \ m$. The charset discussed in our paper is ASCII, so the corresponding size of the charset is 256. Both of the two transformation functions are needed to found the optimal transformation parameters for each row of the state table. We use the iterative method to find the optimal parameters for each state row, and then records the corresponding character lb of the first successor state in the state row after the transformation and the character ub of the last successor state in the state row after the transformation (for the Fig. 2, lb is 3, ub is 6).

1. XOR transformation

   XOR transformation $f(c) = a \ xor \ c$ is one of the simplest mathematical transformations, and obviously, is a bijective transformation. In our paper, in order to ensure that the transformed characters are less than charset size 256, integer parameter a must satisfy $0 \le a \le 255$.
2. Linear congruence transformation

   Linear congruence transformation $f(c) = (a \times c + b) \ mod \ m$ is a widely used mathematical transformation for that it has low computational complexity and requires only a small amount of extra space to store the parameters of the transformation function. In order to ensure the correctness of the matching algorithm, the transformation function used in our paper needs to satisfy two basic constraints:

(1) $m \ge |\Sigma|$, Σ is alphabet of the pattern set and $|\Sigma|$ is the size of the alphabet. ASCII is the alphabet discussed in our paper, so $|\Sigma|$ equals to 256, and we use 256 to represent $|\Sigma|$ in the rest part of this paper. If $m < 256$, assuming n, that is to say the largest character after the transformation is $n-1$ (less than 255), but we know that the largest character of the original charset is 255. This means that several different original characters will be mapped onto the same character by transformation, and then lead to incorrect matching result. So m must be larger than or equals to $|\Sigma|$ (256). In our paper, we chose m equals to $|\Sigma|$.

(2) a and m must be coprime numbers (can be represented as $(a, m) = 1$), so that the transformation function can be guaranteed to be a bijective function. We can prove it by reductio ad absurdum:

The range of character c is $[0, m)$, so we suppose that $0 \le c_2 < c_1 \le m - 1$, and $(a \times c_1 + b) \ mod \ m = (a \times c_2 + b) \ mod \ m$, that means exiting k_1, k_2, y, that:

$$a \times c_1 + b = k_1 \times m + y \tag{3}$$
$$a \times c_1 + b = k_1 \times m + y \tag{4}$$

From Eqs. 3 and 4, we can get that:

$$a \times (c_1 - c_2) = (k_1 - k_2) \times m \tag{5}$$

Equation 5 shows that $a \times (c_1 - c_2)$ is a multiple of m. According to the knowledge of elementary number theory, because of $(a, m) = 1$, as a multiple of m, the minimum value of $(c_1 - c_2)$ is m. But according to our hypothesis, we know that $0 < c_1 - c_2 \le m - 1$, this fact contradicts the conclusion of Eq. 5. Finally, we can conclude that if $(a, m) = 1$, then for any $c_1 \ne c_2$, $f(c_1) \ne f(c_2)$, that is to say transformation function a bijective function.

Algorithm 2. Pattern preprocessing procedure of CTM

1: **procedure** PREPROCESSING$(P=p^{(1)}, p^{(2)}, ..., p^{(r)}, m)$
2:     construct original state transition table S for pattern $P=p^{(1)}, p^{(2)}, ..., p^{(r)}$
3:     $n \leftarrow$ number of row of state transition table S
4:     **for** $i=1$ to n **do**
5:         $parameters \leftarrow$ BestParameter(S, i, m)
6:     **end for**
7:     construct CTM state transition table CS
8:     **return** CS
9: **end procedure**

3.3   Implementation of CTM

Like the original string matching algorithm, CTM also includes pattern prepro-cessing stage and string matching stage, Algorithm 2 shows the preprocessing stage and Algorithm 3 shows the matching stage. During the pattern preprocess-ing stage, we firstly construct the state transition table of the original automata, and then change the distribution of non-empty elements in the state table by using bijective transformation on the charset, finally construct the compressed automata. The number and distribution of non-empty elements of each state transition row are different, so we need to find the optimal transformation param-eters for each row. During the matching stage, for each character t_i of input text $T = t_1, t_2, ..., t_n$, firstly, we use the transformation function $f(c)$ to calculate the transformed character c, then get the next state s, according to value of c. If the next state s is a terminal state, then report a match.

Algorithm 3. String matching procedure of CTM method

1: **procedure** MATCHING(CTM_state_table$=S$, $T=(t_1, t_2, ..., t_n)$)
2:     $s \leftarrow$ initstate of S
3:     **for** $pos=0$ to n **do**
4:         $c' \leftarrow f(c)$
5:         **if** $S[s].lb \leqslant c' \leqslant S[s].ub$ **then**
6:             $s \leftarrow S[s].next[c' - S[s].lb]$
7:         **else**
8:             $s \leftarrow$ initstate of S
9:         **end if**
10:        **if** s *is terminal* **then**
11:            *report a match*
12:        **end if**
13:    **end for**
14: **end procedure**

During the preprocessing stage, For each row of the state transition table, we need to find the best transformation parameter to minimize the size of the

---

Algorithm 4. XOR find optimal parameter for one state row

1: **procedure** XORBESTPARAMETER(state_table=S, row=k)
2:     $min\_interval \leftarrow 255$
3:     **for** $i=0$ to 255 **do**
4:         $inf \leftarrow min\{i\ xor\ c | S[k].next[c]! = -1, c \in [0, 255]\}$
5:         $sup \leftarrow max\{i\ xor\ c | S[k].next[c]! = -1, c \in [0, 255]\}$
6:         **if** $min\_interval > (sup - inf)$ **then**
7:             $a \leftarrow i$
8:             $lb \leftarrow inf$
9:             $ub \leftarrow sup$
10:            $min\_interval \leftarrow (sup - inf)$
11:        **end if**
12:    **end for**
13:    **return** (a, lb, ub)
14: **end procedure**

---

interval $[lb, ub]$ for both of the XOR transformation add LCT transformation. Optimal parameter a for the XOR transformation $f(c) = (a\ xor\ c)$, and optimal parameter (a, b) for LCT $f(c) = (a \times c + b)\ mod\ m$. Algorithm 4 describes the optimal parameter finding procedure of XOR transformation for one state row. The candidate value of parameter a ranges from 0 to 255, we need to find the value by minimizing the interval $[lb, ub]$, then assigns this value to parameter a and records corresponding lb and ub for the current state row. Algorithm 5 describes the optimal parameter finding procedure of LCT for one state row. The candidate value of a is odd number between 1 and 255, and the candidate value of b is integer between 0 and 255, we need to find the combination (a, b) by minimizing the interval $[lb, ub]$, then also records corresponding lb and ub for the current state row.

4   Experiment and Evaluation

We implement XOR and LCT for AC and BOM algorithm, and evaluate the performance on this two algorithms. The hardware and software environment of the experiment is as follows: CPU is Intel Xeon E5-2667 (3.20 GHz), main memory size is 125 GB, and operating system is CentOS 7.2 (64 bit). The algorithms are written in C++ and executed by single thread. Charset chose in our experiment is ASCII with the size of 256 (1 byte).

The patterns are generated by random algorithm, the characters in patterns and text both obey the independently identically distribution, each character of the patterns are uniformly drawn from range [0, 255]. The length of patterns is 8, and scale changes from 100,00 to 200,000. The patterns are searched against a random text of 200 MB generated in the same way.

Table 1 shows the detailed experimental results on the above dataset. We compare the tested algorithms in two aspects:

Algorithm 5. LCT find optimal parameter for one state row

1: **procedure** LCTBESTPARAMETER(state_table=S, row=k, mod_pa=m)
2:     $min\_interval \leftarrow 255$
3:     **for** $i=1$ to 127 **do**
4:         **for** $j=0$ to 255 **do**
5:             $inf \leftarrow min\big\{((2 \times i + 1) \times c + j) \bmod m \big| S[k].next[c]! = -1,\ c \in [0, 255]\big\}$
6:             $sup \leftarrow max\big\{((2 \times i + 1) \times c + j) \bmod m \big| S[k].next[c]! = -1,\ c \in [0, 255]\big\}$
7:             **if** $min\_interval > (sup - inf)$ **then**
8:                 $a \leftarrow i$
9:                 $b \leftarrow j$
10:                $lb \leftarrow inf$
11:                $ub \leftarrow sup$
12:                $min\_interval \leftarrow (sup - inf)$
13:            **end if**
14:        **end for**
15:    **end for**
16:    **return** (a, b, lb, ub)
17: **end procedure**

Table 1. Detailed experimental results of XOR and LCT transformation for AC and BOM algorithm.

Pattern scale	Algorithm	Memory (MB)	Matching speed (MB/s)	Algorithm	Memory (MB)	Matching speed (MB/s)
10000	AC	136.6	40.7	BOM	136.7	35.4
	BandedRow-AC	4.0	44.4	BandedRow-BOM	15.6	42.4
	CTM-LCT-AC	3.4	42.0	CTM-LCT-BOM	4.5	43.5
	CTM-XOR-AC	3.7	51.1	CTM-XOR-BOM	10.1	38.4
50000	AC	654.4	15.0	BOM	654.1	16.4
	BandedRow-AC	24.5	19.0	BandedRow-BOM	77.4	17.3
	CTM-LCT-AC	15.7	20.1	CTM-LCT-BOM	36.7	16.3
	CTM-XOR-AC	20.1	19.6	CTM-XOR-BOM	57.4	16.7
100000	AC	1270.4	12.2	BOM	1269.7	14.1
	BandedRow-AC	53.1	13.5	BandedRow-BOM	113.7	14.8
	CTM-LCT-AC	32.5	15.4	CTM-LCT-BOM	71.0	14.2
	CTM-XOR-AC	42.8	14.7	CTM-XOR-BOM	91.8	13.8
150000	AC	1872.5	11.3	BOM	1871.2	13.1
	BandedRow-AC	79.9	11.6	BandedRow-BOM	141.3	13.6
	CTM-LCT-AC	50.3	13.2	CTM-LCT-BOM	95.5	12.8
	CTM-XOR-AC	65.3	12.4	CTM-XOR-BOM	116.6	13.1
200000	AC	2468.0	12.3	BOM	2466.4	12.9
	BandedRow-AC	104.1	10.8	BandedRow-BOM	168.6	13.1
	CTM-LCT-AC	68.5	12.3	CTM-LCT-BOM	115.0	11.9
	CTM-XOR-AC	86.6	11.5	CTM-XOR-BOM	139.0	12.3

(1) *Memory usage.* We compared the memory usage of original AC algorithm, original BOM algorithm, banded-row algorithm and proposed CTM algorithm (including XOR and LCT) in different pattern scale. Figure 3 shows the specific memory usage of AC and BOM automata after compressed by banded-row, CTM-LCT and CTM-XOR, and sub-figure *a* of Fig. 3 for AC automata, sub-figure *b* of Fig. 3 for BOM automata. From Fig. 3, we can see that memory usage of LCT and XOR are both smaller than original banded-row, where memory usage of LCT is smaller than XOR. Figure 4 shows the compression rate increasing of the CTM, compared to banded-row, sub-figure *a* for AC automata, and sub-figure *b* for BOM automata. Figure 4 shows that the compression rate of CTM-LCT is better than CTM-XOR, take the AC automata as the example, compared to banded-row, compression rate of CTM increased by an average of 32%, but for CTM-XOR is 16.3%.

(2) *Matching speed.* We have mentioned that multiple string matching algorithm is a core technology in network intrusion detection system, it needs to process high speed network traffic, matching speed is the most important factor for practical applications. When designing a compression algorithm, we must not only achieve the purpose of space compression, but also must maintain the matching speed of the original algorithm. We can see the detailed matching speed of different pattern scale in Table 1, result show that matching speed of CTM can be kept at the same level as the original AC algorithm, even slightly faster than AC. Take the pattern scale 500,00 and AC automata as the example, the matching speed of original AC is 15 MB/s, of banded-row is 19 MB/s, of CTM-LCT is 20.1 MB/s, of CTM-XOR is 19.6 MB/s, speed of CTM-LCT is the fastest.

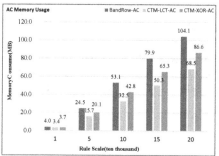
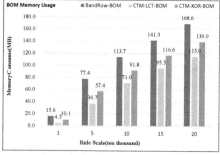

a. Memory usage of AC automata compressed by banded-row, CTM-LCT and CTM-XOR

b. Memory usage of BOM automata compressed by banded-row, CTM-LCT and CTM-XOR

Fig. 3. Memory usage of AC and BOM automata after compressed by banded-row, CTM-LCT and CTM-XOR, with different pattern scale.

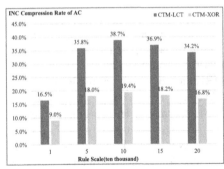
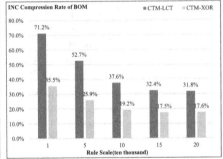

a. Increased compression rate of CTM-LCT and CTM-XOR for AC   b. Increased compression rate of CTM-LCT and CTM-XOR for BOM

Fig. 4. Increased compression rate of CTM for AC and BOM.

5   Conclusion

Multiple string matching algorithm is a core technology in network intrusion detection system. Automata-based multiple string matching algorithms such as AC and BOM are widely used in practical systems because of their excellent matching performance, but the huge memory usage of automata restricts them to be applied to large-scale pattern set. We proposed a space-efficient multiple string matching algorithm CTM, which plays the character transformation on the charset of the patterns to increase the continuity of distribution of non-empty elements in the automata, and then uses the banded-row method to compress the automata. The proposed algorithm can significantly reduce memory usage and maintain the matching speed of the original multiple string matching algorithm. We have designed linear congruence transformation and XOR transformation in this paper, and we have known that CTM is independent of the specific string matching algorithm, so in the future, we can design better transformation functions to further increase the automata compression rate.

Acknowledgement. This work is partially supported by the National Key Research and Development Program of China (Grant No. 2017YFC0820700), and Strategic Priority Research Program of Chinese Academy of Sciences (Grant No. XDC02030000).

References

1. Aho, A.V., Corasick, M.J.: Efficient string matching: an aid to bibliographic search. Commun. ACM **18**(6), 333–340 (1975)
2. Allauzen, C., Crochemore, M., Raffinot, M.: Factor oracle: a new structure for pattern matching. In: Pavelka, J., Tel, G., Bartošek, M. (eds.) SOFSEM 1999. LNCS, vol. 1725, pp. 295–310. Springer, Heidelberg (1999). https://doi.org/10.1007/3-540-47849-3_18
3. Raffinot, M.: On the multi backward DAWG matching algorithm. In: Proceedings of the 4th South American Workshop on String Processing, pp. 149–165 (1999)

4. Norton, M.: Optimizing pattern matching for intrusion detection. www.idsresearch. org (2004)
5. Karp, R.M., Rabi, M.O.: Efficient randomized pattern-matching algorithms. IBM J. Res. Dev. **31**(2), 249–260 (1987)
6. Wu, S., Manber, U.: A fast algorithm for multi-pattern searching, TR-94-17, Tucson. Department of Computer Science, University of Arizona, AZ (1994)
7. Baeza-Yates, R.A., Ricardo, A., Gonnet, G.H.: A new approach to text searching. Commun. ACM **35**(10), 74–82 (1992)
8. Navarro, G., Raffinot, M.: Fast and flexible string matching by combining bit-parallelism and suffix automata. ACM J. Exper. Algorithmics **5**(4), 1–36 (2000)
9. Dencker, P., Dorre, K., Heuft, J.: Optimization of parser tables for portable compilers. ACM Trans. Program. Lang. Syst. **6**(4), 546–572 (1984)
10. Tan, L., Sherwood, T.: A high throughput string matching architecture for intrusion detection and prevention. ACM SIGARCH Comput. Archit. News **33**(2), 112–122 (2005)
11. Vakili, S., Langlois, J.M.P., Boughzala, B., et al.: Memory-efficient string matching for intrusion detection systems using a high-precision pattern grouping algorithm. In: Proceedings of the 2016 Symposium on Architectures for Networking and Communications Systems, pp. 37–42 (2016)
12. Aho, A.V., Sethi, R., Ullman, J.D.: Compilers: Principles, Techniques, and Tools. Addison-Wesley Publishing, Boston (1986)
13. Aoe, J., Morimotoo, K., Sato, T.: An efficient implementation of trie structures. Softw. Pract. Exper. **22**(9), 695–721 (1992)
14. https://en.wikipedia.org/wiki/Finite-state_machine
15. https://www.snort.org

An Image Mathcrypt - A Flawless Security via Flawed Image

R. Anushiadevi[1], Veeramuthu Venkatesh[1],
and Rengarajan Amirtharajan[2(✉)]

[1] School of Computing, SASTRA Deemed University, Thanjavur 613 401, India
[2] School of Electrical and Electronics Engineering,
SASTRA Deemed University, Thanjavur 613 401, India
amir@ece.sastra.edu

Abstract. The present scenario of the medical field is that sending the healthcare images through the internet is so far exposed to security threats. Hence, there is a need for an efficient and secure procedure to exchange healthcare images over the Internet. The Digital Image and Communication in Medicine (DICOM) provides security features for image header information but not for the pixel information. Hence to send the pixel information in a highly secured manner, the pixels need to be encrypted by using a suitable encryption algorithm. The number of pixel changing rate (NPCR) and the unified averaged changed intensity (UACI) are well-known encryption evaluation metrics to analyse the differential attack in image encryption. These two values are used to calculate the average number of pixel changes and intensity changes between two encrypted images before and after modifying any one pixel in a plaintext image respectively. If these two values are high, then the image encryption can resist the differential attacks. In this paper, a theoretical value of NPCR and UACI are computed for DICOM image encryption concerning different significant levels. An encryption algorithm with Gould transform, RC5, logistic map and DNA Diffusion is proposed for DICOM image to increase the NPCR, and UACI value and this method offered an efficient security strategy for DICOM pixel information. Finally, the computed theoretical value of NPCR and UACI are compared with the existing and proposed algorithm.

Keywords: DICOM encryption · Randomness test · Differential attacks · DICOM encryption metrics · UACI · NPCR

1 Introduction

Imaging the inner human parts are essential for diagnosing patient disease; however, it is indeed a complicated task. The unique technique which is used to capture the image of a human's inner body parts is called medical imaging. After obtaining the information by applying DICOM, Picture Archiving and Communication Systems (PACS), they are used to convert the medical images in the form of digital values [1, 2]. DICOM is the commonly recommended standard. The digital medical information offers a useful tool for treatment, and it is beneficial for surgery when compared to analogue data. To take the accurate diagnostics about the patient disease, the medical image has

© Springer Nature Singapore Pte Ltd. 2019
V. S. Shankar Sriram et al. (Eds.): ATIS 2019, CCIS 1116, pp. 16–31, 2019.
https://doi.org/10.1007/978-981-15-0871-4_2

to be sent for the concern of specialised experts. Hence in the medical field, an enhancing requirement for communicating medical images through the internet [3, 4]. In the present technology, addressing the medical images has been made simple and easy for a third person to hack the details.

Already existing methods like Advanced Encryption Standard (AES), Data Encryption Standard (DES) and International Data Encryption Algorithm (IDEA) are used to send the medical images securely. There are several properties of DICOM like large data size, many numbers of pixels, highly correlated pixels, great redundancy and low resolution. The efficiency of these methods is either vulnerable or takes the high computational time to protect the pixel information. Various conventional encryption methods have been suggested by many researchers [5–9]. There have been a lot of attacks on the encrypted image. The differential attack is the most usual attack. To overcome this issue, the differential cryptanalysis is invented by Israeli researchers Eli Biham and Adi Shamir for Data Encryption Standard (DES) [10]. They have proposed various attacks on a block cipher, and also they defined the possible limitation on DES [11, 12]. The well-designed encryption algorithm will give utterly different ciphertext for a single bit changed the plain text. If the encryption algorithm is not suitable, the relationship between the two ciphertexts before and after a one-bit change of plaintext will lead to finding the key.

In an image encryption algorithm, the differential attack is examined by NPCR and UACI [13–35]. The NPCR and UACI are developed to evaluate the number of modifying pixels and the average modified intensity between ciphertext images respectively. When the distinction between plaintext images is simple, these two values are compactly described and easy to determine. But analysed ratings are hard to understand in the sense of whether the efficiency is good enough. For example, if the upper-bound of NPCR value is hundred percentage, then NPCR value of a protected cipher should be very near to this upper-bound, but we don't know which range of NPCR values can resist the differential attack. Hence there is a need for NPCR and UACI ratings for an image cipher. Wu et al. [25] proposed the theoretical value of NPCR and UACI for grayscale image encryption. The proposed work focuses on to get the theoretical value of NPCR and UACI for DICOM image encryption and also a straightforward image encryption technique was implemented to show how the NPCR and UACI value can be improved.

Existing methods provide good Image Encryption [26–35], but NPCR and UACI value can be improved and the obtained values are not guaranteed for optimum benefits. Inspired by the above discussions the proposed algorithm suggests optimum values for NPCR, UACI to DICOM Images.

The main contribution of the proposed algorithm involves

- The theoretical value of the NPCR and UACI are computed for DICOM image
- It shows the way to improve the NPCR and UACI value
- The proposed method can resist the differential attacks
- The proposed method has both confusion and diffusion
- Gould transform, RC5 with logistic map and DNA (XOR and XNOR) extended diffusion to increase the proposed method performance.

2   Materials and Methods

The encryption algorithm consisted of four stages and presented in Fig. 1, which are

1. Bitwise XOR and XNOR operation;
2. Gould Transform
3. RC5 Encryption
4. Enhanced diffusion algorithm.

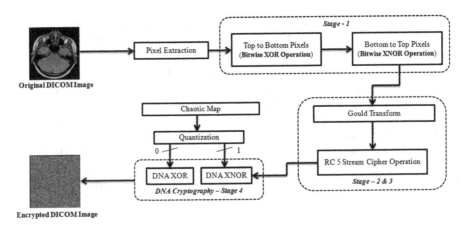

Fig. 1. The proposed encryption algorithm

2.1   Bitwise XOR and XNOR Operation

This stage has two steps. The first step performs the XOR operation from top to bottom as shown in Algorithm 1. The second step performs the XNOR operation from bottom to top as shown in Algorithm 1. Hence, if anyone pixel is changed in the plain image, then all the pixel values in the encrypted image are affected and NPCR, UACI value is increased. If the first-pixel value is changed, then all the pixel values are affected by both XOR and XNOR. If the last pixel value is changed, the entire pixel values are affected by the only XNOR. If the middle pixel is replaced, and then half of the pixels are affected by both whereas half of the pixels are only affected by XNOR. Hence the encryption algorithm should be designed in such a way that if the one-pixel value is changed, that will affect all the pixel values.

Algorithm 1:

> **Step 1:** divide all the pixels into four 4 bit pieces Pi_1, Pi_2, Pi_3, Pi_4
>
> **Step 2:** Loop s=First pixel to the last pixel-1
>
> > If 's' is odd
> >
> > $$Pi_1{}^{s+1}= Pi_4{}^s \oplus Pi_1{}^{s+1}; \quad Pi_2{}^{s+1}= Pi_3{}^s \oplus Pi_2{}^{s+1}$$
> > $$Pi_3{}^{s+1}= Pi_1{}^s \oplus Pi_3{}^{s+1}; \quad Pi_4{}^{s+1}= Pi_2{}^s \oplus Pi_4{}^{s+1}$$
> >
> > If 's' is even
> >
> > $$Pi_1{}^{s+1}= Pi_3{}^s \oplus Pi_1{}^{s+1}; \quad Pi_2{}^{s+1}= Pi_4{}^s \oplus Pi_2{}^{s+1}$$
> > $$Pi_3{}^{s+1}= Pi_2{}^s \oplus Pi_3{}^{s+1}; \quad Pi_4{}^{s+1}= Pi_1{}^s \oplus Pi_4{}^{s+1}$$
>
> **Step 3:** Encrypt the first pixel
>
> > $$Pi_1{}^1= Pi_1{}^1 \oplus Pi_1{}^{last}; \quad Pi_2{}^1= Pi_2{}^1 \oplus Pi_2{}^{last}$$
> > $$Pi_3{}^1= Pi_3{}^1 \oplus Pi_3{}^{last}; \quad Pi_4{}^1= Pi_4{}^1 \oplus Pi_4{}^{last}$$
>
> **Step 4:** Loop s=last pixel to the second pixel
>
> > If 's' is odd
> >
> > $$Pi_1{}^{s-1}= \overline{Pi_2{}^s \oplus Pi_1{}^{s-1}}; \quad Pi_2{}^{s-1}= \overline{Pi_1{}^s \oplus Pi_2{}^{s-1}}$$
> > $$Pi_3{}^{s-1}= \overline{Pi_4{}^s \oplus Pi_3{}^{s-1}}; \quad Pi_4{}^{s-1}= \overline{Pi_3{}^s \oplus Pi_4{}^{s-1}}$$
> >
> > If 's' is even
> >
> > $$Pi_1{}^{s-1} \overline{Pi_3{}^s \oplus Pi_1{}^{s-1}}; \quad Pi_2{}^{s-1}= \overline{Pi_4{}^s \oplus Pi_2{}^{s-1}}$$
> > $$Pi_3{}^{s-1}= \overline{Pi_2{}^s \oplus Pi_3{}^{s-1}}; \quad Pi_4{}^{s-1}= \overline{Pi_1{}^s \oplus Pi_4{}^{s-1}}$$
>
> **Step 5:** Encrypt the Last pixel
>
> > $$Pi_1{}^{last}= \overline{Pi_1{}^1 \oplus Pi_1{}^{last}}; \quad Pi_2{}^{last}= \overline{Pi_2{}^1 \oplus Pi_2{}^{last}}$$
> > $$Pi_3{}^{last}= \overline{Pi_3{}^1 \oplus Pi_3{}^{last}}; \quad ;Pi_4{}^{last}= \overline{Pi_4{}^1 \oplus Pi_4{}^{last}}$$

2.2 Gould Transform

Le et al. in 2006 [26] invented the DGT to provide authentication and better security. It has the special property of identifying the variation between neighboring pixels, if the hackers carried out any exploitation; its non-existence shows that the image has been changed. The transform matrix GT with size $N \times N$ can be defined as $GT_{xy} = -1^{x+y} \binom{po}{x-y}$, for x, y $= 0, 1, \ldots, N-1$, where po is a positive integer.

For example, for po = 1 and N = 2, the GT matrix equals to $\frac{1}{2}GT = \begin{bmatrix} 1 & 0 \\ -1 & 1 \end{bmatrix}$ For extra security, Gould transform is applied to provide authentication and tamper proofing as in [27].

2.3 RC5 Encryption Algorithm

Ronald Rivest invented RC5 in 1994 for RSA security. It has a different key size stretching from 0 to 2040 bits; the total of rounds also differs from 0 to 255, and it can have three different block size 32, 64 and 128-bit word. In this paper, RC5-32/12/16 is used to encrypt 64-bit block in 12 rounds using the 16-byte secret key. This algorithm gives high protection for differential attack because in each round the bits are rotated to "random" positions depending on the input, and it is not a deliberate one. This is shown in Algorithm 2 where A and B are w-bit register input blocks, and S is the expanded key array.

Algorithm 2:
A=A+S[0]   ; B=B+S[1]
loop i=1 to r do
     A= ((A⊕ B)<<<B)+S[2i];   B=((A⊕ B)<<<A)+S[2i+1]

2.4   Enhanced Diffusion Algorithm

Enhanced diffusion is carried out as the final step of the encryption algorithm. This unit utilises the 1D logistic maps and DNA coding. As the first stage of enhanced diffusion, two chaotic sequences are generated from the logistic map. The representation of the logistic map is,

$$X_{n+1} = \mu \times X_n(1 - X_n)$$

The chaotic series generated from the logistic map are quantised to act as a key for DNA diffusion as follows,

Step 1: Key sequence 1, $K1 = \{X_1, X_2, \ldots\ldots, X_{m \times n}\}$,
Key sequence 2, $K2 = \{Y_1, Y_2, \ldots\ldots, Y_{m \times n}\}$,
Step 2: Quantized key sequence 1, $Q1 = ((K1 \times 10^{14}) \bmod 2) + 1$,
Quantized key sequence 2, $Q2 = ((K2 \times 10^{14}) \bmod 8) + 1$.
Step 3: Initially, the encrypted image from Sect. 2.3 is encoded into equivalent DNA code using R. Let R be the user-defined number (R ∈ [1, 8]). The DNA encoding rules are given in the following Table [35].

Eight sets of DNA encoding rule.

Rule 1	Rule 2	Rule 3	Rule 4	Rule 5	Rule 6	Rule 7	Rule 8
00-A	00-A	00-C	00-C	00-G	00-G	00-T	00-T
01-C	01-G	01-A	01-T	01-A	01-T	01-C	01-C
10-G	10-C	10-T	10-A	10-T	10-A	10-G	10-G
11-T	11-T	11-G	11-G	11-C	11-C	11-A	11-A

Step 4: The key set Q1 is used to choose the operation on DNA encoded matrix. If Q1 is 1, then DNA XOR operation is chosen for diffusing the DNA matrix, else DNA XNOR operation is selected. The DNA XOR and XNOR operations are tabulated in the following tables.

Example for DNA XOR matrix.

EX-OR	A	G	C	T
A	A	G	C	T
G	G	A	T	C
C	C	T	A	G
T	T	C	G	A

Example for DNA XNOR matrix.

EX-NOR	A	G	C	T
A	C	T	A	G
T	T	A	G	C
C	A	G	C	T
G	T	C	G	A

Once the type of operation is selected for a particular pixel, the quantised key sequence Q2 is used to select a specific rule set for diffusing the pixel.

Step 5: As a final step of enhanced diffusion, the DNA diffused matrix is then decoded using R to get the encrypted image.

2.5 Critical Value Calculation of NPCR and UACI for DICOM Image Encryption

(i) Definition of NPCR and UACI

The NPCR and UACI are the best metrics to analyse the diffusion features of image encryption algorithms. Both metrics are analysing the algorithm by comparing the ciphertext images CT_1 and CT_2 of plaintext images earlier and subsequently the one-pixel change. Equations (1) and (3), can explain the NPCR and UACI. Where $C(g,h)$ defined by Eq. (2) and $CT_1(g,h), CT_2(g,h)$ represents the pixel values of the images CT_1 and CT_2 at positions g, h respectively where symbols G, H represent the height and width of the image and 'IN' represents the maximum intensity value of an image. For binary image the maximum intensity value is 1 for gray scale and the, DICOM image is 255, 65535 respectively.

$$NPCR = \frac{\sum_{g,h} C(g,h)}{G \times H} \times 100\% \tag{1}$$

$$C(g,h) = \begin{cases} 0 & \text{if } CT_1(g,h) = CT_2(g,h) \\ 1 & \text{if } CT_1(g,h) \neq CT_2(g,h) \end{cases} \tag{2}$$

$$UACI = \frac{1}{G \times H} \sum_{g,h} \frac{|CT_1(g,h) - CT_2(g,h)|}{IN} \times 100\% \tag{3}$$

This paper deals with the statistical analysis of NPCR and UACI for the ideally encrypted image. The ideally encrypted image means that the numbers of occurrences of all the pixel values are same. For example, in 256×256 grayscale image, the number of existence of each pixel value is 256. For 512×512 grayscale image, the number of presence of each pixel value is 1024.

(ii) Theorem 1

IEI_1 and IEI_2 are two ideally encrypted images. The pixel value at (g, h) defines a random variable 'R'.

$$R = \begin{cases} 0 & \text{if } IEI_1(g,h) = IEI_2(g,h) \\ 1 & \text{if } IEI_1(g,h) \neq IEI_2(g,h) \end{cases}$$

where R is the random variable that follows one of the unique cases of two-point distribution called Bernoulli distribution with the parameter $\rho = \frac{IN}{IN+1}$.

Proof

The Bernoulli distribution is defined by $fn(y) = q^y(1-q)^{1-y}$, 'y' = 0, 1, where 'q' represents the probability occurrence of the event.

$$P[R = 0] = P[IEI_1(g,h) = IEI_2(g,h)]$$

$$= \sum_{l=0}^{IN} P[IEI_1(g,h) = l] \cdot P[IEI_2(g,h) = l]$$

$$= (IN+1)\frac{1}{(IN+1)}\frac{1}{(IN+1)} = \frac{1}{(IN+1)}$$

$$P[R = 1] = 1 - \frac{1}{(IN+1)} = \frac{IN}{(IN+1)}$$

(iii) Theorem 2

The sum of all $C(g, h)$ of two ideally encrypted images defines the random variable 'V'. It follows a Binomial distribution with the parameter $\rho = \frac{IN}{(IN+1)}$ and it is defined by $V = \sum_{g=0}^{G-1} \sum_{h=0}^{H-1} C(g,h)$.

Proof: The ideally encrypted image size is $G \times H$ and the value of C (g, h) is either 0 or 1 and by using Theorem 1 the probability of 'V' can be defined in the following equation.

$$P[V = s] = \binom{GH}{s}\left(\frac{IN}{IN+1}\right)^s\left(\frac{1}{IN+1}\right)^{GH-s}$$

which represents the Binomial distribution.

The Eqs. (4) and (5) defined the mean and variance of the variable 'V'

$$\mu_V = GH \cdot \rho = GH \frac{IN}{(IN+1)} \tag{4}$$

$$\sigma_V^2 = GH \cdot \rho \cdot (1-\rho) = GH \left(\frac{IN}{(IN+1)^2} \right) \tag{5}$$

$$NPCR(IEI_1, IEI_2) = \frac{1}{G \times H} \sum_{g,h} C(g,h) = \frac{V}{GH} \tag{6}$$

Hence the probability of NPCR can be defined as

$$P \left[NPCR(IEI_1, IEI_2) = \frac{s}{GH} \right] = \binom{GH}{s} \left(\frac{IN}{IN+1} \right)^s \left(\frac{1}{IN+1} \right)^{GH-s} \tag{7}$$

$$\mu_{npcr} = \frac{\mu_V}{GH} = \frac{IN}{IN+1} \quad from\,(4) \tag{8}$$

$$\sigma_{npcr}^2 = \frac{\sigma_V^2}{(GH)^2} = \frac{IN}{GH(IN+1)^2} \quad from\,(5) \tag{9}$$

(iv) Critical value for NPCR

The hypothesis H_0 for $NPCR(IEI_1, IEI_2)$ with 'α' level significance is μ_{npcr}. Where we accept H_0 when $NPCR(IEI_1, IEI_2) \geq NPCR_*^\alpha$ where $NPCR_*^\alpha$ is the critical value of NPCR with 'α' level significance which is defined by Eq. (10). Critical value of NPCR for different sizes of DICOM is shown in Table 1 and NPCR value of proposed methodology is tabulated in Table 3. Further this value is compared with several existing methodologies in Table 5.

$$NPCR_*^\alpha = \mu_{npcr} - \varphi^{-1}(\alpha)\sigma_{npcr}$$
$$= \left(IN - \varphi^{-1}(\alpha) \sqrt{\frac{IN}{GH}} \right) / (IN+1) \tag{10}$$

where φ^{-1} is the inverse cumulative density function (CDF) of normal standard distribution $N(0, 1)$.

(v) 2.5.5 Theorem 3

The random variable defines the absolute difference between IEI_1, IEI_2 and it follows discrete distribution. If $d = D(g, h) = |IEI_1(g, h) - IEI_2(g, h)|$ which is the pixel value, difference between two encrypted images $IEI_1(g, h)$ and $IEI_2(g, h)$ at position g, h.

$$P[d=k] = \begin{cases} \frac{1}{IN+1} & \text{if } k = 0 \\ \frac{2(IN+1-k)}{(IN+1)^2} & \text{if } k \geq 1 \text{ and } k \leq IN \end{cases}$$

Proof

When d = 0 from Theorem 1 P [d = 0] = 1/(IN + 1)

When $k \epsilon (0, IN+1]$

$$P[d=k] = P[|IEI_1(g,h) - IEI_2(g,h)|]$$
$$= P[IEI_1(g,h) - IEI_2(g,h) = k] + P[IEI_2(g,h) - IEI_1(g,h) = k]$$

$$P[IEI_1(g,h) - IEI_2(g,h) = k] = \sum_{i=0}^{IN} P[IEI_1(g,h) = i] \cdot P[IEI_2(g,h) = i - k]$$

$$= \sum_{i=0}^{IN} P[IEI_1(g,h) = i] \cdot P[IEI_2(g,h) = i - k]$$

$$= \sum_{i=k}^{IN} P[IEI_1(g,h) = i] \cdot P[IEI_2(g,h) = i - k]$$

$$= (IN - k + 1)\frac{1}{IN+1}\frac{1}{IN+1};$$

Similarly

$$P[IEI_2(g,h) - IEI_1(g,h) = k] = (IN - k + 1)\ \ \frac{1}{IN+1}\frac{1}{IN+1}$$

Hence $P[d=k] = 2(IN+1-k)/(IN+1)^2$ which gives the probability and density function of the random variable d.

$$\mu_d = \sum_{k=1}^{IN} \frac{2k(IN+1-k)}{(IN+1)^2}$$

$$= 2/(IN+1)^2 \sum_{k=1}^{IN} k(IN+1-k);$$

$$= 2/(IN+1)^2 \left((IN+1)\sum_{k=1}^{IN} k - \sum_{k=1}^{IN} k^2 \right)$$

$$= \frac{2}{(IN+1)^2} \left(\left(\frac{(IN+1)\ IN\ (IN+1)}{2} \right) - \left(\frac{IN\ (IN+1)(2IN+1)}{6} \right) \right)$$

$$= \frac{1}{(IN+1)^2} \left((IN+1)\ IN\ (IN+1) - \left(\frac{IN\ (IN+1)(2IN+1)}{3} \right) \right)$$

$$= \frac{1}{(IN+1)} \left(IN\left((IN+1) - \frac{(2IN+1)}{3} \right) \right) = \frac{IN}{(IN+1)} \left(\frac{3IN+3-2IN-1}{3} \right) = \frac{IN(IN+2)}{(3IN+3)}$$

$$\sigma_d^2 = \sum_{k=1}^{IN} \frac{2k^2(IN+1-k)}{(IN+1)^2} - \mu_d^2$$

$$= \frac{2}{(IN+1)^2} \sum_{k=1}^{IN} k^2(IN+1-k) - \mu_d^2 = \frac{2}{(IN+1)^2}\left(\left((IN+1)\sum_{k=1}^{IN}k^2\right) - \sum_{k=1}^{IN}k^3\right) - \left(\frac{IN(IN+2)}{(3IN+3)}\right)^2$$

$$= \frac{2}{(IN+1)^2}\left(\frac{(IN+1)IN(IN+1)(2IN+1)}{6}\right) - \frac{\left(IN^2(IN+1)^2\right)}{4} - \left(\frac{IN(IN+2)}{(3IN+3)}\right)^2$$

$$= \frac{IN(2IN+1)}{3} - \frac{IN^2}{2} - \left(\frac{IN(IN+2)}{(3IN+3)}\right)^2 = \frac{2IN^2+IN}{3} - \frac{IN^2}{2} - \left(\frac{IN(IN+2)}{(3IN+3)}\right)^2$$

$$= \left(\frac{IN(IN+2)}{6}\right) - \frac{\left(IN^2(IN+2)^2\right)}{(3IN+3)^2} = \frac{(3IN+3)^2 IN(IN+2) - 6\left(IN^2(IN+2)^2\right)}{6(3IN+3)^2}$$

$$= IN(IN+2)\left(\frac{(3IN+3)^2-6IN(IN+2)}{6(3IN+3)^2}\right) = IN(IN+2)\left(\frac{9(IN+1)^2-6IN(IN+2)}{54(IN+1)^2}\right)$$

$$= IN(IN+2)\left(\frac{3(IN+1)^2-2IN(IN+2)}{18(IN+1)^2}\right) = IN(IN+2)\left(\frac{(IN^2+2IN+3)}{18(IN+1)^2}\right)$$

Let $U = \sum_{g=0}^{G-1}\sum_{h=0}^{H-1}\frac{|IEI_1(g,h)-IEI_2(g,h)|}{GH}$ which is the mean value of D(g, h).
That is, $U = \sum_{g=0}^{G-1}\sum_{h=0}^{H-1}\frac{D(g,h)}{GH}$.

(vi) **Theorem 4**

If $U = \sum_{g=0}^{G-1}\sum_{h=0}^{H-1}\frac{|IEI_1(g,h)-IEI_2(g,h)|}{GH}$ is the scaled version of UACI between

$IEI_1(g,h), IEI_2(g,h)$ with $\mu_U = \mu_d = \frac{IN(IN+2)}{(3IN+3)}$; and $\sigma_U^2 = \frac{\sigma_d^2}{GH} = \frac{IN(IN+2)(IN^2+2IN+3)}{18(IN+1)^2 GH}$,
then the mean and variance of UACI are

$$\mu_{UACI} = \frac{\mu_U}{IN} = \frac{(IN+2)}{(3IN+3)}; \sigma_{UACI}^2 = \frac{\sigma_U^2}{IN^2} = \frac{(IN+2)(IN^2+2IN+3)}{IN\left(18(IN+1)^2 GH\right)}$$

(vii) **Critical value for UACI**

The hypothesis H_0 for $UACI(IEI_1, IEI_2)$ with 'α' level significance is μ_{UACI}. Where we Accept the H_0 when $UACI(IEI_1, IEI_2) \in (UACI_{*-}^\sigma, UACI_{*+}^\sigma)$ where $UACI_{*-}^\sigma, UACI_{*+}^\sigma$ are the critical value of UACI with 'α' level significance which are defined in Eqs. (11) and (12).

$$UACI_{*-}^\sigma = \mu_{UACI} - \varphi^{-1}(\alpha/2)\sigma_{UACI} \tag{11}$$

$$UACI_{*+}^\sigma = \mu_{UACI} + \varphi^{-1}(\alpha/2)\sigma_{UACI} \tag{12}$$

The critical value of UACI for different size of Dicom image is shown in Table 2, the UACI values is tabulated in Table 4 based on proposed one. Further, this value is compared with several existing methodologies in Table 6 and also shown in Fig. 4.

3 Results and Discussions

The 16 bit MRI images with size 256 × 256 and 512 × 512 is proposed and implemented. The tested images and its equivalent encrypted images are shown in Figs. 2a–e and 3a–e respectively.

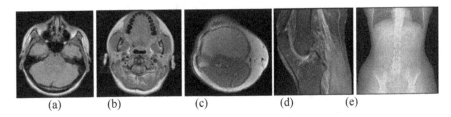

Fig. 2. Test images: (a) MR_Image1 (b) MR_Image2 (c) MR_Image3 (d) MR_Image4 (e) OT_Image5

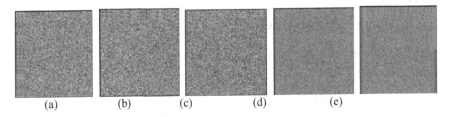

Fig. 3. Encrypted images: (a) MR_Image1 (b) MR_Image2 (c) MR_Image3 (d) MR_Image4 (e) OT_Image5

Table 1. Numerical results of DICOM image for NPCR randomness test

M × N	μ_{npcr}	σ_{npcr}	$NPCR_*^{0.05}$	$NPCR_*^{0.01}$	$NPCR_*^{0.001}$
64 × 64	99.9985	0.00610	99.9884	99.9843	99.9796
128 × 128	99.9985	0.00305	99.9935	99.9913	99.9890
256 × 256	99.9985	0.00153	99.9960	99.9949	99.9938
512 × 512	99.9985	0.00076	99.9972	99.9967	99.9961
1024 × 1024	99.9985	0.00038	99.9978	99.9976	99.9972

Table 2. Numerical results of DICOM image for UACI randomness test

M × N	μ_{UACI}	σ_{UACI}	$UACI_{*-}^{0.05}$	$UACI_{*-}^{0.01}$	$UACI_{*-}^{0.001}$	$UACI_{*+}^{0.05}$	$UACI_{*+}^{0.01}$	$UACI_{*+}^{0.001}$
64 × 64	33.3338	0.3682	32.6119	32.3851	32.1218	34.0557	34.2826	34.5459
128 × 128	33.3338	0.1841	32.9729	32.8594	32.7278	33.6948	33.8082	33.9399
256 × 256	33.3338	0.0921	33.1534	33.0967	33.0308	33.5143	33.5710	33.6369
512 × 512	33.3338	0.0460	33.2436	33.2153	33.1823	33.4241	33.4524	33.4853
1024 × 1024	33.3338	0.0230	33.2887	33.2745	33.2581	33.3790	33.3931	33.4096

Table 3. NPCR for proposed DICOM image encryption

DICOM IMAGE	256 × 256	$NPCR_*^{0.05} = 99.9960$	$NPCR_*^{0.01} = 99.9949$	$NPCR_*^{0.001} = 99.9938$
	512 × 512	$NPCR_*^{0.05} = 99.9972$	$NPCR_*^{0.01} = 99.9967$	$NPCR_*^{0.001} = 99.9961$
Image	Result	0.05 level	0.01 level	0.001 level
Image1 256 × 256	99.9991	Pass	Pass	Pass
Image2 256 × 256	99.9989	Pass	Pass	Pass
Image3 256 × 256	99.9998	Pass	Pass	Pass
Image4 512 × 512	99.9987	Pass	Pass	Pass
Image5 512 × 512	99.9986	Pass	Pass	Pass

Table 4. UACI for proposed DICOM image encryption

DICOM IMAGE	256 × 256	$UACI_{*-}^{0.05} = 33.1534$ $UACI_{*+}^{0.05} = 33.5143$	$UACI_{*-}^{0.01} = 33.0967$ $UACI_{*+}^{0.01} = 33.5710$	$UACI_{*-}^{0.001} = 33.0308$ $UACI_{*+}^{0.001} = 33.6369$
	512 × 512	$UACI_{*-}^{0.05} = 33.2436$ $UACI_{*+}^{0.05} = 33.4241$	$UACI_{*-}^{0.01} = 33.2153$ $UACI_{*+}^{0.01} = 33.4524$	$UACI_{*-}^{0.001} = 33.1823$ $UACI_{*+}^{0.001} = 33.4853$
Image	Result	0.05 level	0.01 level	0.001 level
Image1 256 × 256	33.3510	Pass	Pass	Pass
Image2 256 × 256	33.2839	Pass	Pass	Pass
Image3 256 × 256	33.2120	Pass	Pass	Pass
Image4 512 × 512	33.3365	Pass	Pass	Pass
Image5 512 × 512	33.2438	Pass	Pass	Pass

Table 5. NPCR randomness test for DICOM image encryption

512 × 512 DICOM IMAGE		$NPCR_*^{0.05} = 99.9972$	$NPCR_*^{0.01} = 99.9967$	$NPCR_*^{0.001} = 99.9961$
Methods	Result	0.05 level	0.01 level	0.001 level
Sathiskumar [28]	98.4309	Fail	Fail	Fail
Mahmood [29]	99.6501	Fail	Fail	Fail
Fu [30]	99.6391	Fail	Fail	Fail
Lima [31]	99.6082	Fail	Fail	Fail
Padmapriya [23]	99.88	Fail	Fail	Fail
Weijiacao [33]	99.6011	Fail	Fail	Fail
Dhivya [34]	99.997	Pass	Pass	Pass
Parvees [32]	99.9992	Pass	Pass	Pass
Proposed method	99.9987	Pass	Pass	Pass

Table 6. UACI randomness test for DICOM image encryption

512 × 512 DICOM IMAGE		$UACI_{*-}^{0.05} = 33.2436$ $UACI_{*+}^{0.05} = 33.4241$	$UACI_{*-}^{0.01} = 33.2153$ $UACI_{*+}^{0.01} = 33.4524$	$UACI_{*-}^{0.001} = 33.1823$ $UACI_{*+}^{0.001} = 33.4853$
Methods	Result	0.05 level	0.01 level	0.001 level
Sathiskumar [28]	−0.0083	Fail	Fail	Fail
Fu [30]	33.5141	Fail	Fail	Fail
Lima [31]	33.4682	Fail	Fail	Pass
Parvees [32]	50.0857	Fail	Fail	Fail
Padmapriya [23]	33.49	Fail	Fail	Fail
Weijiacao [33]	33.4811	Fail	Fail	Pass
Dhivya [34]	33.3731	Pass	Pass	Pass
Proposed method	33.2901	Pass	Pass	Pass

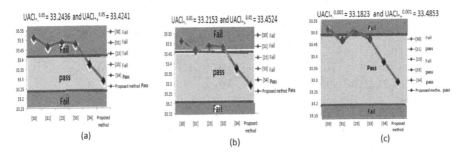

Fig. 4. Comparison of UACI DICOM image Encryption: (a) $UACI_{*-}^{0.05} = 33.2436$ and $UACI_{*+}^{0.05} = 33.4241$ (b) $UACI_{*-}^{0.01} = 33.2153$ and $UACI_{*+}^{0.01} = 33.4524$ (c) $UACI_{*-}^{0.001} = ,33.1823$ and $UACI_{*+}^{0.001} = 33.4853$

This proposed method is implemented using JDK 1.8 in windows 7. For all tested images the NPCR and UACI values are calculated. The $NPCR_*^\sigma$ value of DICOM size 256×256 and 512×512 for $\sigma = 0.05$ are 99.9960, 99.9972 respectively and for $\sigma = 0.01, 0.001$ the values are 99.9949, 99.9967, 99.9938, 99.9961 respectively. For the proposed method, all five tested images NPCR values are higher than this estimated value. Hence the proposed method passes the NPCR randomness test in Table 3.

The $UACI_{*-}^\sigma$ value of the DICOM with size 256×256 and 512×512 for $\sigma = 0.05$ are 33.1534, 33.2436 respectively and for $\sigma = 0.01$, $\sigma = 0.001$ the values are 33.0967, 33.2153, 33.0308, 33.1823, respectively. All five tested images UACI values are higher than this estimated value. The estimated $UACI_{*+}^\sigma$ value of the DICOM with size 256×256 and 512×512 for $\sigma = 0.05$ are 33.5143, 33.4241 respectively and for $\sigma = 0.01$, $\sigma = 0.001$ the values are 33.5710, 33.4524, 33.6369, 33.4853, respectively. All five tested images UACI values are lower than this estimated value. Most of the existing method fails the NPCR and UACI randomness test.

4 Conclusion

The key contribution of this paper is to improve the DICOM security. This article concentrates on security challenges in patient's clinical information in the field of the digital medical system. A novel approach is confronted with efficient encryption algorithms to ensure the security and confidentiality of patients' clinical data. The proposed method deals with the NPCR and UACI randomness assessments for DICOM encryption. The hypothesis assessments with α level significance are made for NPCR and UACI. With these two hypothesis assessments, it is easy to just Agree or Decline the null hypothesis that test cipher text images are random-like. Therefore, such assessments offer qualitative outcomes rather than quantitative outcomes for DICOM image security. After analysing the findings of various researches in this field, it shows that many of the examined methods are challenging or at least not mathematically random-like. Based on the result obtained from the proposed algorithm it shows that it is statistically random –like. Hence the suggested DICOM cryptosystem acquires an appealing quantity of safety for real-time medical image security programs.

Acknowledgements. Authors wish to express their sincere thanks to acknowledging SASTRA Deemed University, Thanjavur, India for extending infrastructural support to carry out this work.

References

1. Armbrust, L.J.: PACS and image storage. Vet. Clin. N. Am. - Small Anim. Pract. **39**, 711–718 (2009). https://doi.org/10.1016/j.cvsm.2009.04.004
2. Bidgood, W.D., Horii, S.C.: Introduction to the ACR-NEMA DICOM standard. Radiographics **12**, 345–355 (1992). https://doi.org/10.1148/radiographics.12.2.1561424
3. Mishra, S.K., Kapoor, L., Singh, I.P.: Telemedicine in India: current scenario and the future. Telemed. J. E Health **15**, 568–575 (2009). https://doi.org/10.1089/tmj.2009.0059

4. Raghupathi, B.W., Tan, J.: Strategic IT applications in health care. Commun. ACM **45**, 56–61 (2002)
5. Alfalou, A., Brosseau, C., Abdallah, N., Jridi, M.: Assessing the performance of a method of simultaneous compression and encryption of multiple images and its resistance against various attacks. Opt. Express **21**, 8025–8043 (2013)
6. Moumen, A., Bouye, M., Sissaoui, H.: New secure partial encryption method for medical images using graph coloring problem. Nonlinear Dyn. (2015). https://doi.org/10.1007/s11071-015-2253-4
7. Vinoth Kumar, C., Natarajan, V., Poonguzhali, P.: Secured patient information transmission using reversible watermarking and DNA encryption for medical images. Appl. Math. Sci. **9**, 2381–2391 (2015). https://doi.org/10.12988/ams.2015.53219
8. Pareek, N.K., Patidar, V.: Medical image protection using genetic algorithm operations. Soft. Comput. **20**, 763–772 (2014). https://doi.org/10.1007/s00500-014-1539-7
9. Khan, M.A., Ali, A., Jeoti, V., et al.: A chaos-based substitution box (S-Box) design with improved differential approximation probability (DP). Iran J. Sci. Technol. Trans. Electr. Eng. **42**, 219 (2018). https://doi.org/10.1007/s40998-018-0061-9
10. Biham, E., Shamir, A.: Differential cryptanalysis of DES-like cryptosystems. J. Cryptol. **4**, 3–72 (1991). https://doi.org/10.1007/BF00630563
11. Biham, E., Shamir, A.: Differential cryptanalysis of the full 16-round DES. In: Brickell, Ernest F. (ed.) CRYPTO 1992. LNCS, vol. 740, pp. 487–496. Springer, Heidelberg (1993). https://doi.org/10.1007/3-540-48071-4_34
12. Biham, E., Shamir, A.: Differential fault analysis of secret key cryptosystems. In: Kaliski, Burton S. (ed.) CRYPTO 1997. LNCS, vol. 1294, pp. 513–525. Springer, Heidelberg (1997). https://doi.org/10.1007/BFb0052259
13. Behnia, S., Akhshani, A., Mahmodi, H., Akhavan, A.: A novel algorithm for image encryption based on mixture of chaotic maps. Chaos, Solitons Fractals **35**, 408–419 (2008). https://doi.org/10.1016/j.chaos.2006.05.011
14. Chen, G., Mao, Y., Chui, C.K.: A symmetric image encryption scheme based on 3D chaotic cat maps. Chaos, Solitons Fractals **21**, 749–761 (2004)
15. Huang, C.K., Nien, H.H.: Multi chaotic systems based pixel shuffle for image encryption. Opt. Commun. **282**, 2123–2127 (2009). https://doi.org/10.1016/j.optcom.2009.02.044
16. Kumar, A., Ghose, M.K.: Extended substitution-diffusion based image cipher using chaotic standard map. Commun. Nonlinear Sci. Numer. Simul. **16**, 372–382 (2011)
17. Khanzadi, H., Eshghi, M., Borujeni, S.E.: Arab J. Sci. Eng. **39**, 1039 (2014). https://doi.org/10.1007/s13369-013-0713-z
18. Liao, X., Lai, S., Zhou, Q.: A novel image encryption algorithm based on self-adaptive wave transmission. Signal Process. **90**, 2714–2722 (2010). https://doi.org/10.1016/j.sigpro.2010.03.022
19. Zhang, Q., Guo, L., Wei, X.: Image encryption using DNA addition combining with chaotic maps. Math. Comput. Model. **52**, 2028–2035 (2010). https://doi.org/10.1016/j.mcm.2010.06.005
20. Kaur, M., Kumar, V.: Arab J. Sci. Eng. **43**, 8127 (2018). https://doi.org/10.1007/s13369-018-3355-3
21. Palacios-Luengas, L., Pichardo-Méndez, J.L., Díaz-Méndez, J.A., et al.: Arab J. Sci. Eng. **44**, 3817 (2019)
22. Zhu, Z., Zhang, W., Wong, K., Yu, H.: A chaos-based symmetric image encryption scheme using a bit-level permutation. Inf. Sci. (Ny) **181**, 1171–1186 (2011)
23. Praveenkumar, P., Kerthana Devi, N., Ravichandran, D., et al.: Transreceiving of encrypted medical image – a cognitive approach. Multimed. Tools Appl. **77**, 8393–8418 (2018). https://doi.org/10.1007/s11042-017-4741-7

24. Wang, X., Liu, C.: A novel and effective image encryption algorithm based on chaos and DNA encoding. Multimed. Tools Appl. **76**, 6229–6245 (2017)
25. Wu, Y., Member, S., Noonan, J.P., Member, L.: NPCR and UACI randomness tests for image encryption. Cyber J. Multidisc. J. Sci. Technol. J. Sel. Areas. Telecommun. **1**, 31–38 (2011)
26. Le, H.M., Aburdene, M.F.: The discrete Gould transform and its applications. In: Proceedings of SPIE-the Image Processing: Algorithms and Systems, Neural Networks, and Machine Learning. International Society for Optics (2006). http://doi.org/10.1117/12.643278
27. Praveenkumar, P., Amirtharajan, R., Thenmozhi, K., Rayappan, J.B.B.: Triple chaotic image scrambling on RGB - a random image encryption approach. Secur. Commun. Netw. **8**, 3335–3345 (2015). https://doi.org/10.1002/sec.1257
28. Sathishkumar, G.A., Bhoopathybagan, K., Sriraam, N., Venkatachalam, S.P., Vignesh, R.: A novel image encryption algorithm using two chaotic maps for medical application. In: Meghanathan, N., Kaushik, B.K., Nagamalai, D. (eds.) CCSIT 2011. CCIS, vol. 133, pp. 290–299. Springer, Heidelberg (2011). https://doi.org/10.1007/978-3-642-17881-8_28
29. Mahmood, A., Dony, R., Areibi, S.: An adaptive encryption based genetic algorithms for medical images. In: 2013 IEEE International Workshop on Machine Learning for Signal Processing (MLSP), pp. 1–6 (2013). https://doi.org/10.1109/mlsp.2013.6661920
30. Fu, C., Zhang, G., Bian, O., et al.: A novel medical image protection scheme using a 3-Dimensional chaotic system. PLoS ONE **9**, e115773 (2014). https://doi.org/10.1371/journal.pone.0115773
31. Lima, J.B., Madeiro, F., Sales, F.J.R.: Encryption of medical images based on the cosine number transform. Signal Process Image Commun. **35**, 1–8 (2015)
32. Parvees, M.Y.M., Samath, J.A., Bose, B.P.: Secured medical images - a chaotic pixel scrambling approach. J. Med. Syst. **40**, 232 (2016). https://doi.org/10.1007/s10916-016-0611-5
33. Cao, W., Zhou, Y., Chen, C.L.P., Xia, L.: Medical image encryption using edge maps. Signal Process. **132**, 96–109 (2017). https://doi.org/10.1016/j.sigpro.2016.10.003
34. Ravichandran, D., Praveenkumar, P., Balaguru Rayappan, J.B., Amirtharajan, R.: Chaos based crossover and mutation for securing DICOM image. Comput. Biol. Med. **72**, 170–184 (2016). https://doi.org/10.1016/j.compbiomed.2016.03.020
35. Ravichandran, D., Praveenkumar, P., Rayappan, J.B.B., Amirtharajan, R.: DNA chaos blend to secure medical privacy. IEEE Trans. Nanobiosci. **16**(8), 850–858 (2017). https://doi.org/10.1109/TNB.2017.2780881

Secure ATM Device Design by Control Command Verification

Hisao Ogata[1,2(✉)], Tomoyoshi Ishikawa[1], Norichika Miyamoto[1], and Tsutomu Matsumoto[2]

[1] Hitachi-Omron Terminal Solutions, Corp., 1-6-3 Osaki, Shinagawa-ku, Tokyo 141-8576, Japan
hisao_ogata@hitachi-omron-ts.com
[2] Yokohama National University, 79-7 Tokiwadai, Hodogaya-ku, Yokohama, Kanagawa 240-8501, Japan
tsutomu@ynu.ac.jp

Abstract. Recently, criminals frequently utilize logical attacks to Automated Teller Machines (ATMs) and financial institutes' networks to steal cash. An ATM security measure called "Control Command Verification" has been proposed to cope with the issues. The measure utilizes peripheral devices to prevent logical attacks "unauthorized cash withdrawals" for smart card transactions. When this measure is applied to magnetic stripe card transactions, there are a variety of implementable systems because of less implementation constraints resulted from the existing security standards for magnetic stripe card transactions. Properly implementable systems should be selected from these systems in terms of three viewpoints: preventing a wide range of logical attacks in a transaction, harmonizing with existing ATM operations, and minimizing the number of peripheral devices to be modified. This paper proposes a systematic implementation design method of the measure to satisfy those three viewpoints. Three proper systems out of the 135 implementable systems can be selected by applying the design method to magnetic stripe card transactions.

Keywords: ATM · Cryptography · Device · Malware · Network · Security

1 Introduction

Recently, criminals frequently carry out logical attacks to Automated Teller Machines (ATMs) and financial institutes' networks to steal cash in more than 30 countries, and these attacks resulted in serious social issues. In general, an ATM consists of a PC and peripheral devices, such as a card reader and a dispenser. The PC and a peripheral device are connected with a USB/RS-232C cable, and the PC and the host computer are connected via the financial institute's Wide Area Network (WAN). Major attack surfaces of those logical attacks are the financial institute's WAN [1], the PC [2–5], and the USB/RS-232C cables [1, 6–8]. Eventually, unauthorized cash dispensing commands are sent to the dispenser to withdraw cash from the ATM.

© Springer Nature Singapore Pte Ltd. 2019
V. S. Shankar Sriram et al. (Eds.): ATIS 2019, CCIS 1116, pp. 32–50, 2019.
https://doi.org/10.1007/978-981-15-0871-4_3

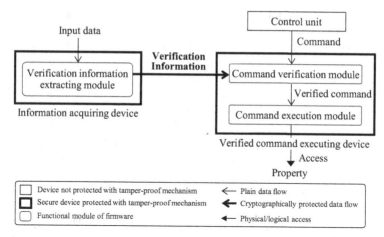

Fig. 1. Primary model of Control Command Verification

The existing security measures [1, 8–12] try to protect the WAN, the PC, and the USB/RS-232C cables, and especially secure integrity of executable files in the PC. However, there is an issue that those measures could be bypassed or disabled by criminals since frequent physical/logical accesses inside ATMs are required in existing ATM operations. For example, periodical cash replenishment and collection for cash services once a few days to a week, and quarterly periodical software/content updating for better services. ATM management costs could increase if integrity of the executable files is assured by tight ATM operational managements to cope with that issue. Furthermore, it is difficult to secure the integrity by limited human resources 24 h 7 days when a financial institute operates more than ten thousand ATMs. To solve the issue, an ATM security measure [13] was proposed, in which controlled peripheral devices themselves verify commands sent from the PC before executing the commands to access property. The proposed measure is called "Control Command Verification" in this paper, and the primary model is depicted in Fig. 1. The information acquiring device extracts verification information to verify a command from input data, and securely sends the information to the verified command executing device. The command verification module verifies a command sent from the control unit with the received information, and the command execution module accesses the property according to the verified command. The primary model was applied to smart card transactions to prevent unauthorized cash withdrawal, and a prototype system of the primary model was developed with an existing ATM system to confirm the operational feasibility [13].

The Control Command Verification should be also applied to widespread magnetic stripe card transactions since there are many logical attacks targeting those transactions. When the Control Command Verification is applied to magnetic stripe card transactions, there are a variety of implementable systems because all transaction sub-processes in a cash withdrawal transaction must be protected due to poor existing security mechanisms. In smart card transactions, the Control Command Verification is applied to prevent only unauthorized cash dispensing commands sent from the PC since the card number and transaction messages transferred between an ATM and the host computer, are protected in accordance with EMV®[1] specifications [14]. In magnetic stripe card transactions, properly implementable systems of the Control Command Verification should be selected from the variety of the implementable systems in terms of three viewpoints: preventing a wide range of logical attacks in a transaction, harmonizing with existing ATM operations, and minimizing the number of peripheral devices to be modified. In general, ATMs are composed of a set of peripheral devices, which are supplied as one of multiple models by multiple device vendors, in conformity to the required specifications of the financial institute and the country regulations. Thus, many devices equipped with greatly modified functions for the control command verification result in increased costs and delayed delivery times. Minimization of the number of peripheral devices to be modified is required, and device/system design to implement the Control Command Verification should be standardized to meet a lot of financial institutes' requirements. This paper proposes a systematic implementation design method of the control command verification to satisfy the three viewpoints described above. By applying the design method to magnetic stripe card transactions, three proper systems out of the 135 implementable systems can be selected.

The remainder of this paper is organized as follows. Section 2 addresses existing ATM systems, the issue of existing measures, and the conditions to implement the Control Command Verification. Section 3 presents the design method to implement the Control Command Verification. Section 4 describes implementation for magnetic stripe card transactions. Section 5 concludes this paper.

2   Control Command Verification

2.1   An ATM System and Magnetic Stripe Card Transaction

Figure 2 outlines an example of an ATM system and data flow of an existing cash withdrawal transaction with a magnetic stripe card. An ATM consists of a PC and peripheral devices. The PC logically consists of three layers: multi-vendor application, a standardized ATM platform [9] to control the peripheral devices, and an Operating System (OS). It is noted that the ATM platform and the OS are not shown in the figure. The ATM platform is vulnerable to unauthorized APIs accesses due to unencrypted APIs and its openness to the public. Encrypting PIN Pad (EPP) is a peripheral device used by an ATM user to enter Personal Identification Number (PIN). The EPP outputs an encrypted PIN [15] and the PIN is transferred to a Hardware Security Module (HSM) connected with the host computer. Then the HSM extracts a PIN from the encrypted PIN to verify the PIN for the user's authenticity. The HSM and EPPs must be a tamper-proof secure cryptographic device meeting the PCI PIN requirements [16–18]. It is supposed that the multi-vendor application includes "transaction application" (hereinafter called "transaction AP") processing transaction messages and "cash dispensing application" (hereinafter called "cash dispensing AP") controlling the dispenser.

---

[1] EMV is a registered trademark in the U.S. and other countries and an unregistered trademark elsewhere. The EMV trademark is owned by EMVCo, LLC.

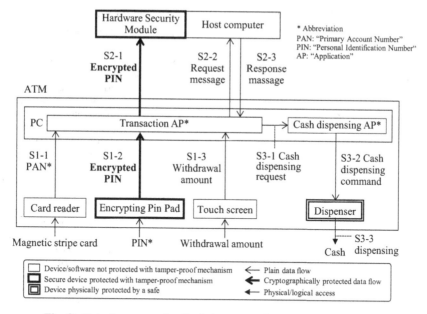

Fig. 2. Data flow example of existing magnetic stripe card transaction.

A transaction consists of three sub-processes: (1) generating a transaction request message, (2) communicating with the host computer, and (3) executing cash dispensing. An example of the three sub-processes is described as follows:

(1) Generating a transaction request message

The transaction AP receives an S1-1 Primary Account Number (PAN) stored on a magnetic stripe card from the card reader, an S1-2 encrypted PIN from the EPP, and an S1-3 withdrawal amount from the touch screen. And then, the AP generates a transaction request message (hereinafter called "request message") from the PAN and the withdrawal amount.

(2) Communicating with the host computer

The transaction AP sends the S2-1 encrypted PIN and the S2-2 request message to the host computer. When the host computer receives them, the hardware security module verifies the encrypted PIN. And then, the host computer decides whether authorizes the transaction or not by confirming the user's account balance. The host computer sends an S2-3 "transaction response message" (hereinafter called "response message"), including the host authorization flag which indicates the host computer's decision, back to the transaction AP.

(3) Executing cash dispensing

The transaction AP provides the cash dispensing AP with an S3-1 cash dispensing request in accordance with the host authorization flag. The cash dispensing AP sends an S3-2 cash dispensing command to the dispenser. The dispenser dispenses cash according to the command.

Table 1. Logical attacks to steal cash from ATMs

No.	Sub-process	Attack objective	Attack method	Targeted property	Outline of logical attack
A1	Generating request message	Manipulation of request message for fraudulent withdrawal	Malicious device	S1-1 PAN, S1-3 withdrawal amount	– A malicious device on a USB/RS-232C cable manipulates a PAN for a reverse brute force attack to fraudulently withdraw cash from other users' accounts – A malicious device manipulates a withdrawal amount for cash robbery from a confused ATM user
A2			Malware	Request message in Transaction AP	– Malware manipulates a PAN for a reverse brute force attack to fraudulently withdraw cash from other users' accounts – Malware manipulates a withdrawal amount for cash robbery from a confused ATM user
B1	Communicating with the host computer	Unauthorized cash withdrawal	Man-in-the-Middle	S2-2 request message, S2-3 reply message	– Same as A2 – Fake host responses are generated to withdraw cash without debiting the fraudsters' accounts
C1	Executing cash dispensing	Unauthorized cash withdrawal	Malware	S3-1 cash dispensing request, S3-2 cash dispensing command in PC	Malware forces the ATM to cash out
C2			Malicious device	S3-2 cash dispensing command on USB/RS-232C	An external computer connected to the dispenser forces it to cash out
D1		Making a false trouble for fraudulent cash dispensing	Malware	Transferring time of S3-2 cash dispensing command in PC	Either cash dispensing request or cash dispensing command is temporarily held by malware to make a false trouble, and then is sent again by operating the malware to steal cash after a user leaves the ATM
D2			Malicious device	Transferring time of S3-2 cash dispensing command on USB/RS-232C	A cash dispensing command is temporarily held by a malicious device on the USB/RS-232C cable to make a false trouble, and then sent to the dispenser again by operating the malicious device to steal cash after a user leaves the ATM

2.2   Issues of Existing Security Measures

The standard security measures in Fig. 2 are described below. The EPP and the HSM are protected with a tamper-proof mechanism and a PIN is protected cryptographically. The dispenser is supposed to be secure against unauthorized physical manipulation because it is physically protected with a safe. Except for those devices and the data flow, the PC, the peripheral devices, the USB/RS-232C cables in an ATM, and the WAN between ATMs and the host computer could be targets of the logical attacks to steal cash from ATMs in each sub-process of a transaction, which are described in Table 1. It is noted that logical attacks to peripheral devices are omitted since protection of peripheral devices is included in the Control Command Verification.

The existing measures [1, 8–12] try to protect executable files in the PC against A2, C1, and D1. Furthermore, those measures try to cryptographically protect the WAN from B1, and the USB/RS-232C cables from A1 and C2. However, cryptographic communication does not work to prevent D2 since it is a kind of a replay attack that a command is temporarily held by a malicious device to make a false trouble in order for the ATM user to leave the ATM for stealing cash. A malicious person steals cash dispensed from the ATM with operating the malicious device. It is noted that cryptographic protection of the communication also depends on the PC's security because the cryptographic keys are stored in the PC. There are issues of increasing management costs if integrity of the executable files is assured by tight ATM operational managements as explained in Sect. 1.

2.3   Conditions to Implement Control Command Verification

When the Control Command Verification is applied to magnetic stripe card transactions, there are a variety of implementable systems explained in Sect. 1. Properly implementable systems should be selected among the variety of the systems from following three viewpoints.

(1) Preventing a wide range of logical attacks in a transaction
Various logical attacks targeting property in each transaction sub-process shown in Table 1 should seamlessly be prevented in a whole transaction.
(2) Harmonizing with existing ATM operations
Implemented systems should be harmonized with existing ATM operations to minimize an impact on the operations. In particular, cryptographic key setting implementation for cryptographic communication in an ATM system should be minimized because such key settings could be an attack target [19] and tightly controlled key settings are required. Such key settings should be minimized from viewpoints of working efficiency since maintenance staffs may exchange a troubled part in an ATM with a service part for trouble shooting, which requires cryptographic key settings in some cases.
(3) Minimizing the number of peripheral devices to be modified

The number of peripheral devices to be modified in order to be equipped with functions of application and other peripheral devices should be minimized so that the Control Command Verification can easily be applied to various systems. For example, if the input data in Fig. 1 is a request/reply message, the information acquiring device must parse the messages and it is an application function. As explained above, many peripheral devices having application functions and specifications of other peripheral devices could result in complicated device modification and could affect costs and delivery times. Thus, the number of peripheral devices to be modified should be minimized.

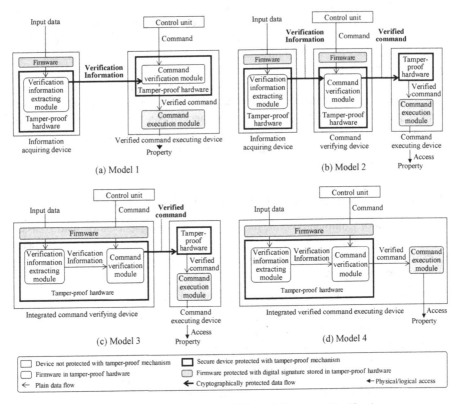

Fig. 3. Implementation models of Control Command Verification

Table 2. Comparison of implementation models for magnetic stripe card transactions

No.	Features	Model 1	Model 2	Model 3	Model 4
1	Cryptographic communication between peripheral devices	One	Two	One	Zero
2	Authenticity of command from a viewpoint of command transfer time	Verifiable	Not verifiable	Not verifiable	Verifiable
3	Authenticity of command except a viewpoint of command transfer time	Verifiable	Verifiable	Verifiable	Verifiable
4	Peripheral device modification to support many vendors' peripheral devices	Good	Poor	Poor	Good

☐ Recommended model

3 Design Method to Implement Control Command Verification

3.1 Implementation Models

To design properly implementable systems of the Control Command Verification, the features of implementation models derived from the primary model shown in Fig. 1 should be clarified. The implementation models are depicted in Fig. 3. Each device consists of tamper-proof hardware and an existing control mechanism including firmware. Authenticity of the firmware is supposed to be assured by digital signatures stored in the tamper-proof hardware although the signatures are not shown in the figure. Cryptographic functions implemented in the devices are also not shown in the figure. "Verification information extracting module" receives input data through the firmware in the device. It is supposed that data flowed in the devices are protected with the firmware or a physical measure such as a safe. Figure 3(a) shows the model 1 that each device corresponds to the device of the primary model. Figure 3(b) shows the model 2 that the verified command executing device in Fig. 3(a) is split into two devices: a command verifying device and a command executing device. Figure 3(c) shows the model 3 that the information acquiring device and the command verifying device in Fig. 3(b) are integrated into one device, namely an integrated command verifying device. Figure 3(d) depicts the model 4 that all devices in Fig. 3(b) are integrated into one device.

Table 2 summarizes the features of each implementation model in Fig. 3 for magnetic stripe card transactions. In conclusion, the model 1 and the model 4 are recommended since they have preferable features. The preferable point of each feature in Table 2 is explained as follows. In terms of No.1 feature, a smaller number is better from a viewpoint of minimizing cryptographic communication as explained in the condition (2) of Sect. 2.3. Accordingly, the model 2 is not preferable. Although the model 4 is the most preferable, the model can be adopted only when a command can be verified with input data of one device. Thus the model 1 and the model 3 should be also acceptable. In terms of No. 2 feature, "verifiable" is preferable. The model 2 and the model 3 are not verifiable since it is difficult to verify command transfer time to detect a command being temporarily held. The command executing device is not equipped with a function to verify transfer time of the received command in these models. In terms of No. 3 feature, "verifiable" is preferable, and all the models can verify a command except a viewpoint of command transfer time. In terms of No. 4 feature, "good" is preferable. The model 2 and the model 3 are also not preferable because the command verification module and the command execution module are not in one device. The command verification module in the (integrated) command verifying device must support command specifications of the command executing device in order to parse the command for verifying it. In this way, the model 2 and the model 3 do not meet the condition (3) of Sect. 2.3.

3.2 Outline of Implementation Design Method

The implementation design method is introduced to systematically design properly implementable systems of the primary model to meet the three conditions described in Sect. 2.3. The method consists of three implementation steps and guidance.

Step 1: Enumerate property and logical attacks targeting the property in all transaction sub-processes

Guidance 1. Each logical attack targets property of a different transaction sub-process in a whole transaction to steal cash. To prevent such logical attacks, ensuring consistency in each transaction sub-process is required throughout a whole transaction. Since targeted property is different for each transaction sub-process to ensure the consistency, each property and logical attacks targeting the property should be enumerated for all transaction sub-processes.

Step 2: Identify information to verify a command accessing the property, identify the source of the information, and decide a device to securely acquire the information

Guidance 2. Information to verify a command accessing the property should be acquired in a secure form and in a device as close as possible to the information source in order to ensure the authenticity of the information.

Step 3: Decide devices to verify a command accessing the property and devices to execute the verified command in light of recommended implementation models of the Control Command Verification

Guidance 3-1. Select proper devices to verify a command to prevent target logical attacks. Data and parameters included in a command are also targets of authenticity verification. The proper device should be selected carefully if the authenticity is verified from the viewpoint of command transfer time since the only two implementation models can verify the authenticity.

Guidance 3-2. Select implementation models to harmonize with existing system operations. One of points of harmonization is to minimize cryptographic communications in an implemented system so as to mitigate tight and complicated cryptographic key setting in system operations.

Guidance 3-3. Minimize the number of peripheral devices with application functions and the functions of other devices so that many vendors can be easier to supply peripheral devices.

Guidance 3-4. Select proper devices which can seamlessly verify a command accessing property in each transaction sub-process. 'Seamlessly' means that a device verifying a command in a transaction sub-process becomes a device providing information to verify a command in the following transaction sub-process. As a result, those selected devices provide a chain of consistency among transaction sub-processes to protect property in a whole transaction process.

4 Implementation

4.1 Implementation for Magnetic Stripe Card Transaction

In this section, a design process is explained to implement the Control Command Verification to a magnetic stripe card transaction in accordance with the implementation design method.

Step 1:   Enumerate property and logical attacks targeting the property in all transaction sub-processes

The property and logical attacks targeting the property are enumerated in Table 3 for each transaction sub-process. Protecting a PAN is required for a magnetic stripe card trans- action although is not required for a smart card transaction. An altered PAN in a request message can be detected in a smart card transaction according to the EMV specifications [14].

Table 3. Logical attacks and targeted property

No	Sub-process	Logical attack	Targeted property
1	Generating request message	A1 Malicious device	S1-1 PAN, S1-3 withdrawal amount
		A2 Malware	Request message in transaction AP
2	Communicating with the host computer	B1 Man-in-the-Middle	S2-2 Request message, S2-3 Reply message
3	Executing cash dispensing	C1 Malware	S3-1 Cash dispensing request, S3-2 cash dispensing command in PC
		C2 Malicious device	S3-2 Cash dispensing command on USB/RS-232C
		D1 Malware	Transferring time of S3-1 cash dispensing request, Transferring time of S3-2 cash dispensing command in PC
		D2 Malicious device	Transferring time of S3-2 cash dispensing command on USB/RS-232C

Step 2:   Identify information to verify a command accessing the property, identify the source of the information, and decide a device to securely acquire the information

Information to verify a command and information acquiring devices are summarized in Table 4. Since ATMs work in accordance with inputs from peripheral devices and communication with the host computer, the information to verify a command

Table 4. Information to verify command and information acquiring device

No	Sub-process	Targeted property	Verification Information	Information acquiring device
1	Generating request message	S1-1 PAN, S1-2 withdrawal amount	S1-1 PAN, S1-2 withdrawal amount	Card reader, EPP
		Request message in transaction AP	S1-1 PAN, S1-2 withdrawal amount	Card reader, EPP
2	Communicating with the host computer	S2-2 request message	MAC1 for S2-2	Either card reader, EPP, or dispenser
		S2-3 reply message	MAC2 for S2-3	Host computer
3	Executing cash dispensing	S3-1 Cash dispensing request, S3-2 Cash dispensing command in PC	Authorized amount (withdrawal amount in S2-2, host authorization flag in S2-3)	Either card reader, EPP, or dispenser
		S3-2 Cash dispensing command in PC	Same as above	Same as above
		Transferring time of S3-2 Cash dispensing command in PC	Reply message receiving time (reference time)	Either card reader, EPP, or dispenser
		Transferring time of S3-2 Cash dispensing command on USB/RS-232C	Same as above	Same as above

should be acquired in the peripheral devices and a counterpart device of the host computer communication. A withdrawal amount should be input not in the touch screen but in the EPP supporting cryptographic functions according to the guidance 2. A verified request message and a verified reply message need to be acquired in a secure device to make a certain link between cash dispensing and debiting the user's account. However, there are no existing devices of an ATM to securely communicate with the host computer in magnetic stripe card transactions. Therefore, either the card reader, the EPP, or the dispenser should be selected to implement the functions securely acquiring the messages in order to be consistent with the step 3. To prevent unauthorized cash withdrawal with a cash dispensing command, an authorized amount is required, which is derived from the withdrawal amount in the request message and the host authorization flag in the reply message. The authorized amount is compared with dispensing

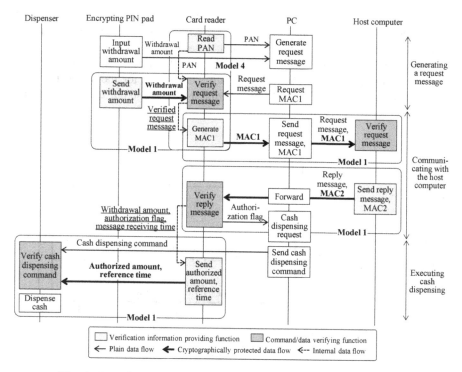

Fig. 4. Data flow ensuring consistency among transaction sub-processes

amount in the command. To prevent a replay attack to a cash dispensing command, a reference time to measure command transferring time is required to detect whether the command is temporarily held or not. The reference time should be the time when either the card reader, the EPP, or the dispenser receives the reply message.

Step 3: Decide devices to verify a command accessing the property and devices to execute the verified command in light of recommended implementation models of the Control Command Verification

According to the guidance 3-1, 3-2 and 3-3, the model 1 and the model 4 should be selected as preferable models referring to Table 2. Since a peripheral device communicating with the host computer must parse a request/reply message to verify them, which is an application function, only one device should have such functions to conform to the guidance 3-3. When the card reader is selected, the whole transaction process is depicted in Fig. 4. The following functions are implemented in each sub-process pursuant to the guidance 3-4.

(a) Sub-process generating a transaction request message

The card reader verifies the request message with a PAN internally transferred in the card reader and a withdrawal amount securely transferred from the EPP (Fig. 5). It is a combination of the model 1 and the model 4 (Fig. 4). The card reader generates a MAC (hereinafter called "MAC1") for the verified request message through the underlined verified request message so that the host computer can seamlessly verify the request message in accordance with the guidance 3-4.

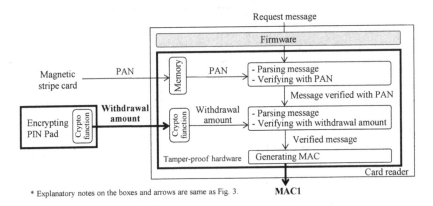

* Explanatory notes on the boxes and arrows are same as Fig. 3.   **MAC1**

Fig. 5. Implementation example of card reader communicating with the host computer

(b) Sub-process communicating with the host computer

The host computer verifies the request message with the MAC1, which is categorized to the model 1. The card reader verifies the reply message with a MAC (hereinafter called "MAC2") for the reply message received from the host computer, which is also categorized to the model 1.

(c) Sub-process executing cash dispensing

The card reader generates an authorized amount from the underlined withdrawal amount in the request message and the underlined host authorization flag in the reply message so that the dispenser can seamlessly verify the cash dispensing command sent from the PC with the authorized amount. The card reader also generates a reference time from the underlined message receiving time so that the dispenser can seamlessly verify the command transfer time. These two kinds of verification with the authorized amount and the reference time are categorized to the model 1. The applied implementation models for each transaction sub-process are summarized in Table 5. Each gray level in Table 5 shows applied implementation models when either peripheral device is selected as the counterpart of the host computer communication. There are three proper systems according to the number of devices selected as the counterpart.

Table 5. Summary of applied implementation models

(a) Sub-process generating a transaction request message

Property		S1-1 PAN, S1-2 withdrawal amount, Request message in transaction AP	
Logical Attack		A1 Malicious device, A2 Malware	
Verification information		PAN	Withdrawal amount
Information acquiring device		Card reader	EPP
Verifying device	Card reader	Model 4	Model 1
	EPP	Model 1	Model 4
	Dispenser	Model 1	Model 1

(b) Sub-process communicating with the host computer

Property		S2-2 Request message		
Logical Attack		B1 Man-in-the-Middle		
Verification information		MAC1		
Information acquiring device		Card reader	EPP	Dispenser
Verifying device	Host computer	Model 1	Model 1	Model 1
Property		S2-3 Reply message		
Logical Attack		B1 Man-in-the-Middle		
Verification information		MAC2		
Information acquiring device		Host computer		
Verifying device	Card reader	Model 1		
	EPP	Model 1		
	Dispenser	Model 1		

(c) Sub-process executing cash dispensing

Property		S3-1 Cash dispensing request, S3-2 Cash dispensing command		
Logical Attack		C1 Malware, C2 Malicious device		
Verification information		Authorized amount		
Information acquiring device		Card reader	EPP	Dispenser
Verifying device	Dispenser	Model 1	Model 1	Model 1
Property		Transferring time of S3-2 cash dispensing command		
Logical Attack		D1 Malware, D2 Malicious device		
Verification information		Reference time		
Information acquiring device		Card reader	EPP	Dispenser
Verifying device	Dispenser	Model 1	Model 1	Model 4

4.2 Detailed Data Flows of the Proper Systems

The data flows of the implementation examples are shown in Fig. 6 for each peripheral device selected as the counterpart of the host computer communication. There is no physical communication cable between existing peripheral devices. An encrypted communication between the peripheral devices is implemented by utilizing existing USB/RS-232C cables between peripheral devices and the PC. "Data Transfer Library" (hereinafter called "DTL") is newly introduced in the PC to simply provide a communication path between the peripheral devices. DTL is supposed to be installed in a layer below the standardized APIs. Figure 6(a) illustrates the data flow of the implementation example that the card reader is the counterpart device communicating with the host computer. The system related with a PIN is omitted in this section. A programmable tamper-proof secure element providing the cryptographic functions is installed in the proposing card reader, the proposing EPP and the proposing dispenser while a HSM is implemented in the proposing host computer. The cryptographic key

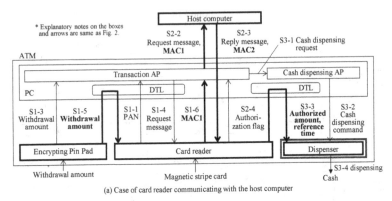

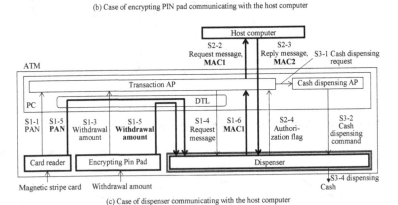

Fig. 6. Implementation examples of the Control Command Verification

management and a session creation for each encrypted communication are supposed to conform to either the PCI requirements [16–18, 20] or the EMV specifications [14] to meet confidentiality, integrity, and authenticity. A session of each encrypted communication is supposed to be preliminarily created. The detailed process flows of Fig. 6(a) are described as follows.

(1) Generating a transaction request message

The card reader sends an S1-1 PAN to the transaction AP, and stores it in the secure element. The EPP sends an S1-3 withdrawal amount to the transaction AP, and stores the amount in it. The transaction AP sends an S1-4 request message to the card reader through DTL so as to make it to generate a MAC1 for the message. When the DTL receives the message, the DTL requests the EPP to send the S1-5 withdrawal amount in an encrypted form and forwards it to the card reader. The card reader verifies the message with the PAN stored in the secure element and the S1-5 withdrawal amount. The card reader generates an S1-6 MAC1 for the verified message and sends it to the transaction AP. The card reader also stores the withdrawal amount in the secure element.

(2) Communicating with the host computer

The transaction AP sends the S2-2 request message and the MAC1 to the host computer, and then the host computer verifies the message. The host computer generates an S2-3 reply message including a host authorization flag and a MAC2, and sends them back to card reader through the transaction AP. When the card reader receives them, it stores the message receiving time as the reference time. The card reader verifies the message with the MAC2, and returns the S2-4 authorization flag to the transaction AP. The card reader also generates an authorized amount with the flag and the withdrawal amount stored in the secure element.

(3) Executing cash dispensing

The transaction AP provides the cash dispensing AP with an S3-1 cash dispensing request, and the cash dispensing AP sends an S3-2 cash dispensing command to the dispenser through the DTL. The DTL requests the card reader to send the S3-3 authorized amount and the reference time in an encrypted form, and then forwards them to the dispenser. The dispenser receives the command and the S3-3 data, and calculates the command transfer time with the reference time. And then the dispenser verifies the command with the authorized amount to confirm whether the dispensing amount in the command is identical to the authorized amount. The dispenser also verifies the command transfer time to confirm whether the transfer time exceeds a predetermined threshold. If they are successfully verified, the dispenser dispenses cash.

Figure 6(b) shows data flows of the implementation example that the EPP is the counterpart device communicating with the host computer. The functions of the EPP and the card reader are inversely positioned in Fig. 6(a) and (b). Figure 6(c) depicts the implementation example that the dispenser is the counterpart device communicating with the host computer. The detailed data flows of those examples are omitted. Deciding the most recommended implementation in Fig. 6 depends on the development costs and harmonization with the detailed specifications of the existing system and the operations. However, it is out of scope in this paper.

4.3   Evaluation of the Design Method

The number of all implementable systems of the Control Command Verification is estimated to evaluate the effect of the design method. The model 2 of Fig. 3(b) is utilized to estimate that number since the model consists of the three elementary devices. There are two steps to estimate the number. The first step is to estimate the number of peripheral device combinations in each transaction sub-process with three devices: the card reader, the EPP, and the dispenser. In the sub-process generating a transaction request message, information acquiring devices are the card reader outputting a PAN and the EPP outputting a withdrawal amount. Since those devices are fixed, there is one device combination. On the other hand, the command verifying devices can be selected from the three devices. A verifying device for PAN and a verifying device for a withdrawal amount can be independently selected from the three devices. Since the request message is sequentially verified by a verifying device for PAN and by a verifying device for a withdrawal amount, there are 9 (= 3 × 3) verifying device combinations. Order of the verifying devices can be transposed except that the both verifying devices are identical. Thus, there are additional 6 (= 3 × 3–3) combinations and total 15 combinations. The command executing device, namely, a device generating MAC1 for the request message can be selected independently among the three devices. Therefore, the number of the total device combinations is 45 (= 1 × 15 × 3).

In the sub-process communicating with the host computer, a device communicating with the host computer should coincide with the device generating MACs since a cryptographic session for MACs must be established between the device and the host computer, and there is only one device combination. In the sub-process executing cash dispensing, the information acquiring device should also coincide with the communicating device. The command verifying device can be selected from the three devices. The command executing device must be the dispenser. In this way, the number of the device combinations is 3 (= 1 × 3 × 1). The second step is to multiply the estimated numbers of the peripheral device combinations in each sub-process. That is 135 (= 45 × 1 × 3). By designing the systems pursuant to the proposed design method, three proper systems out of the 135 implementable systems can be selected as described in the previous section.

5   Conclusion

In this paper, we proposed an implementation design method of the Control Command Verification, which is a verification method of control commands by controlled devices themselves. When the Control Command Verification is applied to magnetic stripe card transactions, there are a variety of implementable systems because the Control Command Verification must protect all transaction sub-processes in a cash withdrawal transaction due to poor existing security mechanisms. Proper systems can be selected with the proposed design method from the variety of the systems in terms of three viewpoints: preventing a wide range of logical attacks in a transaction, harmonizing with existing ATM operations, and minimizing the number of peripheral devices to be modified. The proposed design method to select proper systems consists of three design steps. The step 1 is to enumerate logical attacks and targeted property in all transaction sub-processes. The step 2 is to decide proper devices providing information to verify a command accessing the property. The step 3 is to decide proper devices verifying the command with the provided information so that consistency in each transaction sub-process is ensured with recommended implementation models throughout a whole transaction process. By applying the implementation design method to magnetic stripe card transactions, three proper systems out of the 135 implementable systems can be selected. We expect that the implementation design method can also be applied not only to ATM deposit and remittance with a magnetic stripe card, but also ticketing machines and vending machines operating with payment transactions. They are going to be proposed as future works.

References

1. European law enforcement agency: Guidance and recommendations regarding logical attacks on ATMs. https://www.ncr.com/content/dam/ncrcom/content-type/brochures/EuroPol_Guidance-Recommendations-ATM-logical-attacks.pdf. Accessed 07 July 2019
2. Symantec: Backdoor.Padpin. Press Release, Symantec Security Response (2014). https://www.symantec.com/security_response/writeup.jsp?docid=2014-051213-0525-99&tabid=2. Accessed 07 July 2019
3. Kaspersky Lab.: Tyupkin Virus (Malware) | ATM Security. https://www.kaspersky.com/resource-center/threats/tyupkin-malware-atm-security-malware. Accessed 07 July 2019
4. Symantec Official Blog: Backdoor.Ploutus Reloaded – Ploutus Leaves Mexico. http://www.symantec.com/connect/blogs/backdoorploutus-reloaded-ploutus-leaves-mexico. Accessed 07 July 2019
5. The Times of India: ATM JACKPOT WITH MALWARE. TIMES NATION | Politics & Policy (2015). http://www.pressreader.com/india/the-times-of-india-mumbai-edition/20150-509/282003260992233. Accessed 07 July 2019
6. EUROPOL: 27 arrested in successful hit against ATM Black Box attacks. Press Release (2017). https://www.europol.europa.eu/newsroom/news/27-arrested-in-successful-hit-against-atm-black-box-attacks. Accessed 07 July 2019
7. The European Association for Secure Transactions (EAST): EAST reports 2016 crime stats for Europe's ATMs; black box attacks up 287 percent. (2017). https://www.atmmarketplace.com/news/east-reports-2016-crime-stats-for-europes-atms-black-box-attacks-up-287-percent/. Accessed 07 July 2019
8. NCR: ATM security EXPL a ining attack vectors, defense strategies and solutions. (2018). https://www.ncr.com/content/dam/ncrcom/content-type/white_papers/12518fin-b-atm_security_attack_vectors_and_solutions_update-fin-web.pdf. Accessed 07 July 2019
9. CEN: Extensions for Financial Services (XFS) interface specification Release 3.30 - Part 1: Application Programming Interface (API) - Service Provider Interface (SPI) - Programmer's Reference. European Committee for Standardization (2015). ftp://ftp.cen.eu/CWA/CEN/WS-XFS/CWA16926/CWA%2016926-1.pdf
10. China Zhijian Publishing House: GA 1280-2015, Security requirements for automatic teller machines. (in Simplified Chinese) https://www.spc.org.cn/online/GA%25201280-2015/

11. ATM marketplace: ATMs left behind as Windows XP support ends (2014). https://www.atmmarketplace.com/articles/atms-left-behind-as-windows-xp-support-ends/. Accessed 07 July 2019
12. Bräuer, J., Gmeiner, B., Sametinger, J.: A risk assessment of logical attacks on a CEN/XFS-based ATM platform. Int. J. Adv. Secur. **9**(3&4), 122–132 (2016). ISSN 1942-2636
13. Ogata, H., Ishikawa, T., Miyamoto, N., Matsumoto, T.: An ATM security measure for smart card transactions to prevent unauthorized cash withdrawal. IEICE Trans. Inf. Syst. **102**(3), 559–567 (2019). https://search.ieice.org/bin/pdf_link.php?category=D&lang=E&year=2019&fname=e102-d_3_559&abst
14. EMVCo, LLC: EMV Integrated Circuit Card Specifications for Payment Systems Book 2 Security and Key Management Version 4.3 (2011). https://www.emvco.com/terms-of-use/?u=wp-content/uploads/documents/EMV_v4.3_Book_2_Security_and_Key_Management_20120607061923900.pdf
15. International Organization for Standardization: ISO 9564-1:2017, ISO 9564-2:2014, Financial services – Personal Identification Number (PIN) management and security. https://www.iso.org/standard/68669.html. https://www.iso.org/standard/61448.html
16. PCI SSC: Payment Card Industry (PCI) PIN Transaction Security (PTS) Point of Interaction (POI) Modular Security Requirements Version 5.1 (2018). https://www.pcisecurity-standards.org/documents/PCI_PTS_POI_SRs_v5-1.pdf
17. PCI SSC: Payment Card Industry (PCI) PIN Security Requirements and Testing Procedures Version 3.0 (2018). https://www.pcisecuritystandards.org/documents/PCI_PIN_Security_Requirements_Testing_v3_Aug2018.pdf
18. PCI SSC: Payment Card Industry (PCI) PIN Transaction Security (PTS) Hardware Security Module (HSM) Modular Security Requirements Version 3.0 (2016). https://www.pcisecuritystandards.org/documents/PCI_HSM_Security_Requirements_v3_2016_final.pdf
19. IOActive, Inc.: IOActive Security Advisory (2017). https://ioactive.com/pdfs/ATM_security-advisory_FINAL_v4-davis_cm.pdf. Accessed 07 July 2019
20. PCI SSC: Payment Card Industry (PCI) Point-to-Point Encryption: Solution Requirements and Testing Procedures Version 2.0 (Revision 1.1) (2015). https://www.pcisecurity-standards.org/documents/P2PE_v2_r1-1.pdf

Construction of Two Dimensional Cubic-Tent-Sine Map for Secure Image Transmission

Sujarani Rajendran[1] and Manivannan Doraipandian[2(✉)]

[1] Department of Computer Science and Engineering, Srinivasa Ramanujan Centre, SASTRA Deemed University, Kumbakonam 612001, India
rsujarani@src.sastra.edu
[2] School of Computing, SASTRA Deemed University, Thanjavur 613401, India
dmv@cse.sastra.edu

Abstract. A fusion two dimensional Cubic Tent Sine (CTS) map is formulated and its dynamic range is analysed. To explore its application in secure electronic data transmission, an image cipher is developed under the architecture of confusion and diffusion. A new dual form of chaos series based confusion with fast and efficient method is employed in this cipher. Chaotic key image with excellent random behaviour is utilized for diffusion phase. The proposed cryptosystem entails higher key space and single round structural design to achieve fast and efficient cipher. The random evaluation of CTS proves that the generated key series has more complicate chaotic conduct. Simulation outcomes demonstrates that the proposed cipher possesses better performance than other image ciphers. Security assessment proves the cipher strength that can resist against various attacks.

Keywords: Chaos · Image encryption · Cubic map

1 Introduction

In recent generation there has been an increase in the amount of information sharing on networks, particularly high sensitive images are transferred over public networks. However, security demand of these images is an important issue on both transmission and storage. So a good image cipher is required for confidentiality on image exchange through unsecured networks. Conventional encryption algorithms such as AES, DES, IDEA are proved as insufficient to protect images [1], because of the intrinsic features of images like huge data, high redundancy and high correlation. In past era, many research groups identified that chaos based cryptosystem is more opt for image security [2, 3], because of its special characteristics like ergodicity, randomness, high sensitivity to seed key value and deterministic. Many chaos based image ciphers has been devloped for secure image transmission and storage [4–6]. Different dimensions of chaotic maps "single-dimensional chaotic map" and "multi-dimensional chaotic map" are available and chosen based on the requirement of security. Single dimensional map has better performance, efficient utilization of resources and better execution time. But smaller key space is the main obstacle of this types of map. On the contrary, multi-dimensional maps has higher key space but complex execution structure slows down the execution time.

© Springer Nature Singapore Pte Ltd. 2019
V. S. Shankar Sriram et al. (Eds.): ATIS 2019, CCIS 1116, pp. 51–61, 2019.
https://doi.org/10.1007/978-981-15-0871-4_4

To enhance the key size in single dimensional chaotic map, some researchers combined multiple single–dimensional chaotic maps to generate effective chaotic series. The hybrid chaotic system overcome the key size limitation and also generate long period chaotic series. In [7] two single dimensional hybrid chaotic maps are proposed by combining logistic, Tent and Sine map and the cipher achieved good result of encryption with less computational cost and better performance. Wang et al. [8] combined four single dimensional chaotic map to encrypt the color image and achieved good level of security. Even these techniques developed single chaotic map by combining multiple maps. They are lack in key size, short period of randomness, limited range of control parameters and some of the image ciphers which employed one-dimensional map has weakness in ability to fight against some potential attacks. In [9] authors pointed the weakness of single dimensional map. So to overcome this, many researchers developed two dimensional maps which are have large key size and two random series are dependent to each other and have long period of random behavior, some of the newly developed two dimensional chaotic maps is discussed in the following section.

2 Literature Review

Liu et al. [10] developed a new two–dimensional map by combining Chebyshev and sine map, in that color image is encrypted by applying the chaotic series generated by the newly developed map and proved to be fast and effective. In [11] authors developed a new 2D SIMM map by combining Logistic and Sine map and proved the random behavior by lyopunav exponent and bifurcation analysis, then by using the chaotic series of 2D SIMM image is encrypted in efficient manner. Stoyanov et al. [12] developed a new pseudorandom bit generator by utilizing Rotation equation, which is used for pixel permutation and Chebyshev map is employed in substitution process to achieve good level of image security. A new spatiotemporal cross (STC) chaotic system [13] has developed by combining one dimensional coupled-map lattices and sine map, randomness has proved by applying different evaluation technique such as Lyapunav exponent, complexity and correlation, image cryptosystem has developed by utilizing the chaotic streams of STC system, which is especially designed for color images. Wu et al. [14] developed a new two dimensional Henon Sine Map (2D-HSM) by combining Henon and Sine map, the chaotic series of 2D-HSM is utilized for permutation and DNA computation is employed in diffusion to protect the image at the time of transmission. Modal et al. [15] developed a novel image cryptosystem by employing 2D Baker's map, one of the high random behavior chaotic map. Pixels of image is permutated by the pseudorandom series of Baker's map and XOR operation is executed between pixels and chaotic series to increase the security level.

By inspired on the above studies, we have developed a hybrid two dimensional chaotic map by combining three single chaotic maps and achieved good random behavior and encryption result. A new Two Dimensional (2D) Cubic-Tent-Sine (CTS) map is proposed by combining three one dimensional chaotic map such as Cubic, Tent and Sine map. Its dynamical structure is analyzed and proved to be chaotic. The number of control parameters and its range is expanded, so the key size is enhanced which is sufficient to adopt it in image cipher. A new dual form confusion method is presented in this paper and the chaotic series generated by 2D CTS map is used as a key image for diffusion process to attain better security and efficiency than other existing technique.

The article is organized as follows. Section 2 discuss the preliminaries and the mathematical expression of the seed maps. Detailed explanation of proposed CTS image cryptosystem is given in Sect. 3. Simulation results are exposed in Sect. 4. Security scrutinize analysis is executed in Sect. 5. Developed cryptosystem is concluded in Sect. 6.

3 Preliminaries of Proposed CTS Map

3.1 Mathematical Expressions

All the seed maps such as Cubic [16], Tent and Sine [17] are discrete-time maps, CTS is the combination of these three maps. This section describe the short summary of these three chaotic maps. Their mathematical forms are defined in Eqs. (1–3)

$$\text{Cubic map} - p_{n+1} = rp_n^3 + (1 - r)p_n \tag{1}$$

Where $p_n \in [0, 1]$ and $r \in (0, 4]$. The chaotic series is in random form only when $r \in [3.57, 4]$.

$$\text{Tent map} - p_{en+1} = \begin{cases} p_i/r & 0 < p_i \le 0.5 \\ (1 - p_i)/(1 - r) & 0 < p_i \le 0.5 \end{cases} \tag{2}$$

Where r is the control parameter $r \in (0, 1)$ and $r \ne 0.5$

$$\text{Sine map} - p_{n+1} = r\sin(\pi p_n)/4 \tag{3}$$

Where the system parameter range should be $r \in (0, 4]$

Even these system has good chaotic behaviour but the key size is still required to enhance. So the developed hybrid CTS map include all the parameters of aforementioned maps and that will be considered as a keys of proposed cryptosystem. The CTS map mathematical representation is given in Eq. (4). The three maps are not combined as it is, we have done some changes to achieve worthy random chaotic key series.

$$\begin{aligned} p_{n+1} &= mod(\alpha(fp^3) + (1 - \alpha)p_n \\ q_{n+1} &= \beta * \sin(\pi(fq)) \end{aligned} \tag{4}$$

$$fp = \begin{cases} q_n/\gamma & 0 < q_n \le \gamma \\ (1 - q_n)/(1 - \gamma) & \gamma < q_n \le 1 \end{cases} \quad fq = \begin{cases} p_n/\gamma & 0 < p_n \le \gamma \\ (1 - p_n)/(1 - \gamma) & \gamma < p_n \le 1 \end{cases}$$

Here α, β and γ are act as control factors and p_0 and q_0 are the seed values and their range should be $0 < \alpha, \gamma, p_0, q_0 \le 1$ and $\beta > 2$. The chaotic series is in chaotic state only in these ranges. These three parameters and two seed value totally 5 values act as keys, so if we take the maximum size of each key as 10^{-15} for 64 bit processor, then the total size of the key will be $(10^{15})^5 = 10^{75} > 2^{256}$, so key size is sufficiently enough to fight against bute-force attack. Trajectories of CTS presented in Fig. 1 proves that the chaotic series of the proposed map is random in nature.

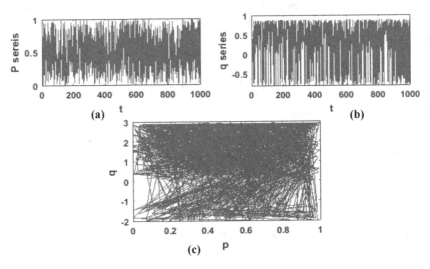

(a)

(b)

(c)

Fig. 1. Trajactories of CTS map (a) P series with 1000 iterations (b) Q series with 1000 iterations (c) correlation of P and Q

4   2D-CTS Map Based Image Cryptosystem

The proposed algorithm employs confusion done by scrambling the image in random manner depends on the index of CTS chaotic series. Diffusion is executed by applying XOR operation between the key image and confused image. Key image is the combination of two chaotic series in odd and even column format. The entire flow diagram of the cryptosystem shown in Fig. 2 and the step by step description of the cryptosystem is presented in the form of Algorithm 1 and Algorithm 2 is given below.

> **Step 1**: Elect the encryption keys $\{\alpha, \beta, \gamma, p_0, q_0\}$ which act as a parameters and seed input of 2D-CTS
> **Step 2:** Choose an image $PI_{M \times N}$ and two chaotic key streams such as $P = \{p_1, p_2, p_3 \ldots \ldots p_{size}\}$ and $Q = \{q_1, q_2, q_3 \ldots \ldots q_{size}\}$ are generated with respect to the seed value and parameters. Here $size = (M \times N)/2$, M and N indicates the height and width of the input image.
> **Step 3**: Permutate PI with Algorithm 1 to gain a confused image PI'
> **Step 4**: Diffuse PI' with Algorithm 2 to gain an encrypted image EI

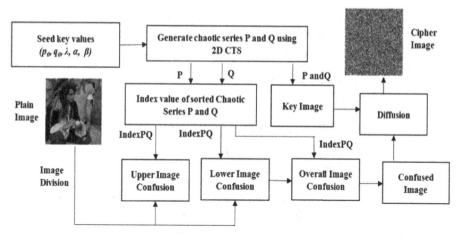

Fig. 2. Overall structure of proposed CTS image cryptosystem

Algorithm 1 Confusion process of developed cryptosystem

Input: Plain image PI_{MN} and Key stream
$$P = \{ p_1, p_2, p_3 \dots\dots p_{M/2} \} and \quad Q = \{ q_1, q_2, q_3 \dots\dots q_{M/2} \}$$
Output: Confused image PI'

1. Divide the image horizontally as two parts
$$upper_{x,y} = \{ PI_{1,1}, PI_{1,2} \dots\dots PI_{x,y} \} \ where \ x = 1,2 \dots\dots M/2 \ and \ y = 1 \dots N$$
$$lower_{z,y} = \{ PI_{z,1}, PI_{z+1,2} \dots\dots PI_{M,N\}} \ where \ z = \left(\frac{M}{2}\right) + 1, \left(\frac{M}{2}\right) + 2 \dots\dots M$$

2. Select first M chaotic series $P1 = p_1, p_2 \dots\dots p_M$ and $Q1 = q_1, q_2 \dots\dots q_M$
   $[sortp1, indexp1] = sort\ (P1); [sortq1, indexq1] = sort(Q1)$

3. Permute the upper part of the image.
$$upper_{x,y} \Leftrightarrow upper_{indexp1(x),indexq1(y)}$$
4. Select next M chaotic series
   $$P2 = p_{M+1}, p_{M+2}, \dots\dots p_{2M} \ and \ Q2 = q_{M+1}, q_{M+2}, \dots\dots q_{2M}$$
   $[sortp2, indexp2] = sort\ (P2); [sortq2, indexq2] = sort(Q2)$

5. Permute the lower part of the image
$$lower_{z,y} \Leftrightarrow lower_{indexp2(i),indexq2(j)} \quad where \ i, j = 1,2,\dots\dots M\ or\ N$$
6. $MPI = merge\ (upper, lower)$
7. Permute the whole merged image MPI by choosing another M chaotic series from P and Q by applying the same logic then we get the final confused image PI'

Algorithm 2: Diffusion process of developed cryptosystem

Input: Confused image and Key streams

$P = \{ p_1, p_2, p_3 \ldots \ldots p_{size} \}$ and $Q = \{q_1, q_2, q_3 \ldots \ldots q_{size} \}$

Output: Encrypted Image EI

1. Convert single dimensional P and Q series in to two dimensional key image
2. Create key image KI by convert decimal form chaotic series into integer form which is eligible for diffusion.

$$KI_{i,j} = \left((P \times 10^{14}), mod\ 256\right) \quad if\ \left((j\ mod\ 2) == 0\right)$$
$$KI_{i,j} = \left((Q \times 10^{14}), mod\ 256\right) \quad if\ \left((j\ mod\ 2) \neq 0\right)$$
$$where\ i, j = 1, 2, \ldots \ldots M \times N$$

3. Diffuse the image PI' by applying XOR operation with KI
$$EI = KI \oplus PI'$$

4. Final Encrypted image EI is obtained

In decryption process the chaotic key stream is common as it is in sender side. The keys are communicated securely. At the time of decryption, first the diffusion process Algorithm 2 is executed with the cipher image and then permutation logic Algorithm 1 is applied to the result of diffusion process, finally plain image is obtained.

5 Experimental Results

Within this section, outcome of the proposed CTS image cryptosystem results are evaluated and compared to finalize the level of security. Experiments are executed in Matlab 2017 platform in Core 2 Duo 2.40 GHz CPU with 4 GB RAM. Standard benchmark images from SIPI database of size 256×256 is employed to carry out the evaluation and comparison. Figure 3 shows the outcome of each process.

6 Security Analysis

6.1 Statistical Attack Analysis

The most critic analysing methods to test the randomness of the cipher image is Correlation coefficient (CC), Entropy and Histogram analysis. In the following subsections these methods are applied to the CTS cryptosystem to identify the security level.

6.1.1 Correlation Coefficient Analysis

The vital goal of image cryptosystem is to maximum reduction of correlation between adjacency pixels in the plain image [18]. This will be identified by the well-known test called CC analysis. For the good image cryptosystem the CC value of image cipher should be equal or nearest to 0. The calculation part of CC is explained in Eq. (5)

$$cr_{p,q} = \frac{N.cov(p,q)}{\sqrt{\sum_{i=1}^{N}\left(p_i - E_p\right)^2 . \sum_{i=1}^{N}\left(q_i - E_q\right)^2}} \tag{5}$$

$$\text{Where} \begin{cases} E_x = \frac{1}{N}\sum_{i=1}^{N} p_i \\ cov(p,q) = E\left(\left(p - E_p\right)\left(q - E_q\right)\right) \end{cases}$$

Here p and q represents the three directional adjacent pixel values. Table 1 shows the CC results of cipher image in all the directions. It can be recognized that all the result values are nearest to 0. Sample of horizontal correlation of plain image and

Fig. 3. Simulation results (a) Input image (b) Upper image confusion (c) Lower image confusion (d) Overall image confusion (e) Diffusion process (f) decrypted image

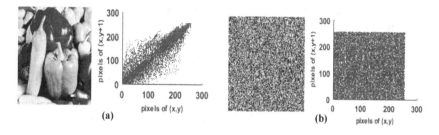

Fig. 4. CC result analysis: horizontal correlation of (a) plain image (b) cipher image

Table 1. Comparison of CC results with existing methods of image size 256 × 256

Image	Direction				
Plain image	Horizontal	0.9735	0.8981	0.8038	0.9115
	Vertical	0.9820	0.9699	0.8183	0.9452
	Diagonal	0.9582	0.9155	0.8090	0.8833
Proposed scheme	Horizontal	0.0036	−0.0021	−0.0016	0.0080
	Vertical	−0.0054	0.0038	0.0018	0.0036
	Diagonal	−9.803e^{-04}	0.0104	−0.0035	0.0023
Ref. [14]	Horizontal	0.0016	0.0056	0.0026	0.0001
	Vertical	0.0059	0.0037	0.0009	0.0031
	Diagonal	0.0034	0.0032	0.0052	0.0015
Ref. [19]	Horizontal	0.0037	0.0023	0.0059	0.0073
	Vertical	0.0258	0.0019	0.0041	0.0109
	Diagonal	0.0079	0.0011	0.0028	0.0016
Ref. [20]	Horizontal	0.0021	0.0041	0.0055	0.0073
	Vertical	0.0218	0.0021	0.0015	0.0216
	Diagonal	0.0096	0.0009	0.0041	0.0035

cipher image is given in Fig. 4 which proves that the CTS cryptosystem greatly reduced the correlation among the pixels.

6.1.2 Histogram Analysis

In plain image each pixel frequency is different, so based on histogram intruders identify the frequency and possible to hack the plain image by applying some statistical attacks. So an efficient cryptosystem should provide equal frequency of all pixels in cipher image [21]. To demonstrate that our CTS cryptosystem is more robust histogram of plain image and cipher images are presented in Fig. 5

6.1.3 Entropy Analysis

This analysis is used to test whether the outcome image of the cryptosystem is fully random. A general entropy value for grayscale random image is 8, so an entropy value of good cryptosystem cipher image should be nearest or exactly 8 [22]. The mathematical part of entropy is defined in Eq. (6).

$$H(P) = \sum_{i=0}^{2^M-1} Prob(p_i)log\frac{1}{Prob(p_i)} \tag{6}$$

Where p_i is the ith pixel value, $prob(p_i)$ finds the probability of p_i in image and M represents the pixels count in image. Table 2 displays the entropy results of different cipher image and comparison proves the randomness of the cipher image better than existing one.

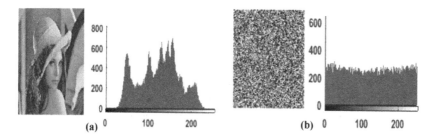

Fig. 5. Histogram Analysis: Histogram of (a) plain image (b) Cipher image

Table 2. Comparison of entropy results

Image				
Plain image	7.7277	7.4436	6.6962	7.1770
Proposed	7.9964	7.9954	7.9960	7.9945
Ref. [14]	7.9974	7.9976	7.9971	7.9971
Ref. [19]	7.9958	7.9975	7.9938	7.9941
Ref. [20]	7.9909	7.9913	7.9912	7.9907

6.2 Exhaustive Attack Analysis

Key size and sensitivity are the two main analysis to find the cryptosystem able to resist exhaustive attack.

6.2.1 Key Space Analysis

The proposed CTS image cipher depends on the following keys $\alpha, \beta, \gamma, p_0, q_0$. The effective cryptosystem should have efficient key space to withstand exhaustive attacks [23]. Here each keys can have a maximum double precision of 10^{-15}, so the maximum key size will be $(10^{15})^5 = 10^{75}$ which will be $> 2^{256}$. Thus our cryptosystem has secure against exhaustive attacks.

6.2.2 Key Sensitivity Analysis

A small bit change in the key should drastically affect the cipher image, so every good cryptosystem should be sensitive to keys [24]. The proposed CTS image cryptosystem is completely sensitive to its initial seed values and parameters. To prove that sensitivity two set of keys are chosen with tiny changes and encrypt the same image. K1 = {p_0 = 0.56786739485345, q_0 = 0.39823452678976, α = 0.867, β = 5.6534565 3298798, γ = 2.69} and k2 = {same value for all parameter except β = 5.6534256 53298798}. From the two images 50 pixels are taken for testing their dissimilarities. Figure 6 depicts that the two images are entirely different, it's proved that CTS image cryptosystem has high key sensitivity.

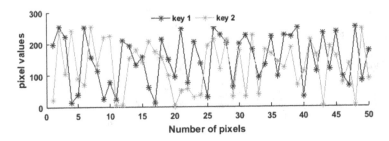

Fig. 6. Key Sensitivity analysis

7   Conclusion

This article suggested a proficient image cryptosystem with effective confusion and diffusion process. Pixels are permutated dynamically in these two process, these dynamical order form is specified by the chaotic series. The proposed chaos cryptosystem employed three chaotic maps Cubic, Tent and sine map, by modifying and combined these three maps, we have developed a new chaotic map called CTS map with good random behaviour and efficient key size. The main observation of the proposed system is, the combination of different single dimensional chaotic system greatly increases the random behaviour of the chaotic system for a long period of time and key size is sufficiently increased to resist brute force attack. Simulation outcomes and scrutinize the security level proved that the developed image cipher has efficient features and well performed against assorted attacks. Hence, the developed CTS image cryptosystem is surely appropriate for real time secure image communication and storage.

References

1. Luo, Y., Zhou, R., Liu, J., Qiu, S., Cao, Y.: An efficient and self-adapting colour-image encryption algorithm based on chaos and interactions among multiple layers. Multimedia Tools Appl. **77**, 26191–26217 (2018)
2. Teng, L., Wang, X., Meng, J.: A chaotic color image encryption using integrated bit-level permutation. Multimedia Tools Appl. **77**, 6883–6896 (2018)
3. Ullah, A., Jamal, S.S., Shah, T.: A novel scheme for image encryption using substitution box and chaotic system. Nonlinear Dyn. **91**, 359–370 (2018)
4. Gong, L., Qiu, K., Deng, C., Zhou, N.: An image compression and encryption algorithm based on chaotic system and compressive sensing. Opt. Laser Technol. **115**, 257–267 (2019)
5. Maddodi, G., Awad, A., Awad, D., Awad, M., Lee, B.: A new image encryption algorithm based on heterogeneous chaotic neural network generator and dna encoding. Multimedia Tools Appl. **77**, 24701–24725 (2018)
6. Wang, X., Zhao, H., Wang, M.: A new image encryption algorithm with nonlinear-diffusion based on Multiple coupled map lattices. Opt. Laser Technol. **115**, 42–57 (2019)

7. Ravichandran, D., Praveenkumar, P., Balaguru Rayappan, J.B., Amirtharajan, R.: Chaos based crossover and mutation for securing DICOM image. Comput. Biol. Med. **72**, 170–184 (2016)

8. Wang, X., Qin, X., Liu, C.: Color image encryption algorithm based on customized globally coupled map lattices. Multimedia Tools Appl. **78**(5), 6191–6209 (2018)

9. Norouzi, B., Mirzakuchaki, S., Seyedzadeh, S.M., Mosavi, M.R.: A simple, sensitive and secure image encryption algorithm based on hyper-chaotic system with only one round diffusion process. Multimed. Tools Appl. **71**, 1469–1497 (2014)

10. Liu, H.: Construction of a new 2D Chebyshev-Sine map and its application to color image encryption. Multimedia Tools Appl. **78**, 15997–16010 (2019)

11. Liu, W., Sun, K., He, S.: SF-SIMM high-dimensional hyperchaotic map and its performance analysis. Nonlinear Dyn. **89**, 2521–2532 (2017)

12. Stoyanov, B., Kordov, K.: Image encryption using chebyshev map and rotation equation. Entropy **17**, 2117–2139 (2015)

13. Miao Zhang, X.T.: A new algorithm of the combination of image compression and encryption technology based on spatiotemporal cross chaotic map. Multimed. Tools Appl. **74**, 11255–11279 (2015)

14. Wu, J., Liao, X., Yang, B.: Image encryption using 2D Hénon-Sine map and DNA approach. Sig. Process. **153**, 11–23 (2018)

15. Mondal, B., Kumar, P., Singh, S.: A chaotic permutation and diffusion based image encryption algorithm for secure communications. Multimedia Tools Appl. **77**, 31177–31198 (2018)

16. Mokhtar, M.A., Sadek, N.M., Mohamed, A.G.: Design of image encryption algorithm based on different chaotic mapping. In: Proceedings of the National Radio Science Conference NRSC, pp. 197–204 (2017)

17. Baoa, L., Zhoub, Y., Chenb, P., Liua, H.: A new 1D chaotic system for image encryption. Sign. Proces. **97**, 172–182 (2014)

18. Zhang, D., Liao, X., Yang, B., Zhang, Y.: A fast and efficient approach to color-image encryption based on compressive sensing and fractional Fourier transform. Multimedia Tools Appl. **77**, 2191–2208 (2018)

19. Enayatifar, R., Abdullah, A.H., Isnin, I.F., Altameem, A., Lee, M.: Image encryption using a synchronous permutation-diffusion technique. Opt. Lasers Eng. **90**, 146–154 (2017)

20. Li, C., Luo, G., Qin, K., Li, C.: An image encryption scheme based on chaotic tent map. Nonlinear Dyn. **87**, 127–133 (2017)

21. Rajendran, S., Doraipandian, M.: Biometric template security triggered by two dimensional logistic sine map. Procedia Comput. Sci. **143**, 794–803 (2018)

22. Parvaz, R., Zarebnia, M.: A combination chaotic system and application in color image encryption. Opt. Laser Technol. **101**, 30–41 (2018)

23. Han, C.: An image encryption algorithm based on modified logistic chaotic map. Optik (Stuttg). **181**, 779–785 (2019)

24. Alawida, M., Samsudin, A., Teh, J.S., Alkhawaldeh, R.S.: A new hybrid digital chaotic system with applications in image encryption. Sign. Proces. **160**, 45–58 (2019)

Confused Memory Read Attracts Synthetic Diffusion on the Fly – A Lightweight Image Encryption for IoT Platform

Vinoth Raj[1], Siva Janakiraman[2(✉)], Sundararaman Rajagopalan[2], and Amirtharajan Rengarajan[2]

[1] Research Scholar, SASTRA Deemed University, Thanjavur 613 401, India
[2] Faculty, Department of ECE, School of EEE, SASTRA Deemed University, Thanjavur 613 401, India
siva@ece.sastra.edu

Abstract. The analogous growth of threat and data communication among the connected devices invites specialised security algorithms for Internet of Things (IoT). The minimal computational capabilities and resource constraints of the processing devices used in IoT architecture do not afford the overhead incurred by the conventional encryption schemes. This paper proposes a lightweight image encryption algorithm that can be realised as an embedded software to run on microcontroller architectures suitable for IoT applications. The proposed algorithm uses the pseudo-random numbers produced by the Linear Feedback Shift Register (LFSR) to perform inherent confusion on the fly via random memory read. A synthetic image generated by extracting the random bits produced by the digitised Lorenz attractor has been used to diffuse the confused pixels on the fly. The proposed algorithm has been realised as embedded software to run on microcontrollers suitable for Internet of Things (IoT) applications. The proposed algorithm achieves better results than similar reliable encryption schemes in terms of security parameters such as entropy, correlation, histogram, PSNR, NPCR and UACI. Further, eliminating the storage of confusion and diffusion key beside the storage of encrypted image employing on the fly encryption process proposed in our algorithm reduces the demand on RAM for about 48 KB as compared to the conventional storage-based encryption schemes.

Keywords: ARM · Chaotic · Embedded · Encryption · Security · Synthetic image

1 Introduction

The strength of any data security algorithm primarily relies on the randomness of the keys used in it. Key generation using True Random Number Generators (TRNGs) may offer a very high level of randomness. Considering its tendency to recreate the values when used with known beginning stage, Pseudo Random Number Generators (PRNGs) are broadly used over TRNGs in applications such as symmetric key cryptography. The modern PRNGs have started exploiting the sensitive character of chaotic maps to its initial conditions that earn excessive randomness in their output [1]. The discretised

© Springer Nature Singapore Pte Ltd. 2019
V. S. Shankar Sriram et al. (Eds.): ATIS 2019, CCIS 1116, pp. 62–73, 2019.
https://doi.org/10.1007/978-981-15-0871-4_5

version of the chaos based PRNGs has been predominantly implemented on software platforms such as MATLAB [2]. The intricacy involved in handling the floating-point input and output variables has been the major bottleneck in realising the chaotic PRNGs in embedded platforms such as microcontrollers and Field Programmable Gate Arrays (FPGAs).

Recently, researchers have started analysing the feasibility of realising chaotic maps in embedded platforms where the 32-bit binary version of float values are represented as per standard IEEE 754 format. Hardware scheme for the fast and robust realisation of chaotic maps on microcontroller silicon was proposed by Harsha [3]. In contrast, software-based algorithmic approaches for chaotic map implementation in resource-constrained microcontroller platforms for image encryption applications have also been analysed [4, 5]. To widen the range of the sensitive inputs and as well to expand the interval between repetitions in output values, chaotic attractors have been proposed [6]. In [7] the practicality of realising digital Lorenz chaotic attractor on PIC32MX7 microcontroller has been demonstrated by generating a visual output of its discrete-time chaotic behaviour. Further, the cost of implementing digital Lorenz attractor on PIC18F452 microcontroller has been examined in terms of memory utilisation and execution time [8]. Although attractors have been implemented on microcontrollers [7, 8], the real randomness of the IEEE 754 compliant binaries generated by such digital chaotic attractor implementations on microcontrollers has not been analysed so far.

In image encryption algorithms, synthetic images with random pixels values are well suited to accomplish the diffusion process [9–11]. Synthetic images constructed using PRNGs are to be analysed for its randomness before their usage in image encryption process to achieve proper diffusion. Internet of Things (IoT) is a typical system that brings wireless connectivity among devices having minimal storage and computational resources [12, 13]. Steganography or cryptography schemes with lightweight properties are predominant to integrate security via confidentiality in such IoT systems [14–24].

Considering the typical limited availability of storage space (memory) in processing devices used in IoT applications, there is a definite need to device new security algorithms that can handle larger data sizes with minimal demand on storage. This paper proposes an algorithm with lightweight computations and minimises the demand on memory resource by performing encryption on the fly. The same has been implemented on an ARM-based microcontroller suitable for IoT applications. Finally, the security and performance analyses were carried out and the results are validated against the recent reliable encryption schemes reported in the literature.

2 Micro-Controller Board (MCB) for IOT

The STM32F407IG microcontroller has a 32-bit ARM Cortex-M4 core with 512 KB of on-chip FLASH memory for code storage and 198 KB of on-chip SRAM as data storage. The device can be operated at a maximum frequency of 168 MHz. The MCB also houses a 240 × 340 TFT display in it. The software development for the MCB using embedded C language is supported by KEIL-MDK μvision4 Integrated Development Environment (IDE) comprising an efficient ARMCC compiler. A JTAG based

ULINK debugger unit facilitates the porting of embedded software (Hex file) in the FLASH program memory of the device.

3   Synthetic Image Generation on MCB

The Euler's discretised version of the Lorenz attractor equations given by (1)–(3) [7] has been implemented as embedded C code to generate synthetic images using STM32F407IG microcontroller. In our implementation, all the initial conditions are set to a value of 0.01 with the control parameters a, b, c has been chosen as 16, 45 and 4 respectively with step size equals to 0.001.

$$X_n = X_{n-1} + T_s(a \times y_{n-1} - a \times X_{n-1}) \tag{1}$$

$$Y_n = Y_{n-1} + T_s(c \times X_{n-1} - Y_{n-1} - (X_{n-1} \times Z_{n-1})) \tag{2}$$

$$Z_n = Z_{n-1} + T_s(X_{n-1} \times y_{n-1} - b \times Z_{n-1}) \tag{3}$$

The preferred STM32F407IG microcontroller supports floating point operations in rounded, single precision 32-bit binary format as per standard IEEE 754 representation. For the construction of synthetic images, the eight Least Significant Bits (LSBs) were extracted during each iteration of the Lorenz attractor from one of its output variables to form a random 8-bit grayscale pixel value. Pointers and type casting operations have been performed to extract pixel values from one of the output variables of the Lorenz attractor. For initial testing, the extracted pixels of the synthetic images are initially

Fig. 1. Snapshot of MCB hardware showing generated chaotic synthetic image on TFT screen.

stored in the on-chip RAM of the microcontroller as a stream of bytes. The stored pixel values are then read to display them as a two-dimensional image on the on-board TFT display. Figure 1 depicts the snapshot of the MCB embedded hardware with the generated 128×128 synthetic image on the TFT screen. The pixel values of the generated synthetic image can serve as a key to perform pixel diffusion in an image encryption process.

4 Confused Memory Read Using LFSR

Any ex-or based n-bit Linear Feedback Shift Register (LFSR) circuit constructed using D-Flip Flops produces all the possible values in the range of 1 to 2^n-1 in a pseudo-random manner. The random sequence generated by these PRNGs gets completed by the insertion of zero at the end. The 14-bit LFSR circuit shown in Fig. 2 is realised as embedded software to run on MCB. Two dimensional (2D) digital images are usually handled in MCBs by storing their pixel values in the form of 2D array in the memory. Reading these pixel values from the memory addresses in an appropriate order facilitate the reconstruction of images. Any change in the actual order of accessing the memory during pixel read may scramble the position of pixels in the image. Therefore, image confusion is possible during pixel read operation by accessing all the memory addresses corresponds to the pixels of an image in a pseudo-random fashion without any repetition.

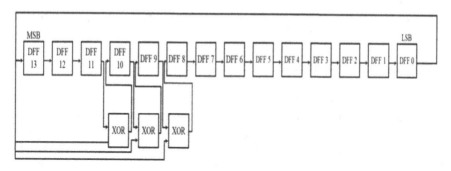

Fig. 2. LFSR PRNG for confusion key generation.

5 Proposed Lightweight Image Encryption for IOT Systems

The limited memory and computational resources are the major bottlenecks in implementing lightweight image encryption schemes on MCBs suitable for IoT systems. Any image encryption scheme has to perform confusion and diffusion processes with possibly different keys. The confusion and diffusion processes may follow each other in any order as per the algorithm. The space required by the keys and the intermediate results obtained from the confusion or diffusion block increases the demand on memory storage beyond the affordable limits of MCBs used in IoT. The proposed lightweight algorithm performs grayscale image encryption through on the fly confusion and diffusion operations on STM32F407IG MCB. The PRNG sequence generated by an LFSR and a chaotic synthetic image generated by the digitised Lorenz attractor is used as keys for accomplishing the confusion and diffusion processes respectively. The steps for the proposed lightweight image encryption are given below.

Step 1: Store the 8-bit pixels of a 128×128 grayscale plain image as 2D array constants in the on-chip FLASH memory of the microcontroller.

Step 2: Initialize the seed value for 14-bit LFSR

Step 3: Initialize the control parameters and initial conditions for the digitised Lorenz attractor

Step 4: Initialize a pointer 'I' to the base address of the 2D plain input image array in FLASH memory

Step 5: Run the LFSR once to obtain a random number 'R'

Step 6: Run the attractor once to extract an 8-bit pixel value 'S' for the grayscale synthetic image

Step 7: Use the LFSR output from Step 5 as offset along with the base address of the pointer to read a random pixel 'P' form address $(I + R)$ to accomplish confusion on the fly

Step 8: Obtain the encrypted pixel 'E' via diffusion on the fly by XORing the confused pixel 'P' obtained in Step 7 with the synthetic pixel value 'S' obtained in Step 6 $(E = P \oplus S)$

Step 9: Communicate the encrypted pixel 'E' by transmitting it via on-chip USART of the microcontroller

Step 10: Repeat the Steps 5 to 9 until all the pixels of the plain image are encrypted

6   Results and Discussions

A sample synthetic image generated by the MCB is shown in Fig. 3a. A 128×128 plain image (Lena) shown in Fig. 4a has been taken as input for the proposed lightweight encryption algorithm. The encrypted images are shown in Fig. 5a–5c has been obtained using three different synthetic images as keys generated respectively from the output variables X, Y and Z of the Lorenz attractor running on the MCB. The generated synthetic images and various encrypted images were subjected to pixel distribution, correlation, entropy, statistical similarity and differential analysis. The encrypted pixels that are serially transmitted from the MCB were obtained in the form of the text file and all the analysis has been carried out using MATLAB 2016b.

6.1   Randomness Analysis via NIST Test Suite on the Generated Synthetic Image

The randomness of the generated synthetic image shown in Fig. 3a was analysed to authenticate the firmness against statistical attacks. A binary string of more than one lakh bits constituted from the pixels of the generated synthetic images has passed all the tests to certify the randomness when subjected to the NIST test suite as given in Table 1.

Table 1. Results of the **NIST** test performed on the synthetic images generated by **MCB**

Statistical test	Pixels from Lorenz O/P Variable X		Pixels from Lorenz O/P Variable Y		Pixels from Lorenz O/P Variable Z		Result Status (Pr ≥ 0.8) Pass
	P	Pr	P	Pr	P	Pr	
Frequency	0.534146	0.9	0.008879	0.9	0.534146	1.0	Pass
Block frequency	0.122325	1.0	0.066882	1.0	0.534146	1.0	Pass
Cumulative sums 1	0.911413	0.9	0.066882	0.9	0.534146	1.0	Pass
Cumulative sums 2	0.911413	0.9	0.066882	1.0	0.739918	1.0	Pass
Runs	0.213309	1.0	0.534146	1.0	0.911413	0.9	Pass
Longest run	0.534146	1.0	0.911413	1.0	0.911413	1.0	Pass
Rank	0.213309	1.0	0.213309	1.0	0.035174	0.9	Pass
FFT	0.213309	1.0	0.350485	1.0	0.122325	1.0	Pass
Approximate Entropy	0.213309	1.0	0.017912	1.0	0.350485	1.0	Pass
Serial 1	0.534146	1.0	0.739918	1.0	0.911413	1.0	Pass
Serial 2	0.739918	1.0	0.739918	1.0	0.739918	1.0	Pass
Linear complexity	0.534146	1.0	0.350485	1.0	0.534146	1.0	Pass
Non overlapping template	0.911413	1.0	0.739918	1.0	0.739918	1.0	Pass
Overlapping Template	0.066882	1.0	0.534146	1.0	0.122325	1.0	Pass

6.2   Pixel Distribution Analysis

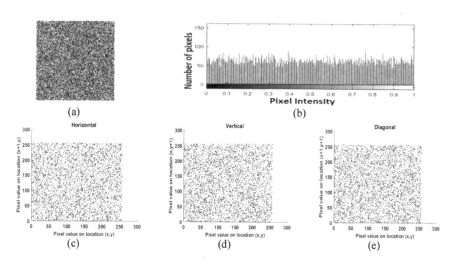

Fig. 3. Synthetic image analysis (a) 128×128 chaotic synthetic image generated by MCB (b) Histogram of the synthetic image in Fig. 3a (c) Horizontal correlation of synthetic image in Fig. 3a (d) Vertical correlation of synthetic image in Fig. 3a (e) Diagonal correlation of synthetic image in Fig. 3a

The horizontal and vertical axis of the histograms individually portrays the pixel intensity levels and the number of pixels in the images. In Fig. 3b the uniform distribution of pixel count in the entire intensity range affirms the rigidity of the generated synthetic image against distribution analysis. Histograms in Fig. 5d–5f corresponds to the encrypted images shown in Fig. 5a–5c respectively confirms the equal distribution of pixel count in all intensity levels. Figure 4b shows the confused Lena image obtained trough confused memory read based on the pseudo-random sequence generated by the LFSR shown in Fig. 2. As the confusion process merely rearrange the pixel positions without affecting the pixel values, the histogram of the confused image does not differ from the histogram of the original image as shown in Fig. 4c.

6.3   Correlation Analysis

The relationship between the progressive pixel values of each image has been assessed through correlation analysis. Figure 3c–3e correspondingly shows the graphical view of association among the pixels in horizontal, vertical and diagonal axes of the generated synthetic image given in Fig. 3a. Similarly, the correlation graph in Fig. 5g–5o with the negligible relationship among the neighbouring pixels in each axis as listed in Table 2 also upholds the sternness of the encrypted images in Fig. 5a–5c opposed to correlation values reported in earlier works. In contrast, the inability of mere confusion process to break the correlation among the confused pixels can be seen in Fig. 4d–4f.

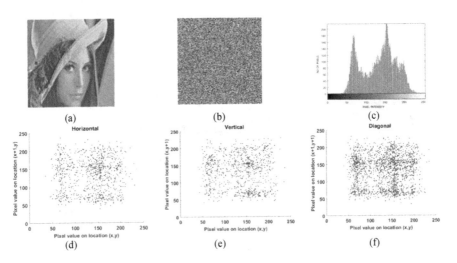

Fig. 4. Confusion analysis (a) Plain image Lena, (b) Confused image obtained from random memory read using LFSR (c) Histogram of Fig. 4a and 4b (d) Horizontal correlation graph of a confused image in Fig. 4b (e) Vertical correlation graph of confused image in Fig. 4b (f) Diagonal correlation graph of confused image in Fig. 4b

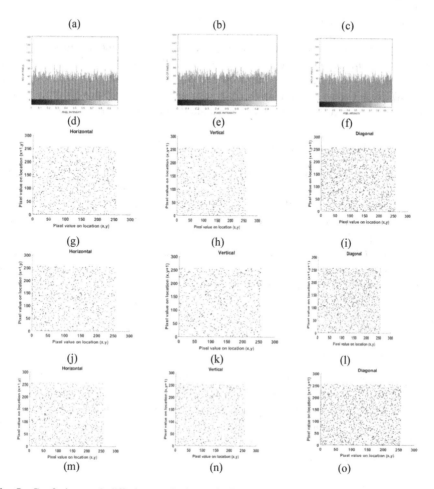

Fig. 5. Confusion and diffusion analysis (a–c) Encrypted images, (d–f) Histograms of the encrypted images (g–i) Correlation graphs for the encrypted image 5a (j–l) Correlation graphs for the encrypted image 5a (m–o) Correlation graphs for the encrypted image 5a

Table 2. Results of the correlation analysis on the encrypted images

Algorithm		Correlation		
		Horizontal	Vertical	Diagonal
Proposed	X	−0.0046	−0.0057	−0.0012
Lorenz O/P	Y	−0.0089	0.0058	−0.0043
Variable Used	Z	−0.0046	−0.0057	−0.0012
Ref. [19]		−0.0510	−0.0408	−0.0369
Ref. [10]		0.0106	−0.0040	0.0131

6.4 Entropy Analysis

When comprising all possible 256 values with equal likelihood, the maximum entropy of a grayscale image having 8-bit depth pixels will be 8. From Table 3, all the encrypted images obtained from the proposed algorithm achieve an entropy value ($7.98 \approx 8$) greater than the similar recent image encryption schemes reported in the literature. Greater entropy is a yet another standard to defend statistical attacks.

6.5 Statistical Similarity Analysis

A good encryption algorithm has to encrypt the images such that the encrypted images do not contain any traces of the plain image. This can be statistically analysed by finding the similarity between the plain image and the encrypted image. An error metric known as Mean Square Error (MSE) estimates the difference between the plain and encrypted images. MSE can be used to obtain a similarity metric known as Pear Signal to Noise Ratio (PSNR) [15, 20, 21]. The higher value of MSE that results in a lower value of PSNR indicates the maximum difference between the plain and encrypted images. The estimated PSNR values are listed in Table 3. For all the encrypted images in our proposed work PSNR < 10 dB ensures better encryption [5] against the other image schemes.

6.6 Differential Analysis

Number of Pixels Change Rate (NPCR) and Unified Average Changing Intensity (UACI) is used to evaluate the strength of encrypted images against differential attacks [5]. Between the original and encrypted image, the rate of change in pixel position given by NPCR > 99 and change in average pixel intensity values with UACI > 33 presented in Table 3 guarantees the strength of encrypted images against differential attacks compared to recent image encryption schemes.

Table 3. Performance comparison of existing chaos-based image encryption schemes.

Algorithm	Entropy	PSNR (dB)	NPCR	UACI
Proposed (Fig. 5a)	7.98	8.30	99.58	33.38
Proposed (Fig. 5b)	7.99	7.73	99.64	33.50
Proposed (Fig. 5c)	7.99	7.80	99.60	33.18
Ref. [5]	7.92	8.37	99.76	31.33
Ref. [15]	7.30	9.20	–	–
Ref. [19]	7.97	–	99.63	33.28

6.7 Memory & Performance Analysis of the Embedded Software on ARM Microcontroller Platform

Memory utilisation and computational time involved in the realisation of digitised Lorenz attractor and the proposed lightweight image encryption scheme on MCB with STM32F407IG ARM microcontroller has been analysed. Table 4 compares the microcontroller realisation of Euler's discretised Lorenz attractor reported in the literature with our implementation. Based on Table 4, it is apparent that the proposed implementation is highly optimised in terms of ROM and RAM utilisation. On comparing in a standard scale with an operating frequency of 10 MHz, the proposed application is effective as well in the timing aspect.

Table 4. Memory and performance comparison of digitised Lorenz attractor implementations on microcontrollers

Lorenz (Euler method)	Target Device (Microcontroller)	ROM (Bytes)	RAM (Bytes)	Time per Iteration (µs)
Proposed	STM32F407IG	2016	40	3.36
Ref. [8]	PIC18F452	2049	92	350
Ref. [7]	PIC32MX7	–	–	1090

On the fly encryption process implemented in the proposed scheme that eliminates the storage of keys by PRNG sequence from LFSR and synthetic image from Lorenz attractor has saved about 32 KB of RAM area. Further, substituting the storage of encrypted pixels by the instantaneous transmission of the same has avoided another 16 KB of RAM requirement. The timing analysis presented in Table 5 has been made when the microcontroller was operated at its highest frequency (i.e., 168 MHz) while excluding the time taken for the serial transmission of the encrypted pixels.

Table 5. Memory and performance analysis of the proposed on the fly lightweight image encryption scheme

Proposed Algorithm	Target Device (Microcontroller)	ROM Data (Bytes)	ROM Code (Bytes)	RAM Data (Bytes)	Time per Iteration (ms)
128 × 128 image	STM32F407IG	16810	2562	72	26.13

7 Conclusion

A lightweight image encryption algorithm that performs confusion and diffusion on the fly has been proposed. The proposed algorithm is intended to minimise the computational and memory overhead to facilitate its implementation as embedded software to run on microcontroller architectures suitable for IoT application. In addition, the chaotic bit stream generated by Euler's digitised Lorenz attractor has been affectively used to generate synthetic images with random pixel values. The NIST test suite substantiates the randomness of the generated synthetic image and validates its usage as key to perform pixel diffusion during image encryption. The set of parameters pertaining to the security aspects of the encrypted images has been analysed and validated against the comparable ones available in the literature. Further, the performance of the proposed lightweight algorithm as embedded software on a IoT based microcontroller board has been analysed in terms of memory footprint and execution time. Image encryption algorithms using transform domain operations may enhance the security. Developing such lightweight algorithms using integer based transform operations such as Integer Wavelet Transform (IWT) that are suitable for microcontrollers will be agenda for future work. However, the on-chip memory of microcontrollers imposing a restriction on the size of input images handled by these algorithms can be viewed as a major limitation.

References

1. Lambić, D.: Security analysis and improvement of the pseudo-random number generator based on quantum chaotic map. Nonlinear Dyn. **94**(2), 1117–1126 (2018)
2. Huynh, V.V., Ouannas, A., Wang, X., Pham, V.-T., Nguyen, X.Q., Alsaadi, F.E.: Chaotic map with no fixed points: entropy, implementation and control. Entropy, **21**(3), art. no. 279 (2019)
3. Harsha, P.: A novel micro-architecture using a simplified logistic map for embedded security. IEEE Embed. Syst. Lett. **9**(2), 41–44 (2017). https://doi.org/10.1109/LES.2017.2672858
4. Castañeda, C.E., et al.: Discrete-time neural synchronization between an Arduino microcontroller and a Compact Development System using multiscroll chaotic signals Chaos. Solitons Fractals **119**, 269–275 (2019)
5. Janakiraman, S., Thenmozhi, K., Rayappan, J.B., Amirtharajan, R.: Lightweight chaotic image encryption algorithm for real-time embedded system: Implementation and analysis on 32-bit microcontroller. Microprocess. Microsyst. **1**(56), 1–2 (2018). https://doi.org/10.1016/j.micpro.2017.10.013
6. Volos, C.K., Jafari, S., Kengne, J., Munoz-Pacheco, J.M., Rajagopal, K.: Nonlinear dynamics and entropy of complex systems with hidden and self-excited attractors. Entropy, **21**(4), art. no. 370 (2019)
7. Méndez-Ramírez, R., et al.: A new simple chaotic Lorenz-type system and its digital realization using a TFT touch-screen display embedded system. Complexity **2017**, 1–13 (2017). https://doi.org/10.1155/2017/6820492
8. Köse, E., Mühürcü, A.: Realization of a digital chaotic oscillator by using a low cost microcontroller. Eng. Rev. **37**(3), 341–348 (2017). https://doi.org/10.30765/er
9. Ravichandran, D., et al.: Encrypted biography of biomedical image-a pentalayercryptosystem on FPGA. J. Signal Process. Syst. 1–27 (2018). https://doi.org/10.1007/s11265-018-1337-z
10. Rajagopalan, S., et al.: Cellular automata+LFSR+synthetic image: a trio approach to image encryption. In: ICCCI 2017, IEEE Xplore, pp. 1–6 (2017). https://doi.org/10.1109/ICCCI.2017.8117702
11. Sundararaman, R., et al.: Cellular automata with synthetic image a secure image communication with transform domain. Defence Sci. J. **69**(3), 259–265 (2019). https://doi.org/10.14429/dsj.69.14422
12. Arunkumar, S., Vairavasundaram, S., Ravichandran, K.S., Ravi, L.: RIWT and QR factorization based hybrid robust image steganography using block selection algorithm for IoT devices. J. Intell. Fuzzy Syst. **36**(5), 4265–4276 (2019)

13. Noura, H., Chehab, A., Sleem, L., Noura, M., Couturier, R., Mansour, M.M.: One round cipher algorithm for multimedia IoT devices. Multimedia Tools Appl. **77**(14), 18383–18413 (2018)
14. Jiménez, M., Cano, M.E., Flores, O., Estrada, J.C.: A portable embedded system for point-to-point secure signals transmission. Microprocess. Microsyst. **61**, 126–134 (2018)
15. Noura, H., Chehab, A., Noura, M., Couturier, R., Mansour, M.M.: Lightweight, dynamic and efficient image encryption scheme. Multimedia Tools Appl. **78**(12), 16527–16561 (2019)
16. Noura, H.N., Noura, M., Chehab, A., Mansour, M.M., Couturier, R.: Efficient and secure cipher scheme for multimedia contents. Multimedia Tools Appl. **78**(11), 14837–14866 (2019)
17. Devi, A.A., Ramana, A.V.: Chaotic based lightweight image encryption algorithm for real-time application systems. Int. J. Recent Technol. Eng. **7**(6), 590–595 (2019)
18. Shifa, A., Asghar, M.N., Noor, S., Gohar, N., Fleury, M.: Lightweight cipher for H.264 videos in the internet of multimedia things with encryption space ratio diagnostics. Sensors (Switzerland), **19**(5), art. no. 1228 (2019)
19. Das, A.K., Hajra, S., Mandal, M.K.: RGB image encryption using microcontroller ATMEGA 32. Microsyst. Technol. 1–9 (2018). https://doi.org/10.1007/s00542-018-3980-5
20. Janakiraman, S., Sree, K.S., Manasa, V.L., Rajagopalan, S., Thenmozhi, K., Amirtharajan, R.: On the diffusion of lightweight image encryption in embedded hardware. In: 2018 International Conference on Computer Communication and Informatics, ICCCI 2018, art. no. 8441229 (2018)
21. Janakiraman, S., Roshini, P., Rajagopalan, S., Thenmozhi, K., Amirtharajan, R.: Permutated symmetric key for perfect lightweight image encryption. In: Proceedings of the 4th International Conference on Devices, Circuits and Systems, ICDCS 2018, pp. 80–83 (2019). art. no. 8605175
22. Janakiraman, S., Thenmozhi, K., Rayappan, J.B.B., Amirtharajan, R.: Light weight steganography on RISC platform-implementation and analysis. Asian J. Sci. Res. **8**(3), 278–290 (2015). https://doi.org/10.3923/ajsr.2015.278.290
23. Janakiraman, S., Thenmozhi, K., Rayappan, J.B.B., Amirtharajan, R.: Indicator-based lightweight steganography on 32-bit RISC architectures for IoT security. Multimedia Tools Appl. 1–29 (2019). https://doi.org/10.1007/s11042-019-07960-z
24. Janakiraman, S., Thenmozhi, K., Rayappan, J.B.B., Paramasivam, V.M., Amirtharajan, R.: Realization of chaos-based private multiprocessor network via USART of embedded devices. In: Singh, A.K., Mohan, A. (eds.) Handbook of Multimedia Information Security: Techniques and Applications, pp. 323–340. Springer, Cham (2019). https://doi.org/10.1007/978-3-030-15887-3_14

Network Security

Insider Attacks on Zigbee Based IoT Networks by Exploiting AT Commands

Waqas Ahmad Piracha[1(✉)], Morshed Chowdhury[1], Biplob Ray[2], Sutharshan Rajasegarar[1], and Robin Doss[1]

[1] Deakin University Centre for Cyber Security Research and Innovation Deakin University-Geelong, Victoria, Australia
wpiracha@deakin.edu.au
[2] Centre for Intelligent Systems (CIS), School of Engineering and Technology, Central Queensland University, Rockhampton, Australia

Abstract. This paper has presented three insiders attacks on Zigbee protocol – a protocol used for wireless communication for the Internet of Thing (IoT) devices. The end-user's communication in IoT networks are sensor oriented as the user objects in IoT networks are embedded with sensors and actuators. Most of the sensors communicate with wireless medium among which many of them use Zigbee protocol. Security is an important element of IoT objects to protect user's privacy and counter malicious attacks but difficult to guarantee due to its limited capabilities, wireless communication and unpredicted users' actions. In this paper, we have evaluated Zigbee protocol stack for security vulnerabilities which revealed security weakness of remote AT commands. By using remote AT commands in an IoT network, we have devised three successful insider attacks to make unauthorized change of the destination address of a packet, change of node ID, and the change of PAN ID. These attacks detail will be very useful for IoT researches and practitioners in the security domain to design appropriate countermeasures for Zigbee IoT networks.

Keywords: Zigbee · Remote AT command · Node ID · PAN ID · Destination ID

1 Introduction

The Internet is interconnected with a vast variety of devices, and Internet of Things (IoT) devices are playing a pivotal role in the Internet revolution. The Internet is used to facilitate multiple segments of day to day life ranging from personal use including social media and web surfing, to banking, commercial, educational and stock sector [2]. As a result of this Internet revolution, the Internet is populated with multiple IoT enabled objects with different functionalities which always remain connected to the Internet. We have already witnessed various popular IoT enabled object categories such as smart watches, cell phones, tablets, and devices used for healthcare.

Regarding the concept of IoT, Common sensors are used to collect the data from the real world, and these sensors share the accumulated data across a channel by communicating and interacting with other nodes [2]. The deployment of IoT devices is

© Springer Nature Singapore Pte Ltd. 2019
V. S. Shankar Sriram et al. (Eds.): ATIS 2019, CCIS 1116, pp. 77–91, 2019.
https://doi.org/10.1007/978-981-15-0871-4_6

done to achieve a wide range of purposes, such as the automation of home devices as well as industrial automation. In the context of home automation, IoT serves the purpose to ensure connectivity of daily appliances and objects such as heating and cooling sensors, light bulbs, fire sensors, and internally installed cameras for security purposes. The IoT devices are encompassed with the ability to support various communication protocols which include Ethernet, Zigbee, and Wi-Fi [2]. The communication protocols used in this paper is the Zigbee device which is the most widely used radio device in the Do-it-Yourself scenarios [16].

The Zigbee protocol ensures a two-way communication based on the fundamentals that minimum power is consumed with tradeoff of low data transmission rate [2]. Although, the Zigbee devices have security protection, certain security tradeoffs have been made to ensure that the device consumes minimal energy, uses very less power, and highly compatible [1]. Therefore, a few areas of the device's security are implemented with lapses and exploiting those vulnerabilities leads to security risks.

In the past, a wide range of attacks have been conducted to exploit the vulnerabilities present in the Zigbee devices [2, 4–7]. Vulnerabilities in the Zigbee devices have been exploited by using frameworks such as Killer-bee [4]. The Killer-bee has built-in tools to analyze the network traffic and execute attacks in order to obtain the Zigbee network keys. The Zigbee network keys are shared by all the devices in the network and are used for broadcast communication. Similarly, by using Killer-bee framework Zigbee devices can be exploited by executing the Replay attacks. Many other attacks have been conducted on these devices such as the denial of service attacks, the ghost attack, and the distributed denial of service attack. However, very little work has been done to explore the Zigbee vulnerabilities associated with AT commands in detail. With majority of the existing work in Zigbee revolving around the common exploits such as the denial of service and replay attacks, very little work explored attacks specific to Zigbee parameters such as the Node ID, the Destination ID, and the PAN ID.

In this paper, we have evaluated the sensors networks using Zigbee protocol for security weakness and identified three vulnerabilities using remote AT commands in Zigbee IoT networks. During the study, the key aspect pertaining to the security of the Zigbee device were found known as remote AT command attack. We have then crafted three remote AT command attacks based upon changing the node ID which is the name associated with a particular node, destination address which is the address of a packet, and Personal Area network (PAN) ID which identifies a particular group of Zigbee nodes. The aim of these attacks is to make unauthorize changes in basic configuration parameters of the Zigbee IoT network or nodes without having physical access to that network node. To test these attacks, we have setup an experimental IoT network and executed these attacks successfully. The experiment has proven the viability of these attacks and reveal the working flow of them. The paper has presented the finding of our evaluation and experiment which can be very valuable to design countermeasure to counter these attacks and prevent them from occurring.

2   Editing Protocol Stack

The Zigbee wireless standard, IEEE 802.15.4, was developed by the Zigbee Alliance. It is primarily used for Wireless Personal Area (PAN) Networks. The Zigbee protocol is a communication protocol used to ensure a two-way reliable communication and is characterized by excessively low data transmission rate and low power consumption. The Zigbee protocol reduces the frequency of battery replacement by up to two years and has a data transfer rate of up to 250 kbps for a radius of approximately 1000 m [2].

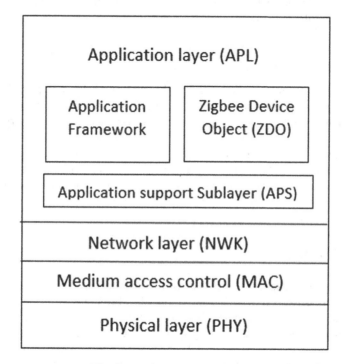

Fig. 1. The Zigbee protocol stack

Due to various positive incentives like low power consumption, higher reliability, simpler and cheaper working mechanism, the Zigbee standard has higher popularity of implementing for IoT enabled sensors at a larger scale, compare to rest of the Wireless Network PAN standards [1].

The Zigbee protocol constitutes of the Physical Layer, MAC layer, Network layer, and the application layer as illustrated in Fig. 1.

In the Zigbee wireless standard, the physical layer is responsible for the modulation and demodulation and supports the following frequencies [2]:

1. 2.4 GHz frequency, with the ability to support sixteen channels and a maximum communication rate of 250 kbps.
2. 868 MHz, with the ability to support a single channel at a maximum data transmission rate of 20 kbps.

3. 915 MHz, supporting up to 10 channels and a transmission rate of 40 kbps.

The MAC layer of a Zigbee device is responsible for ensuring secure and reliable communication by deploying Carrier Sense Multiple Access with Collision Avoidance to control physical level access [3]. The Zigbee protocol network layer is responsible for the implementation of network topologies, management of new devices, and handling security threats.

The network layer deals with network functions such as connecting, disconnecting, and setting up networks. It will add a network, allocate addresses, and add/remove certain devices. This layer makes use of star, mesh and tree topologies. The routing protocol used by the network layer is Ad hoc On-Demand Distance Vector Routing (AODV) [3].

The Application Framework layer depicts the interface of the user and is composed of the following components [2]:

1. The interface between the network and the application layer is provided by the Application Support Sublayer, and it is responsible for managing the sent and received data by other protocol layers. It aims to provide exceptional encryption and transmission of packets.
2. Zigbee Device Objects is responsible for declaring APS procedures and facilitates the network layer of the Zigbee to perform discovery of newly added nodes.
3. The Application framework provides a feasible environment for the application objects.

3 Related Work

The wide adoption of Zigbee devices has led to major concerns regarding the security of Zigbee based networks. The Zigbee protocol has been studied in detail by many security experts who have underlined various threats that target the Zigbee protocol. An extreme emphasis has been laid on Zigbee threats. One of the threats regarding the Zigbee protocol is via the Remote AT commands due to possibility of sending Remote AT commands at the MAC layer [2]. The vulnerability in the Zigbee protocol merely resides in the fact that working at lower layers such as the MAC layer essentially means that the packets are not filtered or processed in the application layer [18]. Vaccari et al. [2], have identified a vulnerability impacting the AT commands in regard to the IoT networks. They used ATID command to target the nodes. The functionality of the ATID command is that it helps to set the network identifier of a Zigbee module. The research involved the execution of the Remote AT command (ATID); the attacker executes the ATID command to send a fake identifier with an ATID packet to force a node to join a different network. The attack was executed on a very small network compromising of only four nodes. These nodes include the coordinator, two end devices, and a malicious node which was used to conduct the attack. Therefore, the dept of the network was small. Moreover, no router was used in the topology and hence the impact of Remote AT Command on the router was undetermined.

Significant work has been done in context of exploiting Zigbee vulnerabilities by using tools such as Killer-bee. Wright [4] has proposed a Killer-bee framework which possesses certain tools that can be used to exploit the Zigbee protocol by analyzing the network traffic and processing recovered packets. The Killer-bee platform also enables to execute multiple attacks on a Zigbee network. The authors of [5] and [6] have discusses the possibility of such attacks. For instance, there is a high probability of retrieving a network key when sent as clear text. However, retrieving the network key in such a manner implies the condition that the attacker is present near the network nodes being attacked. Therefore, the attacker can sniff the keys being exchanged. The authors of [5] and [6] have also discussed other possible threats via replay attacks or injection attacks. However, in order to successfully use the Killer-bee framework it is imperative that the software is integrated well with hardware components such as the Atmel AVR USB Stick or the TelosB mote models. Both these hardware modules are difficult to procure and are extremely expensive in comparison to a Raspberry Pi.

There are other attacks that may interrupt a Zigbee based network by using denial of service mechanisms. For example, Cambiaso et al. [7] elaborate the execution of Denial of Service (DoS) activities to disengage a node form the network. The DoS attacks have gained popularity in the contemporary Internet [7] world named IoT [8], among which, many aims to reduce the battery lifetime of the Zigbee protocols by targeting the battery powered sensors. In this regard, it is possible to keep the Zigbee sensors active [10] to drain battery by executing the Zigbee end-device sabotage. The sensors are kept active whenever a broadcast message is being sent hence waking the device from its sleep status. This essentially forces the sensor being attacked to respond to the malicious attacker resulting in the delay of the next sleep interval and hence draining the battery rapidly. Another similar attack is referred to as the Ghost attack which has been presented by Shila in [11]. The ghost attack aims to diminish the lifetime of the node being targeted. This is achieved by crafting various fake messages and sending them to the victim. It is also possible to discharge the sensor batteries if the malicious attacker is aware of the adopted sensor polling rate as demonstrated by Vidgren et al. in [12]. The feasibility of Distributed Denial of Services (DDoS) attacks against an IoT environment was also discussed by Pacheco et al. in [13]. Vidgren et al. further proposed another form of DoS attack on a Zigbee sensor [12] which exploits the Zigbee frame counter. The frame counter is used by various network protocols to thwart threats including replay attacks. Regarding the frame counter exploitation of a Zigbee sensor, an attacker might send a parameter compromising of the maximum value of the allowed frame counter. This frame counter size is four bytes which forces the victim to revert the frame counter value to the received value. Every genuine packet received after the malicious packet will be rejected by the victim if the Message Integrity Check (MIC) is not implemented by the victim [14].

Sastry et al. have demonstrated same-nonce attack which is pertinent to Zigbee sensor [15]. The attack is executed if the Co-Coordinator/Trust center, which is a Zigbee node type responsible for ensuring the reliability, issues an analogous nonce encrypt with the same network key two successive times during the process of key exchange. In this case, part of the plain text may be retrieved by the malicious attacker; this may be done by sniffing two packets and calculating them with *XOR* operation. It is possible to achieve this scenario by enforcing a power failure by draining the batteries of the - Coordinator [14].

Ray et al. [18] has proposed a malware detection-based solution to counter similar attacks in actuators, but this solution is not effective for neither for insider attacks nor for MAC and lower layers attack. M. Jason et al. have proposed authentication-based solution using neural network-based specific emitter identification (SEI) in physical layer to counter similar attacks but it is not applicable for insider attacks [19].

During our research, we have analyzed and researched various security aspects pertaining to the Zigbee networks. By analyzing the various threats pertinent to the Zigbee protocol we discovered that threats related to Remote AT commands were not investigated in depth in the literature. The AT command exploitation allows the malicious attacker to forward confidential and sensitive information to unintended nodes. The attackers can also reconfigure device settings and information by changing the node id, the destination id, and the pan id. Moreover, device setting such as the baud rate and the configuration of various Zigbee pins can also be changed by using AT commands. These commands are extremely scalable in that they can be executed from various software such as the XCTU and can also be executed by using hardware setups such as Raspberry Pi and Arduino. The AT commands can also be used to conduct the more traditional attacks such as the DoS attack or the Sinkhole attack.

In the next section, we are detailing the IoT experimental test bed which is used for our security evaluation and attacks on sensors using Zigbee communication protocol.

4 Experimental Test Bed

In this section, we will discuss about the hardware used to design the IoT sensor network model for evaluating our proposed attacks. The IoT network topology depicts the routes taken by the sensors in order to forward normal data from one node to another so that the entire data packets are transmitted from the source towards the destination.

4.1 Hardware Specifications of the Test Bed

A networked Raspberry Pi 3 was used to connect XBee sensor devices. A Xbee USB explorer was used to mount the coordinator, the end-devices and the routers to our Raspberry Pi 3 network. The Xbee USB explorer is compatible with both the Xbee Series 1 and Series 2.5. The FT231X USB to Serial converter pin is used to translate the data between the raspberry pi and the Xbee devices. The voltage regulator ensures that sufficient power is supplied to the Xbee, and the reset button enables to manually reset the configurations of the sensors which were then connected to LCD (liquid crystal display) screen for display. After mounting the coordinator, the end-devices and the routers to the Raspberry Pi 3 network, a hub was used to connect the network with LCD (liquid crystal display) screen for display.

Raspberry Pi 3 was used to execute a python script in order to setup XBee sensors as a router or an end device, or a coordinator. The objective of the python script was to forward and store the data packets from the end-device to the coordinator. The XBee devices were set up according to the topology illustrated in Fig. 2 and configured as detailed in 'testbed configuration' section. We have used a python scripts to collect normal data traffic and to execute remote AT commands for evaluating possible weaknesses.

4.2   IoT Network Model Used for Evaluation

This section detailed setup of IoT sensor networks which is used for evaluation and attack implementation in this paper.

The topology in Fig. 2 consists of a coordinator (c), five routers $(R_1 \ldots \ldots R_5)$, and seven end-devices $(E_1 \ldots \ldots E_7)$. During the normal operation of the sensor network in Fig. 2:

The End-devices E_6 and E_7 forward the data packets to the Router R_5 which is connected to the Router R_4. The Router R_5 relay the traffic from End-device E_7 and E_6 to Router R_4. In addition, the End-device E_4 also forwards traffic to the router R_4. All the traffic i.e. from End dvices E_4 E_6 and E_7 is now forwarded from the Router R_4 to Router R_3. In addition, Router R_3 now also has data packets being forwarded to it via End-device E_3.

The traffic from the second branch of the topology is forwarded to the first branch of the Zigbee network. This branch consists of the Coordinator, the Router R_2, the End device E_2, the R_1, and the E_1. All the traffic received from the R_2 is forwarded to the Coordinator. An example of normal data flow from E_6 and E_7 to the coordinator presented sequentially in Table 1. The collection of data during normal operation of the network is essential to ensure that all Xbee modules are operational and are sending data packets as intended to the neighboring nodes.

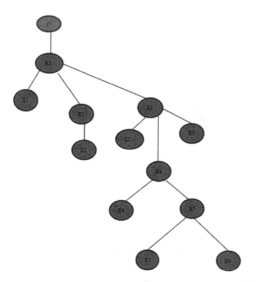

Fig. 2. Sensor network topology of the testbed

During the normal operation of the network, if the data packets are dropped or not been forwarded to the designated nodes it implies that there was an incorrect configuration of destination addresses on the source node, an improper firmware update, or simply because the Zigbee devices have entered into a sleep mode to ensure that minimum power is consumed.

Table 1. Normal Flow of data in the Network Topology

Data flow (- >) sequence before attack
E_7 - > R_5 - E_6 - > R_5 - R_5- > R_4 - E_4- > R_4 - R_4 - > R_3 - E_3 - > R_3
E_1 - > R_1-E_2 - > R_2 - R_1 - > R_2- R_3 - > R_2 - R_2 - > C

After the XBee devices were set up according to the topology illustrated in Fig. 2 and configured as detailed in 'testbed configuration' section, we have used a python scripts to collect normal data traffic and to execute remote AT commands for evaluating possible weaknesses.

5   Testbed Configuration

5.1   Configuring Routers

We have used XBee sensor devices which uses Zigbee wireless communication standard. Initially, Xbee device is detected and assigned a port by the laptop one which let us read the initial device settings of the Xbee and change them as required. The XCTU console mode interface is used to configure Xbee devices as routers XCTU was used to change various parameters [17]. Initially, the firmware update was done by the help of the XCTU software. While performing the firmware update, Zigbee Router's API function set was used and 23A7 (newest) was selected as the function set as illustrated in Fig. 3.

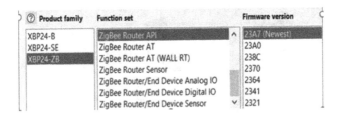

Fig. 3. Firmware update of a router

The Node Identifier parameter was set to R_1 which represents the name of the device. Hence, the Node Identifier parameter was unique to every device. The Destination Low (*DL*) Address was set to *FFFF*, and the Destination High (*DH*) was set to 0. In order to configure an Xbee device as a Router the *API* enable option is set to the default (transparent) mode using the XCTU software. Moreover, the *CE* (Coordinator Enable) parameter is also set to 0, and the JV channel verification is enabled for a router. For the purposes of this experiment, the baud rate was selected as 115200, and the baud rate remained consistent for all the devices including the end devices and the coordinator. The PAN ID was selected as 1234, and this too remained consistent for all the devices. After all the parameters are configured, the device settings are saved, and the Xbee device is now configured as a Router.

5.2 Configuring End Devices

The end devices are also configured by using the XCTU software. In the case of an end device, the PAN ID is set to 1234 which is analogous to the routers and the coordinator. For the end devices, the JV channel verification is set to disable, the CE Coordinator enable setting is also set to disable. The *DH* and *DL* values are set as the *DH* and *DL* values of the routers to which they are connected. This essentially means that the *DH* and *DL* values of an End-Device are those values of the router to which an end device forwards its data packets. The *API* enable parameter for an end device is set to the default (transparent) mode, and the baud rate is kept at 115200. The firmware update of an end device is illustrated in Fig. 4.

⑦ Product family	Function set	Firmware version
XB24-B	ZigBee Coordinator API	28A7 (Newest)
XB24-SE	ZigBee Coordinator AT	28A0
XB24-ZB	ZigBee End Device API	288C
	ZigBee End Device AT	2870
	ZigBee End Device Analog IO	2864
	ZigBee End Device Digital IO	2841
	ZigBee End Device PH	2821

Fig. 4. Firmware update of an end device

5.3 Configuring Coordinator

In order to configure a coordinator using XCTU, all the settings are to remain the same as mentioned for the router and the end device. However, the parameter *CE* (Coordinator Enable) is set to enable or 1. Also, for the coordinator it is imperative that the parameter JV channel verification is set to disable. The firmware update of the Xbee coordinator is illustrated in Fig. 5.

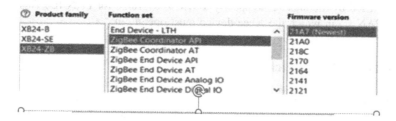

⑦ Product family	Function set	Firmware version
XB24-B	End Device - LTH	21A7 (Newest)
XB24-SE	ZigBee Coordinator API	21A0
XB24-ZB	ZigBee Coordinator AT	218C
	ZigBee End Device API	2170
	ZigBee End Device AT	2164
	ZigBee End Device Analog IO	2141
	ZigBee End Device Digital IO	2121

Fig. 5. Firmware update of a coordinator

6   Remote aT Command Attacks

After the execution of the Python script for the normal data collection as mentioned in the previous section, another Python script was executed to exploit vulnerabilities of remote AT command identified during evaluation for conducting security attacks.

A total of three remote attacks were executed on Node ID, Destination Address and PAN ID where the Node ID, Destination Address, and PAN ID parameters were read and altered using Remote AT commands. The sub-sections below are explaining the methods that are used for the attacks to fetch the original parameters, and then alter the parameters to execute the attacks.

6.1   Node ID

Node ID is a form of cached parameter, and out of all the various cached parameters it is the only parameter which can be changed. Pertaining the node ID, the command 'set_node_id' enables an attacker to change the Node ID of a device. The command configures the Xbee device with the node identifier provided by the attacker by updating the previous cached value and replacing it with the new value.

6.2   Destination Address

The destination address is a non-cached Xbee parameter. The destination address is the default address of an Xbee module which compromises of 64 bits. This address is used by Xbee nodes to transmit the generated data by the nodes. The data and the default destination address can be read by using the 'get_dest_address' method in the python code. This method provides the 64-bit address of the Zigbee device to which the data of the Xbee will be reported. The 'set_dest_address' method changes the default destination address of the Xbee, and this will now be the new 64-bit address to which the data of the device will be reported to.

6.3   Pan ID

Pan ID refers to the Personal Area Network (PAN) ID. Each personal area network has an ID which the Xbee's uses to operate in. The 'get_pan_id' method returns the ID of the PAN which is being used by the Xbee devices to operate in. The 'set_pan_id' method is used by the attacker to specify a byte array value for PAN ID. This is now the new PAN ID in which the Xbee device must operate in.

7   Impact of the Attacks

The results of the three attacks using Remote AT command is detailed in this section. The attacks which have been conducted include the change of destination address, change of PAN ID, and change of node ID. These attacks are unique in that they are conducted remotely by executing the Remote AT commands. However, attacks such as change of destination ID and change of PAN ID are analogous to the more traditional

Denial of Service and the Wormhole attacks. For instance, researchers in the past have executed the Denial of Service attacks on Zigbee modules by draining the battery of the sensors. In the context of AT command, the Denial of Service attack can be conducted by allocating a false destination id to a Zigbee node so that it stops the transmission of its packets or sends packets to a destination which is not present in the network forcing it to drop all the packets. Similarly, the DoS can be executed by changing the PAN ID of the device; this would force the Zigbee device to disassociate itself immediately from the network and would disrupt the overall flow of the traffic within the network. Moreover, the devices within the topology that relies on the associated Zigbee device would be unable to perform their functionalities hence it creates a widespread consequence on the overall functioning of the topology.

7.1 Change of Destination ID

The Destination Low Address of the Routers are set to FFFF which means that Routers can broadcast. By executing the Remote AT command, the destination of nodes used in the topology was changed. The XCTU software is used to verify the parameters being changed after the execution of the remote AT commands. The XCTU is also be used to set the parameters of the nodes in the first case e.g. the PAN ID of Xbee devices is set using XCTU software. The Fig. 6 presents the original DL address of R_4.

The destination addresses of R_4 was changed remotely by using remote AT commands from another node e.g. E_4 or R_2.

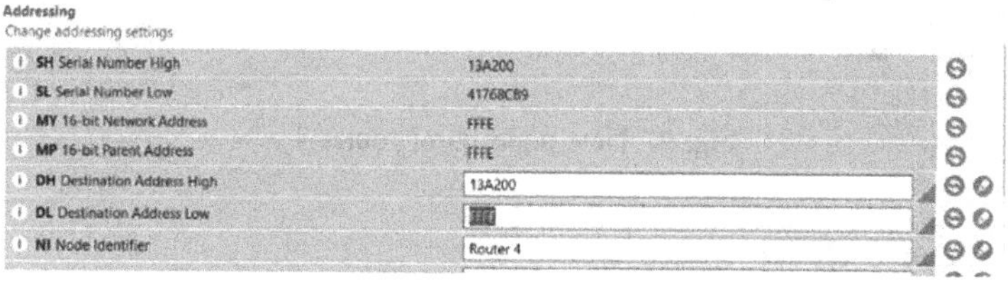

Fig. 6. DL Address of Router 4 as seen on XCTU

After the execution of Remote AT commands, the change in Destination address i.e. DL is verified on XCTU. The results of the Remote AT command attack resulting in the change of DL is presented in Fig. 7.

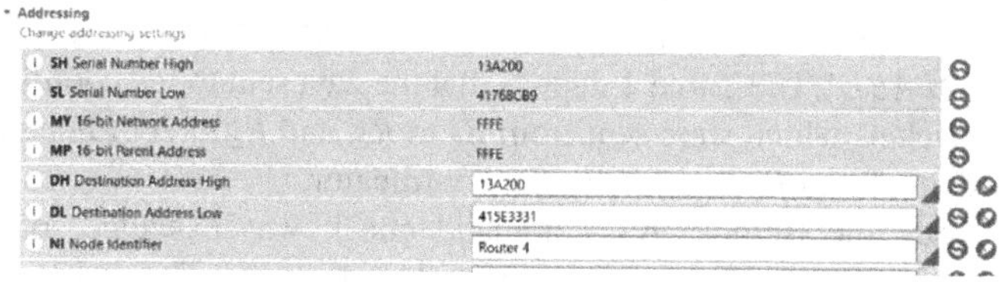

Fig. 7. New destination low address of router 4

7.2   Change of Node ID

The node ID of an Xbee device can also be altered by using Remote AT commands. Initially, the node ID of Router 4 can be seen as 'Router 4'. The Fig. 8 presents the original node ID of router 4. However, by executing the Remote AT command code the node ID of Router 4 was changed to 'pqrst'.

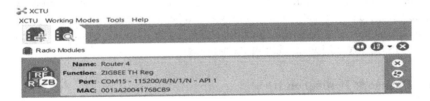

Fig. 8.   Original node ID of router 4

After the execution of the Remote AT commands the node ID of Router 4 was changed to 'pqrst' as presented in Fig. 9.

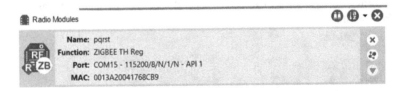

Fig. 9.   New node ID of router 4

7.3   Change of PAN ID

All the nodes which are present with in the topology must be in the same PAN ID as the coordinator to operate normally. Therefore, changing the PAN ID of the coordinator remotely using Remote AT commands essentially means that the PAN ID at which the coordinator operates is different from the PAN ID of the nodes compromising of the routers and end devices in the topology. Hence, these routers and end devices will not be able to forward or send data to the coordinator because of the difference in PAN ID.

For the purpose of this experiment, the Remote AT command attack was executed to change the PAN ID on E_2 from E_1. Initially, the PAN ID of E_2 was 1234 and this was changed to '*BABE*'. The Table 1 depicts that the data sent to the coordinator before the attack had packets which were sent from E_2 to R_2, and R_2 to coordinator as well as packets from E_1 to R_1 to R_2 and finally the coordinator.

However, after the Remote AT command attack was executed to change the PAN ID, the coordinator did not receive any packets from E_2. This is because E_2 now operates at a different PAN ID from the coordinator. Hence, E_2 cannot forward its data to R_2, and therefore R_2 won't receive any packets from E_2. The data which is forwarded to the Coordinator by R_2 would compose of data sent to R_2 by R_1 and R_3 only and not from E_2. The results are shown in Table 2 which demonstrates the data received by the Coordinator after the execution of the attack.

Table 2. Data flow of the network after PAN ID change

Data flow (- >) sequence after attack
E_7 - > R_5 - E_6 - > R_5 - E_4 - > R_4 - R_5 - > R_4 - R_4 - > R_3 - E_3 - > R_3 - R_5 - > R_3 - E_1 - > R_1 - R_1 - > R_2 -
R_3 - > R_2 - R_2 - > C

8 Analysis

The vulnerabilities pertaining to remote AT commands with in Zigbee modules were successfully exploited in this research. In order to conduct all the Remote AT command attacks the presence of an attacker with in the network is essential. Hence, the Remotely conducted AT command attacks are also referred to as Insider attacks because without the presence of a malicious attacker with in the network it is impossible to successfully execute these attacks.

The Zigbee devices send beacon requests to discover networks. The Zigbee coordinator or trust centre undergo the device identification and network discovery process to identify newly established networks. This enables them to avoid any PAN ID conflicts. Even though this process infuses many threats to the Zigbee network, this process is essential for the Zigbee devices to form association with a particular network and discover other Zigbee devices. A malicious attacker may randomly send beacon requests to discover adjacent networks. The beacon requests sent by Zigbee devices are fundamental to the network discovery process and cannot be disabled. In order to prevent random devices from sending beacon requests in order to join the network it is possible to deploy intrusion detection and prevention systems with in a Zigbee network. These intrusion detection systems would analyse the beacon requests sent from internal and external devices with respect to the network and will be triggered in case a malicious request is sent.

The Zigbee Coordinator is also tasked with authenticating requests sent from Zigbee nodes that wish to join the network, and therefore grants permission to the nodes willing to join the network. A successful mitigation approach in order to prevent these attacks would be to preload a network security key in all the Zigbee devices before they are deployed. This would enable the coordinator to only accept requests sent by secure nodes and grant access to these nodes only. Moreover, all the Zigbee nodes without the secure network key would not be able to form a device association with the coordinator.

The experimental test bed composed of thirteen nodes in total. It is to be noted that if these commands are executed on a large network there might be serious repercussions in terms of identity theft as a malicious attacker may pose as a genuine entity to communicate with other nodes and take part in data transfer with other nodes. More-over, the attacker can change the PAN ID of a node in a large network and completely disrupt the data flow of the entire network depending upon the node been attacked. This may result in the loss of important data and information.

9   Conclusion

The paper has presented a security evolution of Zigbee based sensors in IoT networks which is followed by test bed design and configuration for experimental testing of Zigbee based IoT networks. Based on the discovery during evaluation, the paper has also executed remote AT commands in the testbed to compromise IoT network using Zigbee based sensors. The executed attacks involve change of destination address, change of Node ID, and the change of PAN ID parameters of the network. The parameters which were changed as a result of the attack were verified by using the XCTU software. Although, the attacks were generated in a smaller scale within the testbed, with minor modification, these attacks can be executed on a larger scale. We believe, the experiment and data presented in this paper will be very helpful to over-come remote AT command-based security attacks in Zigbee networks. Therefore, our future work may involve setting of attacks on a large-scale Zigbee based sensors in IoT networks. In final note, Zigbee based sensors in IoT networks require security evaluation in firmware level, device configuration level, and external level to ensure security of the network.

References

1. Fan, X., Susan, F., Long, W., Li, S.: Security Analysis of ZigBee. MIT Press, cambridge (2017)
2. Vaccari, I., Cambiaso, E., Aiello, M.: Remotely exploiting AT command attacks on ZigBee networks. Secur. Commun. Networks **2017**, 1–9 (2017)
3. Baronti, P., Pillai, P., Chook, V.W., Chessa, S., Gotta, A., Hu, Y.F.: Wireless sensor networks: a survey on the state of the art and the 802.15. 4 and ZigBee standards. Comput. Commun. **30**(7), 1655–1695 (2007)
4. Wright, J.: Killerbee: practical zigbee exploitation framework (2009)
5. Stelte, B., Rodosek, G.D.: Thwarting attacks on zigbee-removal of the killerbee stinger. In: Proceedings of the 9th International Conference on Network and Service Management (CNSM 2013), pp. 219–226. IEEE (2013)
6. Biswas, A., Alkhalid, A., Kunz, T., Lung, C.-H.: A lightweight defence against the packet in packet attack in ZigBee networks. In: 2012 IFIP Wireless Days, pp. 1–3. IEEE (2012)
7. Cambiaso, E., Papaleo, G., Chiola, G., Aiello, M.: Slow DoS attacks: definition and categorisation. Int. J. Trust Manag. Comput. Commun. **1**(3–4), 300–319 (2013)
8. Suo, H., Wan, J., Zou, C., Liu, J.: Security in the internet of things: a review. In: 2012 International Conference on Computer Science and Electronics Engineering, vol. 3, pp. 648–651. IEEE (2012)

9. Jhaveri, R.H., Patel, S.J., Jinwala, D.C.: DoS attacks in mobile ad hoc networks: a survey. In: 2012 Second International Conference on Advanced Computing & Communication Technologies, pp. 535–541. IEEE (2012)

10. Kandoi, R., Antikainen, M.: Denial-of-service attacks in OpenFlow SDN networks. In: 2015 IFIP/IEEE International Symposium on Integrated Network Management (IM), pp. 1322–1326. IEEE (2015)

11. Shila, D.M., Cao, X., Cheng, Y., Yang, Z., Zhou, Y., Chen, J.: Ghost-in-the-wireless: energy depletion attack on zigbee. arXiv preprint arXiv:1410.1613 (2014)

12. Vidgren, N., Haataja, K., Patino-Andres, J.L., Ramirez-Sanchis, J.J., Toivanen, P.: Security threats in ZigBee-enabled systems: vulnerability evaluation, practical experiments, counter-measures, and lessons learned. In: 2013 46th Hawaii International Conference on System Sciences, pp. 5132–5138. IEEE (2013)

13. Pacheco, L.A.B., Gondim, J.J.C., Barreto, P.A.S., Alchieri, E.: Evaluation of distributed denial of service threat in the internet of things. In: Proceedings of the 15th IEEE International Symposium on Network Computing and Applications, NCA 2016, pp. 89–92, November 2016

14. Li, H., Jia, Z., Xue, X.: Application and analysis of ZigBee security services specification. In: 2010 Second International Conference on Networks Security, Wireless Communications and Trusted Computing, vol. 2, pp. 494–497. IEEE (2010)

15. Sastry, N., Wagner, D.: Security considerations for IEEE 802.15. 4 networks. In: Proceedings of the 3rd ACM Workshop on Wireless Security, pp. 32–42. ACM (2004)

16. Faludi, R.: BuildingWirelessSensorNetworks: with ZigBee, XBee, Arduino, and Processing, O'ReillyMedia Inc, Sebastopol (2010)

17. Digi International Inc. How XBee devices communicate (2019)

18. Ray, B., Huda, S., Chowdhury, M.U.: Smart RFID reader protocol for malware detection. In: 2011 12th ACIS International Conference on Software Engineering, Artificial Intelligence, Networking and Parallel/Distributed Computing, Sydney, NSW, pp. 64–69 (2011)

19. McGinthy, J.M., Wong, L.J., Michaels, A.J.: Groundwork for neural network-based specific emitter identification authentication for IoT. IEEE Internet Things J. Early access Published on 03 April 2019

A Survey on Various Integrity Verification Schemes on the Data Outsourced to Cloud Storage

S. Milton Ganesh[1]([⊠]) and S. P. Manikandan[2]

[1] Department of Computer Science and Engineering, University College of Engineering Tindivanam, Tindivanam 604 001, Tamil Nadu, India
softengineermilton@gmail.com
[2] Department of Computer Science and Engineering, Jerusalem College of Engineering, Velachery Main Road, Pallikaranai, Narayanapuram, Chennai 600 100, Tamil Nadu, India
csehod@jerusalemengg.ac.in

Abstract. The cloud storage is available on-demand, flexible resource provisioning with pay-as-you-go pricing methodologies powered by data centers and virtualization technologies. One of the major applications from cloud service providers is that of the cloud storage. The service providers are ensuring reliability in such a way that, if one server crashes or currently down, a backup server is some other location facilitates continued service-provisioning for the customers. In such an environment, the customers data are stored in a single cloud server or multiple cloud servers. In the current trend, the data has become more valued than the hardware. Hence, verification of data uploaded to the cloud servers at regular intervals is important. This research work strives to provide a wide range of methods which offer this integrity verification service with their merits and demerits.

Keywords: Remote data · Provable data possession · Integrity verification · Cloud storage

1 Introduction

The idea of cloud computing was introduced in 20th century after the invention of mainframes, minicomputers, personal computers, laptops and other handheld devices [1]. The technology converge of web service, grid service, autonomic computing, parallel processing, distributed computing for high performance and high throughput applications have necessitated the need for outsourcing the computing power, storage space, primacy memory technologies [2, 3].

Since the invention of virtualization technologies by VMWare in late 1990s for sharing the hardware resources of a single computer, the thirst for outsourcing the virtualized resources have been extensively studied [4]. As a result, the web service based outsourcing the technology called the cloud computing has successfully been invented with much needed virtualization support by hardware and software from multiple vendors of the computer business [5].

The advent of cloud introduced may vendors to get the service from cloud as ready-made applications with only the database being uploaded to the cloud storage [6, 7].

© Springer Nature Singapore Pte Ltd. 2019
V. S. Shankar Sriram et al. (Eds.): ATIS 2019, CCIS 1116, pp. 92–99, 2019.
https://doi.org/10.1007/978-981-15-0871-4_7

In such a cloud technology prevalent scenario, hackers and intruders are keenly watching the cloud service providers to catch hold of the confidential business data available in cloud servers. If they win this game of intruding the cloud servers, they may do harm to the data by deleting some important portions of it for fun or for business rivalry [8, 9]. Apart from multi-national companies like Amazon, Microsoft, Google, Cloud Fare, many young entrepreneurs are venturing into cloud service provision to the market.

Hence, a proper technique to ascertain the data integrity the in the cloud storage is essential for proper functioning of the businesses and for ensuring confidentiality of the individual users [10]. Recently, the accounts of Facebook users was hacked by intruders which made Facebook look at the vulnerability issues in its application and to seal them as soon as possible. Accordingly, there must be a way for the businesses and laymen to verify their data stored in the outsourced storage areas.

Many authors have proposed their schemes for providing storage verification using different mathematical principles. Each principle makes their scheme stronger than others, but yet to seal all the vulnerabilities from the hackers' illegal attempts.

Some of the related survey works are brought forward to the notice of the researchers in Sect. 2. Various approaches proposed by different authors in the past are presented in Sect. 3. Section 4 details with the analysis and gaps in the present works. Current challenges and directions for future research are presented in subsequent sections. Section 6 concludes this research work.

2 Related Works in the Literature

One of the very recent works is introduced by Liu et al. in 2019. The authors have clearly noted the importance of the need for data integrity verification ranging from the work done before two decades to the current scenario. They have analyzed the work based on the procedures on blockless verification, public verifiability of the proposed schemes, coarse-grained and fine-grained nature of the schemes and the authentication of the nodes among other attributes. Their work puts forwards the facts such as much work is needed to improved efficiency, multi-tenancy based cloud storage, scalability of the data center provisioning [11].

Shin and Kwon [12] in the recent past have studied extensively on the remote data possession schemes proposed. Their work focuses on the performance due to publicly verifiable and batch auditing schemes on the cloud storage. The comparison criteria for the notable works being the computational cost incurred by the works due to cloud service providers, third party auditors, communication cost during challenge to the cloud server and response from the cloud server and finally the probability of the successful findings of data fiddling.

Rani and Ragha [13] have surveyed the previous works in terms of dynamic verification ability, ability to store and verify over the data stored with multiple replicas, identity based schemes and hash table based schemes. They claim that a cheating cloud service provider may sell the data for a price to the hacker and behave dishonestly. The presence of a good auditing method will resolve the dispute the data owner and the cloud service provider.

Zhou et al. in 2018 [14] claim that the verification strategies can be divided into seven major ones. Each category is thoroughly analyzed with respect to the list of services provided including auditing service, data privacy, data dynamicity, auditing operation in batch mode and multi-user setting based verification procedures. They have also attempted to collect the works based on the copies with a user including one copy with one user, multiple copies of data with one user and multiple copies of data with multiple users. This survey is astounding which gives a clear pictures of the works done in the past and the need for new directions in this area.

Another novel survey by Chaudhuri et al. in 2018 [15] highlights the fact that the users are not aware of the verification procedures which are handy to the cloud server providers. They based their survey on traditional methods, Merkle-hash tree methods, signature based methods which are prevalent in auditing strategies.

Though multiple survey with fruitful findings have already been put forward, this research work will complement to identify further research findings and will be helpful to the young researchers to further explore the concepts of integrity verification strategies.

3   Survey on Various Integrity Verification Schemes

3.1   Provable Data Possession

The possession of data by the cloud servers was successfully verified by many approaches in the past. Some of the notable contributions are presented here.

Ateniese et al. in 2007 [16] came out with one of the early verification schemes for proof of verification for the data outsourced to cloud servers. Two schemes were introduced and both of them proved to be more efficient than the similar works in this literature. One of the significant finding of this research work is that of attributing the performance of the verification scheme to disk input and output rather than the complexity in cryptographic formulations.

Sebé et al. in 2008 [17] introduced a possession verification scheme suitable for airports, defense systems and other mission-critical infrastructures. This work allows for repeated verification if needed with minimal cost and allows the use to setup a maximum verification time during the commencement of the cloud outsourcing process.

A recent work proposed by Ghoubach et al. in 2019 [18] allows handheld devices such as mobile phones, tablets to do the verification of the outsourced data. Since these devices come with limited power backups, this work strives to do the integrity check with minimal computation and communication cost than the previous works.

Erway et al. in 2015 [19] introduced a version control scheme for updating the outsourced data to the cloud storage. This scheme is a novel work with relatively less computational cost. The novelty in this research work is that of the usage of authenticated dictionaries containing the ranking details.

3.2   Data Dynamics

Only very few works strive to provide the data dynamicity such as updating, deleting, modifying, inserting blocks into the already uploaded files.

Ren et al. in 2018 [20] allowed for cloud storage data possession by external parties with secure data dynamic operations. Since the existing works suffer from vulnerabilities, this work makes use of rb23Tree technique for it and avoids them showing reduced computational cost for dynamic operation compared to the previous works.

A work proposed by Wang et al. in 2009 [21] based on Merkel hash tree provides prominent support of improved version of data dynamic operations handling mechanisms for the outsourced data. Since prior works provide either data possession verification procedure or dynamic operation procedure, this work provides both of the services at low computational cost.

Hao et al. [22] extended the work proposed by Sebé et al. [17] and allowed for both public verification of data and support data dynamic operations. The significance of this approach is that the data owner does the verification procedure without delegating it to an external auditor. Thus this work can be useful for confidential data handling contexts.

Chen et al. in [23] invented a scheme utilizing the homomorphic hashing method. The Merkle hash tree was used for supporting the data dynamic operations. This tree structure is used to log the details of each data operation being done on the outsourced data.

3.3   Batch Auditing

Under some circumstances, it is necessary that the possession of data be verified for multiple users under consideration. Some of the typical works in this line are included in this research article.

The work proposed by Saxena and Dey [24] made use of more than one third party auditors for doing the auditing process for multiple users. The work introduces its novelty by making use of homomorphic tags and batch code techniques and also avoids the single point of failure of a third party auditor.

Wang et al. in 2013 [25] have conducted a serious study on data integrity verification for data stored in the cloud storage provided by Amazon. The work is free from the vulnerabilities identified in the previous works and it provides multi-user setting option in the Amazon EC2 server for batch auditing.

The work proposed by Yu et al. in 2014 [26] is an improvised version of the previous work done by Chen et al. This work proves that the previous work is susceptible to attacks such as forgery and replace attacks. The proposed protocol fixes the identified problems and surfaces well with less computational overhead.

3.4   Identity Based PDP

Liu et al. in 2017 [27] based on their work on proposing a novel scheme which is free from quantum computer attacks. They have formulated their work using lattice based cryptographic techniques to avoid those attacks without using certificates. This reduces huge computational overhead during the auditing process.

Wang et al. in 2014 [28] setup an environment for multi-cloud storage based integrity verification methods based on identity based signatures. This work is computationally efficient and support the verification by private user, a user in a delegated environment or a public user.

The work done by Yu et al. in 2017 [29] avoid the use of costly public key infrastructure which hinder the usage of the remote data verification protocol. The idea of identity based key-homomorphic initiatives were used to realize the verification process. The proposed protocol preserves perfect data privacy from the external auditor.

3.5 Verification Over Multi-cloud Storage

The data uploaded to cloud are stored in multi-cloud storage provided by the data centers. Works in this direction are very important for real-world implementation scenarios.

In the work proposed by Curtmola et al. [30], a client may wish to keep multiple copies of data in multiple cloud servers to increase the data reliability. In such a scenario, this work strives to avoid any collusion based attack by the cloud servers. Another novel feature of this work is that of increasing the replicas of the copies on demand.

Since the cloud storage area may migrate data due to various migration policies, the work proposed by Zhu et al. in 2012 [31] gains importance. The auditing is provable over the data stored in multiple clouds with zero-knowledge privacy. Moreover, the computational and communication overheads compared to the previous literary works are relatively less.

Wei et al. in 2016 [32] have provided a means of ensuring verification of multiple copies of data stored in different cloud servers in different data centers. This multi-cloud concept is being followed by businesses to increase the availability of the outsourced data to its customers. This scheme makes use of homomorphic technique create multiple copies of the data. It supports auditing and block dynamic data operations.

4 Analysis of the Findings and Identifying the Gaps for Future Research Direction

This section provides a condensed view of the findings of this exhaustive research work and the gaps to be filled in this direction are provided to assist young researches, scientists and academicians to put forward more research in the verification procedures on the cloud storage. The details analysis and the gaps are tabulated in Table 1.

Table 1. Advantages of various integrity verification methods and identified gaps

Sl. No.	Schemes	Advantages	Gaps identified
1.	ID based schemes	Relatively more secure	Improvement on multi-user batch auditing based research works are very less
2.	PDP schemes	Mandatory for current cloud storages	User authentication provided by very few works. Works on storages other than cloud are very few
3.	Multi-cloud storage schemes	Supports replicas providing availability and reliability for business continuity	Very few works available. More research needed in privacy based works
4.	Batch-auditing schemes	Multi-user auditing for hierarchical auditing scenario	More works needed in Hadoop framework and Amazon web services needed as they are wide-spread among cloud user community
5.	Schemes on data dynamics	Provides a real time environment for cloud users	Authenticity during dynamicity is not available. More works not available

5 Research Challenges

One of the major challenges in developing a protocol for secure data storage in cloud servers is that of attacks from hackers and intruders in terms of Man-in-the-Middle attack, collusion attack and message modification attack. The recent work proposed by Nayak and Tripathy in 2018 [33] has been proved to be vulnerable to attack. Similarly, a work pertaining to batch auditing with less computation complexity is a daunting task for a researcher [26] with less computational complexity. Initiating verification on multi-cloud storage is another research challenge which is yet to be resolved.

6 Conclusion

The survey provides a comprehensive view of the various major techniques from a great grand past to the current literature. This article will serve as an eye-opener for the young researches and academicians who want to explore the research works carried out in this arena. The prominent works with the nature of the protocols used by the authors along with their ability for doing the proof verification over the audit response provides a overall picture of the significance of works carried out in different dimension with regard to the verification procedure. The gaps identifies simply portray that, though multiple schemes have been proposed in the literature, the question of providing an attack-resistant and computationally efficient scheme for ensuring the integrity verification yet to be provided in the future.

References

1. Armbrust, M., et al.: A view of cloud computing. Commun. ACM **53**, 50–58 (2010)
2. Ekanayake, J., Fox, G.: High performance parallel computing with clouds and cloud technologies. In: Avresky, D.R., Diaz, M., Bode, A., Ciciani, B., Dekel, E. (eds.) CloudComp 2009. LNICSSTE, vol. 34, pp. 20–38. Springer, Heidelberg (2010). https://doi.org/10.1007/978-3-642-12636-9_2
3. Keahey, K., Foster, I., Freeman, T., Zhang, X.: VirtualWorkspaces: achieving quality of service and quality of life in the grid. Sci. Program. J. **13**(4), 265–276 (2005)
4. Foster, I.: The anatomy of the grid: enabling scalable virtual organizations. In: Sakellariou, R., Gurd, J., Freeman, L., Keane, J. (eds.) Euro-Par 2001. LNCS, vol. 2150, pp. 1–4. Springer, Heidelberg (2001). https://doi.org/10.1007/3-540-44681-8_1
5. Gavrilovska, A., et al.: High-performance hypervisor architectures: virtualization in HPC systems. In: 1st Workshop on System-Level Virtualization for High Performance Computing (2007)
6. Li, Z., He, Q., Zhang, X.: Study on cloud storage system based on distributed storage systems. In: International Conference on Computational and Information Sciences, Chengdu, China, pp. 1332–1335 (2010)
7. Gu, Y., Grossman, R.L.: Sector and Sphere: the design and implementation of a high-performance data cloud. Philos. Trans. R. Soc. **367**, 2429–2445 (2009)
8. Yurukonda, N., ThirumalaRao, B.: A study on data storage security issues in cloud computing. J. Procedia Comput. Sci. **92**, 128–135 (2016)
9. Balduzzi, M., Zaddach, J., Balzarotti, D., Kirda, E., Loureiro, S.: A security analysis of amazon's elastic compute cloud service. In: Proceedings of the 27th Annual ACM Symposium on Applied Computing, Trento, Italy, pp. 1427–1434 (2012)
10. Yang, K., Xia, X.: An efficient and secure dynamic auditing protocol for data storage in the cloud computing. IEEE Trans. Parallel Distrib. Syst. **24**(9), 1717–1726 (2013)
11. Liu, C., Yang, C., Zhang, X., Chen, J.: External integrity verification for outsourced big data in cloud and IoT: a big picture. Future Gener. Comput. Syst. J. **49**, 58–67 (2015)
12. Shin, S., Kwon, T.: A survey of public provable data possession schemes with batch verification in cloud storage. J. Internet Serv. Inf. Secur. **5**(3), 37–47 (2015)
13. Rani, R.S.M., Ragha, L.: Dynamic public data auditing schemes on cloud: a survey. Int. J. Adv. Res. Comput. Sci. Softw. Eng. **8**(1), 76–78 (2018)
14. Zhou, L., Fu, A., Yu, S., Su, M., Kuang, B.: Data integrity verification of the outsourced big data in the cloud environment: a survey. J. Netw. Comput. Appl. **122**, 1–15 (2018)
15. Chaudhari, S., Pathuri, S.K.: A comprehensive survey on public auditing for cloud storage. Int. J. Eng. Technol. **7**(2.7), 565–569 (2018)
16. Ateniese, G., et al.: Provable data possession at untrusted stores. In: ACM Conference on Computer and Communications Security, Alexandria, Virginia, USA, pp. 598–609 (2007)
17. Sebé, F., Domingo-Ferrer, J., Martinez-Balleste, A., Deswarte, Y., Quisquater, J.: Efficient remote data possession checking in critical information infrastructures. IEEE Trans. Knowl. Data Eng. **20**(8), 1034–1038 (2008)
18. Ghoubach, I.E., Abbou, R.B., Mrabti, F.: A secure and efficient remote data auditing scheme for cloud storage. J. King Saud Univ. Comput. Inf. Sci. (accepted for publication)
19. Erway, C.C., Küpçü, A., Papamanthou, C., Tamassia, R.: Dynamic provable data possession. ACM Trans. Inf. Syst. Secur. **17**(4), 15 (2015)
20. Ren, Z., Wang, L., Wang, Q., Xu, M.: Dynamic proofs of retrievability for coded cloud storage systems. IEEE Trans. Serv. Comput. **11**(4) (2018)

21. Wang, Q., Wang, C., Li, J., Ren, K., Lou, W.: Enabling public verifiability and data dynamics for storage security in cloud computing. In: Backes, M., Ning, P. (eds.) ESORICS 2009. LNCS, vol. 5789, pp. 355–370. Springer, Heidelberg (2009). https://doi.org/10.1007/978-3-642-04444-1_22
22. Hao, Z., Zhong, S., Yu, N.: A privacy-preserving remote data integrity checking protocol with data dynamics and public verifiability. IEEE Trans. Knowl. Data Eng. 23(9), 1432–1437 (2011)
23. Chen, L., Zhou, S., Huang, X., Xu, L.: Data dynamics for remote data possession checking in cloud storage. Comput. Electr. Eng. J. 39(7), 2413–2424 (2013)
24. Saxena, R., Dey, S.: A generic approach for integrity verification big data. Cluster Comput. 22(2), 529–540 (2018)
25. Wang, C., Chow, S.M., Wang, Q., Ren, K., Lou, W.: Privacy-preserving public auditing for secure cloud storage. IEEE Trans. Comput. 62(2), 362–375 (2013)
26. Yu, Y., Ni, J., Au, M.H., Liu, H., Wang, H., Xu, C.: Improved security of a dynamic remote data possession checking protocol for cloud storage. J. Expert Syst. Appl. 41(17), 7789–7796 (2014)
27. Liu, Z., Liao, Y., Yang, X., He, Y., Zhao, K.: Identity-based remote data integrity checking of cloud storage from lattices. In: International Conference on Big Data Computing and Application, Chengdu, China (2017)
28. Wang, H.: Identity-based distributed provable data possession in multicloud storage. IEEE Trans. Serv. Comput. 8(2), 328–340 (2014)
29. Yu, Y., et al.: Identity-based remote data integrity checking with perfect data privacy preserving for cloud storage. IEEE Trans. Inf. Forensics Secur. 12(4), 767–778 (2017)
30. Curtmola, R., Khan, O., Burns, R., Ateneise, G.: MR-PDP: multiple-replica provable data possession. In: International Conference on Distributed Computing Systems, Beijing, China (2008)
31. Zhu, Y., Hu, H., Ahn, G., Yu, M.: Cooperative provable data possession for integrity verification in multicloud storage. IEEE Trans. Parallel Distrib. Syst. 23(12), 2231–2244 (2012)
32. Wei, J., Liu, J., Zhang, Ru., Niu, X.: Efficient dynamic replicated data possession checking in distributed cloud storage systems. Int. J. Distrib. Sens. Netw. 12(1) (2016)
33. Nayak, S.K., Tripathy, S.: SEPDP: secure and efficient privacy preserving provable data possession in cloud storage. IEEE Trans. Serv. Comput. 1–13 (2018)

Prognostic Views on Software Defined Networks Based Security for Internet of Things

Antony Taurshia$^{(\boxtimes)}$, Jaspher W. Kathrine, and D. Shibin

Karunya Institute of Technology and Sciences, Coimbatore, India
antony18@karunya.edu.in,
{kathrine, shibin}@karunya.edu

Abstract. Security is very crucial to enhance the privacy and secrecy of the data and applications that are used in routine life. Human life, has been transformed into a much smarter one with the advent of several smart applications based on Internet of Things (IoT). The evolution of the Internet of computer to the Internet of Things was made possible by the involvement of Radio Frequency Identification (RFID), Wireless Sensor Networks (WSN), Lightweight Communication Protocols (LWCP) and cloud services. These major technologies enable IoT to associate with cloud technologies in order to provide advanced real-time applications that could improve our day to day life activities. Software-Defined Networks (SDN) is a technology capable of providing a bird's eye view of the network. Integrating SDN with IoT has several benefits including security. This paper studies the state of art research efforts in securing the IoT environment with SDN based solutions and highlights the advantages of using SDN for security. Further, a novel SDN based framework which segregates the IoT network based on applications with similar security needs is also proposed to enhance the overall security of the system.

Keywords: Security · Internet of Things · Protocol · Software Defined Networks

1 Introduction

The term 'Internet of Things' was first fabricated by Kevin Ashton in 1999 at the time of his tenure at Procter and Gamble [1]. The term was further popularized by RFID Auto-ID center, the RFID tags when attached to a device makes it uniquely identifiable and these devices, when connected to the internet, can perform smart functions. The basic concept of 'Internet of Things' is smart objects getting connected to the internet thereby providing some useful inferences. For example, in smart city application, the water tanks can be made to update their water usage data for efficient water management in drought-affected cities. Further, IoT uses up the advantage of sensor networks, to sense the environmental data and perform functions based on the sensed data. Cloud is an effective service platform which is capable of providing ubiquitous service to the IoT based devices. Since IoT comprises a network of various devices getting connected anytime, anywhere, it is anticipated that the number of devices connected to the internet may reach billion in 2020 [2]. Securing this massive network of devices with limited

© Springer Nature Singapore Pte Ltd. 2019
V. S. Shankar Sriram et al. (Eds.): ATIS 2019, CCIS 1116, pp. 100–116, 2019.
https://doi.org/10.1007/978-981-15-0871-4_8

resources is a great challenge. Moreover, IoT uses different lightweight communication protocols like IEEE 802.15.4, Ipv6 over Low-Power Wireless Personal Area Network (6LoWPAN), ZigBee, Z-wave and application protocols like Constrained Application Protocol (CoAP), Message Queuing Telemetry Transport (MQTT) in contrast to traditional networks [3]. The protocols come with their own vulnerabilities and providing common security methods for these heterogeneous networks is tedious. Various researchers have provided solutions like light-weight cryptography, block and stream ciphers, light-weight security protocols, key management protocols and thus along [4–6]. Even so, the area of securing the IoT network is still in its infancy and issues like providing standard security algorithms for these heterogeneous resource-constrained devices needs to be addressed.

Software Defined Network (SDN) is an emerging technology that segregates the control plane and the data plane. It gives a global view of the network to the users. The decisions regarding routing are determined by the centralized SDN controller while the switches forward the packets based on the decision of the controller. SDN when integrated into the fog and edge paradigm of IoT, can have significant impact on the latter's performance. With SDN, upgrading becomes easier when compared to traditional networks, the network is more flexible, can detect flaws and make decisions on the fly, and support features like Network Function Virtualization (NFV) which in-turn leads to improved network performance [7]. The logically centralized control provided by SDN greatly benefits the heterogeneous IoT networks as it provides more control over the network. In this regard a novel generic framework for handling the heterogeneous network of IoT using SDN for security enhancement is proposed. Despite the fact that the SDN paradigm itself is prone to various attacks, the benefits of securing the IoT environment using SDN are inevitable. This paper reviews on the various research efforts made so far to secure the IoT environment using SDN and highlights its benefits over traditional methods. Further scope for future work is also enclosed.

The contribution of this work unfolds as follows. Section 2 gives an overview of IoT architecture and its vital facilitating technological components. Section 3 categorizes the ways for securing IoT and gives the reason for using SDN for IoT security. Section 4 reviews the various SDN based security solutions and lists out their merits and limitations. Section 5 provides an analysis of the security solutions by listing out the distinctive advantages it carries over conventional methods. Section 6 proposes a novel generic framework for security enhancement in IoT system. Section 7 presents the conclusion.

2 IOT System

The basic architecture of IoT is a simple three-layered architecture as depicted in Fig. 1 with perception layer as the bottom layer, which is responsible for sensing and gathering of status information from the device and its environment [2, 3]. The middle network layer is responsible for transmission and communication of data between devices and applications. The upper layer is the application layer, responsible for delivering services to applications based on the data collected.

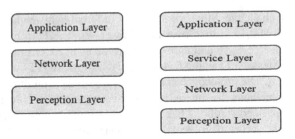

Fig. 1. Basic and Service Oriented Architecture

Another important architecture for IoT is the Service Oriented Architecture (SOA) with an additional service layer [3]. This service layer performs service discovery, service composition, and management. It also provides interfaces for services. Some of the essential components of IoT which works under these layers are listed below.

Perception Layer: RFID, embedded devices and sensor networks form the essential components of this layer. The devices in IoT is resource-constrained with 8-bit, 16-bit and 32-bit microcontrollers used in common. RFID tags are attached to these devices for unique identification and tracking purpose using radio waves, while sensor networks sense and gather the status of devices and environmental data like pressure, humidity, light, etc. [3].

Network Layer: Several lightweight communication protocols are used for communication in the resource constrained IoT environment. The protocols used are IEEE 802.11, IEEE 802.15.4, Zigbee, Z-wave, 6LoWPAN, CoAP, MQTT, etc. [3, 8].

Service Layer: Cloud is a promising service platform which provides unlimited computing and storage capabilities ubiquitously [9, 10]. Still, it has certain limitations like limited network bandwidth and latency problem [11]. Fog, edge and cloudlet, the branches of cloud, are used in collaboration with one another to overcome these limitations [12].

Application Layer: This layer includes some efficient applications like smart grid, intelligent transportation, health monitoring, building automation, smart manufacturing, Industry 4.0, etc. [3].

3 Software Defined Network (SDN)

Software Defined Network is an emerging technology, which uses software applications for programming the network inducing network virtualization [12]. SDN overcomes the drawbacks of the traditional network by possessing a logically centralized architecture which divides the control plane from the data plane. The decision regarding routing of packets is made by SDN controllers whereas the network devices only take responsibility for forwarding the packets based on the controller's decision. SDN architecture consists of three layers namely infrastructure layer, control layer and, application layer as in Fig. 2. The infrastructure layer includes networking devices like switches and routers, the control layer consists of controllers with software for network programmability and the application layer includes applications like traffic monitoring and load balancing which makes use of the underlying functions. Interaction between the infrastructure layer and control layer is done through southbound Application Programming Interfaces (APIs) like OpenFlow and NetConf. Northbound APIs like Frentic is used for interaction between the control layer and the application layer [7]. First, the SDN controller establishes a connection with the networking devices through southbound APIs and based on the information received, builds a global view of the network. The features of SDN, when integrated with fog, can help resolve issues like irregular connectivity, high packet loss rate, and collisions [12].

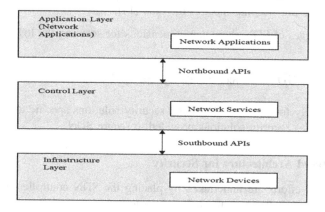

Fig. 2. SDN architecture

The network of 'Internet of Things' is heterogeneous, with unlimited number of devices getting connected anytime, anywhere, the traditional methods of security are not sufficient for securing it. Henceforth, many novel methods are proposed by researchers to secure this resource-constrained heterogeneous network of things [4–6, 13]. Based on the works so far we try to classify the ways for securing IoT into five categories as depicted in Fig. 3.

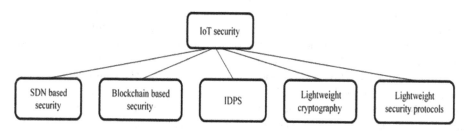

Fig. 3. IOT security solutions

Among the ways of securing, using software defined networks for IoT security is the hot topic prevalent nowadays. The reasons for the need for SDN to secure IoT environment comes as follows,

- SDN provides centralized control over the network, hence it can efficiently tackle several security issues.
- SDN also supports virtualization of services and network components. Hence it is capable of providing fast response to security threats by supporting mechanisms like traffic rerouting, intrusion detection and prevention, security policy deployment, authentication and, access control on the fly [7].
- SDN having a global network view can manage the sleep/wake cycles of IoT devices which are sleeping most of the time [14].

These privileges of SDN show new dimensions for securing the IoT environment.

4   Review on SDN Based Security for IoT

This review solely focuses on SDN based security solutions specific to IoT environment and excludes security solutions provided to secure SDN.

4.1   SDN Based Architecture for Security

Several research efforts are undertaken by placing the SDN controllers and network devices in different patterns in the IoT system to tackle several security issues. The authors in [15] proposed an architecture based on a distributed grid of security concept. The network is divided into domains which may include wired, wireless, ad-hoc and sensor networks. Each domain contains a root controller called the border controller. The security rules and routing functions are distributed on border controllers and are in connection with other domain border controllers. Whenever the border controller encounters a new flow it starts authenticating it, allowing only secure traffic. A similar network-based approach for security has been proposed in [16] where the IoT network is segregated into clusters and each cluster governed by a cluster head with an SDN controller integrated into it. A new routing protocol is proposed for inter-domain cluster communication and an OpFlex based distributed firewall is proposed for IoT systems. Flow visor, a novel SDN based architecture is proposed in [17] where a specialized SDN controller is used for logically segregating the smart grid network into different slices. This segregation privileges the use of several controllers in the same network. Slicing of the network leads to mitigation of several security issues like trust, authentication, availability, authorization, and confidentiality. The controller sends the metering data encrypted using AES-128. Long-Term Evolution (LTE) is used for sending 24-h metering data to the utility which is then compared with the last 24-h metering sum data provided by SDN switches ensuring non-repudiation and integrity.

In IoT network, there are devices that use wireless access point for network access and devices that use cellular networks. A new SDN based security architecture [18] for both kinds of devices is proposed. The architecture uses a gateway controller between OpenFlow switches and SDN main controller. The gateway controller supports

Intrusion Detection and Prevention System (IDPS), Deep Packet Inspection (DPI) and other generic rules for safeguarding the network. The main controller is in constant touch with the gateway controller and is responsible for rerouting the traffic. Since both the inbound and outbound traffic passes via gateway controller only secure traffic is allowed to go further, thus protecting the system from (Denial of Service) DoS and ARP spoof attack. The main SDN controller is responsible for encryption and decryption of information passing through it to avoid data theft in IoT networks.

Another novel SDN based security architecture called RolSec [19] has been proposed which distributes the controller based on security rules. The SDN IoT gateway is managed by many controllers and is in communication with other gateway controllers in addition to its own domain. In RolSec the SDN controllers are separated into intrusion controller for detecting intrusion, key controller for key management and cyptocontroller for ensuring confidentiality, integrity, privacy, authentication and identity management. A distributed blockchain-based cloud and fog architecture is proposed in [20] where the SDN controllers are distributed in fog node in blockchain fashion. The distributed SDN in the fog layer performs analysis of flow rule and packet migration. It also provides an interface for network management operators to provide networking capabilities. The SDN switch is placed in the multi-interfaced base station at the edge of the network to constitute a wireless gateway. The edge of the network is equipped with provision for detecting saturation attack. The blockchain-based SDN architecture improves the overall security of IoT network.

Through SDN, security can be provided as a service. Service Function Chain (SFC) is a technology supported by SDN and NFV which guides the user traffic flow through service applications based on user needs. The authors in [21] proposes an architecture for on-demand security service based on SFC technology. The source traffic is allotted to pass through a set of virtualized security functions like intrusion detection and prevention system, firewall, etc., before reaching the destination based on the demands of the user. Another framework for security services is proposed in [22] where security service applications like Distributed Denial of Service (DDoS) attack mitigator and firewall are deployed on top of the SDN controller. The service applications are centralized and are responsible for protecting the network resources from suspicious traffic by dropping packets based on probability. Table 1 lists out the merits and limitations of the above said SDN architectures for securing IoT.

4.2   SDN Based Virtual Authentication Authorization and Accounting (AAA)

The network of IoT is heterogeneous and the devices use different types of addressing like IP, ZigBee and MAC address based on the type of network for identification purpose. In view of this, a common identity-based authentication scheme [23] is proposed for all networks by integrating a trusted certificate authority along with the SDN controller as it provides centralized control over the network. Key establishment is done using Elliptic Curve Cryptography (ECC) and the authority provides a virtual-IPv6 based identity for the devices which tries to register. This identity can be used for further authentication and nounce is used to avoid replay attack. The proposed scheme is efficient against man-in-the-middle, masquerade and replay attacks.

Table 1. SDN based architecture for security

Research effort	Methodology	Merits	Limitations
SDN based architecture for security [15]	The network is divided into domains with a border controller for each domain	Architecture for both Ad-Hoc and IoT network. Failure recovery is easier as domains are independent. The domains are distributed all over network to prevent attacks and deny unauthorized users to communicate	The architecture is not simulated and the performance is not evaluated
SDN-based security framework grid [16]	The network is divided into clusters with an SDN controller as cluster head	Clusters ensure easy failure recovery. A new routing protocol for communication and provision for distributed firewall	Lack of performance analysis
SDN/LTE based architecture (Flow visor) for smart grid security [17]	The smart grid network is divided into slices using SDN. LTE is used for transferring metering data	Allows use of multiple controllers in the same network. Ensures non-repudiation and integrity of data by cross checking	Framework specific only to smart grid. Lack of performance analysis on communication overhead
SDN and edge computing based security architecture [18]	Gateway controller is placed between the main SDN controller and switches	Gateway controller equipped with IDPS and DPI allowing only secure traffic. Prevention from DoS and ARP spoof attack	The architecture is not simulated and tested. Performance analysis not done. Single point of failure problem. No detailed information on encryption and decryption of information by SDN controller
RolSec [19]	SDN controller is divided into cryptocontroller, intrusion controller and key controller	More efficient and secure as SDN controllers are distributed based on security rules	The architecture is not simulated and tested. No detailed explanation on the working and communication between different distributed controllers

(*continued*)

Table 1. (*continued*)

Research effort	Methodology	Merits	Limitations
A software defined distributed blockchain architecture for IoT [20]	SDN controllers, distributed in Block chain fashion	Improves overall security of the system. Reduced delay, increased throughput, scalability and real-time attack detection capability. Efficient solution for data offloading to cloud	Performance evaluation is done only for saturation attack
Security service on-demand architecture using SDN [21]	A framework for Security as a service using SFC technology	On- demand, dynamic and flexible security service	The framework is not simulated and performance analysis is not performed
A framework for security services based on software-defined networking [22]	Security service applications built on top of SDN controller	Provision for DDoS attack mitigation and firewall	The single, centralized controller leads to overhead during failure recovery. The architecture is not simulated or tested. Lack of performance analysis

As SDN supports virtualization a framework for virtual authentication, authorization and accounting (vAAA) [24] is proposed using SDN and NFV. The network authenticators are deployed at the edge as virtualized network functions (VNFs) for providing authentication service. An IoT device can send requests to the controller for authentication via a virtual switch. The controller then deploys dynamically a VNF of protocols like Extensible Authentication Protocol (EAP) for authentication. After authenticating, the device can derive keys for bootstrapping and receive credentials for authorization. Accounting can be done for generated traffic to prevent excess usage of resources. The proposed framework provides centralized channel protection and provision for dynamic key distribution for Machine-to-Machine (M2M) communications. Table 2 analyses the merits and limitations of the above said research efforts.

Table 2. SDN based virtual AAA

Research effort	Methodology	Merits	Limitations
Identity-based authentication scheme using SDN [23]	A trusted certificate authority is integrated with SDN controller for authentication	Provides a virtual identity common for all networks. Provides a Trusted certificate authority. Resistant to replay attack, Man-in-the-Middle attack and masquerade attack	Lack of performance analysis on memory and communication overhead
Managing AAA with NFV/SDN [24]	A framework for virtual AAA using NFV	Provision for virtual authentication, authorization and accounting at network edge. Provides channel protection and dynamic key distribution for M2M communication	The framework is not tested and evaluated

4.3   SDN Based Black Network

The purpose of a black network is to obscure information from malicious users. An SDN based black network is proposed [25] where the metadata along with the payload is encrypted. Grain 128a authenticating cipher is used for encryption due to its efficiency in IoT networks and a trusted third-party SDN controller is used for secure routing. The packets are broadcasted and only the destined receiver can decrypt the message while others cannot. Broadcasting the packets obscures the destination node. This method promises high security against eavesdropping and packet modification attacks with compromise in network efficiency and overhead due to complicated routing and symmetric key management.

Another SDN based black network is proposed [26] where the source, destination, and routing path is obscured. The source node is obscured through blank tokens originating from random nodes in the path between source and destination. These blank tokens are packets which are empty and of fixed length. When these tokens reach the source after traveling through a predestined path, the source fills the tokens with the payload and resend it back through the same path. In this way, the source node can be obscured. In order to obscure the destination node, the packets are made to hop a random number of nodes after reaching the destination node. The routing path is obscured by the usage of nodes called join nodes. These nodes use a random shuffling method instead of the traditional way of using First in First out (FIFO) order for forwarding the packets. The proposed method improves security with overload in network traffic. Analysis of the research efforts on SDN based black networks is depicted in Table 3.

Table 3. SDN based black networks

Research effort	Methodology	Merits	Limitations
Black SDN [25]	Encrypts the meta-data along with source and destination address. SDN controller is used for secure routing	Resistant against data gathering attack and traffic analysis attack. Broadcasting helps in obscuring the destination	Communication overhead due to routing and key management
Black routing and node obscuring using SDN [26]	Encrypts the metadata with source and destination IP address. Mechanisms for node obscuring using SDN	Obscures source node, destination node and routing path	Network-traffic overload

4.4 SDN Based Data Transfer Security

The author in [27] proposes an algorithm for optimal placement of middlebox like IDPS and firewall in IoT network and model for data transfer security based on middlebox called Middlebox-Guard (M-G). In M-G, the SDN enabled switch is granted to bind a port to one or more MAC addresses to avoid MAC spoofing attack. MAC flooding attack is mitigated by allotting limits to the number of MAC addresses associated with a switch port. The VLAN spoofing attack is mitigated by allotting ports as user-to-network interfaces (UNIs) and network-to-network interfaces (NNIs) and VLAN tags are removed from the packets of NNIs. Finally, IP spoofing is mitigated by configuring flow tables with IP-prefixes. The proposed algorithm's analysis is depicted in Table 4.

Table 4. SDN based data transfer security

Research effort	Methodology	Merits	Limitations
Data transfer security with SDN [27]	Algorithm for optimal placement of middlebox like IDPS and Firewall in IoT network	Mitigates MAC spoofing attack, MAC flooding attack, VLAN spoofing attack and IP spoofing attack	During failure and overload, sequences with loops are required for correct policy traversal

4.5 SDN Based Intrusion Detection and Prevention System (IDPS)

An SDN based framework for detecting and mitigating security attacks in smart home networks [28] is proposed. The framework consists of five modules. They are the device manager, sensor element, feature extractor, and mitigation unit. The Device manager maintains a database of home network devices, security risks associated with them, known home network attacks, and their defense mechanisms. The devices in the

Table 5. SDN based IDPS

Research effort	Methodology	Merits	Limitations
A host-based intrusion detection and mitigation framework for smart home [28]	The traffic from home, network devices are made to pass through an inline sensor built on top of SDN controller to perform intrusion detection and mitigation	Provides Host-based IDPS in smart home environment	No appropriate feature selection for current attacks. Protection only for a specific host
An invariant based intrusion detection system [29]	The static properties of devices named invariants are used for anomaly detection using SDN	Detects 29 out of 30 attacks with 96.5% detection rate and 6.5% false positive rate Exhaustive device knowledge is not required	Manual formation of rules for anomaly detection
GA based intrusion detection system [30]	Feature selection is done using GA on the network traffic obtained from SDN. The suspicious traffic is either suspended or redirected to an isolated spot	The algorithms intrusion detection rate is 80%. Processing time is reduced using GA	No analysis on false positive rate
Flow based security with SDN [31]	IOT gateway is integrated with SDN controller and switch	Traffic analysis is done close to network edge	Experiments focused only on TCP and ICMP based attacks

smart home network first register itself with the administrator using their device ID and location. The sensor element, a virtual inline sensor is built on top of the SDN controller. The SDN controller using OpenFlow redirects the traffic of home network device to flow through the sensor element which in turn maintains a log of network activities. The Feature extractor module extracts the features based on problem instances. The detector unit module uses signature-based and anomaly-based detection or stateful protocol analysis either separately or combined to detect attacks and the mitigation unit module mitigates attacks by redirecting the traffic against victim devices using OpenFlow.

Another novel invariant based Intrusion detection system is proposed [29] for industrial IoT. Invariants are defined as properties of a system that tend to remain constant in all scenarios. The static properties of devices are depicted with a logical design. Any deviation from the normal pattern is treated as an anomaly. This method consists of three phases. In the training phase, the data flow patterns are derived from SDN switches. In the next phase, the invariants are designed from the data flow patterns. The final phase is the anomaly detection phase. The SDN switch is integrated with the invariant algorithm and centralized monitoring is done using SDN. Upon simulation, the proposed method is able to detect 29 attacks out of 30 with a 96.5% detection rate.

A biologically inspired Genetic Algorithm (GA) based Intrusion Detection using SDN is proposed in [30]. GA is used for rule generation and feature selection. The algorithm extracts features from SDN provided network traffic and gets a fitness value to detect suspicious traffic. The suspicious traffic is either blocked or redirected to a honeypot using SDN. The simulation results show the algorithm is efficient against several attacks. Another approach for flow-based security is proposed [31] where the IoT gateway is employed as both SDN integrated controller and switch. That way, the system will be capable of providing analysis of traffic and flow rule closer to the network edge. Flow entries are used to detect the network state and actions like blocking, forwarding, and Quality of Service (QoS) is performed if anomalous behavior is detected. Table 5 provides the analysis of intrusion detection and prevention systems for IoT based on SDN.

4.6 SDN Based Resilience

A resilience approach using SDN for IoT communication [32] is proposed. In the proposed model redundant communication lines are used and if the line becomes disabled due to any attack, then SDN controller is used for dynamic switching between communication lines.

The work in [33] proposes combined cybersecurity and resilience-based modeling environment in network design stage to make a fail-safe environment using SDN. The work aims to achieve equilibrium resilience using SDN controllers knowledge on available paths, workload and bandwidth data with details for future implementation of the proposed framework. The analysis of resilience-based research efforts is done in Table 6.

Table 6. SDN based resilience

Research effort	Methodology	Merits	Limitations
Resilience with SDN [32]	Dynamic switching is done between redundant communication lines using SDN controller	Dynamic switching in case of attack or failure. Time elapsed during switching is reduced compared to conventional systems	Evaluation done only for DoS attack
Integrated cybersecurity and resilience based modeling environment for smart manufacturing [33]	Equilibrium resilience is obtained using SDN controllers by redirecting the traffic through safe network paths	Cybersecurity and resilience combined framework to make a fail-safe environment	The framework is not evaluated and tested. Provides only a generic solution

5   Analysis

From the review of research efforts made so far, it is evident that integrating SDN with IoT, not only improves network efficiency, but also has the ability to provide security against several attacks, perform intrusion detection and prevention on the fly, prevent unauthorized users from accessing the resources either through architecture or through virtual AAA and also capable of providing resilience. The analysis of existing SDN based security solutions identifies the following advantages over conventional security methods,

- Ability to provide real time-dynamic attack detection and prevention.
- Ability to provide traffic analysis, threat detection and prevention close to the network edge.
- Ability to provide virtual authentication, authorization, accounting, and access control.
- Capability of providing dynamic key management.
- Ability to provide Security as a service (SECaaS).
- Capability to isolate a malicious device and segregate networks.
- Capable of providing security common for the heterogeneous network of IoT.
- Ability to obscure the source and destination nodes from adversaries.

With centralized control over the network, SDN is also capable of dynamic rerouting of traffic in case of attack, failure or congestion.

6   Proposed Framework

The system of IoT is heterogeneous with different types of devices and technological components working in integration to provide several useful applications like smart home, security surveillance, healthcare, Industry 4.0, and intelligent transportation. As the privileges provided by these applications are different, the security needs of these applications are also different.

In smart home privacy of users, and confidentiality of information comes as crucial security need whereas temporal unavailability is tolerable to an extent. Whereas in a security surveillance application and health monitoring, unavailability is intolerable [34]. Intelligent transportation is latency-sensitive for vehicle-to-vehicle and infrastructure-to-vehicle communication. Sensitive applications like Industry 4.0 needs a well-protected environment safe from intruders and lots of provisions for resilience to make a fail-safe environment [35]. Providing specific security solution to this heterogeneous system is challenging. To tackle this heterogeneity, we propose a generic framework for IoT system using SDN. SDN controller is used to segregate the IoT network based on applications and their security needs as depicted in Fig. 4. The applications with similar security needs can be clustered together. In this way, the security needs of the applications can be handled effectively.

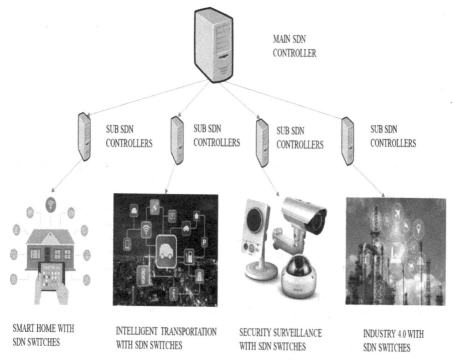

Fig. 4. Proposed framework

Through this framework, Industry 4.0 and healthcare can be segregated from the normal network. Intrusion detection, firewall, and efficient access control policies can be made to reach this network. Sensitive applications can be provided with sufficient resilience facilities to make a fail-safe environment. Applications like intelligent transportation can be concentrated to reduce delay and avoid DoS attacks. The single point of failure problem of the SDN controller can be prevented by using multiple controllers in blockchain fashion.

7   Conclusion

The idea of integrating SDN with IoT not only improves the network efficiency, but also, it is efficient in tackling several security issues. Despite this, SDN based security is still in its infancy and has lots of scope for future work like dynamic key management and distribution, dynamic encryption, dynamic authentication and access control on the way to the destination, and detection of evasive threats like zero day exploits and Advanced Persistent Threats (APTs). The limitations of the existing research works should be rectified and the unexplored areas should be exposed. SDN in itself is prone to new attacks such as newflow attack and threats like comprising of SDN switch and controller. Still, its advantages over conventional security methods, makes SDN based security inevitable for IoT networks. The proposed framework for IoT security is a generic solution and authors have planned to work on this framework for future work.

References

1. Gupta, S., Mudgal, N., Mehta, R.: Analytical study of IoT as emerging need of the modern era. In: 2016 International Conference on Computing for Sustainable Global Development, pp. 233–235 (2016)
2. Riahi Sfar, A., Natalizio, E., Challal, Y., Chtourou, Z.: A roadmap for security challenges in the Internet of Things. Digit. Commun. Networks 4, 118–137 (2018). https://doi.org/10.1016/j.dcan.2017.04.003
3. Lin, J., Yu, W., Zhang, N., Yang, X., Zhang, H., Zhao, W.: A survey on Internet of Things: architecture, enabling technologies, security and privacy, and applications. IEEE Internet Things J. 4, 1125–1142 (2017). https://doi.org/10.1109/JIOT.2017.2683200
4. Singh, S., Sharma, P.K., Moon, S.Y., Park, J.H.: Advanced lightweight encryption algorithms for IoT devices: survey, challenges and solutions. J. Ambient Intell. Humaniz. Comput. 0, 1–18 (2017). https://doi.org/10.1007/s12652-017-0494-4
5. Nguyen, K.T., Laurent, M., Oualha, N.: Survey on secure communication protocols for the Internet of Things. Ad Hoc Netw. 32, 17–31 (2015). https://doi.org/10.1016/j.adhoc.2015.01.006
6. Khan, M.A., Salah, K.: IoT security: review, blockchain solutions, and open challenges. Futur. Gener. Comput. Syst. 82, 395–411 (2018). https://doi.org/10.1016/j.future.2017.11.022
7. Rawat, D.B., Reddy, S.R.: Software defined networking architecture, security and energy efficiency: a survey. IEEE Commun. Surv. Tutorials 19, 325–346 (2017). https://doi.org/10.1109/COMST.2016.2618874
8. Sadeeq, M.A.M., Zeebaree, S.R.M., Qashi, R., Ahmed, S.H., Jacksi, K.: Internet of Things security: a survey. In: ICOASE 2018 - International Conference on Advanced Science and Engineering, vol. 88, pp. 162–166 (2018). https://doi.org/10.1109/ICOASE.2018.8548785
9. Atlam, H.F., Alenezi, A., Alharthi, A., Walters, R.J., Wills, G.B.: Integration of cloud computing with Internet of Things: challenges and open issues. In: Proceeding of the 2017 IEEE International Conference on Internet Things, IEEE Green Computing and Communications, IEEE Cyber, Physical and Social Computing, IEEE Smart Data, iThings-GreenCom-CPSCom-SmartData 2017, January 2018, pp. 670–675 (2018). https://doi.org/10.1109/iThings-GreenCom-CPSCom-SmartData.2017.105
10. Botta, A., De Donato, W., Persico, V., Pescapé, A.: Integration of cloud computing and Internet of Things: a survey. Futur. Gener. Comput. Syst. 56, 684–700 (2016). https://doi.org/10.1016/j.future.2015.09.021
11. Ni, J., Zhang, K., Lin, X., Shen, X.S.: Securing fog computing for Internet of Things applications: challenges and solutions. IEEE Commun. Surv. Tutorials 20, 601–628 (2018). https://doi.org/10.1109/COMST.2017.2762345
12. Hu, P., Dhelim, S., Ning, H., Qiu, T.: Survey on fog computing: architecture, key technologies, applications and open issues. J. Netw. Comput. Appl. 98, 27–42 (2017). https://doi.org/10.1016/j.jnca.2017.09.002
13. Santos, L., Rabadão, C., Gonçalves, R.: Intrusion detection systems in Internet of Things. Found. Sci. Technol. (2016)

14. Chakrabarty, S., Engels, D.W.: A secure IoT architecture for Smart Cities. In: 2016 13th IEEE Annual Consumer Communications & Networking Conference, CCNC 2016, pp. 812–813 (2016). https://doi.org/10.1109/CCNC.2016.7444889

15. Flauzac, O., Gonzalez, C., Hachani, A., Nolot, F.: SDN based architecture for IoT and improvement of the security. In: Proceedings of the IEEE 29th International Conference on Advanced Information Networking and Applications Workshops, WAINA 2015, pp. 688–693 (2015). https://doi.org/10.1109/WAINA.2015.110

16. Gonzalez, C., Charfadine, S.M., Flauzac, O., Nolot, F.: SDN-based security framework for the IoT in distributed grid. In: 2016 International Multidisciplinary Conference on Computer and Energy Science, Split 2016 (2016). https://doi.org/10.1109/SpliTech.2016.7555946

17. Irfan, A., Taj, N., Mahmud, S.A.: A novel secure SDN/LTE based architecture for smart grid security. In: Proceedings of the 15th IEEE International Conference on Computer and Information Technology, CIT 2015, 14th IEEE International Conference on Ubiquitous Computing and Communications, IUCC 2015, 13th IEEE International Conference on Dependable, Autonomic and Secure Computing, pp. 762–769 (2015). https://doi.org/10.1109/CIT/IUCC/DASC/PICOM.2015.112

18. Aggarwal, C., Srivastava, K.: Securing IOT devices using SDN and edge computing. In: Proceedings of the 2016 2nd International Conference on Next Generation Computing Technologies, NGCT 2016, pp. 877–882 (2017). https://doi.org/10.1109/NGCT.2016.7877534

19. Kalkan, K., Zeadally, S.: Securing Internet of Things with software defined networking. IEEE Commun. Mag. 56, 186–192 (2018). https://doi.org/10.1109/MCOM.2017.1700714

20. Sharma, P.K., Chen, M.Y., Park, J.H.: A software defined fog node based distributed blockchain cloud architecture for IoT. IEEE Access 6, 115–124 (2018). https://doi.org/10.1109/ACCESS.2017.2757955

21. Chou, L.D., Tseng, C.W., Huang, Y.K., Chen, K.C., Ou, T.F., Yen, C.K.: A security service on-demand architecture in SDN. In: 2016 International Conference on Information and Communication Technology Convergence, ICTC 2016, pp. 287–291 (2016). https://doi.org/10.1109/ICTC.2016.7763487

22. Jeong, J., Seo, J., Cho, G., Kim, H., Park, J.S.: A framework for security services based on software-defined networking. In: Proceedings of the IEEE 29th International Conference on Advanced Information Networking and Applications Workshops, WAINA 2015, pp. 150–153 (2015). https://doi.org/10.1109/WAINA.2015.102

23. Salman, O., Abdallah, S., Elhajj, I.H., Chehab, A., Kayssi, A.: Identity-based authentication scheme for the Internet of Things. In: Proceedings of the IEEE Symposium on Computers and Communication, August 2016, pp. 1109–1111 (2016). https://doi.org/10.1109/ISCC.2016.7543884

24. Zarca, A.M., Garcia-carrillo, D., Bernabe, J.B., Ortiz, J.: Managing AAA in NFV/SDN-enabled IoT scenarios

25. Chakrabarty, S., Engels, D.W., Thathapudi, S.: Black SDN for the Internet of Things. In: Proceedings of the 2015 IEEE 12th International Conference on Mobile Ad hoc and Sensor Systems, MASS 2015, pp. 190–198 (2015). https://doi.org/10.1109/MASS.2015.100

26. Chakrabarty, S., John, M., Engels, D.W.: Black routing and node obscuring in IoT. In: 2016 IEEE 3rd World Forum Internet Things, WF-IoT 2016, pp. 323–328 (2017). https://doi.org/10.1109/WF-IoT.2016.7845477

27. Liu, Y., Kuang, Y., Xiao, Y., Xu, G.: SDN-based data transfer security for Internet of Things. IEEE Internet Things J. 5, 257–268 (2018). https://doi.org/10.1109/JIOT.2017.2779180

28. Nobakht, M., Sivaraman, V., Boreli, R.: A host-based intrusion detection and mitigation framework for smart home IoT using OpenFlow. In: Proceedings of the 2016 11th International Conference on Availability, Reliability and Security, ARES 2016, pp. 147–156 (2016). https://doi.org/10.1109/ARES.2016.64

29. Madhawa, S., Balakrishnan, P., Arumugam, U.: Employing invariants for anomaly detection in software defined networking based industrial Internet of Things. J. Intell. Fuzzy Syst. **35**, 1267–1279 (2018). https://doi.org/10.3233/JIFS-169670

30. Mansour, A., Azab, M., Rizk, M.R.M., Abdelazim, M.: Biologically-inspired SDN-based Intrusion Detection and Prevention Mechanism for heterogeneous IoT networks. In: 2018 IEEE 9th Annual Information Technology, Electronics and Mobile Communication Conference, IEMCON 2018, pp. 1120–1125 (2019). https://doi.org/10.1109/IEMCON. 2018.8614759

31. Bull, P., Austin, R., Popov, E., Sharma, M., Watson, R.: Flow based security for IoT devices using an SDN gateway. In: Proceedings of the 2016 IEEE 4th International Conference on Future Internet of Things and Cloud, FiCloud 2016, pp. 157–163 (2016). https://doi.org/10. 1109/FiCloud.2016.30

32. Sándor, H., Genge, B., Sebestyén-Pál, G.: Resilience in the Internet of Things: the Software Defined Networking approach. In: Proceedings of the 2015 IEEE 11th International Conference on Intelligent Computer Communication and Processing, ICCP 2015, pp. 545–552 (2015). https://doi.org/10.1109/ICCP.2015.7312717

33. Babiceanu, R.F., Seker, R.: Cyber resilience protection for industrial Internet of Things: a software-defined networking approach. Comput. Ind. **104**, 47–58 (2019). https://doi.org/10. 1016/j.compind.2018.10.004

34. Ouaddah, A., Mousannif, H., Abou Elkalam, A., Ait Ouahman, A.: Access control in the Internet of Things: big challenges and new opportunities. Comput. Netw. **112**, 237–262 (2017). https://doi.org/10.1016/j.comnet.2016.11.007

35. Ustundag, A., Cevikcan, E.: Industry 4.0: managing the digital transformation (2018). https://doi.org/10.1007/978-3-319-57870-5

Integrity Checking of Cloud Data with an Auditing Mechanism Using ECC and Merkle Hash Tree

T. Suriya Praba and V. Meena$^{(\boxtimes)}$

School of Computing, SASTRA Deemed University, Thanjavur 613401, India
meena@cse.sastra.edu

Abstract. Cloud computing is a major concerning solution for the raising infrastructure costs in IT. There are many benefits of storing data in cloud. Once the data is stored in cloud it can be accessed from any location at any time. Securing the data in cloud is necessary. Cloud data auditing mechanism is very essential to check the data integrity in cloud. The auditing mechanism is very efficient and advantageous because it reduces the computation effort on both client's and server's side. But performing auditing with complete file information is a time-consuming process. In this paper we propose ECC-Merkle Integrity checking system by generating hash values and also, there is no need to retrieve the complete file for auditing. Here Provable data possession also known as PDP is used to check the integrity of data at cloud server which uses a spot-checking technique. Also, it uses Merkle hash tree to generate hash of file. Whenever client wants to check the data integrity, he poses a challenge to the server. The server will generate the hash values as a proof and this will be verified by the client. Secure data transmission is supported by Elliptic Curve Cryptography algorithm, which provides a high level of security with small key size. This provides moderately speed encryption and decryption. Merkle hash tree provides efficient and secure verification of the contents of huge data structures. This concrete methodology makes sure that the data is undamaged, unaltered.

Keywords: Elliptic Curve Cryptography · Merkle hash tree · Tag · Data integrity

1 Introduction

Cloud computing has been visualized as an important and concerning solution when it comes to the storage costs provided by IT. Cloud computing provides a wide variety of information services for its users. There are many services provided by cloud computing among which cloud storage is a prominent one which enables customer to store his data in data centre [1]. some of the data may be confidential and must be protected, while others data should be easily shareable. In all cases, business critical data should be secure and available on demand in the face of hardware and software failures, network partitions and inevitable user errors. Cloud storage solutions have many capabilities to store and process user's data in either data centres owned privately by

© Springer Nature Singapore Pte Ltd. 2019
V. S. Shankar Sriram et al. (Eds.): ATIS 2019, CCIS 1116, pp. 117–128, 2019.
https://doi.org/10.1007/978-981-15-0871-4_9

them or third-party data centers. There are many advantages of storing data in cloud. One of the biggest advantages is that a user can access the data from any geographical location at any time [2]. Another important advantage is pay as you go.

Besides all these advantages of storing data in cloud, data owners have to face some security threats. Cloud service providers are considered as a trusted parties for integrity and accuracy preservation on data [3]. However, User cannot fully trust service provider because they may erase the data that haven't been accessed for a long period so that space can be saved to store other files. The stored data on the cloud could be corrupted because of malicious activities and management errors like server's failure. Once the data is stored in cloud, users have no authority on their stored data. Consequently, traditional methods like digital signatures will not work [4]. So, Integrity of the data stored in cloud should be checked on a periodical basis. There are few factors that may lead to the loss of integrity [5, 6].

To maintain integrity of stored data, the auditing is the state-of-the-art technique in cloud computing. It is a method of verifying data integrity which can be done either by the data owner or by Third Party Auditor, which benefits to maintain the trustworthiness of data stored on cloud [7, 8].

In this paper we propose ECC-Merkle Integrity checking system by generating hash values with spot-checking technique. Provable data possession scheme (PDP) is used to check the integrity of data at cloud server. By using this scheme, without accessing the entire file a user can verify the data integrity. Merkle hash tree is used to generate the tags and proof by which the integrity of whole file can be checked with a probability one. Figure 1 describes over all flow of the proposed work, which supports for both secure data storage and integrity through auditing mechanism.

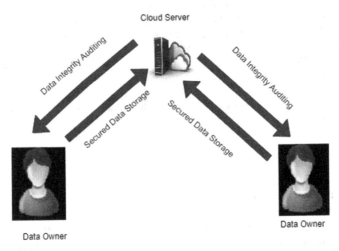

Fig. 1. Secure data storage and integrity through auditing

2   Related Works

In [4] authors had developed a concept of PDP to verify correctness of the data without accessing the whole file. Once the data is stored on cloud, the user has no authority over the data. So many integrity checking algorithms like digital signatures will not work. This was overcome by the concept PDP at untrusted stores. In [9] authors proposed the Proof of Retrievability (POR) concept, prover can generate a proof so that by verifying it verifier can retrieve the file in its entirety. By the proposed concept, the prover will generate a concise proof that is sufficient to retrieve the file and sends it reliably. By this scheme, communication, computation costs reduce, number of accesses to the memory reduces, a storage requirement reduces. This doesn't overcome all the security threats because they don't focus on dynamic data operations. In [10] Shacham and waters proposed two efficient proof retrievability mechanisms which are based on error correcting codes. The first one depends on the Boneh-Lynn-Shacham (BLS) signature. In this, query sent by the client and response generated by the server are very short. This allows public verification that is, whoever acts as the verifier can verify the proof and verifier need not data owner. Second scheme is based on pseudo random functions. Here the server's response is short but the query sent by the client is large compared to first scheme. This allows private verifiability. In [11] Wang et al. proposed a concept which focuses on dynamic data operations and public auditing. They first started with identifying the security problems and difficulties in direct extensions of dynamic data operations. Then they proposed two methods to the difficulties faced in public auditing and dynamic operations on data. They have enhanced the existing proof model by changing the classic Merkle tree implementation for block level verification. In [12] Hao et al. developed a data integrity verifying mechanism which does not include third party auditor (TPA). Many protocols have been proposed with data dynamics and public auditing but do include TPA. This protocol is advantageous for users who require integrity shield and doesn't want any data leakage to other parties. This protocol works efficiently. The communication costs, number of accesses to the memory, the storage requirements are improved when compared to the previous schemes. After the implementation of this work, further enhancements are being done for brace data dynamics. In [13] authors proposed interactive zero knowledge proof system by using Diffie-Hellman assumption and black box knowledge extractor to prevent the fraudulence of prover and leakage of verified data. This method uses optimal parameter to minimize computation overhead of audit services. In [14] authors proposes short signature algorithm which uses Third Party Auditor (TPA) for privacy protection and public auditing. This system mainly focuses on reducing computational overhead on hash value generation. Also, it resists adaptive chosen attacks. To map a value on to a point in the elliptic curve there are a few methods being proposed. Bijective mapping method allows one to one mapping. Map the point at infinity to p, a prime number and maximum limit of ECC [15]. Then we will have a bijective mapping between p + 1 curve element and the integers modulo p + 1. Another method is Elgamal encryption. By this also a value is mapped to a point on the elliptic curve. They require more computation and a method called Koblitz method proposed by Koblitz reduces this. A hash tree is a structure which is used to find quickly the changes made in the parts of a file. There are a variety of hash trees like Tiger hash tree, Merkle hash tree etc. In Merkle hash tree all leaf nodes contain hash values of blocks of data [16]. Every parent node is labelled with hash of child node values. It can be used to verify any type of data stored, handled and transferred in and between computers. The main use of hash tree is, they make sure that blocks received are undamaged, unaltered and other peers doing not send fake blocks.

3 Proposed ECC-Merkle Integrity Checking System

Integrity checking is an essential method used to verify the client's data for its correctness [13]. Many integrity checking models have been proposed but most of them are unable to examine the integrity of whole data. They verify correctness of data with some probability. To overcome this, a scheme is proposed by which integrity of whole can be verified. This scheme uses ECC encryption and Merkle hash tree. This tree identifies if there is a change in even a single block and checks if the whole file is maintained properly or not.

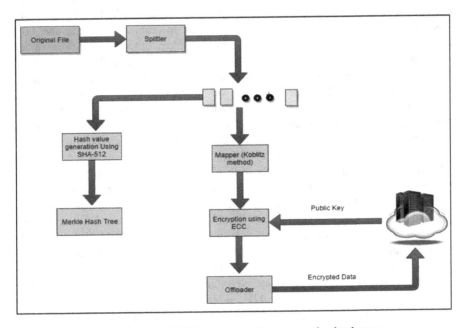

Fig. 2. Proposed ECC based secure data storage in cloud server

Figures 2 and 3 explains overall architecture of proposed system. Figure 2 elucidates phase 1 of the proposed work, which gives insight to data storage mechanism in cloud server with ECC based secure data transmission. The client takes the file to be uploaded and splits it into blocks. Each block is converted to its ASCII representation and then to a big integer value. Then each block's value is mapped to a point on the elliptic curve using Koblitz method. Then the client generates hash values for each block using SHA512 algorithm and produces Merkle hash tree and stores the root node's hash value. The client also encrypts blocks of data with ECC encryption by server public key and transfer the encrypted blocks to the server.

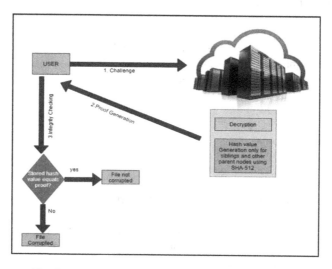

Fig. 3. Proposed auditing system for integrity checking

Figure 3 clarifies phase 2 of proposed auditing structure for integrity checking. The algorithm works as follows, whenever client wants to check the data integrity, he takes a random value 'k'. Using public key of server and 'k' client encrypts the data using ECC, then client poses a challenge to the server. After receiving the challenge, server will take the corresponding file, generates the Merkle hash tree in the same procedure as above. The server sends the proof to the client. The proof generated is verified by the client and checks whether the data integrity is maintained or not.

The algorithm for proposed ECC based Merkle hash tree integrity checking is given below.

Algorithm - ECC-Merkle Integrity checking

Algorithm for Phase 1
Input: File to be uploaded in CS
Output: Secure data storage in CS and Merkle hash tree generation

1: Read stored content
2: Split content into 'n' blocks as $m_0, m_1 m_2 \ldots m_n$
3: for $i = 1$ to m
4: calculate $ASCII[i]$ value for m_i
5: convert $ASCII[i]$ to big integer and map to ECC curve by Koblitz method
6: Mapped point encrypted using ECC algorithm.
7: generate hash for blocks by SHA-512 algorithm.
8: end for
9: generate Merkle hash tree

Algorithm for Phase 2
Input: Challenge by the client
Output: Ensuring Data Integrity

1: Selection random block for integrity to be verified
2: 'G' be a point on elliptic curve
3: Choose private key na and calculate corresponding public key $Qa = na * G$
4: Select random value 'k' and calculate $C1 = k * G$ and $C2 = pm + k * Qa$
5: Challenge posed to server - $(C1, C2)$
6: Decryption at server $pm = C2 - na * C1$
7: Server generates Merkle hash tree
8: Sends siblings and parent hash values alone as proof
9: Client ensures integrity by matching received proof with calculated root value

---

Our construction is inspired from the provable data possession protocol and this scheme incorporates five major steps: **Setup, Tag Generation, Challenge, Proof Generation, Proof Verify.**

The details of these steps are as follows:

- **Setup:** The elliptic curve equation is given as $y^2 \bmod p = (x^3 + a * x + b) \bmod p$. Both cloud user and server choose same values of 'a' and 'b' in a way they satisfy the equation $(4a^3 + 27b^2)! = 0$ where 'p' is a prime number and maximum limit. 'a' and 'b' parameters should be within the range 1 to p − 1. Server randomly selects a point on the elliptic curve say 'G' and generates public key $Q = n_b * G$ where n_b is a random number within the range 1 to p − 1 and a primitive root. User generates a random value 'k' used in the ECC encryption and 'K', an auxiliary parameter used to map a value on to a point in the elliptic curve using Koblitz method. These parameters {a, b, p, Q, k, K} are transferred between both server and the client.

- **Tag_Generation:** This algorithm is run by the cloud user and then he stores his file in the server. The details are as follows:

  1. Given file 'F', split the file into n blocks $F = \{m_0 \| m_1 \| \ldots \| m_{n-1}\}$.
  2. Compute ASCII value for each block and convert it to a big integer within the range 0 to $p - 1$.
  3. For each block, map its big integer value to a point on the elliptic curve using Koblitz method.

- **Koblitz Method**
  - In Koblitz method, an auxiliary parameter 'K' is chosen.
  - For every value m to be mapped on to a point in the elliptic curve, we find $x = mK + 1$ and check if this (x, y) satisfies the elliptic curve equation.
  - If satisfies, (x, y) is the point to which the value is mapped on the elliptic curve.
  - If they don't satisfy, then try x for values of [mK + 2], [mK + 3]......[mK + (K − 1)].
  - Even after substituting [mK + (K − 1)] for 'x', if there don't exist a 'y' value, increment the 'K' value.
  - To decode the original message 'm' after encoding, the quotient of (x − 1)/k gives the value 'm'.

- **ECC Encryption and Decryption**
  - Let 'G' be a point on the elliptic curve.
  - User 'A' chooses a private key 'n_a' and calculates public key $Q_a = n_a * G$.
  - User 'B' chooses a private key 'n_b' and calculates public key $Q_b = n_b * G$.
  - The public keys 'Q_a' and 'Q_b' are transferred between user 'A' and user 'B'.
  - To encrypt the message 'p_m', the user 'A' selects a random value 'k' and calculates C1 $= k * G$, C2 $= {}'p_m + k * Q_b$.
  - The point C = (C1, C2) is the encrypted message.
  - To decrypt the cipher text, the original message pm $= c2 - n_b * C1$.

The tag is generated using Merkle hash tree, which is hash of the wle file. For generation of hash values SHA -512 algorithm is used.

Merkle Hash Tree (MHT): Each file is divided into blocks. The leaf nodes of the MHT contains the hash values of blocks of data. All the parent nodes will have hash of its child nodes. The root MHT will have the hash of the whole file. This concrete methodology makes sure that data is unaltered, undamaged. Figure 4 shows the diagrammatic representation of MHT. The root node's hash value is stored on the client side and the blocks of data are uploaded to the server.

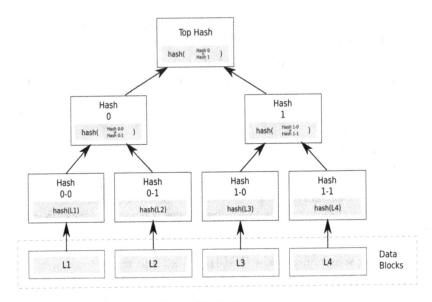

Fig. 4. Merkle hash tree

- **Challenge:**
  Whenever client wants to check his data integrity, he will pose a challenge to the server by sending some random block numbers. The client selects a random value 'c' within [1, n] and generates 'c' random block numbers within [0, n − 1] and send them to the server.

- **Proof_Generation:**
  1. After receiving the random block numbers from the client, server will generate Merkle hash tree with the blocks corresponding to the client's file.
  2. For the block numbers which are present in the challenge, the server will send the hash values of those blocks and their siblings.
  3. For the rest, the cloud server will send the hash values of their parent nodes.
  4. From Fig. 4, if the random block numbers sent by the client are 1 and 3, the server will generate the Merkle tree.
  5. Then for block number 1, the sibling is 0 and for block 3, sibling is 2.
  6. So, the server will send the hash values of 0, 1, 2, 3.
  7. Now for the blocks 4, 5, 6, 7 the server will send the hash values of its parent nodes respectively.

  Figure 5 shows the diagrammatic representation of proof generation.

- **Proof_Verification:** The client will generate the Merkle tree with hash values received from server. The root node's hash value is compared with already calculated hash value. If they both are same, the whole file's data is maintained properly. If not, there is some damage or alteration done to the data.

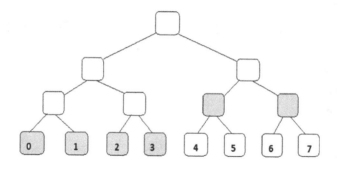

Random blocks: 1, 3

Fig. 5. Proof generation

4 Results and Discussions

The algorithm comprises of tag generation and proof verification. The proof verification time depends on the number of random blocks challenged by the client. The tag generation time depends on the file size and the block size by which the file is split. The proposed system is evaluated for fixed file size of 100 MB with different block sizes varying from 10 MB to 50 MB. Table 1 shows time taken for various operations like Block encryption, transferring encrypted blocks to CS, calculating hash values (SHA 512), Generating Merkle hash tree and for auditing. Results shows that when block size increases there is a decrease in encryption time, MHT generation and auditing time.

Table 1. Tag generation time (in msec) for different block sizes with file size 100 MB

Block size (In MB)	Time for encryption	Time for transferring encrypted file to cloud server	Time for hashing (SHA 512)	Time to form Merkle hash tree	Auditing time
10	13140	8795.7	8502.9	787.4	21411.4
20	13154.9	5906.3	7352.3	1080	16859.4
30	11120.2	4645.2	5815.2	831.7	14610.8
40	10887.6	4363.6	5326.5	951.2	14207.8
50	4841.2	4311.9	3517.8	926	12708.7

Figure 6 is elucidating time taken for various operation of auditing system with different block sizes. Figure 7 depicts the transmission time (in milliseconds) from data owner to the cloud server with various block sizes.

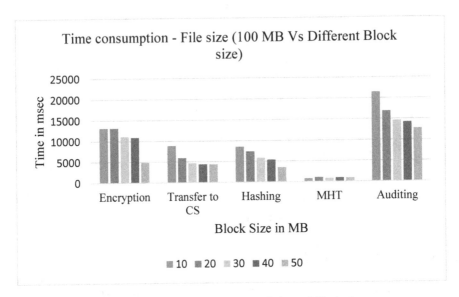

Fig. 6. Time taken for operations of changed block sizes

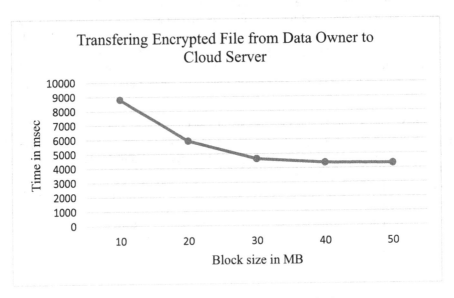

Fig. 7. Transmission time for different block sizes

5 Conclusion

A novel ECC based Merkle hash tree integrity system is proposed for client's data privacy. In this, most secure and efficient encryption algorithm ECC is used for maintaining secrecy in cloud server. ECC algorithm cares competent security even with smaller key size. Client generates MHT and poses a challenge to the cloud server when it desires to verify integrity. Cloud server generates proof and here, there is no need to send the complete hash to the client for integrity checking, which intern reduces the overall time consumption. Results shows, as the block size increases, time taken for block encryption, transferring encrypted blocks to CS, calculating hash values (SHA 512), generating Merkle hash tree and auditing is decreases. This is because, as the block size increases, nodes in the hash tree decreases which intern reduces the computation time.

References

1. Liu, F., Tong, J., Mao, J., Rudall, et al.: (1995). https://doi.org/10.6028/NIST.SP.500-292
2. Sridhar, V., Sheshadri, H.S., Padma, M.C.: Emerging Research in Electronics, Computer Science and Technology: Proceedings of International Conference, ICERECT 2012 (2014). Springer, New Delhi. https://doi.org/10.1007/978-81-322-1157-0
3. Zhang, X., Du, H.T., Chen, J.Q., et al.: Ensure data security in cloud storage. In: Proceedings–2011 International Conference on Network Computing and Information Security NCIS 2011, vol. 1, pp. 284–287 (2011). https://doi.org/10.1109/NCIS.2011.64
4. Ateniese, G., Burns, R., Curtmola, R., et al.: Provable Data Possession at Untrusted Stores, p. 598 (2007). https://doi.org/10.1145/1315245.1315318
5. Bala, I., Bishnoi, S.: Research paper on data integrity checking in cloud computing. Int. J. Enhanc. Res. Manag. Comput. Appl. 4, 2319–7471 (2015)
6. Balasubramanian, V., Mala, T.: Cloud data integrity checking using bilinear pairing and network coding. Cluster Comput. 1–9 (2018). https://doi.org/10.1007/s10586-018-1805-z
7. Yu, Y., Xue, L., Au, M.H., et al.: Cloud data integrity checking with an identity-based auditing mechanism from RSA. Futur. Gener. Comput. Syst. 62, 85–91 (2016). https://doi.org/10.1016/j.future.2016.02.003
8. Jain, N., Jain, P., Kapil, N.: Enhanced data security model for cloud using ECC algorithm and third party auditor, vol. 5, pp. 519–524 (2016)
9. Juels, A., Kaliski Jr., B.S.: PORs: proofs of retrievability for large files. In: Proceedings of ACM Conference on Computer and Communications Security, pp. 584–597 (2007). https://doi.org/10.1145/1315245.1315317
10. Author Asiacrypt2008
11. Wang, Q., Wang, C., Ren, K., et al.: Enabling public auditability and data dynamics for storage security in cloud computing. IEEE Trans. Parallel Distrib. Syst. 22, 847–859 (2011). https://doi.org/10.1109/TPDS.2010.183
12. Hao, Z., Zhong, S., Nenghai, Yu.: A privacy-preserving remote data integrity checking protocol with data dynamics and public verifiability. IEEE Trans. Knowl. Data Eng. 23, 1432–1437 (2011). https://doi.org/10.1109/tkde.2011.62

13. Zhu, Y., Hu, H., Ahn, G.J., Yau, S.S.: Efficient audit service outsourcing for data integrity in clouds. J. Syst. Softw. **85**, 1083–1095 (2012). https://doi.org/10.1016/j.jss.2011.12.024

14. Zhu, H., Yuan, Y., Chen, Y., et al.: A secure and efficient data integrity verification scheme for cloud-IoT based on short signature. IEEE Access **7**, 1 (2019). https://doi.org/10.1109/access.2019.2924486

15. Chakraborty, T.K., Dhami, A., Bansal, P., Singh, T.: Enhanced public auditability & secure data storage in cloud computing. In: Proceedings of 2013 3rd IEEE Int Advance Computing Conference IACC 2013, pp. 101–105 (2013). https://doi.org/10.1109/IAdCC.2013.6514202

16. Saqib Niaz, M., Saake, G.: Merkle hash tree based techniques for data integrity of outsourced data general terms. In: 27th GI-Workshop Found Databases, pp. 66–71 (2015)

Anomaly Detection in Critical Infrastructure Using Probabilistic Neural Network

M. R. Gauthama Raman[1], Nivethitha Somu[2], and Aditya P. Mathur[1(✉)]

[1] iTrust–Centre for Research in Cyber Security, Singapore University of Technology and Design, Singapore, Singapore
gauthamaraman_mr@live.com, aditya_mathur@sutd.sg.edu
[2] Smart Energy Informatics Laboratory (SEIL), Indian Institute of Technology, Bombay, Mumbai, India
nivethithasomu@iitb.ac.in

Abstract. Supervisory Control and Data Acquisition (SCADA) systems forms a vital part of any critical infrastructure. Such systems are network integrated for remote monitoring and control making them vulnerable to intrusions by malicious actors. Such intrusions may lead to anomalous behavior of the underlying physical process. This work presents a Probabilistic Neural Network (PNN) based anomaly detector to detect anomalies arising consequent to a cyber attack. Experimental validation was conducted using the dataset obtained from an operational water treatment testbed, namely Secure Water Treatment (SWaT). The impact of the smoothening parameter on the performance of the PNN-based anomaly detector was analyzed. Experimental evaluations indicate the significance of the PNN-based anomaly detector, compared with several competing detectors, in terms of precision, F-score, false alarm rate, and detection rate.

Keywords: Anomaly detection · Cyber physical systems · Cyber attacks · Industrial control systems · Intrusion detection system · Probabilistic Neural Network

1 Introduction

Critical infrastructure, such as water treatment systems and power grid, consists of an Industrial Control System (ICS) that controls the underlying physical process using sensors and actuators [6,25]. A Supervisory Control and Data Acquisition (SCADA) system is an integral part of ICS. Moreover, such critical infrastructure is also a Cyber Physical System (CPS) that includes cyber and physical components. Increased connectivity through communications network within the ICS components, and possibly through the Internet, exposes such CPS to a range of cyber threats [3,10,23,24,35].

© Springer Nature Singapore Pte Ltd. 2019
V. S. Shankar Sriram et al. (Eds.): ATIS 2019, CCIS 1116, pp. 129–141, 2019.
https://doi.org/10.1007/978-981-15-0871-4_10

A cyber or physical attack on an ICS will likely result in anomalous process behavior. In general, approaches for anomaly-based intrusion detection can be categorized based on rules, statistics, and computational intelligence. Among these, computational intelligence based anomaly detection approaches have gained the attention of researchers as the rest of the approaches require a detailed understanding of the process flow, physical laws, and configuration of components in the CPS [2,14,18]. Moreover, the application of machine learn-

Table 1. Related work.

Technique(s)	Dataset	Performance metrics
Unsupervised anomaly detection approaches		
CNN [19]	SWaT	F-Score
DAE [27]	SWaT; Power grid control system	Precision, F–Score, and Recall
GAN [20]	SWaT	Classification Accuracy, Recall, F–Score, Precision, and False Positive Rate
O-SVM; DNN [16]	SWaT	Precision, Recall, and F–Score
RNN [12]	SWaT	Classification Accuracy
Supervised anomaly detection approaches		
NSA [6]	SWaT	Classification Accuracy
SVM; Artificial immune system [34]	Simulation, KDD Cup 1999	False Positive and False Negative Rates
NB, RF; One R; J48; Non-nested generalized exemplars; SVM [4]	Gas pipeline system at Mississippi State University	Precision and Recall
Neural Network [28]	SWaT	F–Score, NAB Score, Precision, and Recall
Deep belief network; SVM [15]	Real time SCADA network	Classification Accuracy
J48 [29]	IoT security testbed	Classification Accuracy, F–Measure, Recall, Precision
LSTM [8]	Gas and oil plant heating loop	Precision, Recall, and F–Score
RNN [7]	Tennessee Eastman Process	NAB Score
LSTM based Autoencoder [21]	Power demand	True Positive Rate, F–Score, and False Positive Rate
Neural network; SVM; Random forest; J48 [18]	SWaT	Accuracy, Precision, Recall, and False Alarm Rate

ing algorithms for anomaly detection is found to be fast and relatively easy to develop since the behaviour and process flow of the entire CPS system can be learned with reasonable accuracy from the multivariate historical data [27]. A summary of research on computational intelligence based anomaly detection approaches is given in Table 1.

This work describes a study wherein the Probabilistic Neural Network (PNN) framework is selected as a modeling approach for the design of an anomaly detector. Competing approaches include Convolutional Neural Network (CNN), Deep Neural Network (DNN), Naives Bayes (NB), One class-Support Vector Machine (O-SVM), Random Forest (RF), Recurrent Neural Network (RNN), Long Short Term Memory (LSTM), Deep Autoencoders, and others. PNNs are unique in their characteristic of mapping the input variables to class labels using Bayesian strategy [12,17,21,31]. Unlike other variants of neural networks, PNN is robust, faster, mostly independent of parameters, and has the ability to handle imbalanced datasets- a key reason for exploring it in this work. PNN has been effectively used for the design of anomaly detectors in various applications [9,13,32,33] however to the best of our knowledge, this is the first work to employ PNN for anomaly detection in an ICS, especially in a SwaT operational plant.

Novelty and Contributions: (a) A PNN-based anomaly detector for critical infrastructure, and (b) Validation of the performance of the PNN-based anomaly detector using live data from an operational CPS, namely, SWaT [22].

Organization: This paper is structure as follows. An introduction to PNN is in Sect. 2. Experimental assessment of the effectiveness of a PNN-based anomaly detector in detecting anomalies resulting from cyber attacks, is in Sect. 3. This section contains a description of the architecture of the testbed and its dataset used in the evaluation, impact of smoothening parameter on the performance of PNN, and a detailed comparison with seven other neural network based methods. Conclusions from this work are in Sect. 4.

2   PNN-Based Anomaly Detector

In this section, we provide a detailed insight on the application of PNN for the design of an anomaly detector for CPS. In general, any data driven anomaly detector designed for CPS should be fast, reliable, scalable, and sensitive to noisy data generated by the heterogeneous physical and control components as the CPS environment is dynamic, operates in real time, and the sensor data are often generated at high frequency [27]. Further, the ability to predict the anomalies in the unknown samples based on a similar set of samples in the training dataset forms an important criterion for assessing the performance of a data driven anomaly detector [9,30]. The above mentioned requirements of an anomaly detector for a critical infrastructure led to the choice of PNN in this work.

As shown in Fig. 1, a PNN is comprised of artificial neurons arranged in four layers as detailed below.

1. **Input layer:** Passes the unknown sample X_s to the pattern layer without any computation
2. **Pattern layer:** Number of neurons in this layer corresponds to the number of training samples. Each neuron corresponds to the training samples and its output is defined in Eq. 1.

$$y_k^i = exp\left[\frac{-|X_s - x_k^i|^2}{2\sigma^2}\right] \tag{1}$$

where, x_k^i is the ith training sample of the kth class and σ is the smoothening parameter.

3. **Summation layer:** The average of the pattern layer's output that belongs to the same class is computed using Eq. 2.

$$S_i = \frac{1}{n}\sum_{k=1}^{n} exp\left[\frac{-|X_s - x_k^i|^2}{2\sigma^2}\right] \tag{2}$$

4. **Output layer:** The output layer consists of one neuron that decides the class of the unknown sample using Eq. 3.

$$C = argmax(S_i), \forall i = (1, 2, \dots, C_n) \tag{3}$$

Given the conditional attribute (x), decisional attributes (Y), classes in the training set (C), and smoothening factor (σ), PNN computes the class of the unknown sample [26, 30].

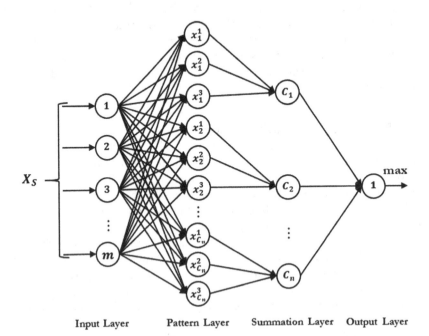

Input Layer   Pattern Layer   Summation Layer   Output Layer

Fig. 1. Probabilistic neural network.

3   Experimental Evaluation

The PNN-based approach proposed in this work was evaluated using the dataset obtain from the SWaT testbed. The architecture of SWaT, summary of the dataset and data preprocessing techniques can be found in [18]. To demonstrate the predominance of the proposed anomaly detector, performance validations were carried out by comparing the effectiveness of the PNN-based anomaly detector with that of the existing machine learning models in terms of classification accuracy, precision, detection rate, F-Score, and false alarm rate. The models used for the comparison include Naives Bayes (NB), Support vector machine (SVM), Random forest (RF), and Multi layer perceptron (MLP).

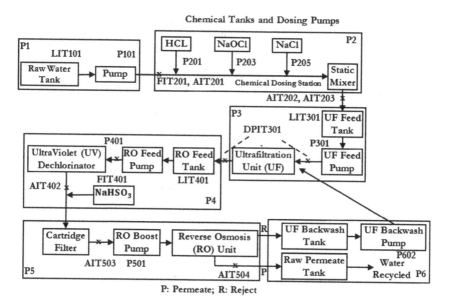

Fig. 2. Stages P1 through P6 in SWaT. AITxxx: chemical property meters, FITxxx: flow rate meters, LITxxx: level sensors; Pxxx: pumps.

3.1   SWaT Architecture

SWaT is a fully operational small footprint water treatment plant at the Singapore University of Technology and Design (SUTD). Details of SWaT are available in [22].

SWaT consists of six stages (P1-P6) as shown in Fig. 2. Each stage comprises of a combination of physical and control components for processing raw water. Each stage is equipped with sensors to measure flow rate, water level in tanks, chemical properties of water, etc., and actuators such as pumps and valves. The cyber part of SWaT consists of a two layered communications network with

Programmable Logic Controllers (PLCs), SCADA workstation, Human Machine Interface (HMIs) and a historian. Level 0 network in the testbed consists of a ring for each stage through which all sensors and actuators transfer measurements, and receive commands, to and from the corresponding PLCs via. wired and wireless links. Similarly, Level 1 network consists of a STAR architecture that enables communications between SCADA workstation and the PLCs.

Table 2. Attacks considered in experiments.

Attack ID	Type	Target	Duration (Secs.)	Expected impact	Unexpected impact
1	SSSP	MV-101	539	Tank overflow	
2	SSSP	LIT-101	300	Tank Underflow; damage P-101	
3	SSSP	MV-504	300	Halt RO shut down sequence; reduce life of RO	
4	SSSP	DPIT-301	500	Backwash process is started again and again; normal operation stops; Decrease in water level of tank 401. Increase in water level of tank 301	
5	SSSP	AIT-504	200	RO shut down sequence starts after 30 min. Water should go to drain	RO did not shut down; water does not drain
6	SSMP	MV-101, LIT-101	501	Tank overflow	
7	MSMP	P-602, DIT-301, MV-302	251	System freeze	
8	MSSP	P-101, LIT-301	251	Stop inflow of tank T-401	
9	MSSP	AIT-402, AIT-502	251	Water enters the drain due to overdosing	Water does not drain
10	SSSP	LIT-302	501	Tank overflow	Rate of decrease of water level reduced after 1:33:25 PM

3.2   SWaT Dataset

For data collection, the entire plant was operated for 11-days. For the first 7-days, the plant was operated under normal mode. Subsequently, for the remaining 4-days, the attacks were launched by spoofing the sensor values, issuing fake commands, etc. Attack timings, target, expected outcome, and effects are available in [11].

During 11-days of data collection, a total of 946,723 labelled records were collected from the historian. Each record consists of 51 attributes corresponding to the individual sensor values. Note that selecting the entire 946,723 instances for the experiment would bias the PNN to the 'normal' class since the normal instance dominates the instances related to the attacks. However, if we consider 449,921, i.e., instances recorded under the attack scenario, reduce the dominating nature and hence the imbalanced nature of dataset is avoided. Therefore, a total of 449,921 records collected during 28th Dec 2015 to 2nd Jan 2016 were used for experimentation.

During the last four days of data collection, a total of ten attacks, referred to as A1-A10 [11], were launched by injecting fake sensor values to the PLCs (Table 2). For each attack, two different subsets of the entire dataset were created using 'random sampling without replacement' to train and validate the learning model. The attacks can be categorized as: (i) Single Stage Single Point attack (SSSP), (ii) Single Stage Multi Point attack (SSMP), (iii) Multistage Single Point attack (MSSP), and (iv) Multi-Stage Multi Point attack (MSMP). Attack duration varies based on the nature of the attack. For example, the duration of attack A1 that targets MV101, and attack A9 that targets chemical sensors AIT 402 and AIT 502, are 539 and 251 s, respectively.

3.3   Results and Discussion

Data was collected from the experiments and analyzed. Results from the analysis are presented next.

Impact of Smoothening Parameter: Note from Eq. 1 that σ is a single tunable parameter which is significant in determining the width of the kernel parameter in the pattern layer which in turn has a significant impact on the performance of the PNN. Since the smoothening parameter relies on the characteristics of the input data, it is important to analyze its impact on the performance of the detector. Therefore, the experiments were conducted by varying σ in the range [0.1,0.9] at intervals of 0.1. For each experiment, the average values of the considered performance metrics were computed. The corresponding plots are given in Figs. 3, 4, 5 and 6. From the plots, it is evident that to achieve the optimal value for the considered performance metrics, σ ought to be in [0.1,0.3].

Analysis of data from the experiments indicates that the identification of multiple optimal values of σ for effective detection of various anomalies in the process flow of SWaT might further enhance the performance of the PNN-based anomaly detector. Therefore, the design of the PNN-based anomaly detector

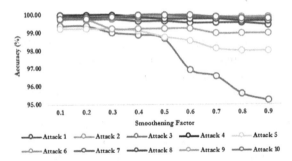

Fig. 3. Smoothening parameter vs. Classification accuracy

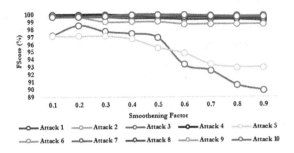

Fig. 4. Smoothening parameter vs. F-score

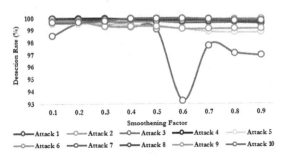

Fig. 5. Smoothening parameter vs. Detection rate

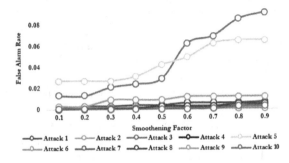

Fig. 6. Smoothening parameter vs. FAR

Table 3. Performance analysis of all classifiers for Attacks 1- 10

Attack ID	Algorithm	Accuracy	Precision	Detection rate	F-Score	False alarm rate
1	NB	97.72	97.8	97.7	97.7	0
	SVM	80.29	84	80.3	78.1	0.03
	MLP	98.92	99	98.9	98.9	0.02
	RF	98.99	99	99	99	0.02
	PNN	**99.8**	**100**	**99.91**	**99.84**	0.001
2	NB	81.7	85.1	81.7	75	0
	SVM	80.22	84.2	80.2	71.8	0
	MLP	95.17	95.4	95.2	94.9	0
	RF	94.03	94.4	94	93.6	0.42
	PNN	**100**	**100**	**100**	**100**	0
3	NB	90.31	90.1	90.3	90.1	0.23
	SVM	92.45	93.1	92.5	91.9	0
	MLP	72.26	87.5	72.3	74.6	1.25
	RF	97.33	97.6	97.3	97.4	0.11
	PNN	**99.38**	**100**	**99.61**	**98.58**	0.013
4	NB	97.52	97.5	97.5	97.5	0.03
	SV	69.43	79.1	69.4	59.4	0
	MLP	95.1	95.2	95.1	95.1	1.13
	RF	91.48	92.5	91.5	91.1	0
	PNN	**100**	**100**	**100**	**100**	0
5	NB	88.94	90.2	88.9	85.4	0
	SVM	87.46	89.1	87.5	82.4	0
	MLP	90.34	89.4	90.3	89	0.3
	RF	91.75	92.5	91.8	90.1	0
	PNN	**99.22**	**100**	**94.44**	**97.14**	0.027
6	NB	88.44	90.2	88.4	87.9	0.18
	SVM	97.11	97.2	97.1	97.1	0.04
	MLP	84.42	86.6	84.4	83.4	0.23
	RF	89.94	91.3	89.9	89.5	0.16
	PNN	**99.79**	**100**	**99.6**	**99.79**	0.001
7	NB	98.65	98.7	98.7	98.7	0.04
	SVM	69.57	79.1	69.6	59.7	0
	MLP	98.05	98.1	98.1	98.1	0.04
	RF	93.9	94.4	93.9	93.7	0
	PNN	**100**	**100**	**100**	**100**	0
8	NB	41.86	76.9	41.9	28.4	0.6
	SVM	40.15	76.6	40.2	24.9	0.6
	MLP	97.05	97.1	97.1	97.1	0.04
	RF	39.84	76.5	39.8	24.3	0.61
	PNN	**100**	**100**	**100**	**100**	0
9	NB	41.86	76.9	41.9	28.4	0.6
	SVM	40.15	76.6	40.2	24.9	0.6
	MLP	97.05	97.1	97.1	97.1	0.04
	RF	39.84	76.5	39.8	24.3	0.61
	PNN	**99.74**	**100**	**99.34**	**99.67**	0.003
10	NB	79.49	84.3	79.5	76.3	0
	SVM	69.3	79	69.3	59.2	0
	MLP	95.1	95.1	95.1	95.1	0.07
	RF	82.97	86.4	83	81	0
	PNN	**100**	**100**	**100**	**100**	0

with multiple σ values and accurate modeling of the physical process of SWaT, resulted in high detection rate and minimal false alarm rate.

Performance Analysis: Performance of PNN was compared with the machine learning techniques mentioned earlier. The results of the comparison are summarized in Table 3. The best values of each metric are highlighted in bold. From the table, it can be noted that PNN outperforms the existing machine learning techniques in terms of all quality metrics expect in a few cases. For example, Naive Bayes and SVM classifier attain the least false alarm rate of 0% when compared with PNN for attack 1 and attack 3.

From the above set of experimental results, some emergent facts observed about data driven anomaly detectors are (i) PNN exhibits an ideal classifier behaviour for attacks 2, 4, 7, 8, and 10, and (ii) The performance of classifiers varies with the nature of the attack, i.e., MLP has a better performance for attacks 1, 2, 4, 5, 7, 8, 9, and 10 when compared with the rest.

Lastly, the performance of the PNN-based anomaly detector over the existing machine learning techniques was analyzed in terms of their respective fault detection ability. In general, attacks 6, 7, 8, and 9 were found to be more difficult to detect as they target multiple sensors across multiple stages. However, PNN achieves 100% detection rate and 0% false alarm rate for attacks 7 and 9. A near optimal outcome was achieved for detecting attacks 6 and 8. This inherent ability of a PNN-based anomaly detector was due to the proper tuning of the smoothening parameter (σ).

To summarize, PNN, and the considered machine learning techniques, either detect the attacks during the initial stage of occurrence or the attack is left undetected. This nature of data driven models is preferred over the existing anomaly detection models, as they do not wait for the behaviour of CPS to exceed any pre-specified threshold for attack identification and therefore possess high detection rate and low false alarm rate [18]. However, they provide worst performance for the attacks that last for a shorter duration since they are left unidentified.

4   Conclusions

A SCADA specific PNN-based anomaly detector is presented. The detector uses a supervised approach to detect anomalies possibly resulting from attacks targeted at a CPS. The novelty of the proposed detector lies in its ability to identify anomalies resulting from single– and multi– stage attacks. Experimental validation on the dataset obtained from SWaT demonstrates the significance of PNN-based anomaly detector over the existing machine learning techniques in terms of various quality metrics. Also analysed in this study was the impact of the smoothening parameter on the performance of the PNN-based anomaly detector.

In the proposed PNN-based anomaly detector, a supervised approach needs training with both attack and normal signatures. However, in an operational plant, especially during the unavailability of appropriate attack patterns, one may employ the supervised learning model in [1] for efficient anomaly detection. In the case of an imbalanced dataset, along with the smoothening parameter, the training samples play a vital role in determining the performance of PNN. Unlike in traditional RNN models, PNN does not rely on the temporal dependencies among the samples. Hence, the application of properties such as hypergraph coarsening, dual hypergraph, etc., for the identification of informative samples, aids in improving the performance of PNN in detecting short term attacks [5]. Further, the analysis and implementation of PNN variants such as heteroscedastic PNN, weighted PNN, arithmetic residue PNN, etc., for efficient anomaly detection in a CPS, is a potential challenge that needs to be focussed.

Acknowledgements. This work was supported by the National Research Foundation (NRF), Prime Minister's Office, Singapore, under its National Cybersecurity R&D Programme (Award No. NRF2016NCR-NCR002-023) and administered by the National Cybersecurity R&D Directorate.

References

1. Adepu, S., Mathur, A.: An investigation into the response of a water treatment system to cyber attacks. In: IEEE 17th International Symposium on High Assurance Systems Engineering, pp. 141–148. IEEE (2016)
2. Adepu, S., Mathur, A.: Distributed attack detection in a water treatment plant: method and case study. IEEE Trans. Dependable Secure Comput. 11 (2018). https://doi.org/10.1109/TDSC.2018.2875008
3. Ball, T.: Top 5 critical infrastructure cyber attacks. https://www.cbronline.com/cybersecurity/top-5-infrastructure-hacks/. Accessed 15 Jan 2019
4. Beaver, J., Borges-Hink, R., Buckner, M.: An evaluation of machine learning methods to detect malicious SCADA communications. In: 12th International Conference on Machine Learning and Applications, pp. 54–59. IEEE (2013)
5. Berge, C., Minieka, E.: Graphs and Hypergraphs. North-Holland Pub. Co., Amsterdam (1973)
6. Clotet, X., Moyano, J., Len, G.: A real-time anomaly-based IDS for cyber-attack detection at the industrial process level of critical infrastructures. Int. J. Crit. Infrastruct. Prot. **23**, 11–20 (2018)
7. Filonov, P., Kitashov, F., Lavrentyev, A.: RNN-based early cyber-attack detection for the tennessee eastman process. arXiv preprint arXiv:1709.02232 (2017)
8. Filonov, P., Lavrentyev, A., Vorontsov, A.: Multivariate industrial time series with cyber-attack simulation: fault detection using an LSTM-based predictive data model. arXiv preprint arXiv:1612.06676 (2016)
9. Gauthama Raman, M., Somu, N., Kirthivasan, K., Sriram, V.: A hypergraph and arithmetic residue-based probabilistic neural network for classification in intrusion detection systems. Neural Networks **92**, 89–97 (2017)
10. Ginter, A.: The top 20 cyber attacks against industrial control systems. https://waterfall-security.com/20-attacks. Accessed 15 Jan 2019
11. Goh, J., Adepu, S., Junejo, K., Mathur, A.: A dataset to support research in the design of secure water treatment systems. In: International Conference on Critical Information Infrastructures Security, pp. 88–99. IEEE (2016)

12. Goh, J., Adepu, S., Tan, M., Lee, Z.: Anomaly detection in cyber physical systems using recurrent neural networks. In: IEEE 18th International Symposium on High Assurance Systems Engineering, pp. 140–145. IEEE (2017)
13. Hajdarevic, A., Dzananovic, I., Banjanovic-Mehmedovic, L., Mehmedovic, F.: Anomaly detection in thermal power plant using probabilistic neural network. In: 2015 38th International Convention on Information and Communication Technology, Electronics and Microelectronics (MIPRO), pp. 1118–1123. IEEE (2015)
14. Han, S., Xie, M., Chen, H., Ling, Y.: Intrusion detection in cyber-physical systems: techniques and challenges. IEEE Syst. J. **8**, 1052–1062 (2014)
15. Huda, S., Yearwood, J., Hassan, M., Almogren, A.: Securing the operations in SCADA-IoT platform based industrial control system using ensemble of deep belief networks. Appl. Soft Comput. J. **71**, 66–77 (2018)
16. Inoue, J., Yamagata, Y., Chen, Y., Poskitt, C., Jun, S.: Anomaly detection for a water treatment system using unsupervised machine learning. In: IEEE International Conference on Data Mining Workshops, pp. 1058–1065. IEEE (2017)
17. Inoue, J., Yamagata, Y., Chen, Y., Poskitt, C., Sun, J.: Anomaly detection for a water treatment system using unsupervised machine learning. In: IEEE International Conference on Data Mining Workshops ICDMW, pp. 1058–1065. IEEE (2017)
18. Junejo, K.N., Goh, J.: Behaviour-based attack detection and classification in cyber physical systems using machine learning. In: Proceedings of the 2nd ACM International Workshop on Cyber-Physical System Security, pp. 34–43. ACM (2016)
19. Kravchik, M., Shabtai, A.: Detecting cyber attacks in Industrial Control Systems using convolutional neural networks. In: ACM Proceedings of the 2018 Workshop on Cyber-Physical Systems Security and PrivaCy, pp. 72–83. ACM (2018)
20. Li, D., Chen, D., Goh, J., Ng, S.: Anomaly detection with generative adversarial networks for multivariate time series. In: 7th International Workshop on Big Data, Streams and Heterogeneous Source Mining: Algorithms, Systems, pp. 1–10. ACM (2018)
21. Malhotra, P., Ramakrishnan, A., Anand, G., Vig, L., Agarwal, P., Shroff, G.: LSTM-based encoder-decoder for multi-sensor anomaly detection. arXiv preprint arXiv:1607.00148 (2016)
22. Mathur, A.P., Tippenhauer, N.O.: SWaT: A water treatment testbed for research and training on ICS security. In: International Workshop on Cyber-physical Systems for Smart Water Networks (CySWater), pp. 31–36. IEEE, USA, April 2016
23. McMillen: Attacks targeting Industrial Control Systems (ICS) up 110 percent. https://securityintelligence.com/attacks-targeting-industrial-control-systems-ics-up-110-percent/. Accessed 15 Jan 2019
24. Myers, D., Suriadi, S., Radke, K., Foo, E.: Anomaly detection for industrial control systems using process mining. Comput. Secur. **78**, 103–125 (2018)
25. Nazir, S., Patel, S., Patel, D.: Assessing and augmenting scada cyber security: a survey of techniques. Comput. Secur. **70**, 436–454 (2017)
26. Raman, M.G., Somu, N., Krithivasan, K., Sriram, V.S.: A hypergraph and arithmetic residue-based probabilistic neural network for classification in intrusion detection systems. Neural Networks **92**, 89–97 (2017)
27. Schneider, P., Bottinger, K.: High-performance unsupervised anomaly detection for cyber-physical system networks. In: ACM Proceedings of the 2018 Workshop on Cyber-Physical Systems Security and PrivaCy, pp. 1–12. IEEE (2018)
28. Shalyga, D., Filonov, P., Lavrentyev, A.: Anomaly detection for water treatment system based on neural network with automatic architecture optimization. arXiv preprint arXiv:1807.07282 (2018)

29. Siboni, S., et al.: Security testbed for the Internet of Things Devices. IEEE Trans. Reliab. **68**, 1–12 (2018)

30. Somu, N., Gauthama Raman, M.R., Kalpana, V., Krithivasan, K., Shankar, V.: An improved robust heteroscedastic probabilistic neural network based trust prediction approach for cloud service selection. Neural Networks **108**, 339–354 (2018)

31. Specht, D.: Probabilistic neural networks. Neural Networks **3**, 109–118 (1990)

32. Tran, T.P., Jan, T.: Boosted modified probabilistic neural network (BMPNN) for network intrusion detection. In: The 2006 IEEE International Joint Conference on Neural Network Proceedings, pp. 2354–2361. IEEE (2006)

33. Yu, S.N., Chen, Y.H.: Electrocardiogram beat classification based on wavelet transformation and probabilistic neural network. Pattern Recogn. Lett. **28**(10), 1142–1150 (2007)

34. Zhang, Y., Wang, L., Sun, W., Green, I., Robert, C., Alam, M.: Distributed intrusion detection system in a multi-layer network architecture of smart grids. IEEE Trans. Smart Grids **2**, 796–808 (2011)

35. Zonouz, S., Davis, C.M., Davis, K.R., Berthier, R., Bobba, R.B., Sanders, W.H.: SOCCA: a security-oriented cyber-physical contingency analysis in power infrastructures. IEEE Trans. Smart Grid **5**(1), 3–13 (2014)

Chaotic Map Based Key Generation and Realistic Power Allocation Technique for Secure MU-MIMO Wireless System

C. Manikandan⬤, S. Rakesh Kumar$^{(\boxtimes)}$⬤,
Kopparthi Nikhith, M. Sai Gayathri, and P. Neelamegam⬤

School of EEE, SASTRA Deemed to be University,
Thanjavur 613401, Tamil Nadu, India
srakesh@eie.sastra.edu

Abstract. Security and reliability are major aspects of any Multi-User Multiple Input Multiple Output (MU-MIMO) wireless communication systems, which have been addressed in this work. Conventional linear precoder and decoder use Total Power Constraint (TPC), which does not limit the power allocated to each transmitting antenna with respect to linearity constraint of an individual power amplifier. To overcome this problem, a joint optimal linear precoder and decoder are designed for 1-D modulation based uplink system with Per Antenna Power Constraint (PAPC) under perfect and imperfect channel state condition. The complexity associated with the coder design is minimized with the help of Minimum Total Mean Square Error (MTMSE) criterion. A novel key generation using chaotic map has been proposed to improve security. It uses a combination of a logistic map with a random pixel-based synthetic color image. Use of logistic map ensures higher randomness in key generation, which improves security. Simulation conveys that the proposed system is able to provide a realistic power allocation on p = 1.76. The generated key is validated with NIST tool and its probability value is observed to be greater than 0.01. This ensures that the proposed key generation technique is suitable for stream cipher encryption/decryption algorithm.

Keywords: MU-MIMO · Chaotic map · Synthetic colour image · TPC ·
PAPC · MTMSE · Perfect CSI · Imperfect CSI

1 Introduction

High data rate and reliability are essential in multi-user communication systems. To meet this requirement, MIMO technology has been introduced in new generation wireless system. In this system, multiple antennas are used at the base station radio and mobile station radios to increase its capacity and reliability of a radio system [1]. MIMO technology incorporated in point to point communication system is called a single-user MIMO system. Similarly inclusion of MIMO configuration at base station and mobile stations is termed as MU-MIMO [2]. Generally, MU-MIMO systems have higher throughput than SU-MIMO system. It makes a significant growth of MU-MIMO wireless systems in various applications like cellular network, wireless LAN, and other

© Springer Nature Singapore Pte Ltd. 2019
V. S. Shankar Sriram et al. (Eds.): ATIS 2019, CCIS 1116, pp. 142–155, 2019.
https://doi.org/10.1007/978-981-15-0871-4_11

networks demanding higher throughput [3]. To improve reliability, several linear and non-linear channel aware precoding technique for MU-MIMO has been reported. Various optimization criteria under a minimum SINR constraint [4, 5], TMSE criterion have been considered to design joint precoder and decoder for MU-MIMO systems [6]. Both Equal power allocation (EPA) and TPC has been used for design of MIMO systems with the presumption that the channel state information (CSI) is perfect [7, 8].

The perfect CSI is unreasonable in practical scenario hence imperfect CSI was considered. It includes the effect of channel estimation error and its correlation for both transmitter and receiver. Two methods were designed to solve Multiuser MIMO uplink transceiver optimization problem under a TPC with imperfect CSI [9]. The first method uses Karush-Kuhn-Tucker (KKT) conditions and other is succession of Semi-definite Programming (SDP). It is found in the literature most of the existing designs of MU-MIMO systems were subject to TPC [10, 11]. The TPC based power allocation does not satisfy a limitation in power allocated to each transmitting antenna with respect to linearity constraint of individual power amplifier [12].

In this work, MU-MIMO is optimized for PAPC using MTMSE criterion. As this MIMO communication system utilizes RF spectrum, hence, a confidential information exchanged can be intercepted by Man-in-the-Middle (MITM) [13]. Hence, there is need for encryption using a cryptosystem. It is a fact that the cryptosystem's strength depends on key complexity. The key generation technique is one of the important aspect in improving the strength of the cryptosystem [14]. To facilitate high security, a key generation using a combination of chaotic map with synthetic digital color image is proposed.

This work majorly contributes to the (i) Generation of cryptographic key using synthetic colour image and logistic map (ii) Design of uplink MU-MIMO transceiver concerning PAPC constraints with perfect and imperfect CSI (iii) Performance analysis of proposed system using standard parameters.

The paper presents the proposed work as follows. Section 2, proposes the design of MU-MIMO uplink system model along with key generation technique. Section 3, evaluates the simulation scenario and their results. Section 4, concludes the paper with a discussion on the future directions.

2 System Model

Figure 1 depicts the MU-MIMO MAC (Multiple Access Channel) case, where more than one mobile station connects to single base station. Let, N_R be the quantity of receiving antennas at the base station. The quantity of mobile nodes are assumed to be K where each mobile station has N_T transmits antennas. The information stream of each user are independent and it is encrypted with help of stream cipher techniques using proposed key generation algorithm. This encrypted plain text is converted to parallel form and modulated before transmission. The cipher streams of each user have a size of B × 1 where B is chosen such that B ≤ min (N_R, N_T). A linear precoder P_K of size N_T × B is employed so that the ciphertext data stream is processed before it sent through the channel. The uplink channel matrix $H_m^{(UL)}$ has size of N_r × N_t is independent for each user where m = 1, 2...K. The entries of $H_m^{(UL)}$ varies at different instants of time. To simulate the real-time scenario, a spatially white complex gaussians noise vector $n_i^{(UL)}$ has size of $N_R \times 1$ is added to the channel matrix. The transmitted data from each user is decoded with a linear decoder D_K sized $B \times N_R$ at the base station radio. Information symbols from the channel is complex in nature and is given to the demodulator for detection process. Then, the detected data is given to serial to parallel converter and decrypted using same key. At last, an estimate of the transmitted symbol is calculated for both the perfect and imperfect case of channel.

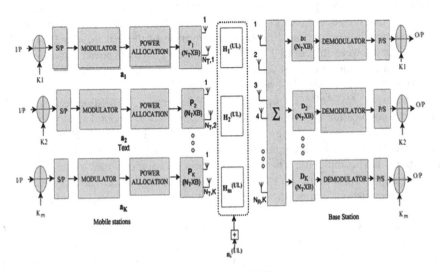

Fig. 1. Proposed MU-MIMO system

2.1 Chaotic Map Based Key Generation

The steps for key generation using logistic map are given below.

Step 1: Select an initial value for x_n and 'ρ' randomly between zero to one and between zero to four respectively.

Step 2: Using $x_{n+1} = \rho x_n(1 - x_n)$ generate 65,536 random values and multiply by 10000.

Step 3: A modulus operation is applied over all the values with eight to get the values in the range 0 to 7 and bias with 1 to set the range 1 to 8.

Step 4: Take each 8 values and store into an array.

Step 5: Sort every 8 values and return their indices.

Step 6: Repeat Step 4 & 5 for 8192 times and stored in a memory array.

Step 7: Get the color image of size 256×256 as in [14] Divide the selected image into three layers namely Red, Green, and Blue.

Step 8: Select the first element from the memory array. The elements in the memory array are considered as the bit locations of the 8-bit pixels from each layer of the color image.

Step 9: Extract one bit from the first pixel of the red, green and blue layer and perform XOR operation on the extracted bits then store the obtained result.

Step 10: Repeat Step 8 and 9 until bits are extracted from all the pixels.

Step 11: Then obtained a result with the size of 65536 is used as key for encryption and decryption process.

2.2 Problem Formulation to Design Joint Optimal Linear Precoder and Decoder

Formulation of the mathematical model for the uplink MU-MIMO system is presented in this section. In this case, the design problem is non-convex [7–9]. Hence the non-convex optimization techniques is used to design joint optimal linear precoder cum decoder for perfect and imperfect case leading to reduced MTMSE with respect to PAPC.

MU-MIMO Uplink System Under Perfect CSI

In this design, a channel matrix H is known perfectly at the transmitter as well as at the receiver. Then, an estimated resultant vector at the receiver is defined as

$$\mathbf{d}_l^{\wedge (UL)} = \mathbf{D}_l \mathbf{y}^{(UL)} \tag{1}$$

With the above assumption the TMSE matrix for uplink is

$$E[\|\mathbf{e}^{(UL)}\|^2] = E[\|\mathbf{d}_l^{\wedge (UL)} - \mathbf{a}_l\|^2] \tag{2}$$

where $\mathbf{d}_l^{\wedge (UL)} = \mathbf{D}_l[\sum_{m=1}^{K} \mathbf{H}_m^{(UL)} \mathbf{P}_m \mathbf{a}_m] + \mathbf{D}_l \mathbf{n}^{(UL)}$.

Substituting the value of $\mathbf{d}_l^{\wedge (UL)}$, we get (3)

$$E[\|\mathbf{e}^{(UL)}\|^2] = E[\|\mathbf{D}_l[\sum_{m=1}^{K} \mathbf{H}_m^{(UL)} \mathbf{P}_m \mathbf{a}_m] + \mathbf{D}_l \mathbf{n}^{(UL)} - \mathbf{a}_l\|^2] \tag{3}$$

Then TMSE calculation is prepared as discussed below:

$$E[\|\mathbf{e}^{(UL)}\|^2] = E\{Tr[[\mathbf{D}_l[\sum_{m=1}^{K} \mathbf{P}_m \mathbf{a}_m \mathbf{H}_m^{(UL)}] + \mathbf{D}_l \mathbf{n}^{(UL)} - \mathbf{a}_l] \\ [\mathbf{D}_l^H [\sum_{m=1}^{K} \mathbf{P}_m^H \mathbf{a}_m^H \mathbf{H}_m^{(UL)H}] + \mathbf{D}_l^H \mathbf{n}^{(UL)H} - \mathbf{a}_l^H]]\} \tag{4}$$

Switch the trace and expectation in (4)

$$E[\|e^{(UL)}\|^2] = Tr\{E[[\mathbf{D}_l[\sum_{m=1}^{K} \mathbf{P}_m \mathbf{a}_m \mathbf{H}_m^{(UL)}] + \mathbf{D}_l \mathbf{n}^{(UL)} - \mathbf{a}_l] \\ [\mathbf{D}_l^H [\sum_{m=1}^{K} \mathbf{P}_m^H \mathbf{a}_m^H \mathbf{H}_m^{(UL)H}] + \mathbf{D}_l^H \mathbf{n}^{(UL)H} - \mathbf{a}_l^H]]\} \tag{5}$$

Define $\sum_{m=1}^{K} \mathbf{H}_m^{(UL)}\mathbf{P}_m\mathbf{a}_m = \mathbf{y}^{(UL),\text{eff}}$ and expand (5)

Using the assumptions made in [7, 8] simplifies the Eq. (5)

After simplification TMSE is defined as

$$E[\|\mathbf{e}^{(UL)}\|^2] = Tr[\mathbf{D}_l[\sum_{m=1}^{K} \mathbf{H}_m^{(UL)}\mathbf{P}_m\mathbf{P}_m^H\mathbf{H}_m^{(UL)H} + \sigma_n^2\mathbf{I}_M]\mathbf{D}_l^H - \mathbf{D}_l\mathbf{H}_l^{(UL)}\mathbf{P}_l$$
$$- \mathbf{P}_l^H\mathbf{H}_l^{(UL)H}\mathbf{D}_l^H + \mathbf{I}_l] \tag{6}$$

The TMSE for all mobile station is specified as

$$E[\|\mathbf{e}^{(UL)}\|^2] = \sum_{l=1}^{K}(Tr(MSE_l^{(UL)})) \tag{7}$$

The objective of this uplink design is to minimize the TMSE concerning PAPC

$$\min_{\{P_l,D_l\}_{l=1}^{l=k}}[\|\mathbf{e}^{(UL)}\|^2] \, s.t \sum_{l=1}^{K}(Tr(\mathbf{P}_l\mathbf{P}_l^H)^p)^{1/p} \leq \alpha \tag{8}$$

Using Lagrangian get the solution for the above-defined problem

$$\eta^{(UL)} = E[\|\mathbf{e}^{(UL)}\|^2] + \mu^{(UL)}\sum_{l=1}^{K}(Tr(\mathbf{P}_l\mathbf{P}_l^H)^p)^{1/p} - \alpha \tag{9}$$

Substitute (6) in (9), we get

$$\eta^{(UL)} = Tr[\mathbf{D}_l[\sum_{m=1}^{K}\mathbf{H}_m^{(UL)}\mathbf{P}_m\mathbf{P}_m^H\mathbf{H}_m^{(UL)H} + \sigma_n^2\mathbf{I}_M]\mathbf{D}_l^H - \mathbf{D}_l\mathbf{H}_l^{(UL)}\mathbf{P}_l - \mathbf{P}_l^H\mathbf{H}_l^{(UL)H}\mathbf{D}_l^H + \mathbf{I}_l]$$
$$+ \mu^{(UL)}\sum_{l=1}^{K}(Tr(\mathbf{P}_l\mathbf{P}_l^H)^p)^{1/p} - \alpha \tag{10}$$

The problem in Eq. (8) is nonconvex and also continuously differentiable. Therefore we are taking the derivatives of $\eta^{(UL)}$ relating to $\mathbf{D}_l$ and $\mathbf{P}_l$. Then the related KKT conditions can be obtained as illustrated below,

First, take the derivate of $\eta^{(UL)}$ with respect to $\mathbf{D}_l$ and equate to zero. Then replace $1 = k(k = 1, \ldots\ldots, K)$ and $m = 1$.

$$\mathbf{H}_k^{(UL)^T}\mathbf{P}_k^T = \mathbf{D}_k^*[\sum_{l=1}^{K}\mathbf{H}_l^{(UL)^T}\mathbf{P}_l^T\mathbf{P}_l^*\mathbf{H}_l^{(UL)^*} + \sigma_n^2\mathbf{I}_M] \tag{11}$$

Taking complex conjugate on both the sides of (11), gives

$$\mathbf{H}_k^{(UL)^H} \mathbf{P}_k^H = \mathbf{D}_K [\sum_{l=1}^{K} \mathbf{H}_l^{(UL)^H} \mathbf{P}_l^H \mathbf{P}_l \mathbf{H}_l^{(UL)} + \sigma_n^2 \mathbf{I}_M] \tag{12}$$

Similarly, take the derivate of $\eta^{(UL)}$ concerning $\mathbf{P}_l$ and make it as zero. The value of l is replaced with k(k = 1, ..., K) and m = l.

$$\mathbf{H}_k^{(UL)^T} \mathbf{D}_k^T = \left(\mathbf{H}_k^{(UL)^T} [\sum_{l=1}^{K} \mathbf{D}_l^T \mathbf{D}_l^*] \mathbf{H}_k^{(UL)^*} \right) \mathbf{P}_k^* + \mu^{(UL)} (\sum_{l=1}^{K} (Tr(\mathbf{P}_l \mathbf{P}_l^H)^p)^{1/p-1} (\mathbf{P}_l^T \mathbf{P}_l^*)^{p-1}) \mathbf{P}_k^* \tag{13}$$

Taking complex conjugate on both the sides of (13) gives

$$\mathbf{H}_k^{(UL)^H} \mathbf{D}_k^H = \left(\mathbf{H}_k^{(UL)^H} [\sum_{l=1}^{K} \mathbf{D}_l^H \mathbf{D}_l] \mathbf{H}_k^{(UL)} \right) \mathbf{P}_k + \mu^{(UL)} \left(\sum_{l=1}^{K} (Tr(\mathbf{P}_l \mathbf{P}_l^H)^p)^{1/p-1} (\mathbf{P}_l^H \mathbf{P}_l)^{p-1} \right) \mathbf{P}_k \tag{14}$$

Where $k = \left(\sum_{l=1}^{K} (Tr(\mathbf{P}_l \mathbf{P}_l^H)^p)^{1/p-1} (\mathbf{P}_l^H \mathbf{P}_l)^{p-1} \right)$.

Multiplying Eqs. (12) and (14) by $\mathbf{D}_k^H$ and $\mathbf{P}_k^H$ respectively

$$\mathbf{D}_k^H \mathbf{H}_k^{(UL)^H} \mathbf{P}_k^H = \mathbf{D}_K [\sum_{l=1}^{K} \mathbf{H}_l^{(UL)^H} \mathbf{P}_l^H \mathbf{P}_l \mathbf{H}_l^{(UL)} + \sigma_n^2 \mathbf{I}_M] \mathbf{D}_k^H \tag{15}$$

$$\mathbf{H}_k^{(UL)^H} \mathbf{D}_k^H \mathbf{P}_k^H = \mathbf{P}_k^H \left(\mathbf{H}_k^{(UL)^H} [\sum_{l=1}^{K} \mathbf{D}_l^H \mathbf{D}_l] \mathbf{H}_k^{(UL)} \right) \mathbf{P}_k + \mu^{(UL)} k \mathbf{P}_k \mathbf{P}_k^H \tag{16}$$

In (15) and (16) take trace on left and right hand side. Finally, summing over k (k = 1, ..., K) results in (17).

$$\mu^{(UL)} = \frac{\sigma_n^2}{\alpha} \sum_{k=1}^{K} Tr(\mathbf{D}_k \mathbf{D}_k^H) \tag{17}$$

The value of the decoder is obtained by considering Eq. (12),

$$\mathbf{D}_k = (\mathbf{H}_k^{(UL)^H} \mathbf{P}_k^H) [\sum_{l=1}^{K} \mathbf{H}_l^{(UL)^H} \mathbf{P}_l^H \mathbf{P}_l \mathbf{H}_l^{(UL)} + \sigma_n^2 \mathbf{I}_M]^{-1} \tag{18}$$

Similarly, the value of precoder is obtained by considering the Eq. (14),

$$\mathbf{P}_k = (\mathbf{H}_k^{(UL)^H} \mathbf{D}_k^H) \left(\mathbf{H}_k^{(UL)^H} [\sum_{l=1}^{K} \mathbf{D}_l^H \mathbf{D}_l] \mathbf{H}_k^{(UL)}] + \mu^{(UL)} k \right)^{-1} \tag{19}$$

Based on KKT conditions (12)–(14) an iterative algorithm is developed to get an optimal solution as in [7, 8] for perfect CSI. Here the Lagrange multiplier is updated based on (17).

MU-MIMO Uplink System Under Imperfect CSI

The TMSE function for the proposed uplink channel with imperfect CSI is defined as follows

$$E[\|\mathbf{e}^{(UL)}\|^2] = E[\left\| \mathbf{D}_l[\sum_{m=1}^{K} (\mathbf{H}_m^{\wedge (UL)} + \mathbf{E}_m^{(UL)})\mathbf{P}_m\mathbf{a}_m] + \mathbf{D}_l\mathbf{n}^{(UL)} - \mathbf{a}_l \right\|^2] \tag{20}$$

Then TMSE calculation in (20) is expanded using Frobenius matrix norm,

$$E[\|\mathbf{e}^{(UL)}\|^2] = E\{Tr[[\mathbf{D}_l[\sum_{m=1}^{K} \mathbf{P}_m\mathbf{a}_m(\mathbf{H}_m^{\wedge (UL)} + \mathbf{E}_m^{(UL)})] + \mathbf{D}_l\mathbf{n}^{(UL)} - \mathbf{a}_l]$$
$$[\mathbf{D}_l^H[\sum_{m=1}^{K} \mathbf{P}_m^H\mathbf{a}_m^H(\mathbf{H}_m^{\wedge (UL)^H} + \mathbf{E}_m^{(UL)^H})] + \mathbf{D}_l^H\mathbf{n}^{(UL)H} - \mathbf{a}_l^H]]\} \tag{21}$$

Switch the trace and expectation in (21)

$$E[\|\mathbf{e}^{(UL)}\|^2] = Tr\{E[[\mathbf{D}_l[\sum_{m=1}^{K} \mathbf{P}_m\mathbf{a}_m(\mathbf{H}_m^{\wedge (UL)} + \mathbf{E}_m^{(UL)})] + \mathbf{D}_l\mathbf{n}^{(UL)} - \mathbf{a}_l]$$
$$[\mathbf{D}_l^H[\sum_{m=1}^{K} \mathbf{P}_m^H\mathbf{a}_m^H(\mathbf{H}_m^{\wedge (UL)^H} + \mathbf{E}_m^{(UL)^H})] + \mathbf{D}_l^H\mathbf{n}^{(UL)H} - \mathbf{a}_l^H]]\} \tag{22}$$

Define $\sum_{m=1}^{K} \mathbf{H}_m^{\wedge (UL)}\mathbf{P}_m\mathbf{a}_m = \mathbf{y}^{(UL),\text{eff}}, \sum_{m=1}^{K} \mathbf{E}_m^{(UL)}\mathbf{P}_m\mathbf{a}_m = \mathbf{e}^{(UL),\text{ch}}$ and expand (22)

Using the assumptions made in [9] simplifies the Eq. (22)

After simplification TMSE is defined as

$$E[\|\mathbf{e}^{(UL)}\|^2] = Tr[\mathbf{D}_l[\sum_{m=1}^{K} \mathbf{H}_m^{\wedge (UL)}\mathbf{P}_m\mathbf{P}_m^H\mathbf{H}_m^{\wedge (UL)H} + \sigma_n^2 I_M]\mathbf{D}_l^H$$
$$+ \mathbf{D}_l[\sum_{m=1}^{K} \sigma_{Em}^2 Tr(\mathbf{P}_m\mathbf{P}_m^H)\sum_m]\mathbf{D}_l^H - D_l\mathbf{H}_l^{\wedge (UL)}\mathbf{P}_l - \mathbf{P}_l^H\mathbf{H}_l^{\wedge (UL)H}\mathbf{D}_l^H + \mathbf{I}_l] \tag{23}$$

The TMSE for all mobile station is specified as

$$E[\|\mathbf{e}^{(UL)}\|^2] = \sum_{l=1}^{K}(Tr(MSE_l^{(UL)}) \tag{24}$$

The aim of the proposed design is to minimize the TMSE concerning PAPC

$$\min_{\{P_l,D_l\}_{l=1}^{l=k}}[\|\mathbf{e}^{(UL)}\|^2] \; s.t \; \sum_{l=1}^{K}(Tr(\mathbf{P}_l\mathbf{P}_l^H)^p)^{1/p} \leq \alpha \tag{25}$$

Using Lagrangian get the solution for the above-defined problem

$$\eta^{(UL)} = E[\|\mathbf{e}^{(UL)}\|^2] + \mu^{(UL)}\sum_{l=1}^{K}(Tr(\mathbf{P}_l\mathbf{P}_l^H)^p)^{1/p} - \alpha \tag{26}$$

Substitute (23) in (26), we get

$$\eta^{(UL)} = Tr[\mathbf{D}_l[\sum_{m=1}^{K}\mathbf{H}_m^{\wedge(UL)}\mathbf{P}_m\mathbf{P}_m^H\mathbf{H}_m^{\wedge(UL)H} + \sigma_l^2\mathbf{I}_M]\mathbf{D}_l^H + \mathbf{D}_l[\sum_{m=1}^{K}\sigma_{Em}^2 Tr(\mathbf{P}_m\mathbf{P}_m^H)\sum_m]\mathbf{D}_l^H$$

$$- \mathbf{D}_l\mathbf{H}_l^{\wedge(UL)}\mathbf{P}_l - \mathbf{P}_l^H\mathbf{H}_l^{\wedge(UL)H}\mathbf{D}_l^H + \mathbf{I}_l] + \mu^{(UL)}\sum_{l=1}^{K}(Tr(\mathbf{P}_l\mathbf{P}_l^H)^p)^{1/p} - \alpha \tag{27}$$

The problem in (25) is nonconvex and also continuously differentiable. Therefore we are taking the derivatives of $\eta^{(UL)}$ relating to $\mathbf{D}_l$ and $\mathbf{P}_l$. Then the related KKT conditions is derived as follows

Take the derivate of $\eta^{(UL)}$ with respect to $\mathbf{D}_l$ and equate to zero. Then replace all 'l' by k(k = 1, ……, K) and m = l.

$$\mathbf{H}_k^{\wedge(UL)T}\mathbf{P}_k^T = \mathbf{D}_k^*[\sum_{l=1}^{K}\mathbf{H}_l^{\wedge(UL)T}\mathbf{P}_l^T\mathbf{P}_l^*\mathbf{H}_l^{\wedge(UL)*} + \sigma_n^2\mathbf{I}_M] + \mathbf{D}_k^*[\sum_{l=1}^{K}\sigma_{El}^2 Tr(\mathbf{P}_l\mathbf{P}_l^H)\sum_l] \tag{28}$$

Applying complex conjugate on both the sides of Eq. (28) gives

$$\mathbf{H}_k^{\wedge(UL)H}\mathbf{P}_k^H = \mathbf{D}_k[\sum_{l=1}^{K}\mathbf{H}_l^{\wedge(UL)H}\mathbf{P}_l^H\mathbf{P}_l\mathbf{H}_l^{\wedge(UL)} + \sigma_n^2\mathbf{I}_M] + \mathbf{D}_k[\sum_{l=1}^{K}\sigma_{El}^2 Tr(\mathbf{P}_l\mathbf{P}_l^H)\sum_l] \tag{29}$$

Similarly, take the derivate of $\eta^{(UL)}$ with respect to $\mathbf{P}_l$ and equate to zero. then replace all l in the resultant equation with k(k = 1, ……, K) and m by l.

$$\mathbf{H}_k^{\wedge(UL)T}\mathbf{D}_k^T = \left(\mathbf{H}_k^{\wedge(UL)T}[\sum_{l=1}^{K}\mathbf{D}_l^T\mathbf{D}_l^*]\mathbf{H}_k^{\wedge(UL)*}\right)\mathbf{P}_k^* + \mathbf{P}_k^*[\sigma_{Ek}^2\sum_{l=1}^{K}Tr(\mathbf{D}_l\sum_l\mathbf{D}_l^H)]$$

$$+ [\mu^{(UL)}\sum_{l=1}^{K}(Tr(\mathbf{P}_l\mathbf{P}_l^H)^p)^{1/p-1}(\mathbf{P}_l^T\mathbf{P}_l^*)^{p-1}]\mathbf{P}_k^* \tag{30}$$

Applying complex conjugate on both the sides of Eq. (30) gives

$$\mathbf{H}_k^{\wedge(UL)^H}\mathbf{D}_k^H = \left(\mathbf{H}_k^{\wedge(UL)^H}[\sum_{l=1}^{K}\mathbf{D}_l^H\mathbf{D}_l]\mathbf{H}_k^{\wedge(UL)}\right)\mathbf{P}_k + \mathbf{P}_k\left([\mu^{(UL)}k] + [\sigma_{Ek}^2\sum_{l=1}^{K}Tr(\mathbf{D}_l\sum_k\mathbf{D}_l^H)]\right)$$
(31)

Multiplying Eqs. (29) and (31) by $\mathbf{D}_k^H$ and $\mathbf{P}_k^H$ respectively

$$\mathbf{D}_k^H\mathbf{H}_k^{\wedge(UL)^H}\mathbf{P}_k^H = \mathbf{D}_k[\sum_{l=1}^{K}\mathbf{H}_l^{\wedge(UL)^H}\mathbf{P}_l^H\mathbf{P}_l\mathbf{H}_l^{\wedge(UL)} + \sigma_n^2\mathbf{I}_M]\mathbf{D}_k^H + \mathbf{D}_k[\sum_{l=1}^{K}\sigma_{El}^2Tr(\mathbf{P}_l\mathbf{P}_l^H)\sum_l]\mathbf{D}_k^H \quad (32)$$

$$\mathbf{H}_k^{\wedge(UL)^H}\mathbf{D}_k^H\mathbf{P}_k^H = \mathbf{P}_k^H\left(\mathbf{H}_k^{\wedge(UL)^H}[\sum_{l=1}^{K}\mathbf{D}_l^H\mathbf{D}_l]\mathbf{H}_k^{\wedge(UL)}\right)\mathbf{P}_k$$
$$+ \mathbf{P}_k\left([\mu^{(UL)}k] + [\sigma_{Ek}^2\sum_{l=1}^{K}Tr(\mathbf{D}_l\sum_k\mathbf{D}_l^H)]\right)\mathbf{P}_k^H$$
(33)

In (32) and (33) take trace on left and right hand side terms. Then, sum over k (k = 1, ..., K) to get an expression for Lagrange multiplier

$$\mu^{(UL)} = \frac{\sigma_n^2}{\alpha}\sum_{k=1}^{K}Tr(\mathbf{D}_k\mathbf{D}_k^H)$$
(34)

The value of the decoder is obtained by considering Eq. (29)

$$\mathbf{D}_k = (\mathbf{H}_k^{\wedge(UL)^H}\mathbf{P}_k^H)\left([\sum_{l=1}^{K}\mathbf{H}_l^{\wedge(UL)^H}\mathbf{P}_l^H\mathbf{P}_l\mathbf{H}_l^{\wedge(UL)} + \sigma_n^2\mathbf{I}_M] + [\sum_{l=1}^{K}\sigma_{El}^2Tr(\mathbf{P}_l\mathbf{P}_l^H)\sum_l]\right)^{-1}$$
(35)

Similarly, the value of precoder is obtained by considering the Eq. (31)

$$\mathbf{P}_k = (\mathbf{H}_k^{\wedge(UL)^H}\mathbf{D}_k^H)\left((\mathbf{H}_k^{\wedge(UL)^H}[\sum_{l=1}^{K}\mathbf{D}_l^H\mathbf{D}_l]\mathbf{H}_k^{\wedge(UL)}) + (\mu^{(UL)}k + \sigma_{Ek}^2\sum_{l=1}^{K}Tr(\mathbf{D}_l\sum_k\mathbf{D}_l^H))\right)^{-1}$$
(36)

Based on KKT conditions (29)–(31) an iterative algorithm is developed to get an optimal solution as similar to [9] for imperfect CSI.

3 Results and Discussion

The proposed key generation algorithm is evaluated using National Institute of Standards and Technology (NIST). Randomness of the generated key is evaluated using a benchmark of 0.01 for the probability value. A probability value obtained in each test is compared with the benchmark and a value greater than the benchmark indicates a pass in the corresponding test. The obtained results are described in Table 1 ensure the generated key using the proposed method has passes the entire randomness tests with the probability value greater than the benchmark (>0.01).

Table 1. NIST result.

Test	Probability	Test	Probability
Frequency	0.739918	FFT	0.122325
Block frequency	0.122325	Non-overlapping template	0.991468
Cumulative sums	0.534146	Approximate entropy	0.534146
Runs	0.350485	Serial	0.991468
Longest run	0.739918	Linear complexity	0.534146
Rank	0.066882		

Similarly, proposed MU-MIMO transceiver is compared with existing MU-MIMO uplink transceiver for its reliability, which is designed for binary phase-shift keying (BPSK) and Multi-level amplitude shift-keying (M-ASK) modulations. To evaluate the reliability, a test condition has been fabricated as follows, the system has been designed for 4 mobile stations and each user containing 4 transmitting antennas ($N_{t1} = N_{t2} = N_{t3} = N_{t4} = 4$). The quantity of receiving antennas at the base station is fixed as sixteen ($N_r = 16$). The data stream is chosen as B = 4, which is the minimum of transmit or receive antennas. The above parameters and values are kept uniform to evaluate the reliability under various scenarios.

The precoder and decoder matrix are updated using an iterative algorithm with respect to the p-norm constraint. This constraint satisfies both SPC and PAPC based power allocation. The p-values must be selected within the interval of 1 to ∞ and also based on the values of α (PAPC) and β (SPC). Hence the proposed systems are examined for three cases namely p = 4.12, 2.36 and 1.76. For p = 4.12, the value of α = 1.1 W and β = 3.16 W. When p = 2.36, the value of α = 2.8 W and β = 6.31 W. Finally when p = 1.76, the value of α = 5.5 W and β = 10 W are chosen.

Figure 2 compares the performance of the proposed uplink system with TPC and PAPC under perfect CSI. It is illustrated that the SNR requirement shows a significant increase by 2 dB and 1 dB for the proposed model than the conventional model when p = 4.12 and 2.36 respectively. For BPSK modulation, SNR is escalated from 14 dB to 16 dB and 11 dB to 12 dB is observed for p = 4.12 and 2.36 respectively. Similarly, 18 dB to 20 dB and 15 dB to 16 dB SNR escalation is observed for 4-ASK. For p = 1.76, The SNR requirement and escalation is observed to be similar at BER level of 10-2. It is observed that proposed system performance becomes close to optimal as p-value decreased to unity.

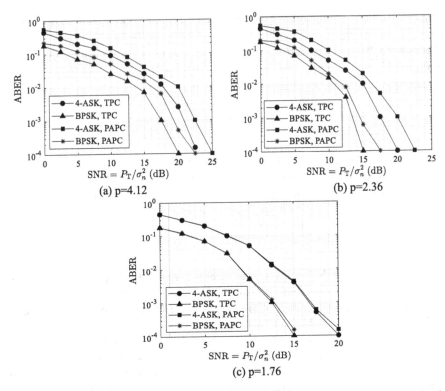

Fig. 2. Performance of TPC and PAPC based MU-MIMO uplink system with perfect CSI, for BPSK and 4-ASK modulations

The proposed uplink system with TPC and PAPC is examined for an imperfect CSI and compared with perfect CSI. To simulate imperfect CSI, transmit and receive correlation matrices are assumed as $\rho_T = 0.5$, $\rho_R = 0.5$ respectively with the channel estimation error of $\sigma_{ce}^2 = 0.015$. A moderate value of σ_{ce}^2 is chosen so that it doesn't lower the system performance to a greater extent. Figure 3 illustrates the behavior of an imperfect CSI with p = 2.36. It is observed that a 2.5 dB difference in the SNR between the perfect and imperfect case and a 1 dB increase between the conventional and proposed design. In BPSK modulation scheme, SNR requirement is increased from 13.5 dB to 14.5 dB and for 4-ASK modulation SNR requirement is increased from 17.5 dB to 18.5 dB at 10^{-2} BER level. This makes the proposed design feasibility for imperfect CSI also.

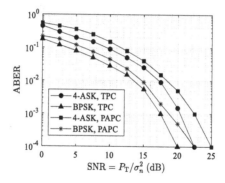

Fig. 3. Performance comparison TPC and PAPC based MU-MIMO uplink system with imperfect CSI, for BPSK and 4-ASK at p = 2.36

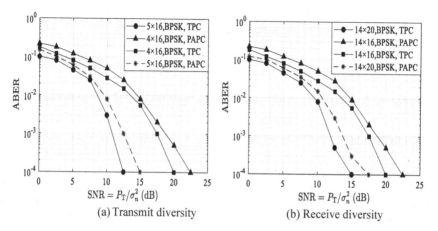

Fig. 4. Effect of transmit diversity and receive for TPC and PAPC based MU-MIMO uplink system with imperfect CSI, at p = 2.36

Figure 4 shows the diversity performance of uplink MU-MIMO system for BPSK modulation. It is found that the SNR requirement has been reduced as the transmit and receive antennas increases.

Figure 5 examines the correlation effects of MU-MIMO for BPSK modulation having B = 4. The channel estimation error, σ_{ce}^2 is maintained at 0.015. Table 2 shows the SNR requirement for various combinations of channel correlations. It is found that at 10^{-2} BER, SNR requirement increases if the transmit and receive correlations increases.

Table 2. SNR requirement for various transmit and receive correlations

ρ_t	ρ_r	SNR (dB)
0.5	0.0	13.5
0.5	0.5	14.2
0.9	0.0	17.5

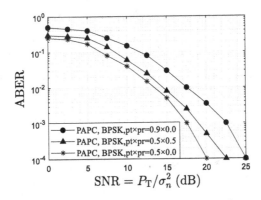

Fig. 5. SNR analysis for transmit and receive correlations of PAPC at p = 2.36

4   Conclusion

This paper addresses the security and reliability aspects of an MU-MIMO system. A novel pseudo-random key generation technique is proposed to implement security. It employs chaotic map to generate random sequence. These sequences are used to generate key from the random pixel value based synthetic color image. Use of chaotic map with synthetic color image enables a highly randomized key generation. The randomness of the generated key is ensured by pass in the entire NIST tests.

Reliability is addressed by the proposed uplink MU-MIMO system employing BPSK and M-ASK modulation with individual antenna power constraint. It uses an iterative algorithm to jointly optimize the precoder and decoder. This minimizes the total mean-square-error subjected to PAPC. The proposed design also increases the data rate with the same amount of reliability as SU-MIMO system. An optimum design is obtained when the value of p approaches unity (p = 1.76) indicating a realistic power allocation. Hence the proposed power allocation scheme meets the requirement of a practical MU-MIMO transceiver design.

References

1. Gesbert, D., Kountouris, M., Heath Jr., R.W., Chae, C.B., Sälzer, T.: Shifting the MIMO paradigm. IEEE Signal Process. Mag. **24**(5), 36–46 (2007)
2. Mietzner, J., Schober, R., Lampe, L., Gerstacker, W.H., Hoeher, P.A.: Multiple-antenna techniques for wireless communications-a comprehensive literature survey. IEEE Commun. Surv. Tutorials **11**(2), 87–105 (2009)
3. Zid, M.B.: Recent Trends in Multi-user MIMO Communications. BoD–Books on Demand. Intech Open, Rijeka (2013)
4. Windpassinger, C., Fischer, R.F., Vencel, T., Huber, J.B.: Precoding in multiantenna and multiuser communications. IEEE Trans. Wireless Commun. **3**(4), 1305–1316 (2004)
5. Codreanu, M., Tolli, A., Juntti, M., Latva-Aho, M.: Joint design of Tx-Rx beamformers in MIMO downlink channel. IEEE Trans. Signal Process. **55**(9), 4639–4655 (2007)
6. Schubert, M., Shi, S., Jorswieck, E.A., Boche, H.: Downlink sum-MSE transceiver optimization for linear multi-user MIMO systems. In: Conference Record of the Thirty-Ninth Asilomar Conference on Signals, Systems and Computers, Pacific Grove, CA, USA, pp. 1424–1428. IEEE (2005)
7. Khachan, A.M., Tenenbaum, A.J., Adve, R.S.: Linear processing for the downlink in multiuser MIMO systems with multiple data streams. In: IEEE International Conference on Communications, Istanbul, Turkey, pp. 4113–4118. IEEE (2006)
8. Serbetli, S., Yener, A.: Transceiver optimization for multiuser MIMO systems. IEEE Trans. Signal Process. **52**(1), 214–226 (2016)
9. Ding, M., Blostein, S.D.: Relation between joint optimizations for multiuser MIMO uplink and downlink with imperfect CSI. In: IEEE International Conference on Acoustics, Speech and Signal Processing, Las Vegas, NV, USA, pp. 3149–3152. IEEE (2008)
10. Li, W., Ke, Y., Han-ying, H., Wei-jia, C.: Robust joint linear transceiver design for MU-MIMO with imperfect CSI. In: Proceedings of the 2010 Global Mobile Congress, New Orleans, LO, USA, pp. 1–6. IEEE Computer Society (2010)
11. Kejalakshmi, V., Arivazhagan, S.: PSO based sum rate optimization for MU-MIMO linear precoder with imperfect CSI. Wireless Pers. Commun. **92**(3), 1039–1051 (2017)
12. Merline, A., Thiruvengadam, S.J.: Design of optimal linear precoder and decoder for MIMO channels with per antenna power constraint and imperfect CSI. Wireless Pers. Commun. **75**(2), 1251–1263 (2014)
13. Chen, Y., Wang, L., Zhao, Z., Ma, M., Jiao, B.: Secure multiuser MIMO downlink transmission via precoding-aided spatial modulation. IEEE Commun. Lett. **20**(6), 1116–1119 (2016)
14. Chinnusamy, M., Sidharthan, R.K., Sivanandam, V., Kommi, S.S.S., Mallari Rao, C., Periasamy, N.: Optimal tracking of QR inspired LEA using particle filter for secured visual MIMO communication based vehicular network. Photonics **6**(3), 1–24 (2019)

Intrusion Detection System

A Survey of Machine Learning Techniques Used to Combat Against the Advanced Persistent Threat

E. Rajalakshmi, N. Asik Ibrahim, and V. Subramaniyaswamy[✉]

School of Computing, SASTRA Deemed University, Thanjavur 613401, India
vsubramaniyaswamy@gmail.com

Abstract. The increased dependence of people on online services has led to a rapid increase in Cybercrime. Nowadays, each device is connected to the internet. Since every device connected to the web is vulnerable to cyber attack, securing these devices has become very crucial. The Advanced Persistent Threat (APT) is a novel techniques used by hackers. It is among the most alarming security threat. It can bypass all kinds of security appliances. The malware is becoming stronger and more redundant, which cause the victim's system/network more damage. To prevent or mitigate such type of attacks, there is some prevention mechanism with the help of Machine Learning (ML) which would help to detect the advanced level threat. These Advanced level threats are much capable of hiding themselves from the firewall or any other defensive mechanism, of uncovering this advanced level threats there are some ML algorithms which would help to detect them with the low false positive rate and a higher level of accuracy. This paper mainly emphasizes on various Machine Learning algorithms and techniques that can be applied to detect Advanced Persistent Threats.

Keywords: Advanced Persistent Threat · Intrusion Detection System · Reconnaissance · Command & Control (C&C) Communication · Privilege escalation · Establishing foothold

1 Introduction

Nowadays, cyberspace has been compromised by one of the new threats called an Advanced Persistent Threat (APT) [15]. These types of threats are invisible to the normal firewall or antivirus; to ensure our system with the high-security mechanism, we defend these threats by the Machine-Learning (ML) methodology. To detect malicious content in the system or network, we ensure the ML algorithms [16] like Decision Tree, K-Means algorithm, Support Vector Machine (SVM) and more which were used in these malware detection mechanisms. Most of the APTs are target based attack. APTs have their defensive mechanism, which is much strong to crack it by the anti-virus software or firewall. The target-based attacks are mostly carried out by the remote access via bot control. The compromised system is capable of acting as a bot, which gives the attacker a way to access the victim system remotely. The APTs have the capacity of controlling the IoT [17] devices as well; it has to inject the payload on

© Springer Nature Singapore Pte Ltd. 2019
V. S. Shankar Sriram et al. (Eds.): ATIS 2019, CCIS 1116, pp. 159–172, 2019.
https://doi.org/10.1007/978-981-15-0871-4_12

the mainframe system to gain control of the IoT devices. The malware has the characteristics to damage the victim's computer system. The modern way to detect and analyze the malware/threat is with the help of machine learning or deep learning algorithms. It can be used to detect and predict the threat in a small period of time with the lower false positive rate and a higher amount of accuracy rate.

Intrusion Detection System (IDS) [18] is a defensive mechanism which is used for defending the machine or network from the malware or threat. It will defend it from the serious damage and detect the threat at an early stage. After the detection of the threat, it will analyze the threat based on the signature-based or pattern based (depends on the level of threat), it will alert the user. Most of the IDS are capable of detecting the Ransomware with the help of the MLP algorithm. RNN [19] (Recurrent Neural Network) is used to detect the threat or malware in the IoT with the assistant of behavior analysis and mining process. Figure 1 shows the normal strategy of how an attack is carried out. The summary of the most dangerous attacks carried out until 2018 is shown in Table 1.

Fig. 1. A normal attack strategy

2   Advanced Persistent Threat

The Advanced Persistent Threat (APT) is among the alarming security threat. These Advanced level threats are much capable of hiding themselves from the firewall or any other defensive mechanism. APTs [11] are done by hackers, working individually or in a group, and are subsidized by some organizations or state in order to get vital information about a target organization or state. The APT attacker has exfiltration of information or obstructing critical features of some mission as its objective. An APT hacker tries to attain the goal repeatedly over a long period of time, bypasses and adapts to all the obstacles, and tries to preserve the interaction that is required to achieve the goal. To obtain the objective, the hacker needs to go through a series of stages of attacks which are mentioned below. Figure 2 shows the stages [20] of an APT attack.

Table 1. Most dangerous attacks carried out until 2018

Year	Organization	What got leaked	No of users affected
2013–2014	Yahoo	Name, telephone number, date of birth and email addresses	500 million
2014–2018	Marriott International	Name, credit card credential, passport credential, and other contact information	500 million
2014	Ebay	Names, date of birth, passwords and, addresses	145 million
2017	Equifax	Social Security Number, driver's license details, date of birth, and address	143 million
2013	Target Stores	Contact information, Credit card details, and Debit card details	110 million
2016	Uber	Phone numbers, credit card details, driver license, etc.	57 million users 600,000 drivers
2014	JP Morgan Chase	Contact information, and internal information	83 million
2012–2014	US Office of Personnel Management (OPM)	Security clearance information, personal information, and fingerprint data	22 million

2.1   Reconnaissance

In this stage, the attacker finds potential user or organization which can be made a target for extracting the useful information. The hacker identifies and researches the target victim using community sources such as social media, websites, etc., and gets ready for launching a customized attack. The attacker sets the attack methodology by analyzing the activities of the victim or the target. The attacker carries out his research with the help of some activities such as identifying the vulnerable website, monitoring the target organization's business activities, their current projects, internal organization, etc.

2.2   Initial Compromise

After the deep analysis about the target, the attacker, somehow, tries to successfully execute exploit or malicious codes on one or a more targeted victim. It tries to find out Point of Entry. The malicious code or the exploit is sent to the victim through Internet sources by one or the other means. It is mostly done by spear phishing. By installing malicious code, the attacker opens a back door which can be used to access the machine whenever they want.

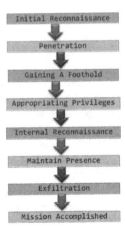

Fig. 2. APT attack stages

2.3 Command & Control Communication (C&C)

It is very important to provide a channel for communication between the attacker's system and compromised machine throughout the APT campaign. The attacker exploits the compromised machine by passing commands and controlling the victim machine. After they gain access to machine, they can do anything with the target machine. They can ex-filtrate data, record keyboard inputs, get important credentials, etc. To make sure that he can maintain the control over the target system, he establishes a foothold by adding other malware required to the compromised machine. The hacker gets access to the valuable information and tries to increase their privileges by executing various techniques such as password hash dumping, recording keystrokes, getting PKI certificates, etc.

2.4 Privilege Escalation

After establishing the foothold, the attacker finds ways to reach valuable information by spreading malware through the victim's network. The hacker always targets the vulnerable machine of the target network at first and then tries to find out the system which has the information he requires. He tries to get access to the system containing valuable information by tracing through the network and raising his privileges. Various ways are used by hackers to escalate their privileges. One of the ways of getting privilege escalation is by finding the vulnerabilities in the configuration of the system such as files having credentials of administrator, services that are misconfigured, intentionally weakened security. The other method which is way more reliable than this method is by attacking the OS kernel, which in turn ends up in the execution of arbitrary code that allows the hacker to bypass all the security obstacles. In some cases, privileges can be escalated by using simpler methods such as brute force attack, recording keystrokes, weak passwords, etc.

2.5 Maintain Access

The hacker maintains continued access to the compromised network. There are various ways to maintain access, which include installation of different kinds of malware, getting access to services that enable remote access like Virtual Private Network. Broadening the access and gaining valuable information by creating a ghost network within the target network, getting access to trace more routes.

2.6 Asset Discovery and Data Ex-Filtration

There are many methods like network analysis and port scanning to discover the potential services and servers that the target's machine has. This stage involves unauthorized access and displacement of information from the target's web to the hacker's system. Upon gaining access to the valuable information required, the information piece is archived, compressed and the archive is encrypted in order to bypass deep packet inspection and to prevent data loss. This step is followed up by data exfiltration from the compromised system.

2.7 Covering the Tracks

When the goal is achieved, the hacker makes sure that he covers up all the traces. The hackers ensure that they don't leave any traces behind. There have been many cases where hackers left the backdoor open for a long time and continued to gain access as and when they require without getting caught.

3 Techniques Used to Bypass Security

Some of the techniques used by the attackers that are used to bypass security are discussed below [10].

3.1 Exploitation of Well-Known Vulnerabilities

Most of the attacks are made using already exposed vulnerabilities. The known vulnerabilities are available in databases like the National Vulnerability Database of NIST and Common Vulnerabilities and Exposures List [13] where each vulnerability is disclosed publicly and has a unique CVD_ID through which it is identified. Deep web and dark web forums [12] also helps the attackers to share and gather vital information about vulnerabilities. It is inferred from a study report [14] it was observed that most of the attacks were made exploiting the known vulnerabilities.

3.2 Use of Malware

Using malware is one of the basic techniques to hijack user's computer very easily. Malware can spread throughout the internet in the form of drive-by download files or through USB sharing. Most of the attacks carried out by the attackers involve the installation of malware on the target machine. There are billions of varieties of malware which can be used very easily, and the user will not even get a hint that malware has been installed in his machine. By installing the malware in the client's machine, the hacker can leave a backdoor open for gaining access to the targeted network in the future.

3.3 Spear Phishing

Spear phishing helps to breach into the web which done using social engineering. In this technique, specially crafted emails that contain disguised exe files are sent to specific targeted individuals or organizations. The recipient of the emails is induced to or convinced to click a hyperlink to an exploited site or download a file attachment that has malicious content or a link to malware using social engineering tactics. The malicious hyperlink may end up in an attack using drive-by download. This malicious code that gets installed on the client's machine without his knowledge can control the machine which is infected and can perform various malicious activities such as stealing stored passwords., record keystrokes, data exfiltration, etc.

3.4 Zero Day Vulnerability

It is a software bug which is unknown to the software builder or known to the software builder, but he couldn't fix it at that point of time [21]. The attackers collect information related software components such as OS version, anti-viruses, and anti malwares installed; patches ran etc. They try to find the vulnerabilities present in those versions so that they can find a route to gain entry to the target machine. However, it's observed [14] that there are very few attacks achieved through this method.

3.5 Watering Hole Attack

The watering hole attack is the one in which the targets one of the intermittently visited websites are infected. In this method, a hacker injects exploits into the websites that are most frequently visited by the target user. Once the target user goes to this infected website, the malicious software gets installed in the target machine, and the hacker waits for it to run. The main challenge in this attack is to hide the execution of malware, and the exploit should be invisible to the anti-viruses and anti-malwares installed in the target system.

4 APT Detection Methods

There are different techniques which are used to detect the threat with the help of Machine Learning (ML) algorithm. Some of them are discussed below.

4.1 Detection of Threat Using Machine-Learning Correlation Analysis

APT is one of the most concerned threats. It potentially causes the system and gains information by compromising the victim's system. MLAPT helps us to find the threat.

It gives the higher level accuracy with the accuracy of 84.8% [1]. The MLAPT runs with the three main phases. The first one is the Threat Detection phase, which has eight sub-module, which helps to find the threat in real time traffic analysis. The second one is Alert Correlation, which gets the output from the detection phase and identifies which type of alert it belongs to. The last phase is Attack Prediction which deals with the machine learning that helps to find the prediction of APT threat at an early stage. This paper defines ways to minimize the FPR (False positive Rate) with the help of a machine learning based system which helps in detection and prediction of the APT attack in a unified approach.

4.2   A Detection of Malware/Threat Using a Recurrent Neural Network Method

Deep Learning has the unique feature which is Recurrent Neural Network (RNN) [19], that helps to analyze the malware content in the IoT device. Algorithms are defined to classify the malware based on the Operational Codes (OpCodes). For evaluation of OpCodes and identification of the optimum feature for malware, detection by applying SVM classifier, and techniques using n-gram methods were used to obtain an accuracy rate of 96% [2]. This method used the n-gram, via text mining, to detect the malicious rate up to 75%. At first, analyze the infected IoT devices and extract the OpCode from that infected device. After that, using the Deep Learning process we can find the True Positive rate (TPR) of advantageous files and True Negative Rate (TPR) of malware correctly identified as malware, FPR of advantageous is defined as malware and FNR is also malware of the advantageous classified files. LSTM approach helps to hunt the malware based IoT with opcode sequence to achieve the detection of 98% accuracy.

4.3   Anomaly-Based Intrusion Detection Systems

Here a unique feature called a Pattern-of-Life from the network was used. It is considered as high prior information to detect the anomaly based intrusion. A new approach called Fuzzy Cognitive Map (FCM), which helps to integrate the detection of Pattern-of-Life, was implemented. By using these methods, we can identify the attack which is currently being carried out. We can integrate this with the FCM into IDS framework to yield the best output/results (99.76%), and it can reduce the number of false alarm (6.33%) [3]. Current IDS system gives protection based on the already defined signatures from the intrusion detection process. In this process, we use the method called Pattern-of-Life (PoL), which gives information about the network resources. These information can be utilized to characterize the PoL which will be useful in the generation of contextual data. In the process to incorporate the PoL into detection process, FCM [22] is applied for the anomaly based detection. The first approach is using FCM to integrate the PoL contextual information and use output of FCM to develop the additional metric. The second approach is using the different metrics from the FCM to characterize the PoL of the network traffic. The last step is the implementation of FCM to gain the high-level data from network user with the high-level accuracy of details with detailed information which produces the best results and reduces the number of false alarm. IDS will provide a minimum false positive and maximum accuracy rate. Additionally, few metrics were used to design the modeled FCM, which gives the effect of the IDS. The metrics were based on the already detected attacks.

4.4   A Detection of Malware by Using the Search Engine

APT is the target based cyber attack, which mostly attacks the victim remotely with the help of bot control to get confidential information. Signature-based or learning based approach on the APT malware detection is weak to detect them. Here they have developed a specific search-engine applying a Hadoop platform for APT investigation to find, uncover victims by referring the known victim [4]. Bot-infected systems are fully remote-controlled, which can access the HTTP log, which contains valuable information about the network such as cookies, etc. Here command and control (C&C) are the HTTP based one which helps the infected bot system to victimize the other system. Normally in another search engine, the HTTP request is logged by the proxy and is then sent to the search-engine operator repeatedly. But in this Hadoop based search engine, the queries are logged in every 2 s. Which prove that the C&C servers are completely prevented from the malware infected computer systems. In an APT investigation, it is proved that the known C&C communication servers are rated under top 10 sites and responding time of each query is reduced in less than 2 s.

4.5   Detection of Malware Based on Deep Learning Algorithm

This deals with the usage of Deep Belief Network (DBN) [23] to detect the malware with the comparison of traditional neural network analysis [6]. The performance of this malware detection is based on SVM, Decision Tree, and the K-nearest algorithm as classifiers [16]. For example, worm contains the payload which has a capacity of accessing the computer via remotely by creating a back-door. To overcome this issue, we have signature-based detection, but it cannot detect the previously unseen threat via a pattern-based approach. To address this problem, the new approach was introduced to detect the malware with the new intelligent technique of machine learning and data mining method to analysis/detect the malware. These experiments prove that the DBN model provides more accurate detection with the help of an auto-encoder and significantly reduce the dimension of feature vectors and expose the disguised exe file with the help of some algorithms like Naïve Bayes classification, SVM and Decision Tree.

4.6   Detection of Malware by Using Frequent Pattern Mining

The attacker will encrypt the computer system, and it will only decrypt after the ransom has been paid. To overcome this problem, here the sequential pattern mining to find the Maximal Frequent Pattern (MFP) of active ransomware was utilized. To detect the malware pattern and get the 99% of accuracy, here the MLP (Multi-Layer Perceptron) algorithm [24] to analyze the threat was implemented. To implement the technique for the detection of ransomware malware they used the MLP algorithm to find the frequent pattern and achieved 99% [8] of accuracy in detection of ransomware from the sample pattern and reduced the period for the detection process to less than 10 s. There are other ransomware families which cannot be detected by this MLP algorithm. This problem can be overcome by using the datasets of Dynamic Link Libraries (DLL) on the sequence pattern mining in order to detect frequent feature of ransomware application logs, which helps to achieve the solution and reduce the false positive. By combing the sequential pattern mining for identification with the classification using machine learning methodology, we can find the ransomware based on the given goodware samples within the first ten seconds of ransomware execution.

4.7   Detection of Malware with the Help of the SPuNge

APT is target based attack, which is burdensome to detect. To beat this issue, then SPuNge [5] based novel system was introduced. This could process the information about the threat from the victim and it used the combination of clustering and correlation technique to identify the machine which is responsible for the malicious resource. The threat information from the potentially targeted attack is used to detect the upcoming attack, by using this methodology, we can reduce the malicious activities and similar threat in the future attack scenario. To implement this approach, the combination of clustering techniques [25] was utilized to identify the malicious request from the unknown resource which were correlated to a group of machines on the computer system. The information can be correlated with the help of k-means and classification algorithm to find the location of the attack operation. SPuNge is a clustering algorithm which oblige to identify the group of malicious hyperlinks that have akin hostnames/domains.

4.8   Robust Malware Detection by Deep "Eigenspace" Learning

Recently IoT is also used in military applications which consist of a wearable combat uniform, etc. Here the objective is to detect the malware from the Internet of Battlefield Things (IoBT) via Operational Code (OpCode) sequence. This can be done by optimizing the deep Eigenspace learning approach with an OpCode via vector space to specify the malicious and benign applications. It also works against the junk code insertion attack, which is detected by the malware detection with the help of machine learning. The attackers who targeted the IoBT devices can exploit the vulnerabilities on particular IoT device and target the nuclear plants. To overcome this issue, this methodology has three main sections which are used to detect and prevent the IoBT device from the malware. OpCode are the more reliable and upgradeable feature for the identification of malware using the machine learning via neural networks and decision tree there would be a 94.93% of accuracy [7]. Using the Bayesian network and K-Nearest neighbor algorithm, there could be a 95.90% of accuracy in malware detection. Deep learning is used to analysis the IoBT devices with the help of a machine learning algorithm correlated with the OpCode to find the malware in the IoBT device. Using OpCode sequence as a feature for classification task in the deep eigenspace learning, the malware can be detected at the 98.37% of accuracy rate and 98.59% of the precision rate, as well as the junk code insertion attack can be mitigated.

4.9   Early-Stage Malware Prediction Using Recurrent Neural Networks

This deals with analyzing the static malware at the endpoint antivirus which matches them with the previously analyzed malicious code. It takes nearly 5 min to capture the malicious payload by that time the malware has been done its work. To overcome this issue, the recurrent neural network that is capable of capturing the executable malicious content within 5 s with the 94% of accuracy was an ensemble. The Recurrent Neural Network (RNN) is applied to detect and find the malware at the early stage with the help of a Behavioral Analysis which analyze the static data for the malware content. An antivirus system is run in a timely manner. Dynamically collected data are taken to the behavioral analysis for the malware detection and then checked with the sandbox that will be helpful for the future analysis. The algorithm for the sequential data analyzing with the help of Recurrent Neural Network and Hidden Markov Models can detect the malware with a higher accuracy rate. This methodology also has a capacity of blocking the malicious payload rather than repairing the damage which is caused by the malware. Dynamic malware detection methods are always one step ahead of traditional malware detection. The malicious payload is detected in advance with the help of Recurrent Neural Network that can significantly reduce the time to less than 5 s for the malware detection to achieve an accuracy of 94% of malware detection and 96% in 10 s. [9]

The techniques discussed here have their own merits and demerits. Table 2 summarizes the merits and demerits of each detection technique discussed in this paper. We can see in Table 2 that each and every method has its own advantages and disadvantages. Though the first method has good accuracy but since it has multiple sub tasks it takes a lot of time for malware detection. The second method is also time consuming and has storage issues when it comes to store OpCodes. The third method has good accuracy but its datasets need different training metrics which makes it a little bit complex. The fourth method uses Hadoop platform which makes the model unique. Its only disadvantage is that the signature-based approach is obsolete in this case. Though the usage of Naïve Bayes and the SVM methods makes the Fifth method highly inevitable but the slow detection process brings its performance based on time down. The sixth method helps to detect even the signature pattern analysis but it is quite complicated when it comes to implementation. The seventh method is a target based attack ant this method also takes a lot of time to detect the attack. Method eight can be advantageous than other methods in terms of speed of detection since it can detect a malware within 5 s but its accuracy is low.

Table 2. Merits and Demerits of the detection methods

S. no.	Methodologies	Merits	Demerits
1	Detection of Threat using Machine-Learning Correlation Analysis	Detection accuracy is accurate	It has several sub level testing, for that it takes time
2	A RNN approach for malware threat hunting	It helps to find the malware in IoT hardware devices	Time-consuming and OpCodes need storage
3	Anomaly-Based Intrusion Detection Systems	Pattern-of-Life (PoL) increase the threat detection accuracy	Datasets have to be trained with different metrics
4	A Novel Search Engine to Uncover malware/threat	Hadoop platform gives the unique level of malware detection	Signature-based approach is obsolete to this method
5	Malware detection Using Deep Learning Algorithm	Using Naïve Bayes method and SVM in DBN. The detection of malware is highly inevitable	Detection process takes time to detect the malware/threat
6	Frequent Pattern Mining for Malware and Threat hunting	It is used to detect the Ransomware based on the signature pattern analysis	Complicate to implement
7	Targeted Attacks Detection With SPuNge	Prevent the target based attack	Time-consuming
8	Early-Stage Predictionof malware Using RNN	It detects the malware within the 5 s	A lower level of accuracy

5   Proposed Work

This paper briefs about the stages of APTs and various approach used by attackers to bypass the security. This paper proposes the different techniques used to detect malware and threat. Intrusion detection system mainly focuses on detecting the advanced persistent threat. This paper deals with various classifications of techniques to prevent the threat with the help of machine learning. Each technique has its advantage and disadvantage. The merits and demerits of each detection technique discussed in this paper are summarized. Continuous filtering System and Defense System helps to protect confidential, sensitive data from APTs. We propose a method to extend better support of monitoring. We intend to decrease the False Positive Rate (FPR). We are going to implement this system in a real-world network and evaluate our approach by applying larger datasets. With this type of implementation, we can reduce the Advanced Persistent Threat. Our proposed model is shown in Fig. 3.

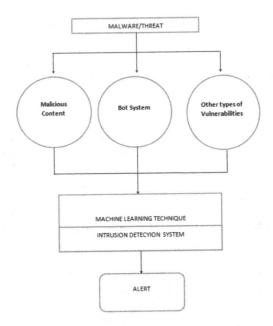

Fig. 3. Implementation of Intrusion Detection System

The APT attacks are conducted step by step. It can be considered as the action of a series of events. These series of events may have taken place for months. The main challenge in detecting an APT is keeping track of various steps that are logged over months of analyzing and monitoring and linking them together. We are going to propose a system in which we are using machine learning techniques for analyzing the threat in detail. We are going to build an application which will detect the threat by inspecting each stage of APT and detect the chain of events in APT thus detecting the threat.

The proposed method deals with keeping track of each event/stage that leads to APT by using some Machine Learning techniques. We will analyze the behavior of the attack and identify the pattern of the attack. While some detection methods discussed in this paper have high accuracy but they take lot of time and on the other hand we have seen some methods have low accuracy but work faster. To overcome this problem we will analyze various combinations of Machine Learning techniques which will help both to increase accuracy as well as reduce the detection time.

6 Conclusion and Future Works

The Advanced Persistent Threat (APT) is one among the dangerous security threat. In this paper, the main concepts of APT are discussed. This paper briefs about various stages involved in APT and how the attack is carried out. It mainly highlights some of the Machine Learning techniques used for detection of APT. Continuous filtering System and Defense System helps to protect confidential and sensitive data from APTs.

By extending the better support of monitoring, the outcome of this detection method and the outcome of alternative detection methods will be correlated in order to raise an alert on APT attack detection and minimize the False Positive Rate (FPR). Here we are planning to build a model using machine learning which will be able to find the APTs by analyzing series and sequence of APT stages carried out. Since APT attacks are carried out in stages, it requires more time to find the place to hide. In future implementation of this work can be done by implementing the Machine learning with the Intrusion detection system to find the APT during the reconnaissance period and also it can be implemented in the real-world network and we will evaluate our approach by applying the model to larger datasets. With this type of implementation, we can reduce the Advanced Persistent Threat.

References

1. Ghafira, I., et al.: Detection of advanced persistent threat using machine-learning correlation analysis **89**, 349–359 (2018)
2. HaddadPajouh, H., Dehghantanha, A., Khayami, R., Choo, K.-K.R.: A deep recurrent neural network based approach for internet of things malware threat hunting. Future Gener. Comput. Syst. **85**, 88–96 (2018)
3. Aparicio-Navarro, F.J., Kyriakopoulos, K.G., Gong, Y., Parish, D.J., Chambers, J.A.: Using pattern-of-life as contextual information for anomaly-based intrusion detection systems. IEEE Access **5**, 22177–22193 (2017)
4. Liu, S.T., Chen, Y.M., Lin, S.J.: A novel search engine to uncover potential victims for APT investigations. In: Hsu, C.-H., Li, X., Shi, X., Zheng, R. (eds.) NPC 2013. LNCS, vol. 8147, pp. 405–416. Springer, Heidelberg (2013). https://doi.org/10.1007/978-3-642-40820-5_34
5. Balduzzi, M., Ciangaglini, V., McArdle, R.: Targeted attacks detection with spunge. In: 2013 Eleventh Annual Conference on Privacy, Security and Trust, pp. 185–194. IEEE (2013)
6. Yuxin, D., Siyi, Z.: Malware detection based on deep learning algorithm. Neural Comput. Appl. **31**(2), 461–472 (2019)
7. Azmoodeh, A., Dehghantanha, A., Choo, K.K.R.: Robust malware detection for internet of (battlefield) things devices using deep eigenspace learning. IEEE Trans. Sustain. Comput. **4**(1), 88–95 (2018)
8. Homayoun, S., et al.: Know abnormal, find evil: frequent pattern mining for ransomware threat hunting and intelligence. IEEE Trans. Emerg. Top. Comput. (2017)
9. Rhode, M., Burnap, P., Jones, K.: Early-stage malware prediction using recurrent neural networks. Comput. Secur. **77**, 578–594 (2018)
10. Alshamrani, A., Myneni, S., Chowdhary, A., Huang, D.: A survey on advanced persistent threats: techniques, solutions, challenges, and research opportunities. IEEE Commun. Surv. Tutor. **21**(2), 1851–1877 (2019)
11. Chen, P., Desmet, L., Huygens, C.: A study on advanced persistent threats. In: De Decker, B., Zúquete, A. (eds.) CMS 2014. LNCS, vol. 8735, pp. 63–72. Springer, Heidelberg (2014). https://doi.org/10.1007/978-3-662-44885-4_5
12. Mell, P., Scarfone, K., Romanosky, S.: Common vulnerability scoring system. IEEE Secur. Priv. **4**(6), 85–89 (2006)

13. Motoyama, M., McCoy, D., Levchenko, K., Savage, S., Voelker, G.M.: An analysis of underground forums. In: Proceedings of the 2011 ACM SIGCOMM Conference on Internet Measurement Conference, 2 November 2011, pp. 71–80. ACM (2011)

14. Ussath, M., Jaeger, D., Cheng, F., Meinel, C.: Advanced persistent threats: behind the scenes. In: 2016 Annual Conference on Information Science and Systems (CISS), 16 March 2016, pp. 181–186. IEEE (2016)

15. Daly, M.K.: Advanced persistent threat. Usenix 4(4), 2013–2016 (2009)

16. Tsai, C.F., Hsu, Y.F., Lin, C.Y., Lin, W.Y.: Intrusion detection by machine learning: a review. Expert Syst. Appl. 36(10), 11994–12000 (2009)

17. Abomhara, M.: Cyber security and the internet of things: vulnerabilities, threats, intruders and attacks. J. Cyber Secur. Mob. 4(1), 65–88 (2015)

18. Liao, H.J., Lin, C.H., Lin, Y.C., Tung, K.Y.: Intrusion detection system: a comprehensive review. J. Netw. Comput. Appl. 36(1), 16–24 (2013)

19. Yin, C., Zhu, Y., Fei, J., He, X.: A deep learning approach for intrusion detection using recurrent neural networks. IEEE Access 12(5), 21954–21961 (2017)

20. Brewer, R.: Advanced persistent threats: minimising the damage. Netw. Secur. 2014(4), 5–9 (2014)

21. Avasarala, B.R., Day, J.C., Steiner, D. (Inventors): Assignee: Northrop Grumman Systems Corporation, System and method for automated machine-learning, zero-day malware detection. United States patent US 9,292,688, 22 March 2016

22. Stylios, C.D., Groumpos, P.P.: Modeling complex systems using fuzzy cognitive maps. IEEE Trans. Syst. Man Cybern. Part A Syst. Hum. 34(1), 155–162 (2004)

23. Hinton, G.E.: Deep belief networks. Scholarpedia 4(5), 5947 (2009)

24. Moradi, M, Zulkernine, M.: A neural network based system for intrusion detection and classification of attacks. In: Proceedings of the IEEE International Conference on Advances in Intelligent Systems-Theory and Applications, pp. 15–18, 15 November 2004

25. Jain, A.K., Murty, M.N., Flynn, P.J.: Data clustering: a review. ACM Comput. Surv. (CSUR). 31(3), 264–323 (1999)

Subtree Hypergraph-Based Attack Detection Model for Signature Matching over SCADA HMI

Sujeet S. Jagtap and V. S. Shankar Sriram$^{(\boxtimes)}$ (iD)

Centre for Information Super Highway (CISH), School of Computing,
SASTRA Deemed University, Thanjavur 613401, Tamil Nadu, India
sriram@it.sastra.edu

Abstract. Layered inter-network communications, and dynamic control mechanisms of intra-connected testbeds in cyber-physical systems (CPS) paves way for controlling the PLCs and HMIs in a distributive manner. This intuits the idea of monitoring and logging the CPS traffic by embedding the motorized sensor/actuator readings into an IP-network packet. Attackers commence the network packet intervention of a CPS traffic as an initial phase for launching cyber-based attacks over critical public infrastructures. Log sequences captured for such an instance, required the security professional to observe the log sub-sequences that might possibly lead to an attack, unlisted in the signature repository of the existing defense mechanisms. Hence, this paper defines a hypergraph based attack detection model where constraints can be parameterized based on the type of CPS traffic in order to provide adaptable degree of representing possible attack incidents for the existing intrusion detection systems. Post defining the model's parameterized constraints; we study the attack scenarios over Secure Water Treatment (SWaT) dataset from SUTD's iTrust lab.

Keywords: Intrusion detection systems · Cyber-physical systems · Hypergraphs · Cyber and physical attacks

1 Introduction

Integrating algorithmically parameterized instructions with the communal physical infrastructures like smart-grid [1], water-distribution/treatment, etc. paves a way to build much smarter Cyber-physical systems (CPS). Such computational intensive algorithms even flagged the distributed command-and-control mechanism for CPS when connected to the World Wide Web. This intense potential of controlling the physical process in a distributed manner leads to intrusive cyber-attacks over the critical infrastructures. This prudentially demanded the design and development of cyber-safe attack detection models that validate the incoming traffic with the pre-defined signature patterns that signify a normal behavior of the overall CPS process. Intrusions in CPS are quite diverse from network-oriented attacks as CPS manages critical infrastructures like metro water-treatment, smart grids, thermal plants, etc. CPS-based intrusions are briefly categorized as an attempt to damage the physical components, or to access information that are unauthorized, or to explore the trajectories

© Springer Nature Singapore Pte Ltd. 2019
V. S. Shankar Sriram et al. (Eds.): ATIS 2019, CCIS 1116, pp. 173–184, 2019.
https://doi.org/10.1007/978-981-15-0871-4_13

(paths) of the network that are bounded by firewalls. The proposed subtree hypergraph-based attack detection model for CPS-based intrusion detection system (IDS) contributes the following:

- Process wise attack vulnerabilities are identified through hyperedge representation;
- The incoming traffic is constrained as elemental graph nodes for the attack identification based on the temporal data;
- The subtree-hypergraphs are deduced from the complete graph to accommodate various possible attack scenarios;
- The whole traffic log is traversed with the suffix-tree (STrie) mechanism. Subsequently, the identified attack patterns from hypergraph model and STrie's pattern has been validated through isomorphic property.

The proposed attack detection model is described in such a manner that the routes in the model from beginning to terminal hyperedges constitute a possible assault over the SCADA testbed (say Tank overflow) and correspond to the subsequences of a specified input log i.e. the log is a series of events (tuples) with a sensor/actuator value and a timestamp.

The vertex of the hypergraph represents either sensor or actuator of the SCADA testbed instance from the log tuple(s), whilst the operational stage-wise sub-processes of the testbed are associatively grouped to form an instance of a hyperedge. The efficiently implementable data-domain module of the suffix-tree is built from the incoming log that compares the pattern of the log with the hypergraph attack models. This extends the intrusion detection model to specify vertex cardinality constraints over tuple groups and hyperedges to raise an alarm when temporal limitations on group connections are bypassed on any one of the testbed's sub-processes.

In practical, signature based rules of Network Intrusion Detection System (NIDS) consider almost all possible threat scenarios before the deployment, since the organization's specified network setup is known and static. Though CPS in WatTest adapts Ethernet/IP and Common Industrial Protocol (CIP) as the control-level protocol stack for network communication, it bypasses the NIDS rules during an attack. Thus, the node traversal of the attack model corresponds to the interdependent security vulnerabilities of the critical infrastructure – since attackers cannot pursue certain list of network routes that are hurdled by strict firewall policies.

Organization: Section 2 summarizes the related work carried out in context of the hypergraph-based attack models. Section 3 formally defines the attack model and instances that are parameterized for the scenarios related to the WatTest testbed described below. The study of the CPS testbed is discussed in Sect. 4 with the stages, components, and communication involved. The overall model's assessment phase is described, tabulated, and illustrated in Sect. 5, and finally Sect. 6 discusses the overall work carried out.

2 Related Work

Most of the security administrators incorporate the idea of hypergraph modeling while designing the traffic flow directions that a particular host machine is authenticated to take [7]. Such functionality of path validation aided the NIDS to pre-model attack graphs to part away from the normal ones [8, 9]. [10] utilizes hypergraph models for correlating attacks, and [11] uses hypergraphs in analyzing the risks associated with the dependencies over the security model of the network. Scenario based intrusion study on [12] focuses on the node connectivity over physical inhibition transcendence. The proposed model is designed with the intention that it mounts compatible with the existing open-source IDS for pattern inference on a parameterized basis. Most of the rule-based IDS infer the transmission information from the traffic log for host-dependency and validate rule policies with the recipient's network [14–16]. However, the network modeling tasks utilize the key benefit of hypergraphs which aids in illustrating voluminous possibilities of attack scenarios for a given network architecture. The proposed model associates each component of the SCADA testbed depicted in Fig. 1 to the hypergraph model instead of associating attack activity step labels to the graph model in [17]. After all, the major intent of this work is to identify and prevent the physical attacks in critical infrastructure. Whereas, the attack weights of the attackers' trajectory were not calculated as stated in the literature.

3 Attack Modeling Using Hypergraphs

Definition 1: Attack model $\mathcal{G}$ defines the attack-patterns for raising alerts when an attacker tries to intervene the data-acquisition process and launch an attack through an MITM based injection on testbed's HMIs. Say for an attempt $\mathbb{A}$ of launching an MITM has a tuple of $\mathcal{G} = \{\mathcal{H}, \theta, \tau, \varepsilon, \mathbb{T}(\mathbf{X})\}$. Where,

- $\mathcal{H} = (V_i, H_e)$ refers to the hypergraph with finite set of vertices (V) and hyperedges (H). The vertices and hyperedges are indexed for the fact that when traffic under investigation is represented as a suffix-trie, malicious patterns can be compared with the attack model though targeted nodes or edge-relations. A targeted hyperedge leads to identify the root node of a specific attack pattern, by way of $h \in H, h \subseteq V$.
- $\theta : V_i \leftarrow (\{\{V^{\wedge}V_i\}, V_i \ll 2^2\} \cup \{\infty\})$ acts as the parameter that decodes the incoming little-endian 32-bit encoded data, which the suffix-trie infers the bits coupled in a reverse order for identifying the pattern from the model. This method of vertex labeling intends the ∞ notation to represent the absence of upper bound for the encoded hexadecimals.
- $\tau : H_e \leftarrow \{(-1)^s \times M \times 2^E; H_e \subseteq H\}$ is a function that constraints the hyperedges to check for the possible changes in: $s \rightarrow$ sign-bit to verify the positive/negative number for the identification of the overflow/underflow situations in the testbed, $M \rightarrow$ a significant fractional threshold that checks for values that drops/raises from the specified range, and $E \rightarrow$ exponent to check for the values that are non-floating point. In addition, the function $H \leftarrow \{\mathbb{N}^+ \cup (\infty)\}$ expresses the sequential constraints, such that $\tau(H_e)$ is defined with upper and lower bounds denoting the hyperedge sets.

- $\varepsilon : H^2 \leftarrow \mathbb{N}^+$ function partially expresses the possible sets as upper bound fractional threshold between hyperedges $\{h_e \in H\}$ of the testbed's distinct sensors/actuators (vertices). Process(P) denotes the hyperedge pair sets which when surpassed an alert is raised by the IDS, given $P(h_{e1}, h_{e2})$ along with either of the logical operators $\{\wedge\}, \{\vee\}, \{\neg\}$ representing the conjunction, disjunction, or negation of the node within an hyperedge for an given process.
- $\mathbb{T}$ a (partial) function which when called by the suffix-trie built from the data recursively returns the $\mathcal{S} \to$ start hyperedge and $\mathcal{T} \to$ terminal hyperedge, given $(x_i \subseteq X) \in (!\varnothing[\mathcal{S}, \mathcal{T}])$.

Definition 2: A path in Model $\mathcal{G} = \{\mathcal{H}, \theta, \tau, \varepsilon, \mathbb{T}(X)\}$. "$\gamma$" is a continuous mapping of hyperedge sequences $\gamma : \{h_{e1}, h_{em}\}$ of H under investigation, where:

  i. Initial hyperedge is an element of the hyperedge set $[\mathcal{S}]$;
  ii. Intermediate hyperedges between $[\mathcal{S}, \mathcal{T}]$ must not be an empty-set;
  iii. $\nexists i \in \{2 \ldots m - 1\}$ where $h_i \ldots h_{j-1}, h_{j+1} \ldots h_m$ satisfies previous conditions;
  iv. Path completion of γ is met when h_m is an element of set $[\mathcal{T}]$.

The sequenced traffic capture of the SWAT testbed's log defines the varied instances of whether the sensor/actuator is operational for the water treatment process. Log sequences l_i contains a tuple of features $\langle \mathbb{N}_1 \ldots \mathbb{N}_n \rangle$ (of HMI_MVxxx say) encoded in the ENIP/CIP protocol with its respective timestamp occurrence. Each log l_x holds the respective feature with $l_x.time\_instance < l_y.time\_instance$, reflecting the fine granularity of time sequences encoded with the type of the sensor/actuator (say HMI_MVxxx) and its respective instance $\mathbb{N}$.

Definition 3: Each hyperedge h_e of the hypergraph H for an particular attack (say Tank-Overflow due to Injection of values) embeds number of sensors/actuators as the node/vertex from different processes of the SCADA testbed. The start and terminal hyperedges $[\mathcal{S}, \mathcal{T}]$ for an particular segment $\overline{\mathcal{S}, \mathcal{T}}$ of the water-treatment's sub-process generates a log sequence $L = \{l_1 : l_m\}$ for which $\overline{\mathcal{S}, \mathcal{T}}$ must be both $\{> 0; \mathbb{N}\}$. An attack segment within a sub-process of the testbed is a set-sequence of $\{[\mathcal{S}_1, \mathcal{T}_1] \ldots [\mathcal{S}_m, \mathcal{T}_m]\} \in \mathbb{N}$ where:

  i. For an given instance i of the particular segment $\overline{\mathcal{S}, \mathcal{T}}$, $segment(L) \leftarrow [\mathcal{S}_i, \mathcal{T}_i]$;
  ii. For attack types like Multi Stage Multi Point attacks the attack's impact might be distinguishable but the hyperedge segments for two different attack instances might be congruent, $[\mathcal{S}_i, \mathcal{T}_i] \cong [\mathcal{S}_j, \mathcal{T}_j]$.

Definition 4: For the traffic generated out of the water-treatment plant, $\mathcal{G} = \{\mathcal{H}, \theta, \tau, \varepsilon, \mathbb{T}(X)\}$ is assumed to be the attack model for an incident $\mathbb{A}$. $\gamma : \{h'_{e1}, h'_{em}\}$ denotes the m-complete path for $\mathcal{G}$, given the log traffic $L = \{l_1 : l_n\}$. $\exists \{[\mathcal{S}_1, \mathcal{T}_1] \ldots [\mathcal{S}_m, \mathcal{T}_m]\}$ segments of the log L when $\{\lim_{i \to m}[l_i] \in \mathcal{G};$ over $\gamma\} \Rightarrow L \vDash_\gamma \mathcal{G}$.

3.1 Identification of Graph Discrepancy from Logs

Generalized attack models do not correspond to the varied variable thresholds of SCADA architecture, assuming the traffic with attack patterns as benign to the host infrastructure. This in turn bypasses the intrusion detection system's signatures and grants the intruder to exploit the SCADA infrastructure and launch an attack. Proposed model was designed with the key intent of identifying the abnormal data traffic and to validate the conditional state of the corresponding sensor/actuator through associative thresholds. Logging of the corresponding timestamp along with its consequent data-packets from the HMI will be the at most primary constraint imposed by the attack model, over the log to be inspected. For this reason, attack graphs had to be designed in correspondence with the attack model must comprise both the process states of each module and its respective timestamps.

Attack pattern is identified from the logs generated through spatial-temporal trajectory that varies for each sensor/actuator over time and type of the testbed's process. SWAT water treatment testbed embeds the sensor/actuator values in an encoded format that will be used to represent the presence of a pattern in the spatial-temporal region either as a normal/abnormal activity by the attack model.

Trajectories plotted out of incoming traffic are compared with the process-wise graph models that will be inferred by the security professional to improve the IDS signatures.

4 Testbed

WatTest [3] is a water treatment test environment designed for the sole purpose of carrying research study on handling cyber-based attack incidents that could possibly cause physical damage and impact over critical infrastructures. Staged process of treating the water helps researchers to model various possible attack scenarios, which could help in experimenting, designed programmable models for in-depth defence, as those outlined in [4–6]. The architecture of WatTest clearly depicts the overall stage-wise treatment of water carried over in a temporal constraint from PLC1-to-PLC6. Programmable Logic Controllers (PLC) controls each stage by its own and logs the data traffic in the Historian server; that can be viewed and controlled through the Human Machine Interface (HMI).

4.1 WatTest Stages

Stage P1 regulates the untreated raw water by opening/closing the motorized valve that links inlet pipe with the tank holding raw water. Untreated water is then pumped to stage P3 for Ultrafiltration (UF) through the chemical dosing plant in stage P2. On completion of ultrafiltration, the UF feed pump transmits water to the supply tank in stage P4 for carrying out Ultraviolet Dechlorination (UV) controlled by PLC-4. After which stage P5 includes the PLC to regulate the process of Reverse Osmosis (RO) for further filtration of water by means of a 2-stage RO process. The pressure fall below 0.4 bar across the UF unit initiates the backwash cycle, once the Differential Pressure Sensors at stage P3 senses the pressure drop [3].

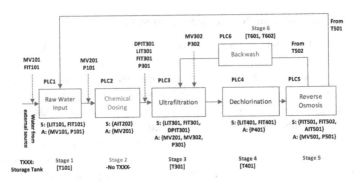

Fig. 1. Stage-wise process of the testbed [WatTest]

4.2   Sensors and Actuators

The overall testbed is embedded with 51 sensors and actuators thru each among the six-stage water treatment process. These sensors and actuators not only record the process dynamics of the entire procedure, but also quantify the water's chemical properties like hardness, *pH* –levels, and conductivity.

4.3   Communication

Based on the number of steps designed for each stage, a set of sensors and actuators have been connected across the testbed to its respective PLCs. Ethernet/IP (EN/IP) is utilized as the control-level protocol which incorporates DeviceNet as the fieldbus [3]. CIP specification is adapted by the EN/IP protocol, which embeds the data recorded from the sensor/actuator in the packet transmitted to HMI. The intra-process communications among the PLCs are communicated using the fieldbus protocol by sending control message requests in level-0 and the data requested is transmitted over level-1 network. Sensor/Actuator data transmitted through packets is encoded in little-endian single-precision floating-point format (Fig. 2).

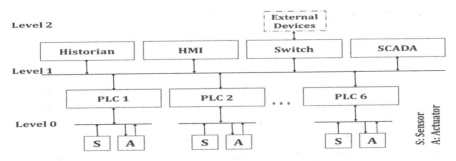

Fig. 2. Communication stack of the testbed [WatTest]

5 Assessment

This section introduces the formal characterization of the problem of detecting intrusions for which the attack model applies. The main objective of the designed attack model is to check for the path instances of an attack, given a process log of the traffic capture to validate with the pre-defined possible attack hypothesis. The SWaT dataset obtained from SUTD's iTrust lab consists traffic capture of 11 whole days. Out of the capture the testbed generated 7-days of normal operation based traffic and 4 days of traffic with various attack scenarios. The traffic capture embeds both the network data and the sensor/actuator readings. Model proposed in this work highlights several most predominant attack scenarios among the overall process due to space constraints, for which the graphs were modeled and defined theoretically.

5.1 Attack Strategy

Attack procedure carried out over the attack model $\mathcal{G}$, to comprehend τ parameter, which are targeted at θ, launched post exploring the set of hyperedges from ε where the testbed is in the initial state of that particular process where attack will be carried out S. Attack strategies studied for the modeled graph are mostly communication channel-attacks, which can be carried out at levels- 0 (I/O-network), 1 (PLC-network), and 2 (SCADA-network) through sensor/actuator value alteration.

Table 1. Attack list

Scenario No.	Attack type	Model	Intent	Start state	Final state	Process
1	MITM	Level 0 Spoofing	Change LIT101 sensor reading	945 mm	700 mm	LIT101
2	MITM	Level 0 Replay	Underflow Tank	945 mm	Bias = −2 mm	LIT101
3	Physical attack	Remove Cable	Blackout frozen HMI	945 mm	XXX	LIT101
4	MITM	Level 0 Stealthy	Underflow Tank	1016	Bias = 0.5 mm	LIT101
5	MITM	Level 0 Multi-Point	Disturb system state	Normal	Abnormal	LIT101, MV101, P101, FIT101
6	Injection	Level 1 Injection	Overflow	975 mm	700 mm	LIT101
7	Injection	Level 1 Spoofing	Change flow indicator	0 cm	1.6 cm and 2.6 cm	FIT101
8	Injection	Level 1 Multi-point	Disturb system state	Normal	P101 ON, LIT101 to 1000 mm	P101, LIT101
9	DoS	DDoS, PLC packet flooding	Delay Communication	LIT101 is 1050 mm	Delay PLC response	PLC1

Attack possibilities at level-0 are Man in the middle attack (MITM), replay, and covert exploitation of sensors or actuators. This is possible when an insider is physically present around the testbed and can directly connect to the I/O network at level 0. Attacker launched the attack by manipulating the EN/IP packets utilized for communication at that level.

At level-1, attacker tries to perform manipulation/replay by injecting control specific values for the process independent PLC or just the level-0 network.

IP-based attacks are possible if and only if the SCADA host machines are connected to the World Wide Web. Based on the levels, nine different attacks were attempted in discrete timestamps, and are summarized in Table 1 [2].

5.2 Procedure

Based on the identified vulnerabilities and the attacks tabulated above, a shell script was developed that initiates the open-source tools like *hping* to launch attacks over the testbed. Levels- 0 and 1 were mainly targeted to launch command injections, DDoS, and covert replay kind of attacks. This whole attack procedure was carried out intervening the network traffic of the above stated levels and transforming the sensor/actuator values above normal threshold.

5.3 Sample Traffic Pattern

The traffic is captured, monitored, and inferred for validating the modeled graph is carried out using tools like wireshark (for monitoring), python (for processing the packet), and tcpdump (for network sniffing). When the testbed is under operation, there will be a packet transmitted between the HMI and PLC.

Example 1: The below traffic gets transmitted when level indicator LIT301 from process 3 has to be invoked through a service code 0x4c from the received CIP message out of ENIP protocol:

. . .

0040 00 00 00 00 00 00 00 00 00 00 00 00 00 00 00 00
0050 00 00 00 00 02 00 a1 00 04 00 6e 56 f6 ff b1 00
0060 12 00 db a7 4c 06 91 0a 48 4d 49 5f 4c 49 54 33
0070 30 31 01 00

. . .

Each process-wise HMI-PLC communications generate a huge traffic from which unusual traffic is identified. The following graphs are modeled for run-time reference from the identified un-usual traffic for identifying an intrusion.

5.4 Attacks and Their Graph Patterns

Attacks like Spoofing, Replay, Stealthy, etc. have been deployed across the testbed. Due to space constraints, graphs for attack leading to "underflow" situation have been demonstrated with captured traffic and subtree hypergraph.

- **Stealthy attack:** This experiment was carried out over the level indicator LIT101 of process-1 through the communication channel of level-0 where the key intent is to reduce the level bias down to -0.5 mm. This leads to the tank underflow situation, further leading to pump damage in the testbed. The attack gets identified as the level indicator is embedded as graph vertex V_i in the attack model $\mathcal{G}$, where the node is constrained with a threshold τ. Values less than/greater than this threshold for more than t time instances will be reported to the IDS (Fig. 3).

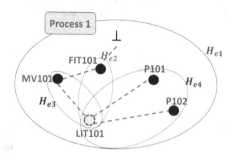

Fig. 3. Hypergraph (HG) representation of Process-1 among 6-stages with H_{e4} as a subtree-HG

5.5 Subtree Reduction

From the graph G with hyperedges H_e threshold fixed for the above scenario will be $v_{LIT101} \leftarrow \tau$. This will be identified and alarmed by reducing the whole graph to subtrees [13], since:

- $\exists Tree$ with vertices $LIT101(root), P101(leaf), P102(leaf)$, such that hyperedge H_{e4} deduces a subtree from the overall graph. The parameters of the subtree are passed to the partial function $\mathbb{T}$ (from the hypergraph model) that will be compared with the incoming live traffic for identifying the attack induced traffic (if any).

5.6 Live Traffic Representation (STrie)

Let $X = \{x_1 \ldots x_n\}$ be the traffic over the process Σ of the testbed. $X = ixj$ be the instance where i and j be the sub-strings of X. From the incoming traffic $X = \{x_i \ldots x_n\}$, $1 \leq i \leq n+1$ represents the suffix of X; $X_{n+1} = \varepsilon$ will represent the empty suffix. Model $STrie(X) = (\mathcal{G} \cup \{\perp\}, root, S_i, f, S_j)$ sequences the incoming traffic into trie based augmented DFA. This transition graph represents $\sigma(X)$ of the traffic to which the suffix function S_j and auxiliary state $\perp$ can be augmented. For a given traffic $X, \{X_i | 1 \leq i \leq n+1\}$ will be inferred as the suffix-links.given traffic $X, \{X_i | 1 \leq i \leq n+1\}$ will be inferred as the suffix-links.

5.7   Identifying Isomorphism

Definition 5: The subtree-hypergraph (modeled for each possible attack) and the transition graph plotted as STrie exhibits *Isomorphism* thereby identifying an attack pattern if, $\mathcal{G} : \theta \equiv root : STrie(X); \mathcal{G} : \tau \ll$ and $\gg \perp : STrie(X); \mathcal{G} : \mathcal{T}_m \equiv S_j : STrie(X)$.

Example 2: Given a traffic log stream $S = \mathbf{12\,00\,db\,a7\,4c\,06\,91\,0a\,48\,4d\,49\,5f\,4c}$ **49 54 33** to $STrie(S)$ the suffix tree keeps traversing for each hexadecimal byte arriving, and raises alert when the one of the suffix matches the aforementioned scenario (*underflow* situation); for which the attack model $\mathcal{G}$ has the patterns (Fig. 4):

$\theta = \mathbf{48\,4d\,49\,5f\,4c\,49\,54\,31\,30\,31}$ // Signature for identifying 'LIT101'
$\tau = \mathbf{00\,00\,00\,bf}$ ... // Pattern signifying ' $-$ 0.5' that initiates alert

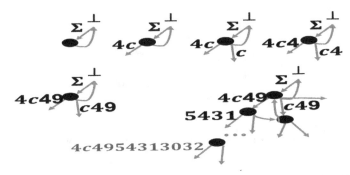

Fig. 4. Suffix-tree construction for the traffic [......**4c 49 54 31 30 31**...]

6   Discussions

Cyber-physical systems capture the sensor/actuator values in a CIP-data packet that are utilized as parameters in the proposed model. Readings that are parameterized in this graph-based model are considered elemental for identifying the trajectory taken by the attackers to reach the target. These trajectories can be exploited even by the attacker to explore the rest of the SCADA testbed. Considerations have to be made of tuning each of the model's parameters as fully-functional rather than being partially functional by just truncating the traffic to a binary source-target node set. The main reason for not considering the functional parameters for each tuple in the hypergraph model is that the attack patterns for known vulnerabilities were prioritized the most in this work than the memory consuming programmable functional arrays (since the traffic generated from the testbed consumes immense storage). The unified model presented in this work was conducted for theoretical analysis of identifying attacks for testbed specific CPS. If the tree representation of the incoming traffic is exploited by the attacker, then flooding the STrie model with traffic from various sources is possible. This in turn paves way for higher computational complexity for STrie model to traverse the whole log traffic and infer the hypergraph attack patterns. There still exist some limitations in running the models and inferring the encoded CPS data at runtime. Model designing and initiating the attack identification process is not presented in this work due to space constraints. Indeed, more unconsidered examples and attack scenarios may exist, out of which the most predominant one from the literature have been borrowed and demonstrated in this work through theoretically defined graph models.

Acknowledgements. This work was supported by The Ministry of Electronics and Information Technology (MeitY), India (AAA-22/7/2018-CSRD-MeitY).

References

1. Chen, Y.C., Gieseking, T., Campbell, D., Mooney, V., Grijalva, S.: A hybrid attack model for cyber-physical security assessment in electricity grid. In: 2019 IEEE Texas Power and Energy Conference (TPEC), pp. 1–6. IEEE, February 2019
2. Shrivastava, S., Adepu, S., Mathur, A.: Design and assessment of an orthogonal defense mechanism for a water treatment facility. Robot. Auton. Syst. **101**, 114–125 (2018)
3. Mathur, A.P., Tippenhauer, N.O.: SWaT: a water treatment testbed for research and training on ICS security. In: 2016 International Workshop on Cyber-Physical Systems for Smart Water Networks (CySWater), pp. 31–36. IEEE, April 2016
4. Adepu, S., Mathur, A.: Distributed detection of single-stage multipoint cyber attacks in a water treatment plant. In: Proceedings of the 11th ACM on Asia Conference on Computer and Communications Security, pp. 449–460. ACM, May 2016
5. Adepu, S., Mathur, A.: Generalized attacker and attack models for cyber physical systems. In: 2016 IEEE 40th Annual Computer Software and Applications Conference (COMPSAC), vol. 1, pp. 283–292. IEEE, June 2016
6. Adepu, S., Mathur, A.: Using process invariants to detect cyber attacks on a water treatment system. In: Hoepman, J.-H., Katzenbeisser, S. (eds.) SEC 2016. IFIP AICT, vol. 471, pp. 91–104. Springer, Cham (2016). https://doi.org/10.1007/978-3-319-33630-5_7
7. Berge, C.: Hypergraphs: Combinatorics of Finite Sets, vol. 45. Elsevier, Amsterdam (1984)
8. Vigna, G.: A topological characterization of TCP/IP security. In: Araki, K., Gnesi, S., Mandrioli, D. (eds.) FME 2003. LNCS, vol. 2805, pp. 914–939. Springer, Heidelberg (2003). https://doi.org/10.1007/978-3-540-45236-2_49
9. Vigna, G., Kemmerer, R.A.: NetSTAT: a network-based intrusion detection approach. In: Proceedings 14th Annual Computer Security Applications Conference (Cat. No. 98EX217), pp. 25–34. IEEE, December 1998
10. Morin, B., Mé, L., Debar, H., Ducassé, M.: M2D2: a formal data model for IDS alert correlation. In: Wespi, A., Vigna, G., Deri, L. (eds.) RAID 2002. LNCS, vol. 2516, pp. 115–137. Springer, Heidelberg (2002). https://doi.org/10.1007/3-540-36084-0_7
11. Baiardi, F., Suin, S., Telmon, C., Pioli, M.: Assessing the risk of an information infrastructure through security dependencies. In: Lopez, J. (ed.) CRITIS 2006. LNCS, vol. 4347, pp. 42–54. Springer, Heidelberg (2006). https://doi.org/10.1007/11962977_4
12. Pieters, W.: ANKH: Information threat analysis with actor-network hypergraphs. University of Twente, Enschede, The Netherlands, Technical report, 71079 (2010)
13. Tuo, Q., Zhao, H., Hu, Q.: Hierarchical feature selection with subtree based graph regularization. Knowl. Based Syst. **163**, 996–1008 (2019)

14. Albanese, M., Jajodia, S., Pugliese, A., Subrahmanian, V.S.: Scalable analysis of attack scenarios. In: Atluri, V., Diaz, C. (eds.) ESORICS 2011. LNCS, vol. 6879, pp. 416–433. Springer, Heidelberg (2011). https://doi.org/10.1007/978-3-642-23822-2_23
15. Albanese, M., Pugliese, A., Subrahmanian, V.S.: Fast activity detection: indexing for temporal stochastic automaton-based activity models. IEEE Trans. Knowl. Data Eng. 25(2), 360–373 (2011)
16. Ammann, P., Wijesekera, D., Kaushik, S.: Scalable, graph-based network vulnerability analysis. In: Proceedings of the 9th ACM Conference on Computer and Communications Security, pp. 217–224. ACM, November 2002
17. Chen, Y., Boehm, B., Sheppard, L.: Value driven security threat modeling based on attack path analysis. In: 2007 40th Annual Hawaii International Conference on System Sciences (HICSS 2007), p. 280a. IEEE, January 2007

Computational CBGSA – SVM Model
for Network Based Intrusion Detection System

Tina Manghnani[1(✉)] and T. Thirumaran[2]

[1] Microsoft Corporation, Bangalore, India
tinaem14@gmail.com
[2] Infoview Technologies Pvt. Ltd., Chennai, India
thirum110@gmail.com

Abstract. The accelerated growth and use of internet-based applications drive the research community towards the development of an appropriate IDS that solely focuses on safeguarding the computer networks from attacks and intrusions by hybridizing various machine learning and statistical intelligent techniques. On considering the open research challenge of designing a robust IDS, this paper proposes an improved Support Vector Machine (SVM) hybridized with Crossover based Binary Gravitational Search Algorithm (CBGSA) for parameter optimization and feature selection. Moreover, the hindrance of local maxima is neglected by introducing the crossover operator during the computation. To illustrate the efficiency of the solution proposed in this paper, CBGSA-SVM has been validated using NSL KDD dataset with the scenarios as follows (i) Training SVM with all the features, and (ii) Training SVM with the optimal feature subset and parameters derived from the CBGSA in terms of detection rate and false alarm rate.

Keywords: Support Vector Machine · Crossover based Binary Gravitational Search Algorithm · Intrusion Detection System

1 Introduction

The growth in internet applications and communication technology over the years has led to the emergence of a dynamic information society. The confidentiality, privacy, integrity and availability of the critical information is compromised when an unauthorized entity attempts to trespass the security mechanisms of the network. According to Accenture's global survey, security breaches have leveled up by 67% in the past five years [1]. It was in 2014, that the DOS attack on American Yahoo causing the halt of its server drew the focus on the acute call for better immunity against malicious attacks like spyware, viruses, Trojan horses, worms etc. in the network traffic [2]. The advancement of the security attacks is such that, it now a matter of *when*, and *not if* a security breach occurs.

Traditional security techniques like security policies, data encryption, firewall, authentication, etc. were proven to be too immature against the advanced and sophisticated nature of new attacks.

© Springer Nature Singapore Pte Ltd. 2019
V. S. Shankar Sriram et al. (Eds.): ATIS 2019, CCIS 1116, pp. 185–191, 2019.
https://doi.org/10.1007/978-981-15-0871-4_14

Variance in the network configurations lead to several IDS technologies primarily classified as anomaly and signature based intrusion detection system. Signature based intrusion detection system includes a d of familiar attacks and any suspicious packet bypassing the security mechanisms is compared with the known patterns. In this case, the unknown abnormalities go undetected and the need for an exclusive dataset make the system insufficient. Whereas in Anomaly based detection system, network administrators use machine learning techniques to determine the normal user behavior which is used as a baseline to differentiate the abnormalities.

Conventional mechanisms such as firewall, antivirus etc. have proved to be an insufficient mechanisms for the emerging cyber-attacks. Intrusion Detection System acts as an additional layer of defense by monitoring the incoming packets to safeguard the system from intruders. The deployment of an efficient IDS in a dynamic environment remains a major area of research. In the recent decades, the design of a robust and an intelligent IDS has been carried out through the integration of several machine learning and statistical techniques such as Neural Networks (NM), K-Nearest Neighbor (KNN), Decision Tree (DT), Bayesian Network (BN), Support Vector Machines (SVM) etc. in an attempt to enhance the intrusion detection rate and minimize false alarm rate. Among these, Support Vector Machine is more operational and yield high accuracy rate since they completely depend on mathematical functions besides providing a multi-label class classification, structural risk minimization and out-of sample generalization. However, few drawbacks such as high algorithmic complexity, curse of dimensionality, choice of the kernel, extensive memory requirement, parameter optimization etc. hinder its performance. To overcome these limitations, it has been hybridized with various meta- heuristic techniques namely Ant Colony Optimization, Particle Swarm Optimization (PSO), Fruit Fly Optimization (FFO), Binary Gravitational Search Algorithm (BGSA), Genetic Algorithm (GA) etc. as listed in Table 1. However, due to high dimensional and massive nature of network traffic, these optimization techniques may have a chance of being trapped at local optima. In order to overcome this issue, we propose cross-over based BGSA (CBGSA) for improving the performance of SVM in IDS. The experimental results are validated on the benchmark NSL-KDD data set and the performance of CBGSA was evaluated in terms of detection rate and false alarm rate.

Table 1. Related works

Authors	Methodology	Application
Peng Chen et al. [4]	Double-chains-quantumgenetic-algorithm	Analogue circuit diagnosis
M. Malvoni et al. [5]	Hybrid PCA–LSSVM	Photovoltaic forecast
Liming Shen et al. [6]	Fruit Fly Optimization	Classification of Medical Data
Cheng-Lung-Huang [7]	Genetic Algorithm	Generic
XiaoLi Zhang et al. [8]	Ant Colony Algorithm	Intelligent Fault Diagnosis of Rotating Machinery
F. Segovia et al. [9]	Partial Least Squares	Early diagnosis of Alzheimer's disease
Xiaohui Yuan et al. [10]	Gravitational Search Algorithm	Short-term wind power prediction

2   CBGSA – SVM Proposed Methodology

This section of the paper talks about the working of the proposed CBGSA-SVM for the design of an effective IDS (Fig. 1). The procedural flow of the proposed approach is mentioned below.

2.1   Initial Population Generation

As the proposed algorithm operates over n dimensional binary search space, the position of each objects were generated randomly. Each generated positions were divided into three parts which represents feature subsets, cc & $\gamma\gamma$ respectively. The binary string corresponding to kernel parameters were converted into equivalent floating point values using the following equation. The detailed explanation of population generation can be found in [3].

$$f_{B2F} = Min + \frac{Max - Min}{2^S - 1} * Dec \tag{1}$$

$$f_{CBGSA-SVM} = W_A[D_R] + W_B[1 - FA_R] \tag{2}$$

Where FA_R and D_R denotes false alarm rate and detection rate respectively and their corresponding weights are represented as W_B & W_A. S denotes the length of binary string and Dec denotes the decimal value representation of the Binary string.

2.2   SVM Train and Test

The training and testing data were generated from the NSL-KDD dataset in the ratio of 80:20 using random sampling without replacement. Employing the feature subsets obtained from step 1 along with the kernel parameters, the Support Vector Machine is trained and tested.

2.3   Fitness Function

To gauge the performance and efficiency of Intrusion Detection System, the proposed work is evaluated with a weighted fitness function. The fitness function is computed as follows,

$$ff_{CCBBCCSSCC-SSSSMM} = WW_{CC}[DD_{RR}] + WW_{BB}[1 - FFCC_{RR}] \tag{3}$$

Where DD_{RR} & $FFCC_{RR}$ denotes the detection rate and false alarm rate respectively and their corresponding weights are represented as WW_{CC} & WW_{BB}.

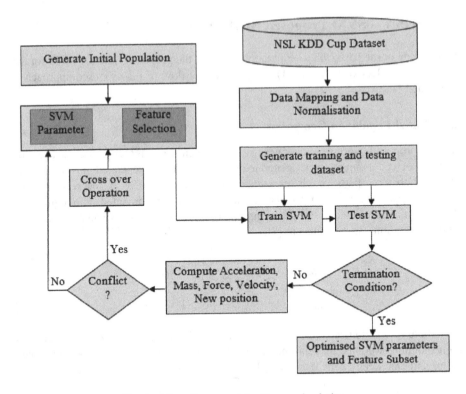

Fig. 1. Flow diagram of the Proposed solution

2.4 Termination Condition

Once the performance of each object is calculated as explained in Sect. 2.3 with the help of a fitness function, the termination condition was verified for obtaining optimal kernel parameters and feature subset.

2.5 Position Update

If the termination condition was not satisfied, then the position of each objects were updated using Eq. 14 in [11]. To avoid the convergence of the proposed solution at a local optima, we have introduced the cross over operator while updating the object's position if the global optimal solution remains same over few number of iterations.

3   Results and Discussions

3.1 Experimental Setup

Optimization of SVM by CBGSA was implemented using Python on a INTEL® Core™ i5 processor @ 2.40 GHz. We used the WEKA tool for carrying out the validation process.

3.2   Dataset Description

KDD Cup 1999 is a standard intrusion detection dataset consisting of 34 numeric and 7 alphanumeric features. The classification of every connection to a network into normal or attack is done by examining these features. The features can be grouped as content, traffic and basic features [4].

3.3   Data Pre-processing

NSL-KDD dataset uses numerical encoding to convert the features from string to numerical values. The corresponding numerical values for all the features have been listed in the table. Consequently, each numerical value is normalized into a value ranging between 0 and 1. Equation 4 below depicts how the normalization is performed.

$$X_{i[0\ to\ 1]} = \frac{x_i - x_{minima}}{x_{maxima} - x_{minima}} \qquad (4)$$

Where x_i represents each data point i, x_{minima} and x_{maxima} is the minimal and maximal of all the data points respectively and $X_i[0\ to\ 1]$ depicts the data point normalized between 0 and 1. This set of data is now further used in the evaluation of the efficiency of the proposed algorithm.

3.4   Results

The proposed solution was applied on the benchmark NSL-KDD dataset considering 80% of the training samples. The evaluation of the effectiveness of this IDS was performed based on the performance metrics such as false alarm rate and detection rate. Furthermore, the experimental results of various other optimization techniques were compared under two scenarios, (i) Taking all features under consideration (Fig. 2) (ii) Considering an optimal feature subset (Fig. 3).

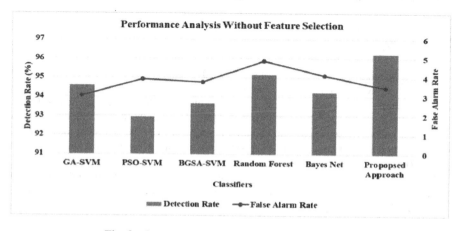

Fig. 2. Comparison Chart without Feature Selection

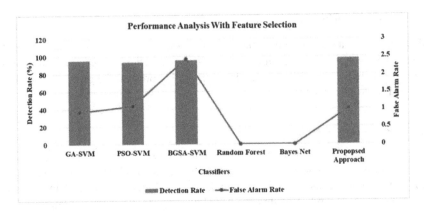

Fig. 3. Comparison Chart with Feature Selection

As depicted by the above comparison charts, the performance of the proposed approach outperforms the modern techniques with respect to the performance metrics of detection rate and false alarm rate.

4 Conclusion

This paper puts forward an IDS which incorporates the Binary Gravitational Search Algorithm for the optimization of the SVM kernel parameters and to obtain a optimal feature subset. The novelty in the proposed methodology is the crossover property which prevents the algorithm from getting trap at a local maxima. The NSL – KDD, a standard Intrusion dataset has been used in the validation of the proposed methodology. The results of this methodology outperform the prevalent machine learning based IDS methodologies in terms of the performance metrics. This methodology was found to be scalable and adaptive even for large datasets. The complexity of the proposed work can be further improved using MapReduce implementation.

References

1. 80 Eye-Opening Cyber Security Statistics for 2019. https://www.thesslstore.com/blog/80-eye-opening-cyber-security-statisticsfor-2019/
2. Yahoo attack exposes web weakness. http://news.bbc.co.uk/2/hi/science/nature/635444.stm
3. Gauthama Raman, M.R., Somu, N., Kirthivasan, K., Liscano, R., Shankar Sriram, V.S.: An efficient intrusion detection system based on hypergraph - Genetic algorithm for parameter optimization and feature selection in support vector machine. Knowl. Based Syst. **134**, 1–12 (2017)
4. Chen, P., Yuan, L., He, Y., Luo, S.: An improved SVM classifier based on double chains quantum genetic algorithm and its application in analogue circuit diagnosis. Neurocomputing **211**(26), 202–211 (2016)

5. Malvoni, M., Congedo, P.M., De Giorgi, M.G.: Photovoltaic forecast based on hybrid PCA–LSSVM using dimensionality reducted data. Neurocomputing **211**(26), 72–83 (2016)
6. Shen, L., et al.: Evolving support vector machines using fruit fly optimization for medical data classification. Knowl. Based Syst. **96**, 61–75 (2016)
7. Huang, C.L., Wang, C.J.: A GA-based feature selection and parameters optimization for support vector machines. Expert Syst. Appl. **31**(2), 231–240 (2006)
8. Zhang, X.L., Chen, W., Wang, B.J., Chen, X.F.: Intelligent fault diagnosis of rotating machinery using support vector machine with ant colony algorithm for synchronous feature selection and parameter optimization. Neurocomputing **167**, 260–279 (2015)
9. Segovia, F., Górriz, J.M., Ramírez, J., Salas-González, D., Álvarez, I.: Early diagnosis of Alzheimer's disease based on partial least squares and support vector machine. Expert Syst. Appl. **40**(2), 677–683 (2013)
10. Yuan, X., Chen, C., Yuan, Y., Huang, Y., Tan, Q.: Short-term wind power prediction based on LSSVM – GSA model. Energy Convers. Manag. **101**, 393–401 (2015)
11. Rashedi, E., Nezamabadi-Pour, H., Saryazdi, S.: BGSA: binary gravitational search algorithm. Nat. Comput. **9**(3), 727–745 (2010)

Attention-Based LSTM for Insider Threat Detection

Fangfang Yuan[1,2], Yanmin Shang[1], Yanbing Liu[1(✉)], Yanan Cao[1], and Jianlong Tan[1]

[1] Institute of Information Engineering, Chinese Academy of Sciences, Beijing, China
{yuanfangfang,shangyanmin,liuyanbing,caoyanan,tanjianlong}@iie.ac.cn
[2] School of Cyber Security, University of Chinese Academy of Sciences, Beijing, China

Abstract. Insider threat is an important cyber security issue for businesses and organizations. Existing insider threat detection methods can be roughly divided into two categories, statistical features based detection methods and action sequence based detection methods. The first kind of method aggregates all actions that a user has performed over one day and uses these aggregated features to find insider threat. This kind of coarse-grained analytics of user behavior may miss anomalous behavior happening within that day. The second kind of method overcomes the coarser-grained problem and uses fine-grained detection to identify insider threat through user actions. However, the second kind of method considers all user operations to be equally important, without highlighting malicious user actions. To solve this problem, we present an attention-based Long Short-Term Memory (LSTM) model to detect insider threat. In our model, we apply the LSTM to capture the sequential information of user action sequence and employ an attention layer that can learn which user actions contribute more to insider threat detection. Extensive studies are conducted on the public dataset of insider threat. Our results demonstrate that the proposed model outperforms other deep learning models and can successfully identify insider threat.

Keywords: Insider threat detection · Recurrent Neural Network · Anomaly detection · Network security

1 Introduction

Insider threat is one of the most serious challenges in cyber security. Malicious insiders who are trusted by organizations, such as an employee advertently abuse their authorized access to organizational information systems and commit attacks, often causing privacy, credibility and reputation issues [1]. How to detect insider threat early has become a research hotspot in cyber security [2].

However, insider threat detection faces several serious challenges. Firstly, system logs are usually used for insider threat detection. How to identify insider threats from a massive amount of system logs is a crucial issue. Secondly, insider

© Springer Nature Singapore Pte Ltd. 2019
V. S. Shankar Sriram et al. (Eds.): ATIS 2019, CCIS 1116, pp. 192–201, 2019.
https://doi.org/10.1007/978-981-15-0871-4_15

threat behavior is widely varying, such as a disgruntled employee deleting data from the hard disk or database, using his privileged access to take sensitive data for financial gain, etc. The threat behavior manifests in various forms, thus increasing the difficulty of insider threat detection. Finally, insider's anomalous behavior usually consists of several subtle actions scattered in a lot of users' normal behavior.

In order to detect insider threat, it is necessary to build the profiles representing normal behaviour and recognize abnormal behavior that deviates from the user's normal behavior profiles. Researchers have proposed many approaches to detect and identify insider's anomalous behavior. Tuor et al. [3] use the user's aggregated action features in one day for insider threat detection. However, some anomalous behavior that happened within a day cannot be detected by using this method. For example, an employee logs in his office computer after hours and copys some sensitive data to the removable disk. In order to overcome the coarser-grained problem, Yuan et al. [4] presented the LSTM-CNN framework to detect insider threat. They used the LSTM to capture the temporal features of user behavior from user's action sequences and used the Convolutional Neural Network (CNN) to identify user's abnormal behavior. However, the framework considers all user operations to be equally important, without highlighting malicious user actions.

In this paper, we propose an attention-based LSTM to detect insider threat. Firstly, we apply the LSTM to capture the sequential information of user behavior as far as possible. Secondly, we employ an attention layer that can automatically judge which user actions have more contributions to the classification decision. In summary, the main contributions of the paper are as follows:

(1) We use the LSTM to capture the sequential information of user action sequences.
(2) We apply the attention layer to let the model to pay more or less attention to individual user action when constructing the representation of the user behavior.
(3) We conduct experiments on the CERT insider threat dataset and the results demonstrate that our model outperforms other deep learning models and can successfully identify insider threat.

The rest of this paper is organized as follows. In Sect. 2, we review the related research in the field of insider threat detection. In Sect. 3, we describe our attention-based proposal in detail. We provide the experimental results in Sect. 4. In Sect. 5, We conclude the paper.

2   Related Work

The topic of insider threat has recently received increasing attention both in academic and industry fields. There has been many studies on insider threat detection.

Insider threat detection based on machine learning is the main direction of current studies. Schonlau et al. [5] built the Schonlau dataset (SEA dataset) based on UNIX user truncated commands and compared six different insider threat detection methods. Maxion et al. [6,7] used the same dataset and showed better performance by using the Naive Bayes classifier to detect insider threat. Oka et al. [8] employed the Eigen Co-occurrence Matrix (ECM) approach for insider threat detection on the SEA dataset. Szymanski and Zhang [9] used One-Class Support Vector Machine (OC-SVM) to detect insider threat. However, their results are not good enough. More recently, Rashid et al. [10] used the Hidden Markov model (HMM) to build each user's normal behavior profile and identify the deviations that may potentially indicate insider threats. The advantage of their model is learning from the sequential data. However, the increasing number of states leads to the increasing computational cost of the HMM model, while the number of the states would highly impact the effectiveness of this method.

Recently, the rapid development of deep neural networks has brought new inspiration to insider threat detection. Veeramachaneni et al. [11] used time-aggregated statistics as features and applied an Autoencoder neural network to insider threat detection. However, they did not explicitly model individual user behavior over time. Lu and Wong [12] used the LSTM to build user's behavior patterns and find anomalous events. However, the LSTM is a biased model, where later user actions are more dominant than earlier user actions. Hence, using the recurrent model to directly classify user's behavior is not efficient. Tuor et al. [3] proposed a deep learning based insider threat detection system. They trained the LSTM models to recognize each user's characteristic and classified user behavior as anomalous or normal. While they aggregated features by one day for each user, this has the potential to miss anomalous behavior happening within a single day. To solve the coarser-grained problem, Yuan et al. [4] presented the LSTM-CNN framework to detect insider threat. However, they failed to highlight the user actions that contribute more to detect insider threat. Instead, our model combines the LSTM and the attention layer. Therefore, our model can identity anomalous behavior happening within a single day and provides insight into which user actions contribute more to insider threat detection.

3   Attention-Based LSTM Model

The aim of our work is to find the user's anomalous behavior which is an indicator of insider threat. The individual operation of a user represents a user action; a user action sequence that the user performs in one day represents user behavior. We firstly feed a user action sequence to the LSTM layer and obtain the abstract feature vectors. Secondly, the abstract feature vectors are fed into the attention layer. Finally, we obtain the representation of user behavior and feed it to the output layer to classify the user behavior as anomalous or normal.

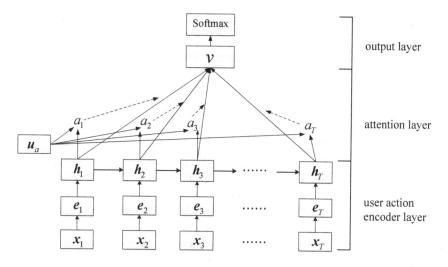

Fig. 1. Structure of attention-based LSTM

Figure 1 shows the structure of the attention-based LSTM model. It contains three layers: a user action encoder layer, an attention layer and an output layer. The different components of the structure are described in detail as follows.

3.1   LSTM-Based Sequence Encoder

Recurrent Neural Network (RNN) extends the conventional feed-forward neural network. Unfortunately, Bengio et al. [13] found that training the RNN to capture long-term dependencies is a difficult task because the vanishing gradient problem or the exploding gradient problem may occur during the training process. In order to address this problem, Hochreiter and Schmidhuber [14] developed the Long Short-Term Memory (LSTM) nerual network. Unlike to the RNN, the LSTM maintains a memory cell that is capable of storing information. The LSTM has three gates which are used to modulate the flow of information inside the unit. The input gate decides how much of the new information should be added to the memory cell. The forget gate modulates how much of the previous cell state should be forgotten. The output gate decides which part of the memory should be seen.

The updation of the LSTM is implemented as follows:

$$i_t = \sigma(\boldsymbol{W}_i \boldsymbol{e}_t + \boldsymbol{U}_i \boldsymbol{h}_{t-1} + \boldsymbol{b}_i) \tag{1}$$

$$\boldsymbol{f}_t = \sigma(\boldsymbol{W}_f \boldsymbol{e}_t + \boldsymbol{U}_f \boldsymbol{h}_{t-1} + \boldsymbol{b}_f) \tag{2}$$

$$\boldsymbol{o}_t = \sigma(\boldsymbol{W}_o \boldsymbol{e}_t + \boldsymbol{U}_o \boldsymbol{h}_{t-1} + \boldsymbol{b}_o) \tag{3}$$

$$\boldsymbol{g}_t = \tanh(\boldsymbol{W}_g \boldsymbol{e}_t + \boldsymbol{U}_g \boldsymbol{h}_{t-1} + \boldsymbol{b}_g) \tag{4}$$

$$\boldsymbol{c}_t = \boldsymbol{f}_t \odot \boldsymbol{c}_{t-1} + i_t \odot \boldsymbol{g}_t \tag{5}$$

$$\boldsymbol{h}_t = \boldsymbol{o}_t \odot \tanh(\boldsymbol{c}_t) \tag{6}$$

where $\boldsymbol{W}_i$, $\boldsymbol{W}_f$, $\boldsymbol{W}_o$ are the weighted matrices and $\boldsymbol{b}_i$, $\boldsymbol{b}_f$, $\boldsymbol{b}_o$ are biases of the LSTM. These parameters are learned during training. σ denotes sigmoid function. $\odot$ is an element-wise multiplication. $\boldsymbol{i}_t$, $\boldsymbol{f}_t$, $\boldsymbol{o}_t$ represent the input gate, the forget gate and the output gate respectively. $\boldsymbol{e}_t$ is the sequence vector at time t, representing the user action embedding vector $\boldsymbol{x}_t$ in Fig. 1. The hidden state is $\boldsymbol{h}_t$.

3.2   Attention Layer

The standard LSTM cannot pick out which is the important part for insider threat detection. To solve the problem, we design that the LSTM is followed by an attention layer that can capture the important user actions.

As Fig. 1 shows, given the user $u_k (k \in [0, K])$, his action sequence on the j-th day can be represented as $S_{u_k} = [\boldsymbol{x}_1, \boldsymbol{x}_2, \ldots, \boldsymbol{x}_T]$, where $\boldsymbol{x}_t (1 \le t \le T)$ denotes the user action at time instance t. Firstly, the user action is embedded into a vector representation $\boldsymbol{e}_t = \boldsymbol{W}_e \boldsymbol{x}_t$, where $\boldsymbol{W}_e$ is the embedding matrix. Next, a single layer LSTM takes the embedded vector $\boldsymbol{e}_t$ as input, and outputs the hidden status $\boldsymbol{h}_t$.

$$\boldsymbol{e}_t = \boldsymbol{W}_e \boldsymbol{x}_t, t \in [1, T] \tag{7}$$

$$\boldsymbol{h}_t = LSTM(\boldsymbol{e}_t), t \in [1, T] \tag{8}$$

Not all user actions contribute equally to detect insider threat. Hence, we employ attention mechanism to self-adaptively pick out important user actions that play key roles in insider threat detection. Specifically,

$$\boldsymbol{u}_t = \tanh(\boldsymbol{W}_a \boldsymbol{h}_t + \boldsymbol{b}_a) \tag{9}$$

$$\alpha_t = \frac{\exp(\boldsymbol{u}_t^T \boldsymbol{u}_a)}{\sum_t \exp(\boldsymbol{u}_t^T \boldsymbol{u}_a)} \tag{10}$$

$$\boldsymbol{v} = \sum_t \alpha_t \boldsymbol{h}_t \tag{11}$$

where $\boldsymbol{W}_a$ is the weighted matrix and $\boldsymbol{b}_a$ is the bias. $\boldsymbol{u}_a$ is a context vector, which is randomly initialized and jointly learned during training.

That is, a one-layer neural network takes the user action hidden status $\boldsymbol{h}_t$ as input and outputs $\boldsymbol{u}_t$ which is the hidden representation of $\boldsymbol{h}_t$. Next, the importance of each user action is measured by computing the similarity of $\boldsymbol{u}_t$ with the context vector $\boldsymbol{u}_a$. Then, we use the softmax function to obtain the normalized importance weights. At last, we compute the user behavior vector $\boldsymbol{v}$ as a weighted sum of the user action hidden status $\boldsymbol{h}_t$. Hence, the user behavior vector $\boldsymbol{v}$ summarizes all the information of the user action sequence.

3.3   Output Layer

The last part of our model is an output layer. For insider threat detection, the user behavior vector $\boldsymbol{v}$ is the whole representation of the user action sequence.

Table 1. Selected user action set

Activities	Actions	The number of actions
Logon activity	Logon	4
	Logoff	4
File activity	Copy exe file	4
	Copy doc file	4
	Copy pdf file	4
	Copy txt file	4
	Copy jpg file	4
	Copy zip file	4
HTTP activity	Visit neutral website	4
	Visit hacktivist website	4
	Visit cloudStorage website	4
	Visit jobHunting website	4
Email activity	Internal email	4
	External email	4
Device activity	Connect	4
	Disconnect	4

The softmax classifier takes the $\boldsymbol{v}$ vector as input,

$$p(\hat{y} = k|\boldsymbol{v}) = \frac{\exp(\boldsymbol{W}_k^T \boldsymbol{v} + \boldsymbol{b}_k)}{\sum_{k'=1}^{K} \exp(\boldsymbol{W}_{k'}^T \boldsymbol{v} + \boldsymbol{b}_{k'})} \tag{12}$$

where $\hat{y}$ is the predicted label of the user action sequence, the number of classes is K, $\boldsymbol{W}_k$ and $\boldsymbol{b}_k$ are the parameters of the softmax function for the k-th class. In order to train our model, we use the standard cross-entropy as training loss,

$$L = -\frac{1}{M} \sum_{i=1}^{M} y_i * log(p(\hat{y}_i)) \tag{13}$$

where y_i is the true label of the i-th user action sequence, M is the number of training user action sequences.

4   Experiments

We evaluate the proposed model on the publicly available CMU-CERT Insider Threat [15]. The model is implemented using Keras [16] with Theano [17] backend. Firstly, we introduce the dataset and comparison of methods. Next, we describe the experiment setup. Finally, we compare the performances of different models.

4.1 Dataset

Since the number of insider threat instances in CERT Insider Threat Dataset version r4.2 is larger than other versions of datasets, we conduct experiments on the version r4.2. The dataset consists of five different types of system logs. We can parse the system logs and obtain detailed user activity information. Furthermore, we find that the user behavior of normal users is different from the user behavior of abnormal users during after hours. Compared with normal users, some abnormal users who did not previously work after hours begin logging on their office computers after hours and copying sensitive data to the removable disk. Therefore, we divide a single day into 2 time segments: working hours (8am–5pm) and after hours (5pm–8am). In addition, we regard user's action performed on an assigned PC and user's action performed on an unassigned PC as two different user actions. Finally, we obtain a total of 64 user actions over five categories. Take an user action for example, a user sends an external email working hours on an unassigned computer. Table 1 shows the full set of user actions.

In our experiments, we use the activity record data of 100 users and build 100 users' specific profiles. After data preprocessing, we obtain a total of 25,274 action sequences among which only 954 action sequences represent the anomalous activities. The entire dataset is splitted into two subsets: 80% of the dataset for training and 20% of the dataset for testing.

4.2 Baselines

We compare our method with several deep learning models. Specifically, we test the RNN, LSTM and GRU model to find out which performs better when constructing the feature vectors of user behavior for each user. In addition, We perform experiments to assess the effectiveness of the attention mechanism. Therefore, we design several deep learning models as baseline methods.

RNN. This model consists of a single layer RNN network and a softmax layer. The RNN layer takes a user action sequence as input and feeds the last hidden state to the softmax layer for insider threat detection.

RNN with attention (RNN-Att). This model combines the basic RNN network with an attention mechanism and is used to compared with the RNN. We use this model to asess the effectiveness of the attention mechanism in the RNN.

GRU. This model consists of a single layer GRU network and a softmax layer. The GRU layer takes a user action sequence as input and feeds the last hidden state to the softmax layer for insider threat detection.

GRU with attention (GRU-Att). This model combines the basic GRU network with an attention mechanism and is used to compared with the GRU. We use this model to asess the effectiveness of the attention mechanism in the GRU.

LSTM. This model consists of a single layer LSTM network and a softmax layer. The LSTM layer takes a user action sequence as input and feeds the last hidden state to the softmax layer for insider threat detection.

Table 2. Parameters of the RNN, LSTM, GRU and Softmax

Models	Input	Hidden layer
RNN	Embedding dimension: 128	Units size: 64(128, 256) Dropout: 0.5 Activate function: tanh
LSTM	Embedding dimension: 128	Units size: 64(128, 256) Dropout: 0.5 Activate function: tanh The offset of forget gate: True
GRU	Embedding dimension: 128	Units size: 64(128, 256) Dropout: 0.5 Activate function: tanh
Softmax	Input dimension: 128	No

4.3 Experiment Setup

The proposed method is an end-to-end architecture. We hand-tuned the hyper-parameters of the RNN, LSTM and GRU by sweeping over a range of possible values. We tune the number of the batch size (between 5 and 30) and the epoch (between 10 and 30). The parameters of the RNN, LSTM, GRU and Softmax are shown in Table 2. The optimizer is the RMSprop optimizer and the loss function is the cross entropy loss. We set the learning rate to be 0.001.

4.4 Results

Figure 2 shows the experimental results on the CERT insider threat dataset version r4.2. As the dataset is imbalanced, we use the AUC-ROC (Area Under Curve - Receiver Operating Characteristics) curve as the evaluation metric. We analyze these results in detail in the following.

We first evaluate the ROC curves of different models under the same parameter settings. We fix the batch size to 30 samples, the epoch number to 20 and the units size to 128. Figure 2(a) shows the ROC curves when the RNN model, the LSTM model and the GRU model, respectively, are used for insider threat detection. Figure 2(b) shows the ROC curves when these models with attention mechanism, respectively, are used for insider threat detection. We can see that the performances of these models differ slightly when using the same parameter settings. The attention-based LSTM (LSTM-Att) is the best performing model and achieves an area under the ROC curve 0.9278.

We compare RNN with RNN-Att, GRU with GRU-Att, LSTM with LSTM-Att, finding that the addition of attention mechanism improves the performance for both the RNN and the LSTM. The attention mechanism improves the performance of the RNN more significantly because it can highlight the user actions

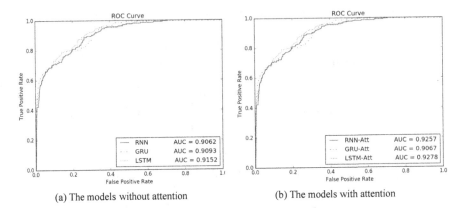

(a) The models without attention   (b) The models with attention

Fig. 2. ROC curves for different models

which are more likely to be malicious user actions. Note that the AUC of GRU-Att is close to that of GRU, we suspect that the GRU-Att will yield superior performance when applied to large-scale dataset with more complicated temporal patterns.

5 Conclusion

In order to achieve fine-grained analysis of user behavior and improve the detection rate of insider threat, we propose an attention-based LSTM for insider threat detection. Since the threat behavior manifests in different forms, we cannot explicitly define the anomalous behavior pattern of insiders. Instead, we build the user's normal behavior profiles and take the user's anomalous behavior as an indicator of insider threat. Our model captures sequential information of user action sequences with the LSTM and constructs the representation of user behavior using the attention mechanism. We evaluate our method on the public CMU-CERT Insider Threat dataset Version r4.2. The experimental results demonstrate that our model outperforms other baseline methods and can successfully identify insider threat.

Acknowledgement. This work was partly supported by the National Key Research and Development Program (Grant No. 2017YFC0820700), Strategic Priority Research Program of the Chinese Academy of Sciences under Grant No.XDC02030000, the National Natural Science Foundation of China under grant No. 61602466.

References

1. Costa, D.L., Albrethsen, M.J. Collins, M.L: Insider threat indicator ontology. Technical report, Carnegie-Mellon University, Pittsburgh, PA, United States (2016)
2. Azaria, A., Richardson, A., Kraus, S., Subrahmanian, V.S.: Behavioral analysis of insider threat: a survey and bootstrapped prediction in imbalanced data. IEEE Trans. Comput. Soc. Syst. **1**(2), 135–155 (2014)
3. Tuor, A., Kaplan, S., Hutchinson, B., Nichols, N., Robinson, S.: Deep learning for unsupervised insider threat detection in structured cybersecurity data streams. In: Workshops at the Thirty-First AAAI Conference on Artificial Intelligence (2017)
4. Yuan, F., Cao, Y., Shang, Y., Liu, Y., Tan, J., Fang, B.: Insider threat detection with deep neural network. In: Shi, Y., et al. (eds.) ICCS 2018. LNCS, vol. 10860, pp. 43–54. Springer, Cham (2018). https://doi.org/10.1007/978-3-319-93698-7_4
5. Schonlau, M., DuMouchel, W., Ju, W.-H., Karr, A.F., Theusan, M., Vardi, Y., et al.: Computer intrusion: detecting masquerades. Stat. Sci. **16**(1), 58–74 (2001)
6. Maxion, R.A., Townsend, T.N.: Masquerade detection using truncated command lines. In: Proceedings International Conference on Dependable Systems and Networks, pp. 219–228. IEEE (2002)
7. Maxion, R.A.: Masquerade detection using enriched command lines. In: Proceedings of 2003 International Conference on Dependable Systems and Networks, pp. 5–14. IEEE (2003)
8. Oka, M., Oyama, Y., Kato, K.: Eigen co-occurrence matrix method for masquerade detection. Publications of the Japan Society for Software Science and Technology (2004)
9. Szymanski, B.K., Zhang, Y.: Recursive data mining for masquerade detection and author identification. In: 2004 Proceedings from the Fifth Annual IEEE SMC Information Assurance Workshop, pp. 424–431. IEEE (2004)
10. Rashid, T., Agrafiotis, I., Nurse, J.R.C.: A new take on detecting insider threats: exploring the use of hidden markov models. In: Proceedings of the 8th ACM CCS International Workshop on Managing Insider Security Threats, pp. 47–56. ACM (2016)
11. Veeramachaneni, K., Arnaldo, I., Korrapati, V., Bassias, C., Li, K.: AI^2: training a big data machine to defend. In: 2016 IEEE 2nd International Conference on Big Data Security on Cloud (BigDataSecurity), IEEE International Conference on High Performance and Smart Computing (HPSC), and IEEE International Conference on Intelligent Data and Security (IDS), pp. 49–54. IEEE (2016)
12. Lu, J., Wong, R.K.: Insider threat detection with long short-term memory. In: Proceedings of the Australasian Computer Science Week Multiconference, p. 1. ACM (2019)
13. Bengio, Y., Simard, P., Frasconi, P., et al.: Learning long-term dependencies with gradient descent is difficult. IEEE Trans. Neural Netw. **5**(2), 157–166 (1994)
14. Hochreiter, S., Schmidhuber, J.: Long short-term memory. Neural Comput. **9**(8), 1735–1780 (1997)
15. Glasser, J., Lindauer, B.: Bridging the gap: a pragmatic approach to generating insider threat data. In: 2013 IEEE Security and Privacy Workshops, pp. 98–104. IEEE (2013)
16. Al-Rfou, R., et al.: Theano: a python framework for fast computation of mathematical expressions. arXiv preprint arXiv:1605.02688 (2016)
17. Chollet, F., et al.: Keras: The python deep learning library. Astrophysics Source Code Library (2018)

Cog-SDN: Mitigation Mechanism for Distributed Denial of Service Attacks in Software Defined Networks

P. Mohana Priya$^{(\boxtimes)}$ (ID) and K. R. Manjula (ID)

School of Computing, SASTRA Deemed University, Thanjavur 613 401, India
mohanapriya@it.sastra.edu, manjula@cse.sastra.edu

Abstract. Software Defined Network is a novel network paradigm that decouples forwarding devices from the controller. Distributed Denial of Service attack is the most common threat found in which an attacker floods request messages to the victim. These attacks saturate control plane and degrade the service for legitimate traffic flows. In this research work, Cognitive-Software Defined Network is proposed which uses an unsupervised Deep Belief Network algorithm to defend against attacks. Deep Belief Network self-learns the flow payload details and detects flooding attacks when the counter exceeds the threshold value. The proposed mitigation method is deployed in the SDN controller which monitors the incoming traffic flows and blocks the malicious hosts. The experimental results show that Cognitive Software Defined Network outperforms in terms of bandwidth consumption, installation of flow entries with attack detection time when compared with SLICOTS.

Keywords: Software Defined Networks · Cognition · Distributed Denial of Service Attack · Self-learning · Deep Belief Network

1 Introduction

Software Defined Networks (SDN) [1,2], is a promising solution to incorporate intelligent metrics during routing as the data and control planes are decoupled from each other. It provides a global view of the network topology in which the controller takes forwarding decisions for unknown requests of data plane switches. The control functions are fed as cognitive security policies from the control plane for the data plane switches to provide secure routing during resource consumption attacks. OpenFlow (OF) [3] the defacto standard of SDN, is an interface which implements network security policies to the controller via North-Bound Application Programming interface (NB-API).

As the core component of SDN is the control plane, these networks are highly subject to security attacks and the threat vector includes vulnerable switches [4], vulnerable controllers communications [5], compromised controllers [6] and lack in trust between the control and management plane. The more specific security attacks in SDN architecture includes unauthorized access [7], side channel attacks in data plane layer, Man-In-The-Middle (MITM) attack in the control-data plane layer, compromised applications

V. S. Shankar Sriram et al. (Eds.): ATIS 2019, CCIS 1116, pp. 202–215, 2019.
https://doi.org/10.1007/978-981-15-0871-4_16

in the application-control layer and Distributed Denial of Service (DDoS) attacks in data-control plane layer [8].

The separation of data and control planes in SDN leads a way to incorporate intelligence in the control plane layer. Conventional defense techniques use packet header fields and Intrusion Detection Systems (IDS) [9] to mitigate DDoS attacks which is highly obsolete. These mechanisms are highly reactive and fail to respond to the network conditions without intelligence (i.e.,) Self-learning capability. Some defense solutions use a supervised learning algorithm that is not suitable for an uncertain network environment. The above said research challenge motivates to mitigate DDoS attacks using an unsupervised learning algorithm. Most of the existing defense solutions use a static threshold value to identify attack traffic flows which result in the increase of False Positive Rates (FPR) during the process of attack identification.

In this paper, Cognitive-SDN (Cog-SDN) mitigation mechanism is proposed using an unsupervised Deep Belief Networks (DBN) algorithm [10] to detect and mitigate DDoS attacks in SDN. DBN algorithm is preferred as it handles massive traffic flows because of dimensionality reduction. In previous research work, Restricted Boltzmann Machine (RBM) algorithm is used where all the network traffic flows are incorporated in the single hidden layer and adding more than a layer based on the protocol nature is found impossible. As DBN is an unsupervised learning algorithm, it can detect zero-day attacks based on the knowledge base provided with traffic flow features. The programmable SDN overcomes security drawbacks with the context of flow payload details of legitimate traffic flows. Network traffic flow metrics include src IP address, dst IP address, src MAC address, dst MAC address, src port number, dst port number and proto type of the participating hosts. These are fed as security and routing app in the application plane of SDN. DBN self-learns the provided metrics and fixes threshold value "K" based on the number of participating hosts and the network conditions. The proposed mitigation mechanism also prevents flow table modification attacks based on the match; action rules of matched Media Access Control (MAC) addresses in OF tables.

Most of the existing research works on SDN uses both supervised and unsupervised ANN algorithms with static threshold value defined for the dynamic networks. Threshold value cannot be a static value, since the network environment is highly dynamic in nature. Dynamic threshold value is assigned automatically by SDN controller for a periodical time based on the amount of incoming network traffic flows generated by SDN switches.

The contribution of proposed mitigation mechanism is listed as follows:

- The proposed Cog-SDN mitigation mechanism is an initiative work to mitigate DDoS attacks in SDN using an unsupervised Deep Belief Network algorithm.
- The proposed mitigation mechanism outperforms SLICOTS with respect to attack detection time, attack mitigation time, bandwidth utilization of controller and an average number of installed flow rule entries in an open flow switch.
- The proposed mitigation mechanism self-learns flow payload details and traffic flow features to detect and mitigate DDoS attack traffic flows with an adaptive threshold value and the proposed Cog-SDN is tested both in centralized and distributed SDN controllers.

The paper is organized as follows. Section 2 presents the related works, Proposed Cog-SDN mitigation mechanism is given in Sect. 3. Section 4 discusses the experimental network. Section 5 details about results and their discussions and future research directions are concluded in Sect. 6.

2 Related Work

Cognitive SDN mitigation mechanism is essential to defend resource consumption attacks that lead in service degradation of SDN resources. Most of the existing defense solutions fail to incorporate machine learning algorithms. Few works include supervised Neural Network (NN) learning algorithm to defend these attacks which increase False Positive Rates (FPR) due to lack of traffic awareness. This section lists some of the defense solutions for mitigation of flooding attacks in SDN.

Wang et al. [11] proposed Flood guard, a protocol-independent defense framework that has two modules namely proactive flow rule analyzer and packet migration to prevent data-control plane saturation attack. Chin et al. [12] proposed a detection approach for Transmission Control Protocol-SYNchronization (TCP-SYN) flooding attacks based on inspecting selective packets on demand. The proposed approach has two key components namely monitors and correlators. Monitors continuously capture the network traffic with SYN traffic flows and correlator is hosted on the SDN controller which correlates the alert message and queries the Open Virtual Switch (OVS) flow table to fetch the details of IP address that follows deep packet inspection.

SPHINX [13] detects SYN flooding attacks with the rate of incoming PACKET-IN request messages to the controller, flow statistics to the parser and assimilator components. If the rate of incoming request packets greater than the threshold specified, it concludes those as attack traffic flows and raises a false alarm for legitimate flows.

Shin et al. [14] proposed AVANT-GUARD that acts as proxy, an added intelligence in SDN data plane switches for every incoming TCP traffic flows. It proxies the entire traffic flows and hence introduces buffer saturation attacks and so the flow tables of data plane switches needs to be updated.

LineSwitch [15] overcomes the limitations of AVANT-GUARD by preventing buffer saturation attacks in data plane switches and controllers. It uses SYN proxy techniques and probabilistic black-listing of IP addresses to prevent SYN flooding attacks. Wei et al. [16] proposed Flow Ranger, a buffer prioritizing algorithm deployed in SDN controller to defend against DDoS attacks. Trust metrics are used to evaluate the likelihood of incoming PACKET-IN request messages.

Wang et al. [17] proposed OF-GUARD, a light-weight defense framework that consist of migration and data plane cache as SDN controller application and data plane. Table miss packets are forwarded to the cache of OF switches which has proactive flow rules that classify attack packets from legitimate packets.

Nugraha et al. [18] combine SFlow and OpenFlow detection mechanism to mitigate SYN flooding attacks in SDN. SFlow agent uses sampling techniques that capture network traffic flows and detects SYN flooding attacks based on the defined threshold value. The detection methodology uses the cumulative sum of incoming packets from every switch and the controller blocks attack traffic flows whose threshold value is greater than the cumulative sum threshold.

Imran et al. [22] proposed various mitigation approaches based on three different classifications namely blocking, delaying and resource management. This research work also highlights the weakness of all mitigation methods and necessary reasons for decreased network efficiency and increase in cost parameter.

RBM based DDoS attack detection system [23] is used to detect the malicious network traffic flows in POX SDN controller using attributes of data and control planes namely energy consumption of switches, bandwidth utilization of controller and modification of flow table entries.

SDN based secure and agile framework for protecting smart applications (SEAL) [24] consist of three types of defense mechanisms along with filters namely proactive, active and passive to compute dynamic threshold value for the incoming network traffic flows in order to detect and mitigate network traffic flows. Surbi et al. [25] discusses a survey on challenges and solutions in design and implementation of SDN. The challenges are considered based on the network parameters like fault tolerance, elasticity and flexibility in deploying the network. Issues regarding the network performance metrics namely latency, delay and consistency is also considered.

3   Proposed COGNITIVE SDN (Cog-SDN)

Figure 1 shows the block diagram of proposed cognitive SDN mitigation mechanism which consists of 3 phases namely flow generation in data plane switches, flow analysis using open source SDN controllers and flow visualization is done through GENI public testbed desktop environment.

In Phase 1, legitimate and attack traffic flows are generated using data plane switches. As a follow-up, in Phase 2, the newly incoming network traffic flows are analyzed through cognitive flow management module that uses Deep Belief Network (DBN) algorithm to identify attack traffic flows based on the knowledge base gained from the context-aware application plane. The proposed security and routing applications are incorporated in the SDN application plane. The context-aware application plane has legitimate context about flow payload details to identify the attack traffic flows.

3.1   Flow Analysis

The process of proposed Cog-SDN and the routing process is carried out at two different levels as illustrated in Fig. 2. In Level 1, SYN flooding attack traffic flows are detected using flow payload details. The metrics considered are, (1) Hit count (Hc) of SYN request packets, the count of packet-in (SYN) message to the controller for unknown traffic flows. (2) Time Out Value (TOV) of a flow rule, the expiration time of a flow rule defined by the controller for the SYN traffic and (3) Age value of a flow, the waiting time of traffic flows in the OF switch for connection establishment. The above-said metrics are compared with their corresponding threshold values. When Hit Count Hc(SYN) > Hc(SYN-ACK), TOV > 5s and age > 5s for a same IP and MAC addresses, those traffic flows are directed to the second level (Level 2) of attack detection.

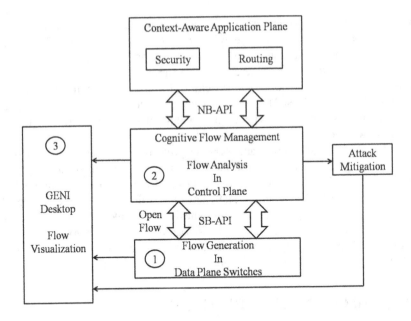

Fig. 1. Proposed cognitive SDN

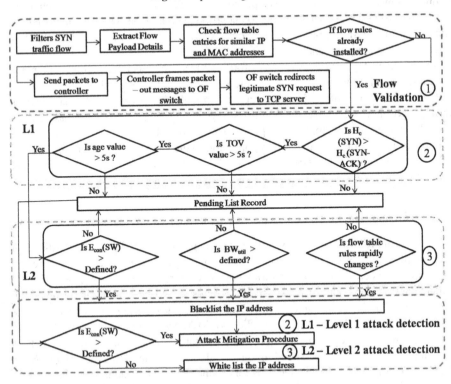

Fig. 2. Process flow of proposed cognitive SDN

In Level 2, the other three detection metrics considered are (4) Energy consumption of switches E(SW), the number of flow rules installed in the OF switch by the controller, (5) Bandwidth utilization of controller, the number of PACKET-IN (SYN) request message to the controller and (6) Rapid change of flow rules in OF table for the specific IP and MAC addresses. When E(SW) > 5000 rules, BWutil: number of SYN requests that are greater than the SYN-ACK messages and frequent change of flow rules in OF table within 5s, for the similar IP and MAC addresses are stored in the pending list. It represents the SYN traffic flows that have not acknowledged. The major problem considered is fixing a static threshold value at different levels of attack detection. The higher threshold value for the said flow metrics will result in a delay of resource consumption attack detection. The lower threshold value results in higher False Positive Rates (FPR), detecting legitimate traffic flows as attack traffic flows before the sequential ACK message reaches the server. The threshold value should act as a better tradeoff between attack mitigation and controller performance.

The proposed method also prevents flow table modification attacks [10] as the controller checks the frequent change of flow rules in OF tables. The match, action rules are checked with the MAC addresses including TOV and age value of flow. Cog-SDN considers MAC addresses and port numbers for detecting attack traffic flows as the IP addresses are highly vulnerable for spoofing attacks. If the incoming packet is ACK, the controller considers it as legitimate traffic and sends the client the notification to finish the established TCP connection. The matched flow payload with the pending list record is blacklisted and the rest MAC addresses are white listed.

DBN self-learns the routing module and flow payload details in order to detect the online traffic flows at a highly dynamic network environment. Hit count of SYN traffic flows and energy consumption of switches of SDN are described below.

Hit count of PACKET-IN request messages to the controller H_c is computed as follows:

$$H_c = sum(Incoming\ request\ traffic\ flows) \tag{1}$$

where,

Here, the value is computed after ten simulation runs of the legitimate and attack traffic flows generation to the OF switch. The average value from the ten simulations runs is considered as a finalized average threshold value. An average threshold value is computed as follows:

$$Average\ threshold\ value = \frac{H_c}{No.of.permitted\ IP's} \tag{2}$$

The attack traffic flows are detected based on energy consumption rate of switches $(E(SW))$ [19]. The energy consumed by compromised switches is higher than the legitimate switches. The energy consumption is computed by number of active switches in the network and enabled interfaces that flood massive request packets as follows,

$$E(SW) = E(SW_{ACT}) + E(Interface_{ACT}) + \sum_{k=1}^{R} n_{ports,r} * E(ports_{enabled}) \tag{3}$$

where,
$E(SW_{ACT})$ = Active switches energy consumption.

$E_{con}(Interface_{ACT})$ = Active interfaces energy consumption.

$n_{ports,r}$ = Total no of ports available in a switch.

$E(ports_{enabled})$ = Enabled ports energy consumption.

The flow table modification attacks are detected by the duration of flows existing in the flow table. The flow rule for attack traffic flow gets changed frequently in the flow table for same IP and MAC addresses. The newly incoming attack traffic flows can be detected by the ML engine using DBN algorithm. Input is a set of flow features from the online traffic flow metrics namely src IP address, dst IP address and dst port number of a switch.

The unsupervised DBN training algorithm involves the process of Restricted Boltzmann Machine (RBM) and sigmoidal belief network algorithm where the top layer forms the RBM and the bottom layers have Bayesian network algorithm. An input to this algorithm is a feature vector that includes traffic flow features such as src IP address, dst IP address, src MAC address, dst MAC address, src port number, dst port number, proto type and output to this algorithm is a reconstructed feature vector. The algorithm begins with training all the internal RBM layers where the weight matrix is assigned separately for each layer. The input of traffic flow features is fed into the hidden layer. The bias values b^k and c^k are considered as an offset vector from the level 1 RBM to the $(n-1)$th layered RBM. The sampling of features is done for all the traffic flow features available in the feature vector.

The joint probability distribution between visible (feature vector) $x = h_0$ and hidden layers for all elements of h^k is given by,

$$P(x, h^1, ..., h^l) = \left(\prod_{k=0}^{l-2} P(h^k | h^{k+1}) \right) P(h^{l-1}, h^l) \tag{4}$$

where,

$x = h^0$ is an observed input vector

$P(h^{k-1}|h^k)$ = conditional probability distribution of visible given hidden units

$P(h^{l-1}, h^l)$ = joint distribution of visible and hidden units at top level RBM.

The greedy layer-wise unsupervised learning is applied to DBN with RBM as the building blocks and the process is given by,

1. The visible layer 1 is trained as an RBM that models vector representation as $x = h^0$.
2. Visible layer 1 acts as second hidden layer as it can be represented by samples of $P(h^{(1)}|h^{(0)})$.
3. Second hidden layer is trained with the features extracted from visible layer 1.
4. Follow steps 2 and 3 for next hidden layers, propagating upward samples.
5. It will produce inference $Q(h_{1i}|x_1)$ for the first hidden layer and $Q(h_{2i}|x_2)$ for the higher hidden layers.

RBM is trained by initializing the visible units (h_0) and parameters. The initialized parameters of visible units namely flow features are learned by Contrastive Divergence (CD) algorithm through Gibb's sampling method. The hidden units are determined by calculating the probabilities of weights and visible units. This phase increases the probability of training data, hence it is called as a positive gradient of the network. The next step is to compute the negative gradient of the network, as it decreases the probability of samples generated by the model. The error values are calculated between generated samples and actual vector after the end of each iteration. After every epoch (completion of positive and negative phase), the values of the weight matrix are updated for the higher hidden layers.

The energy configuration [20] of RBM deployed network is given as follows:

$$E(V,H) = \sum_{i=1}^{m} \sum_{j=1}^{n} w_{m,n} h_n v_m - \sum_{i=1}^{m} a_i v_m - \sum_{i=1}^{n} b_j h_n \qquad (5)$$

where,

$E(V,H)$ = Network energy configuration of visible and hidden layers.

$W_{m,n}$ = Weight matrix of m and n.

a_i, b_j = Bias units.

v_m = Visible units.

h_n = Hidden units.

It extracts features and re-constructs the input for the second RBM stack. The second stack of RBM is trained with the flow payload details which serve as an input for the top level RBMs. RBM uses feature vectors of traffic flows namely src IP address, dst IP address, dst port number to determine the defined flow rules from OF tables.

RBM stacks of DBN self-learn the computed threshold values of bandwidth consumption and delay of SDN routing. Delay of SDN routing is measured by the Round Trip Time (RTT) of the PACKET-IN request message from the switch to the controller and the response packets from the controller to the data plane switches. The unsupervised greedy training procedure of DBN analyzes SDN for a regular time period to find the traffic flows that exceeds the computed minimum and maximum flow values. The newly incoming online traffic flows are fed into DBN algorithm which extracts the features of a flow. It includes src IP address, dst IP address, src port number, dst port number and MAC address of a source and destination switch. The timeout value for each flow has been defined by DBN based on the frequency of incoming IP addresses.

4   Experimental Setup

Experimentations are carried out using GENI testbed [21] both for centralized and distributed controllers to generate low and high rate SYN flooding attack traffic flows. In site-1 at slice attack project, TCP-SYN flooding (or) DDoS attack traffic is generated where the topology comprises of 7 nodes attached to a TCP server. Among the nodes, node-1 is an attacker and the rest of the 7 nodes are participating hosts. The IP address of TCP server is represented by 10.10.9.2 and the corresponding port 22 receives the network traffic flows to and from the neighboring nodes. POX, a python based open source controller is integrated with the data plane topology that is used for network control and management. The maximum rate of SYN packets that can handle in the scenario varies from 50 to 350 packets in static network scenario which results in scalability issue. Here, the maximum rate of TCP-SYN packets handled for each malicious hosts is 360 Packets Per Second (PPS). Log in to all the nodes via Secure SHell (SSH) from the attacker node 1 and execute the script for flooding attacks. Hping3 tool is used to generate malicious TCP-SYN request packets with the spoofed IP address at various rates. The context-aware metric is threshold K, which allow (or) drops the malicious TCP-SYN request packets according to the service availability and degradation of SDN.

SYN packets are flooded to the participating nodes from pc101 (node 1) using the command sudo hping3 -i u1 -s -p 25362 10.10.9.1 at interface (i16) of node 2 where, hping is the tool used to generate malicious TCP SYN packets, -i u1 is the time (i.e. 1 microsecond to transmit next SYN packet), -s is the SYN flag (or) SYN packet to be sent, -p is the port number to receive SYN packets.

The results are evaluated for the metrics namely installation of flow entries, attack detection time and bandwidth utilization of controller during low and high rate of SYN flooding attacks.

5   Results and Discussions

Results are discussed for three different scenarios such as in SLICOTS, COG-SDN mitigation mechanism with the centralized and distributed controllers. Even with SLI-COTS and Cog-SDN, centralized controller infrastructure is vulnerable to single point of failure. If the centralized controller fails, entire network will be collapsed. Hence, the performance of both centralized and distributed SDN controllers is analyzed in cog-SDN and compared with the existing method SLICOT. Figures 3 and 4 are the illustration of attack detection time for the varying rate of SYN request traffic flows. Cog-SDN mitigation mechanism outperforms SLICOTS by adaptive cognitive threshold "K" according to the number of incoming SYN request traffic flows. The attack detection time decreases even if the SYN request traffic flow increases by comparing the MAC addresses with the pending list record.

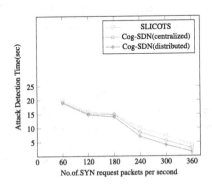

Fig. 3. Attack detection time for low rate SYN packets in S1

Figure 3 shows the attack detection time for low rate SYN flooding attacks in a centralized cog-SDN with a maximum of allowing 360 packets per second (pps).

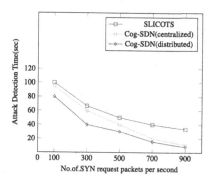

Fig. 4. Attack detection time for high rate SYN packets in S1

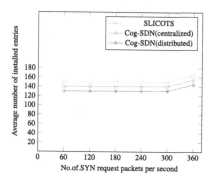

Fig. 5. Installation of flow rule entries for SYN packets in S1

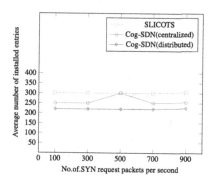

Fig. 6. Installation of flow rule entries for high rate SYN packets in S1

It reduces attack detection time by filtering SYN request traffic flows using self-learning capability of cognitive DBN algorithm. It also checks the flow payload details such as hit count of SYN request to the controller.

The unmatched flows compared by MAC address, TOV and age value greater than the defined threshold are ignored without further analysis that reduces attack detection time than SLICOTS. Hence, it is proactive in attack detection providing service for the legitimate SYN request flows. Figure 4 shows the cog-SDN mitigation mechanism for high rate SYN flooding attacks. The proposed mitigation mechanism also reduces delay in both attack detection and mitigation by blacklisting the MAC address, blocks the corresponding IP address and originated ports.

Figures 5 and 6 shows the average number of flow entries installation during low and high rate SYN flooding attacks, in which detection module blocks the malicious SYN traffic flows. Cog-SDN detects and blocks malicious traffic flows by frequency of PACKET-IN request messages arriving at controller. It also installs forwarding rules for SYN traffic and crosschecks the pending list for known MAC addresses. It does not install forwarding rules for all SYN request traffic, rather it checks for the time out values and age of the flow rules. The proposed mitigation mechanism also prevents Open Flow (OF) switches and flow tables from buffer saturation (or) memory consumption attacks as the mitigation mechanism reduces the number of installed flow rules in the data plane switches.

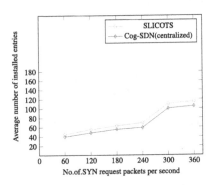

Fig. 7. Bandwidth utilization of controller for low rate attacks

Cog-SDN mitigation mechanism reduces the number of installed forwarding entries in open flow switches as the attack detection routing module checks the corresponding SYN-ACK and ACK messages generated by the controller and TCP server as shown in Fig. 5. The centralized and distributed approach of Cog-SDN mitigation mechanism has almost equally installed forwarding entries for SYN traffic flows. Both SLICOTS and Cog-SDN mitigation mechanism prevents many half-open TCP connections by framing temporary rules and blocking the MAC addresses of participating hosts. Cog-SDN mitigation mechanism reduces the number of forwarding entries both in centralized and distributed approaches than SLICOTS. Figure 6 shows the proposed mitigation mechanism will be effective for high rate SYN packets as the controller

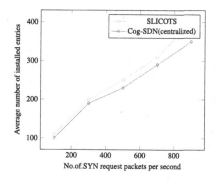

Fig. 8. Bandwidth utilization of controller for high rate attacks

queries OF switch for MAC address of participating hosts, previous SYN and SYN-ACK traffic originated by OF switch and controller.

Figures 7 and 8 demonstrates that the high rate of malicious SYN traffic flows that saturate the SDN control plane and it leads to control plane saturation attack. Both Cog-SDN mitigation mechanism and SLICOTS prevents control plane saturation attacks by blocking malicious users based on MAC address. Cog-SDN mitigation mechanism checks the SYN request and their corresponding SYN-ACK responses of similar IP addresses. If the SYN-ACK response is greater than the hit count of SYN request with similar IP addresses, the proposed mitigation mechanism blocks the host from sending an ACK message to the TCP server. Bandwidth utilization of SDN controller is computed by hit count of incoming PACKET-IN (SYN) requests to SDN controller. Cog-SDN mitigation mechanism does not send SYN-ACK and ACK packets to the malicious host and outperforms SLICOTS as it responds SYN request with corresponding SYN-ACK and ACK packets even for the malicious hosts. SLICOTS frames temporary forwarding rules for incoming SYN traffic flows which result in denial of service for legitimate traffic flows. In comparison, distributed Cog-SDN consumes higher bandwidth than the centralized approach.

6   Conclusion and Future Work

In this research work, cognitive SDN mitigation mechanism is proposed to secure SDN against TCP based DDoS attacks at victim. The proposed mitigation mechanism is deployed in the SDN control plane that continuously monitors incoming network traffic flows to detect malicious traffic flows. The attack detection process is carried out at two different levels by using flow payload and hardware related details of SDN architecture. For each TCP-SYN request, the mitigation mechanism extracts flow metrics and matches with the known list of MAC addresses from the pending list. For the matched flows, further TCP SYN-ACK and ACK messages are generated and the controller terminates established TCP connection by sending FIN flags to the client and is white listed. For the unmatched flows, OF switch queries the flow rules from of table and detection metrics are chosen from second level of attack detection.

Cognitive SDN blocks the unmatched MAC addresses, IP and MAC address conflicts from originated port numbers. The proposed mitigation mechanism is tested under different scenarios of centralized and distributed SDN controllers and compared with the existing SLICOTS defense solution. The proposed mitigation mechanism also prevents buffer saturation attacks by reducing flow entries installation in OF switches, flow table modification attacks using an in-depth analysis. It is sufficient to use an intelligent firewall in which the set of security policies can be incorporated to decide and apply on the incoming network traffic flows. Instead of using an intelligent firewall, SDN is preferred where network customization is achieved based on user needs. The future work is to incorporate cognition in data plane switches to provide a secure edge intelligence to mitigate security attacks in SDN.

References

1. Jammal, M., Singh, T., Shami, A.: Software defined networking: state of art and research challenges. Comput. Netw. **72**, 74–98 (2014). https://doi.org/10.1016/j.comnet.2014.07.004
2. Nunes, B.A.A., Mendonca, M., Nguyen, X.: A survey of software-defined networking: past, present and future of programmable networks. IEEE Commun. Surv. Tutor. **16**(3), 1617–1634 (2014). https://doi.org/10.1109/SURV.2014.012214.00180
3. Li, W., Meng, W., Kwok, L.F.: A survey on OpenFlow-based software defined networks: security challenges and counter-measures. J. Netw. Comput. Appl. **68**, 126–139 (2016). https://doi.org/10.1016/j.jnca.2016.04.011
4. Kim, H., Feamster, N.: Improving network management with software defined networking. IEEE Commun. Mag. **51**, 114–119 (2013). https://doi.org/10.1109/MCOM.2013.6461195
5. Savas, S.S., Tomatore, M., Habib, M.F.: Disaster-resilient control plane design and mapping in software-defined networks. In: Proceedings of IEEE International Conference on High Performance Switching and Routing, Budapest, Hungary, pp. 1–6 (2016). https://doi.org/10.1109/HPSR.2015.7483086
6. Karakus, M., Duressi, A.: A survey: control plane scalability issues and approaches in software defined networking. Comput. Netw. **112**, 279–293 (2016). https://doi.org/10.1016/j.comnet.2016.11.017
7. Scott-Hayward, S., Natarajan, S., Sezer, S.: A survey of security in software defined networks. IEEE Commun. Surv. Tutor. **18**(1), 623–654 (2016). https://doi.org/10.1109/COMST.2015.2453114
8. Brooks, M., Yang, B.: Man in the middle attack against OpenDayLight SDN controller. In: Proceedings of ACM Conference on Research in Information Technology, New York, USA, October, pp. 45–49 (2015). https://doi.org/10.1145/2808062.2808073
9. Chen, P.J., Chen, Y.W.: Implementation of SDN based network intrusion detection and prevention system. In: Proceedings of Carnahan Conference on Security Technology, Taipei, Taiwan, January, pp. 141–146 (2016). https://doi.org/10.1109/CCST.2015.7389672
10. Niyaz, Q., Sun, W., Javaid, A.Y.: A Deep Learning Based DDoS Detection System in Software-Defined Networking. arXiv preprint arXiv:1611.07400 (2016). https://doi.org/10.4108/eai.28-12-2017.153515
11. Wang, H., Xu, L., Gu, G.: Floodguard: a DoS attack prevention extension in software-defined networks. In: Proceedings of IEEE International Conference on Dependable Systems and Networks, Riode Janeiro, Brazil, September, pp. 239–250 (2015). https://doi.org/10.1109/DSN.2015.27

12. Chin, T., Mountrouidou, X., Li, X.: Selective packet inspection to detect DoS flooding using software defined networking. In: Proceedings of International Conference on Computing Systems Workshops, Columbus, OH, USA, July, pp. 95–99 (2015). https://doi.org/10.1109/ICDCSW.2015.27

13. Dhawan, M., Poddar, R., Mahajan, K.: SPHINX: detecting security attacks in software-defined networks. In: Network and Distributed System Security (2015). https://doi.org/10.14722/ndss.2015.23064

14. Shin, S., Yegneswaran, V., Porras, P.: Avant-guard: scalable and vigilant switch flow management in software defined networks. In: Proceedings of ACM SIGSAC Conference on Computer and Communications Security, November, pp. 413–424 (2013). https://doi.org/10.1145/2508859.2516684

15. Ambrosin, M., Conti, M., De Gaspari, F.: Lineswitch: efficiently managing switch flow in software defined networking while effectively tackling DoS attacks. In: Proceedings of ACM Symposium on Information, Computer and Communications Security, pp. 639–644 (2015). https://doi.org/10.1145/2714576.2714612

16. Wei, L., Fung, C.: FlowRanger: a request prioritizing algorithm for controller DoS attacks in software defined networks. In: Proceedings of IEEE International Conference on Communications, London, UK, September, pp. 639–644 (2015). https://doi.org/10.1109/ICC.2015.7249158

17. Haopei, W., Lei, X., Guofei, G.: OF-GUARD: a DoS attack prevention extension in software defined networks. In: Open Network Summit (2014)

18. Nugraha, M., Paramita, I., Musa, A.: Utilizing OpenFlow and sFlow to detect and mitigate SYN flooding attack, pp. 988–994 (2014). https://doi.org/10.9717/kmms.2014.17.8.988

19. Amokrane, A., Langar, R., Boutaba, R.: Flow-based management for energy efficient campus networks. IEEE Trans. Netw. Serv. Manage. **12**(4), 565–579 (2015). https://doi.org/10.1109/TNSM.2015.2501398

20. Mohana Priya, P., Shalinie, S.M., Pandey, T.: Restricted Boltzmann machine based energy efficient cognitive network. In: Snášel, V., Abraham, A., Krömer, P., Pant, M., Muda, A.K. (eds.) Innovations in Bio-Inspired Computing and Applications. AISC, vol. 424, pp. 463–472. Springer, Cham (2016). https://doi.org/10.1007/978-3-319-28031-8_40

21. Berman, M., Chase, J.S., Landweber, L.: GENI: a federated testbed for innovative network experiments. Comput. Netw. **61**, 5–23 (2014). https://doi.org/10.1016/j.bjp.2013.12.037

22. Imran, M., Durad, M.H., Khan, F.A., Derhab, A.: Toward an optimal solution against denial of service attacks in software defined networks. Future Gener. Comput. Syst. **92**, 444–453 (2019). https://doi.org/10.1016/j.future.2018.09.022

23. Mohana Priya, P., Shalinie, S.M.: Restricted Boltzmann machine based detection system for DDoS attack in software defined networks. In: Fourth International Conference on Signal Processing, Communication and Networking, pp. 1–6 (2017). https://doi.org/10.1109/ICSCN.2017.8085731

24. Bawany, N.Z., Shamsi, J.A.: SEAL: SDN based secure and agile framework for protecting smart city applications from DDoS attacks. J. Netw. Comput. Appl. (2019). https://doi.org/10.1016/j.jnca.2019.06.001

25. Saraswat, S., Agarwal, V., Gupta, H.P., Mishra, R., Gupta, A., Dutta, T.: Challenges and solutions in software defined networking: a survey. J. Netw. Comput. Appl. **141**, 23–58 (2019). https://doi.org/10.1016/j.jnca.2019.04.020

Authentication and Key Management System

Password Strength Estimators Trained on the Leaked Password Lists

Cameron R. Schafer[1] and Lei Pan[2(✉)]

[1] InfoSys, Docklands, VIC 3008, Australia
cameron.schafer@infosys.com
[2] School of IT, Deakin University, Geelong, VIC 3220, Australia
l.pan@deakin.edu.au

Abstract. Passwords currently are and will be used as the main authentication mechanism across online applications for the foreseeable future. Estimating the strength of a user's password gives the user a valuable insight into the strength or weakness of their chosen passwords. Current password strength estimators, when giving an estimate on a password's strength, often fail to consider the plethora of leaked lists at an attacker's disposal. This research investigates the effect of training a password strength estimator on a leaked list of 14.3 million passwords, all of which are commonly used in the password cracking world and then observing the effect that it has on the estimation of a password's strength. Through modifying the trained dictionary lists that the zxcvbn classifier is fed, an estimate that accounts for the leaked list was achieved. Our empirical results show that there is a clear need to include leaked passwords in the password strength estimation process and that the accuracy of the estimator should not be sacrificed in order to provide a faster service.

Keywords: Password strength estimation · Leaked passwords · Password dictionary · Multi-factor authentication

1 Introduction

Passwords are used as the main form of authentication. Also on many different websites that these people create accounts on, with no clear standard to govern how these websites determine the strength of a user's password. When creating a new user account, an individual may be faced with a password creation screen that will display the strength of their chosen password. Depending on the requirements of the website and the feedback the user receives, they will choose/create a password to satisfy the websites password strength requirements.

Websites use many different methods to estimate a password's strength. Some websites simply implement a method of calculating a password's strength using the number of Lowercase, Uppercase, Digits and Symbols, also known as the LUDS method. But other websites are starting to adopt complex password strength estimators that employ dictionary lists and other factors to estimate a

© Springer Nature Singapore Pte Ltd. 2019
V. S. Shankar Sriram et al. (Eds.): ATIS 2019, CCIS 1116, pp. 219–231, 2019.
https://doi.org/10.1007/978-981-15-0871-4_17

password's strength. Due to many available types of password strength estimators and their configurations, there is often huge discrepancies between what a site would define as a strong password and what is a weak password. Therein lies the research problem: How can a user gauge whether his/her password is strong in the presence of contradicting estimations provided by different sites?

Estimating password strength is neither a new problem nor a new technology [17]. The zxcvbn password strength estimator has been publicly available since 2012 [25]. zxcvbn is used in the account creation and password change screens of many major websites. Sites such as *Google* [7], *DropBox* [4], *WordPress*, and many others all use this estimator to give their users an estimation of their password's strength. Due to these websites all using the same estimator, one would naturally guess that their outputs are consistent. Unfortunately, this intuition would be incorrect, as we found that they all return different results for the same password. Hence, we believe that the zxcvbn estimator is modified and configured differently across the independent sites.

The main ways that zxcvbn is modified is through editing the type of feedback and replacing zxcvbn's internal password dictionaries. The effect of modifying zxcvbn's internal password dictionaries will be the focus of this paper. This type of modification can effect the performance of the estimator. We choose to observe the accuracy and speed as the performance metrics. Estimators such as zxcvbn only consider a small subset of the leaked passwords while estimating the strength of a password. Thus, we investigate the following questions and try to derive the meaningful answers:

- What is the effect of adding a large leaked list of passwords as an additional trained dictionary list with regards to the estimation of a passwords strength and the speed of the estimator?
- Does the splitting of the list of leaked passwords into smaller sub lists have an effect on the accuracy of password strength estimation and the speed of the estimator?

The contributions of this paper are two-folds: First, this is the first attempt to estimate the strength of the passwords using the real-world leaked lists; second, our empirical studies showed that the password class affects the password strengths significantly. Based on our findings, we recommend the users of the Internet to adopt the complex forms of passwords (such as 3Class or 4Class passwords) if the password length is restricted.

The rest of this paper is organized as follows: Sect. 2 presents a literature review of the password related issues in the cyber security context. Section 3 presents the password strength estimators. Section 4 presents our experiments using the tool zxcvbn [27] with the rockyou list [21] and discusses our findings. Section 5 concludes this paper.

2   Literature Review

Passwords have been and still are used as the mainstream authentication mechanism for online and offline applications. The amount of effort towards finding a complete replacement for passwords is immense, but has had an overall unfruitful outcome [10]. For the average computer user, there are at least three times that they will have to remember a password—during the creation of an account, when logging into an account, and when updating the password. Most types of applications would require the users to remember at least one password. Many online applications have started to or already have introduced two-factor authentication [13] (2FA) as a password supplement to further protect their user accounts. Many times the 2FA feature is still an opt-in choice for the users to decide.

2FA is an authentication mechanism that many online applications use to add an additional layer of protection for an end-user's account. Typically, 2FA uses a combination of a user chosen password combined with an extra verification code or a web link sent via SMS or email. This extra authentication step could be present within the form that the end-users need to authenticate themselves. The websites [13] owned by Facebook, Twitter, and the Commonwealth Bank all employ some form of 2FA for the sole purpose of improving their end-user's account security. Even though there are many applications that employ the use of 2FA, the end-users of these applications more often than not, have to opt into this service. With 2FA authentication in place, it could simplify the level of complexity that a password needs to fulfill. Nevertheless, 2FA is a supplement to what is universally considered a weak method of authentication—the password.

Password authentication systems can be easy to implement in most applications. But this forces the users to create and remember more passwords. Remembering one to five passwords can be challenging enough, but a study [5] in 2007 found that on average a person had created accounts on around 25 different websites. This result was discovered 12 years ago. More and more websites are being made that require a user to sign up and choose a password. More often that not, a user will choose to reuse old passwords from other accounts in order to make this process easier for themselves. This is where password usability degrades [20], that is, if a password on one website gets compromised, then all the other accounts using the same password may also become compromised. If a password has to be continually reset because it has been forgotten, then there is no point of having a system that requires a single password.

A password's complexity refers to how difficult it takes to crack the given password. With online and offline applications, the given password's complexity is typically calculated using one of the two methods—through calculating the entropy of the password, or through calculating a score of a combination of password length and lowercase letters, uppercase letters, digits, and symbols (LUDS). In the password strength calculations, both of these techniques rarely consider any passwords that have been leaked. Instead, the end-user's chosen password will have to conform to the password strength requirements set by the system's administrator. This mandatory check of the password complexity has many drawbacks. For example, this application requires the user to create a password with a minimum of 8 characters with a minimum of 3 character types. While the users are trying to create a password, they may be shown some sort of visual feedback. The most common way that the feedback is shown is through a password strength meter, for example, the stronger the password, the fuller the meter. The accuracy of these meters depends greatly on the strength calculating algorithm used by the application, and by the minimum password requirements set by the system administrator.

Password classes are important to both system administrators and researchers as it gives them the ability to easily define their password complexity requirements and identify the type of password given. Passwords can be sorted by its class and size. The "class" of a password defines how many different types of characters are found within the password, where the size is the number of characters. For example, the password "Abc1@" would be defined as a 4Class5 password; when the password "Abc1@" is broken down, it has four different character types: The Uppercase "A", followed by the Lowercase "bc", followed by the Digit "1", and finally with the Symbol "@". The number five in 4class5 means that there are five characters in total within the given password. We provide a few more examples—password is 1Class8, PaSSworD is 2Class8, 123456841 is 1Class9, and H1G3!sdFp12 is Class11.

Even if a password contains four types of characters, it is not necessarily a stronger password than another password with only three or less character types. Take a 4Class10 password "Password1!" for example, it should not be considered a strong password. When cracking passwords, the attacker usually goes through a dictionary list and mutates those words to find different passwords. Programs used to crack these passwords have built-in rule sets that automate this process to make the cracking of weak strength passwords relatively easy. Therefore, it would be a fair assumption that this password should not be considered strong as it is just a common dictionary word that has "1!" appended at the end. Now, take the password "correcthorsebatterystaple" [26] for example, this password is more than double the length of the previous password. Although this password only has one character type and the previous password has four, the "correcthorsebatterystaple" password should be considered stronger because it uses four seemingly random dictionary words together rather than "Password1!" consisting of a single dictionary word with simple mutations.

Password strength meters in some shape or form are found in nearly every single online application. These meters give the user a visual representation of their passwords' strength. The strength displayed is typically given as a simple visualization of a number of bars or colours ranging from red to green.

Password cracking comes in many forms and can be used for a variety of applications. There are legitimate and illegitimate reasons to crack a password. The type of password cracking that will be examined in this paper is online password cracking. Offline password cracking using programs, including John The Ripper [12], or Hashcat [9]. It is a different matter altogether, as the passwords that are leaked tend to be in a hashed form. This means that the complexity depends on the types of hashing algorithms used rather than just the strength of the underlying password. If the hashing algorithm is weak, then the cracking process will be relatively quick; otherwise, cracking the passwords may be infeasible. Online passwords also have multiple methods of protection, such as rate-limiting [23], [10], 2FA [1], and account lockouts [6].

User data gets leaked all the time caused by many different attacking methods. Attackers can use either active or passive attacks to breach the password data. In an active attack, the attacker will try to gain access to the user's credentials when the user enters them. An active attack can be conducted in many forms—shoulder surfing [20], Krack [15], phishing [11,18], and so on. In a passive attack, the attacker will gain access to passwords through bruteforcing the password. The passive attack usually is performed when the attacker has either the password hashes, or is trying to bypass an authentication control. Credential leaks vary vastly when it comes to how many user accounts are effected.

A method that user data is often leaked is through active attacks. Active attacks come in many forms and therefore have many different methods to mitigate such attacks. The most recent of attacks that has come about is Krack [15]. This attack used a vulnerability within the WPA2 encryption used by many routers that is used to protect users data within a network. This attack allows an attacker to be able to read the previously encrypted data on a network in plain-text, giving them the ability to steal all user credentials that any unsuspecting individuals may enter on web application forms. Shoulder surfing of mobile devices [20] is another tactic that attackers can use to steal a unsuspecting user's credentials. In this attack, the attacker will watch the user typing in a pin or password. This information that is then stolen will be kept and reused at another time. Another way passwords could get leaked is through an insider who has access to the data could leak it themselves. This type of attack can be detrimental to whatever company is effected as most of the user data that they hold could be leaked. All these methods of leaking user data can expose many end-users accounts. For many of these end-users, these leaks may effect multiple different accounts as they may reuse that password across multiple platforms.

Another method that user data is leaked is through that of passive attacks. Passive attacks generally occur once a user database has been attacked and the data has been stolen. This data is usually found hashed so to leak the user data the attacker will need to crack the hashes of the found data. The hashes are cracked using bruteforcing and dictionary attacks [3,22,24] in hash cracking software such as `Hashcat` [9] and `John The Ripper` [12]. Under these attacks, the user data can be leaked with the same after effects as with the active attacks. To protect against these kinds of attacks the application should hash user data using strong hashing algorithms if they have the hardware to handle the load of the hashing calculations.

What is often not considered by many password strength estimators is that passwords get leaked regularly. Passwords are often leaked through the exploitation of a vulnerable database containing the user information of people. These leaked passwords are then free to use by attackers who are trying to crack more and more passwords. This becomes a problem when the password strength estimators does not update what they define as a weak password. Therefore a password strength estimator that was created in 2012, such as `zxcvbn` that has not updated the dictionary lists that it uses to define what is a weak or strong password. This can lead to a reduced accuracy of this classifier.

3   Password Strength Estimation

When a user creates a new account on a website, a web form requesting the username and password is usually needed. When choosing their passwords, they receive some form of feedback from the web application. This feedback is generally based on the strength of the password estimated by a back-end application. The application is written by different programmers according to some rules measuring the combinations of the characters. Thus, the accuracy and the feedback for the chosen password may vary greatly from application to application, where one application will say that the password is strong, but another application may say weak. Feedback-wise, some applications give the user useful tips on how to improve their password choice, but others will merely display a bunch of rules that the applications creator decided upon. If the systems creator decided on using an application such as zxcvbn [27] or whether they decided on using a simple rules based system that employs the use of LUDS (Lowercase letters, Uppercase letters, Digits, and Symbols) will affect on the level of accuracy that the passwords strength will be estimated at and the feedback that the application will be able to give back to the user. Thus, it lacks a uniform standard across the password strength estimators used in the industry.

Two common metrics are used to indicate the accuracy of a password strength estimator—overestimation and underestimation. Both metrics represent inaccuracies in the classification of a passwords strength, but underestimation is more desirable than overestimation for the real-world use [16,25]. That is, when a password's strength is underestimated, it is said to be weaker than what it actually is; on the contrary, when a password's strength is overestimated, then it is said to be stronger than what it actually is. A password strength estimator should be able to estimate the strength to a specific degree of accuracy.

The LUDS system that is used commonly in password strength estimation as a simplified password guide that is easy to implement. It is a rule-based system with and easy to implement integration to the websites. However, the rules may vary from site to site: A site may choose to enforce a minimum of 8 characters with at least three different character types; another site may choose to enforce a minimum of 12 characters with at least two different character types. If a password matches the criteria, then it is automatically accepted; otherwise, automatically rejected. This type of password strength estimation does not calculate the strength of a password. This type of estimator typically only displays the rule set as the feedback for the user to change the password to fulfill the criteria.

The tool zxcvbn is a low-budget password strength estimator [25] to provide users accurate estimates on their password strengths. Wheeler et al. [25] empirically showed that zxcvbn outperformed the LUDS systems. Most LUDS-based system uses a simple entropy calculation, such as the NIST method in [2]—the first character in a password is worth 4 bits, from the second to the eighth character each is worth 2 bits, from the ninth to the twentieth character each is worth 1.5 bits, any extra character after 20 is worth 1 bit; if both uppercase letters and non-alphabetic symbols are used, then its entropy adds 6 more bits;

if a password is not a dictionary word and its length is less than 20, its entropy adds 6 more bits. The tool zxcvbn uses an entropy measure to calculate the chosen passwords strength. That is, zxcvbn breaks the password into segments before each segment is matched against five different categories. A number of sub-patterns are also used, such as tokens, reversed, repeat, keyboard, dates, and so on. This estimator can only recognize the words that are present within one of its dictionaries. If a common word from another language is not present within the dictionary, then it will most likely treat this password as a brute-force only string. This can lead to the overestimation of a password.

The estimation algorithm used in zxcvbn is not based on a probabilistic model but a heuristics model. For example, a password consists of two top-1,000 common words, the 2012 version of zxcvbn estimates that it will take an attacker to guess $1000^2 = 1,000,000$ times as the worst case scenario. Wheeler et al. [25] further improved this heuristics method by training the following model from a given list of passwords:

$$\arg \min_{S \subseteq \mathcal{S}} D^{|S|-1} + |S|! \prod_{m \in S} m.guesses$$

where S is a sequence that fully covers the password, $|S|$ is the length of S, $\mathcal{S}$ is the set of the overlapping patterns, and D is a constant. This model consists of two parts: The first part $D^{|S|-1}$ measures when an attackers knows the pattern sequence with bounds, and the second part $|S|! \prod_{m \in S} m.guesses$ measures how many guesses are needed in the worst case scenario. Once these parameters are learned through the optimization model, the trained zxcvbn can estimate the password strength.

Melicher et al. [16] explored the use of using a neural network (NN) to estimate a passwords strength. In this paper, the NN was compared to the zxcvbn password strength estimator and found that both estimators are able to calculate password strength more efficiently than a LUDS estimator. Melicher et al. [16] found that the NN is slightly more accurate than zxcvbn because it is less likely to overestimate a passwords strength. However, both of these applications do not consider whether or not if a password is matched to a list that it should just be rejected, rather than just giving a low score.

Both zxcvbn and the NN compare their accuracy to that of the Password Guessability Service (PGS) [22]. PGS is a service hosts by Carnegie Mellon University in order to "help researchers estimate how many guesses a particular password-cracking algorithm with particular training data would take to guess a password" [3]. Using this information, anyone can determine how much a specific algorithm or classifier is overestimating or underestimating certain passwords. This services uses multiple password cracking techniques to estimate a passwords strength without actually cracking the password. By comparing the estimations among multiple password cracking techniques, PGS gives an accurate representation of how many guesses a professional would take to crack a specific password.

Different strength estimators have their own strengths and weaknesses. They are beginning to incorporate leaked password lists within their training data in order to give a more accurate representation of how strong or weak a given password is. NIST's recent recommendations [8] on this matter is that all leaked passwords should be automatically rejected. This is due to these passwords all being compromised and available within the attackers toolkit. This research will be based off the assumption that all leaked passwords should be automatically rejected by a password strength estimator. We choose to use the zxcvbn password strength estimator as it is used across many different web applications.

The Rockyou password list is used for the purpose of simulating how real passwords would perform against the zxcvbn password strength estimator. The main purpose of using this password list is that the tests conducted can cover a large variety of passwords that have, at some point been used by individuals. Therefore this password list provides an accurate representation of the kinds of passwords people may still use today. Last but not the least, this leaked password list is readily available on the Internet.

4   Experimental Setups and Results

We conducted a number of experiments on a Windows PC with an Intel I7-4770K CPU, an NVIDIA GTX1070 Strix graphic card, 16 GB of RAM, and a 256 GB SSD with an external 3 TB HDD. The zxcvbn password strength estimator was used to test password strength. The python library for zxcvbn [27] was used.

The Rockyou [21] list is separated into four separate dictionary lists according to password classes. Each list will contain a different Class. In total, it contains approximately 14.3 million unique passwords that once were or still are used by individuals to authenticate themselves on to their user accounts. In the Rockyou dictionary list, there are approximately 6,313,091 1Class passwords, 7,093,412 2Class passwords, 884,638 3Class passwords, and 53,155 4Class passwords. Percentage-wise, 1Class is 43%, 2Class 50%, 3Class 6%, and 4Class below 1%.

The following graphs are the results from each test that were performed during this experiment. There were three tests that were performed for each Class of password. This experiment involved testing the zxcvbn classifier [27] with different sized dictionary lists against the Rockyou dictionary list. The first test used zxcvbn with its default dictionary lists, the second test used zxcvbn with the Rockyou dictionary list as an additional password list, and the final test used zxcvbn with the addition of Rockyou dictionary list divided by password Class into four separate lists.

From Figs. 1, 2, 3, 4, 5, 6, 7, 8, 9, 10, 11 and 12, we plot the password estimation results. Each row of the figures presents the results for each password class—1Class, 2Class, 3Class, and 4Class, respectively; each column of the figures presents the results for each password list—default dictionary, Rockyou dictionary, and class dictionary. The y-axis shows the number of the guesses in terms of $\log_{10}$, and the x-axis shows the size of the password. Each password size has three different bars: The bars shown are for the minimum guesses (blue bar), Mean guesses (red bar), Maximum guesses (green bar).

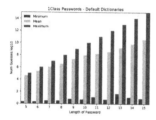

Fig. 1. 1Class passwords with zxcvbn default dictionary lists.

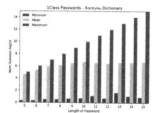

Fig. 2. 1Class passwords with zxcvbn Rockyou dictionary list.

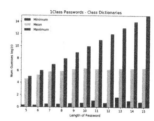

Fig. 3. 1Class passwords with zxcvbn class dictionary lists.

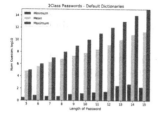

Fig. 4. 2Class passwords with zxcvbn default dictionary lists.

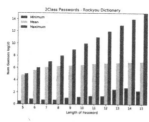

Fig. 5. 2Class passwords with zxcvbn Rockyou dictionary list.

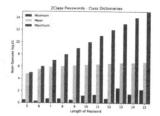

Fig. 6. 2Class passwords with zxcvbn class dictionary lists.

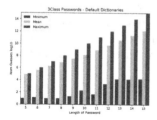

Fig. 7. 3Class passwords with zxcvbn default dictionary lists.

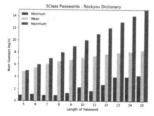

Fig. 8. 3Class passwords with zxcvbn Rockyou dictionary list.

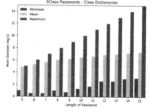

Fig. 9. 3Class passwords with zxcvbn class dictionary lists.

Across the first three tests, there was a marked improvement in what the zxcvbn estimator was able to estimator the password strengths to be. This is due to someone using the Rockyou password list against a website, the 100-th password in that list will not be the one millionth guess as previously reported by zxcvbn. In the final test against the 4Class passwords, there was minimal improvement. This could be due to something like when the special symbols are

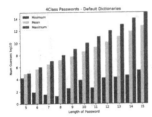

Fig. 10. 4Class passwords with zxcvbn default dictionary lists.

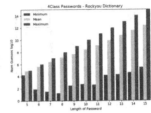

Fig. 11. 4Class passwords with zxcvbn Rockyou dictionary list.

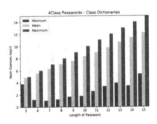

Fig. 12. 4Class passwords with zxcvbn class dictionary lists.

run through the classifier, they do not match up with what is in the dictionary lists, due to how the data is being parsed.

When running the passwords through the zxcvbn password strength estimator, the speed, see Table 1 of each test was taken. This speed includes the reading of the password from a file, testing that password against zxcvbn and then outputting those results to another file. The first test with zxcvbn's default dictionaries took approximately 4 h and 35 min to complete. The second test with the Rockyou dictionary list added took approximately 6 h and 15 min to complete. The final test with the four separate Class based dictionaries took a total of 6 h and 54 min. This shows that there is a large difference in classifier speed when larger dictionary lists are used and also when those dictionary lists are broken into smaller lists. These results show a large increase in time taken to run the full Rockyou Dictionary list against the zxcvbn password strength estimator. This could point to the fact that the Rockyou Dictionary may be too large, or the method of searching through large dictionary lists is not supported by zxcvbn.

Table 1. Test times for each zxcvbn test.

Test	Time taken
Default dictionaries	4 h 35 min
Rockyou dictionary	6 h 15 min
Four class dictionaries	6 h 54 min

There are many different technologies that are often used to help combat the problems of multiple use passwords or where users have to remember multiple strong passwords. One time use passwords [19] can be employed by a web application to remove the user's need to remember a password. This can be done by the web application when generating a new password every time the user wants to log in and then sending that password via email or SMS to the user.

There are also plenty of applications that a user can use to help them create strong passwords that are hard to crack and that they do not have to remember. These Password Managers [14] only require the users to remember a single password that will give them access to all their other passwords. That way the user will only have to remember a single password across all their user accounts.

5 Conclusion

This paper analyzes the password strength estimator zxcvbn and the effects of adding leaked password lists as trained dictionary lists. There was found to be a clear need to include the weakness of leaked passwords into the calculations of a chosen password's strength. These estimators only take into account small lists of leaked passwords, which merely scratch the surface of the millions of leaked passwords openly available to attackers. When a user chooses a password on an online form and then receives feedback from that application, how can the user trust the information given if all the other applications that they use give a different estimate. The feedback that the user receives is instrumental in how they form their passwords and their understanding of what constitutes a strong or weak password. Password strength estimators should check the user's chosen password against the leaked lists in order to provide accurate feedback to the user. Without checking these leaked lists, how will the estimator be able to give the user an accurate assessment of the passwords strength?

This study does not connect specific words to their estimated strength. It only shows the change in password Class strength estimation when a new dictionary list is added. Tests could be done where each password's strength is calculated taken before and after larger leaked lists are added to show how this type of estimator modification works in greater detail. This type of test could also show what types of user generated passwords are inherently stronger than others. Another test that could be implemented is introducing faster dictionary searching algorithms when searching for a specific password. If the password "Help1" is given, then the estimator could search through only the 3Class dictionary list instead of the other 1Class, 2Class, and 4Class dictionary lists. More research could also be done to find the optimal size for the dictionary lists so that it does not slow down the near instantaneous feedback that the user is expecting to receive on their chosen passwords strength. Furthermore a larger set of classifiers could be tested to see how they react to these changes. Whether or not modifying the trained dictionary lists has a similar effect on the estimators and if the estimates that the user receives should be a combination of multiple estimates from multiple estimators for more accurate results.

References

1. Aloul, F., Zahidi, S., El-Hajj, W.: Two factor authentication using mobile phones. In: 2009 IEEE/ACS International Conference on Computer Systems and Applications, AICCSA 2009, pp. 641–644. IEEE (2009)
2. Burr, W., et al.: Nist special publication 800–63-2: Electronic authentication guideline. Technical report, National Institute of Standards and Technology (2013)
3. Password guessability service. https://pgs.ece.cmu.edu/. Accessed 06 July 2019
4. Dropbox landing. https://www.dropbox.com/login. Accessed 06 July 2019
5. Florencio, D., Herley, C.: A large-scale study of web password habits. In: Proceedings of the 16th international Conference on World Wide Web, pp. 657–666. ACM (2007)
6. Florêncio, D., Herley, C., Coskun, B.: Do strong web passwords accomplish anything? HotSec 7(6), 159 (2007)
7. Google: Google landing. https://accounts.google.com/signup/v2/webcreateaccount?continue=accounts.google.com/ManageAccount&gmb=exp&biz=false&flowName=GlifWebSignIn&flowEntry=SignUp. Accessed 06 July 2019
8. Grassi, P.A., et al.: NIST specification 800-63B. In: Digital Identity Guidelines (2017). Accessed 06 July 2019
9. Hashcat. https://hashcat.net/hashcat/. Accessed 06 July 2019
10. Herley, C., Van Oorschot, P.: A research agenda acknowledging the persistence of passwords. IEEE Secur. Priv. 10(1), 28–36 (2012)
11. Huang, C.Y., Ma, S.P., Chen, K.T.: Using one-time passwords to prevent password phishing attacks. J. Netw. Comput. Appl. 34(4), 1292–1301 (2011)
12. John the ripper (JtR). http://www.openwall.com/john/. Accessed 06 July 2019
13. Two factor auth (2FA). https://twofactorauth.org/. Accessed 06 July 2019
14. Li, Z., He, W., Akhawe, D., Song, D.: The emperor's new password manager: security analysis of web-based password managers. In: USENIX Security Symposium, pp. 465–479 (2014)
15. WPA2 krack. https://www.krackattacks.com/. Accessed 06 July 2019
16. Melicher, W., et al.: Fast, lean, and accurate: modeling password guessability using neural networks. In: USENIX Security Symposium, pp. 175–191 (2016)
17. Radhappa, H., Pan, L., Zheng, J.X., Wen, S.: Practical overview of security issues in wireless sensor network applications. Int. J. Comput. Appl. 40(4), 202–213 (2018). https://doi.org/10.1080/1206212X.2017.1398214
18. Ross, B., Jackson, C., Miyake, N., Boneh, D., Mitchell, J.C.: Stronger password authentication using browser extensions. In: USENIX Security Symposium, pp. 17–32, Baltimore, MD, USA (2005)
19. Rubin, A.D.: Independent one-time passwords. Comput. Syst. 9(1), 15–27 (1996)
20. Schaub, F., Deyhle, R., Weber, M.: Password entry usability and shoulder surfing susceptibility on different smartphone platforms. In: Proceedings of the 11th International Conference on Mobile and Ubiquitous Multimedia, p. 13. ACM (2012)
21. Rockyou leak. https://wiki.skullsecurity.org/Passwords. Accessed 06 July 2019
22. Ur, B., et al.: Measuring real-world accuracies and biases in modeling password guessability. In: USENIX Security Symposium, pp. 463–481 (2015)
23. Weir, M., Aggarwal, S., Collins, M., Stern, H.: Testing metrics for password creation policies by attacking large sets of revealed passwords. In: Proceedings of the 17th ACM Conference on Computer and Communications Security, pp. 162–175. ACM (2010)

24. Weir, M., Aggarwal, S., De Medeiros, B., Glodek, B.: Password cracking using probabilistic context-free grammars. In: 2009 30th IEEE Symposium on Security and Privacy, pp. 391–405. IEEE (2009)
25. Wheeler, D.L.: zxcvbn: low-budget password strength estimation. In: USENIX Security Symposium, pp. 157–173 (2016)
26. XKCD comic - password memorability. https://xkcd.com/936/. Accessed 06 July 2019
27. zxcvbn github: Low-budget password strength estimation. https://github.com/dropbox/zxcvbn. Accessed 06 July 2019

Cellular Automata Based Key Stream Generator – A Reconfigurable Hardware Approach

Sundararaman Rajagopalan, Nikhil Krishnaa Sriram, V. Manikandan,
Sivaraman Rethinam, Sridevi Arumugham, Siva Janakiraman,
and Amirtharajan Rengarajan$^{(\boxtimes)}$

Department of ECE, School of EEE,
SASTRA Deemed University, Thanjavur 613 401, India
amir@ece.sastra.edu

Abstract. Rapid developments in network-based application demand a special attention to protect the confidentiality of data. Cryptographic algorithms play a lead role in ensuring confidentiality assisted by key generation architecture. Keys have a fair role in modern cryptography, which can be generated through random number generators. To meet the real-time requirements, cryptographic primitives can be developed on reconfigurable hardware such as Field Programmable Gate Arrays (FPGAs). This work focuses on the development of Pseudo Random Number Generation (PRNG) architecture using Cellular Automata (CA) on Altera Cyclone II EP2C20F484C7 FPGA at an operating frequency of 50 MHz. Significantly, CA based random sequences were generated based on five rules namely R30, R90, R105, R150 and R165. The randomness of the proposed Pseudo Random Number Generator (PRNG) has been confirmed using entropy and NIST 800 − 22 tests. The proposed design has consumed only 461 logic elements which are 3% of total logic elements of target FPGA and also achieves a throughput of 51.603 Mbps for 128-bit PRNG with a power dissipation of 72.26 mW.

Keywords: Confidentiality · PRNG · Cryptography · FPGA and NIST 800 − 22

1 Introduction

Technology development in computer networks has enabled swift growth in digital data communication around the globe. Due to the high-speed internet, trillions of data packets are transferred every day. Information security occupies the centre stage of attention in such scenarios. CIA triad of any security deals with Confidentiality, Integrity and Authentication triangle. In cryptographic applications, random keys have major usage during the encryption as well as decryption processes. Strength of the key is directly related to the strength of the algorithm to resist the attacks. Field Programmable Gate Array (FPGA) is adopted as a fruitful platform for implementing cryptographic primitives due to the advantages namely parallel processing, faster time to market, easy prototyping, reconfigurability, reusability and System on Chip (SoC) features [1].

© Springer Nature Singapore Pte Ltd. 2019
V. S. Shankar Sriram et al. (Eds.): ATIS 2019, CCIS 1116, pp. 232–242, 2019.
https://doi.org/10.1007/978-981-15-0871-4_18

Random Number Generators (RNG) are widely utilized not only for key generation but also for applications such as protocol identification, initialisation vectors, random simulations and lottery [2]. In general, random numbers must satisfy three basic properties namely the equidistribution of zeros and ones, unpredictability and large span of randomness. Pseudo-Random Numbers can be generated through deterministic RNG architectures with these properties. Initially, Middle square technique, Linear Congruential Generator (LCG), Quadratic Congruential Generator (QCG) and Blum Blum Shub generator were employed to generate random numbers. When the Galois Field (GS) was introduced in number theory, researchers started to explore it using polynomial based PRNG such as Linear Feedback Shift Register (LFSR) [3].

LFSR is constructed with Flip-flops and XOR operations to generate the required amount of random numbers in which 2n-1 is the maximum length sequence generated, where 'n' is the number of random bits generated by the LFSR in a single clock cycle. The parameter 'n' is decided by the maximum degree of primitive polynomial utilized for the circuit construction [4]. Deckhakka et al., presented a PN sequence generator using LFSR with 8, 16 and 32 bit polynomials. In this work, the EDA tool Xilinx ISE 10.1 was utilized to develop the design using VHDL. This design required 85.9 s to generate the 232 − 1 random sequences each with 32-bits width at a clock period of 20 ns [5]. LFSR with leap ahead technique has been suggested by Lee et al., to achieve multi LFSR architecture. Segmentation scheme was proposed in this work to increase the span of randomness 2.5 times greater than the existing architectures [6]. Zhang et al. enhanced the LFSR based PRNG with genetic algorithm because of its optimisation capabilities. This work showcases the LFSR perform as a nonlinear operation to generate a new set of random sequences. FIPS 140-1 test has been performed to evaluate the randomness of this proposed design [7].

The unique features of chaos can be utilized for the development of PRNGs. Chaotic maps or attractors are sensitive to seed and initial conditions. Due to the characteristics namely chaoticity, stochasticity and ergodicity, chaotic maps have been adopted in random number generators. One such work was presented by Xiaole Fang et al., using chaotic iterations with required mathematical modelling. Adders and multipliers are the fundamental objects of this design, which has been developed using Verilog HDL and implemented on Altera Cyclone II FPGA. NIST 800 − 22 statistical tests have been carried out to evidence the randomness of the design [8]. In addition to the 1D chaotic maps, multiple chaotic maps have been combined to form a PRNG where chaotic attractors also used for random number generation [9–17].

Though LFSR and chaotic maps produce random numbers, they are not suitable for low power and high-speed cryptographic applications when implemented on FPGA. LFSR has bitshifting effects which reduces its randomness. Chaotic maps are governed by floating point arithmetic so that they consume more area and power. One-dimensional Cellular Automata (CA) has been suggested in this work to yield a high quality of random numbers, which is evident through statistical test suite such as NIST 800 − 22. The main contributions of this proposed algorithm are:

1. Generation of the pseudo-random numbers using Cellular Automata (CA) with five different rules of CA namely R30, R90, R105, R150, R165

2. The keys are generated in the hardware platform of Altera Cyclone II EP2C20F484C7 FPGA at an operating frequency of 50 MHz
3. The randomness of the key was validated through entropy and NIST 800 – 22 tests
4. The proposed algorithm achieves an average power dissipation of 70.48 mW and throughput of 51.603 Mbits/s respectively.

2   PRNG Using Cellular Automata

Cellular Automata is a dynamical system of equations which is used for solving complex digital designs because of its modularity, regularity and locality of interconnection properties. It comprises a linear array like structure having neighborhood cells such as previous, present and next cells called as states to hold 1-bit of value at each time [18]. The next state of any cell is identified using rule which is a major term in CA to control the operations. A rule in Cellular Automata describes the relationship among the neighborhood cells in terms of arithmetic and logical operations with each cell producing a 1-bit value either '0' or '1'. In CA, totally 256 rules are available. Each rule exhibits an unique property. Due to the rule architecture, evolution and population of states, they can provide immense solution to pseudo-random number generation [19, 20].

From a reconfigurable hardware perspective, CA can be constructed using a chain of registers such as flip-flops. The block diagram of PRNG using CA is shown in Fig. 1. The CA generates diffused bits with 50 MHz as operating frequency which has been implemented using five rules such as R30, R90, R105, R150, R165 in separate

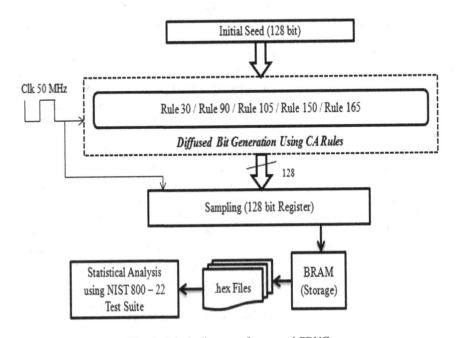

Fig. 1. Block diagram of proposed PRNG

hardware descriptions. Diffused bits are further sampled as 128-bit random numbers and then stored in Block Random Access Memory (BRAM) of size 1024×128. Finally, random numbers from the BRAM are extracted as .hex files and tested using NIST Randomness test suite.

2.1 CA Rules

Rule is a predominant control parameter in CA to construct chain of registers in a digital system. CA can be developed using synchronous or asynchronous rule models. Synchronous rule model of CA consists of the same set of rules to design the system wherein the asynchronous rule model of CA follow a different set of rules to achieve the design [21, 22]. In this work, the synchronous rule model has been adopted to explore the random properties of CA. Among 256 rules of CA, five rules namely 30, 90, 105, 150 and 165 are determined as rules for enhanced randomness during the evolution of random bits [26]. Equations (1–5) express the mathematical model for Rule 30, 90, 150, 105 and 165. Tables 1, 2, 3, 4 and 5 present the state operations of rules mentioned above [23–26].

$$\Psi_i(t+1) = \Psi_{i-1} \, XOR \, (\Psi_i(t) \, OR \, \Psi_{i+1}(t)) \tag{1}$$

$$\Psi_i(t+1) = \Psi_{i-1}(t) \, XOR \, \Psi_{i+1}(t) \tag{2}$$

$$\Psi_i(t+1) = \Psi_{i-1}(t) \, XOR \, \Psi_i(t) \, XOR \, \Psi_{i+1}(t) \tag{3}$$

$$\Psi_i(t+1) = \Psi_{i-1}(t) \, XOR \, \Psi_i(t) \, XOR \, (\overline{\Psi_{i+1}(t)}) \tag{4}$$

$$\Psi_i(t+1) = \Psi_{i-1}(t) \, XOR \, \overline{\Psi_{i+1}(t)} \tag{5}$$

Ψ_i – Present state
Ψ_{i-1} – Previous state
Ψ_{i+1} – Next state

Table 1. Rule 30 state evolution

Present state	111	110	101	100	011	010	001	000
Next state	0	0	0	1	1	1	1	0

Table 2. Rule 90 state evolution

Present state	111	110	101	100	011	010	001	000
Next state	0	1	0	1	1	0	1	0

Table 3. Rule 105 state evolution

Present state	111	110	101	100	011	010	001	000
Next state	0	1	1	0	1	0	0	1

Table 4. Rule 150 state evolution

Present state	111	110	101	100	011	010	001	000
Next state	1	0	0	1	0	1	1	0

Table 5. Rule 165 state evolution

Present state	111	110	101	100	011	010	001	000
Next state	1	0	1	0	0	1	0	1

2.2 Random Number Generation Procedure

The hardware description was developed for the following steps to generate N-bit keys using CA based PRNG. Here 16, 32, 64 and 128-bits are the values of 'N' considered during the generation. Initially, the flip-flops in CA circuit are loaded with a N-bit seed and upon application of clock pulses, new time series of random sequences will evolve from the registers. The bitstream file will be programmed on the target hardware for acquisition of random bits and subsequent storage in memory.

Step – 1: Load the Flip-flops with an N-bit non-zero random initial seed value
Step – 2: Set the reset pin as active low to start the random data generation
Step – 3: Initialize a variable to store the current random value internally
Step – 4: Generate the new flip-flop values based on the Look Up Table entries (1–5) for the N-bit width at a clock frequency of 25 MHz
Step – 5: Store the new random N-bit value in a register
Step – 6: Repeat steps 4 and 5 for generating required number of random numbers.

3 Results and Discussion

This PRNG architecture was developed using Verilog HDL and implemented on Altera Cyclone II EP2C20F484C7 FPGA using Quartus II 8.0 EDA tool. The random bits acquired through PRNG with five different rules were evaluated through entropy analysis. To evaluate the randomness, NIST 800 – 22 tests have been conducted. Resource utilization, power dissipation and throughput analyses have been carried out to validate the design in terms of hardware perspective. Figure 2 presents the RTL view of the PRNG being implemented on the target FPGA.

3.1   Entropy Analysis

Entropy is an important metric to evaluate the equidistribution of zeros and ones in random sequences such that probability of occurrence of zeros and ones are distributed equally. For an ideal case, 1 is the maximum entropy yielded by the random number. However, in a practical scenario, close to $1(\sim 0.99)$ is considered as the maximum entropy to be achieved by any random number generator to produce statistically strong random numbers. Entropy analysis of this proposed work with four set of random numbers is listed in Table 6 wherein the design attained an average entropy of 0.99999.

Table 6. Entropy analysis

Rules	Entropy for different bits			
	128	64	32	16
30	0.99937	0.99731	0.99508	0.99800
90	0.99996	0.99999	0.99996	1
105	1	0.99998	0.99995	0.99995
150	0.99995	0.99993	0.99994	0.99998
165	0.99988	0.99999	0.99998	0.99994

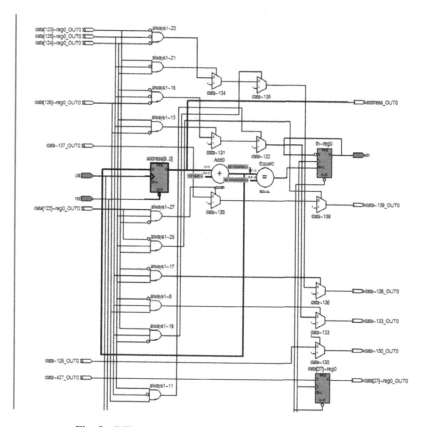

Fig. 2. RTL view of the proposed PRNG using Rule 90

3.2 NIST 800 – 22

The National Institute of Standards and Technology (NIST) has recommended a test suite to evaluate the statistical characteristics of random numbers [27]. It comprises a collection of tests to statistically compute the proportion value through which the status of the test is decided. The random bits were analyzed with NIST Test Suite by considering 10-bit streams each with a bit length of 5000.

The following parameter settings were applied to various tests before performing NIST randomness analyses.

Block frequency Test – Block length (M) = 128
Non-overlapping Template – Block length (m) = 9
Overlapping Template – Block length (m) = 9
Approximate Entropy Test – Block length (m) = 8
Serial Test – Block length (m) = 10
Linear Complexity Test – Block length (M) = 500

NIST test has been performed for the generated random sequences of all the rules and the results are presented in Table 7. The results ensure the statistical independency of proposed PRNG.

Table 7. NIST 800 – 22 Tests

Test	P-values (*0.0000 indicates that the test is failed*)				
	Rule 30	Rule 90	Rule 105	Rule 150	Rule 165
Frequency	0.213309	0.000199	0.534146	0.350485	0.534146
Block frequency	0.008879	0.739918	0.534146	0.350485	0.122325
Cumulative Sums – I	0.000199	0.066882	0.122325	0.534146	0.739918
Cumulative Sums – II	0.000199	0.008879	0.350485	0.017912	0.534146
Runs	0.000000	0.739918	0.213309	0.911413	0.911413
Longest Run	0.000199	0.122325	0.739918	0.911413	0.350485
Rank	0.035174	0.739918	0.350485	0.213309	0.017912
FFT	0.000000	0.350485	0.122325	0.213309	0.991468
Non-overlapping Template	0.911413	0.911413	0.911413	0.911413	0.911413
Overlapping Template	0.213309	0.008879	0.017912	0.122325	0.739918
Approximate Entropy	0.000003	0.000199	0.122325	0.066882	0.008879
Serial – I	0.000003	0.017912	0.534146	0.739918	0.213309
Serial – II	0.000439	0.122325	0.739918	0.350485	0.122325
Linear Complexity	0.911413	0.066882	0.122325	0.911413	0.739918

From the Table 7, Rule 30 has achieved low p-value due to the less randomness. Other rules have yielded adequate high level of p-values indicating the improved randomness.

3.3   Resource Utilization

Resource utilization includes the number of combinational logic elements, registers, dedicated Digital Signal Processing (DSP) blocks, Phase Locked Loops (PLL), memory bits and input-output pins required to implement the PRNG on FPGA. Tables 8, 9, 10 and 11 present the resource utilization. The total power dissipation of the proposed work is estimated as 72.26 mW through Power play power analyser tool of Altera Quartus II.

Table 8. Resource utilization – 128 bit PRNG

Hardware parameters	Rule 30	Rule 90	Rule 105	Rule 150	Rule 165
Combinational functions (18,752)	612	474	487	484	484
Dedicated logic registers	496	369	369	369	369
Memory bits (2,39,616)	1,31,072	1,31,072	1,31,072	1,31,072	1,31,072

Table 9. Resource utilization – 64 bit PRNG

Hardware parameters	Rule 30	Rule 90	Rule 105	Rule 150	Rule 165
Combinational functions (18,752)	513	317	324	322	320
Dedicated logic registers	431	240	239	240	240
Memory bits (2,39,616)	65,536	65,536	65,536	65,536	65,536

Table 10. Resource utilization – 32 bit PRNG

Hardware parameters	Rule 30	Rule 90	Rule 105	Rule 150	Rule 165
Combinational functions (18,752)	461	236	237	237	238
Dedicated logic registers	398	175	174	175	175
Memory bits (2,39,616)	32,768	32,768	32,768	32,768 .	32,768

Table 11. Resource utilization – 16 bit PRNG

Hardware parameters	Rule 30	Rule 90	Rule 105	Rule 150	Rule 165
Combinational functions (18,752)	435	195	195	196	196
Dedicated logic registers	381	142	141	142	142
Memory bits (2,39,616)	16,384	16,384	16,384	16,384	16,384

3.4   Throughput Analysis

Throughput indicates the number of random bits generated per second. It is primarily based on the operating frequency of the PRNG design. This hardware architecture requires 2.54 ms to generate 1024 × 128 bits of pseudo-random numbers which was captured through Zero Plus real-time logic analyser tool as shown in Fig. 3. Further, the throughput is calculated as 51.603 Mbits/s through Eq. (6),

$$Tp = \frac{\text{Total number of bits generated}}{\text{Time taken to generate the bits}} \qquad (6)$$

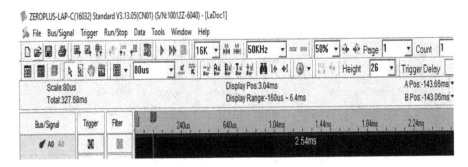

Fig. 3. Time taken for generating 1024×128 bits

Table 12. Performance comparison with other earlier works

System	Ref. [10]	Ref. [11]	Ref. [12]	Ref. [13]	Ref. [14]	Ref. [15]	Proposed work
Target device	Virtex 6	Virtex 6	Virtex II	Spartan 3E	Virtex 7	–	Cyclone II
PRNG scheme	Henon Map	Logistic Map	Lorenz System	Bernoulli Map	Logistic Map	Chaotic Maps	Cellular Automata
LUTs	1600	643	2718	575	510	–	461
Logic registers	64	160	791	108	120	–	398
Throughput	–	1.5 Gbps	124 Mbps	7.380 Mb/s	24 Mbps	–	51.603 Mbps
Power dissipation (mW)	–	–	–	–	–	–	72.26
NIST 800 – 22	PASS	PASS	PASS	PASS	PASS	PASS	PASS

From Table 12, it is inferred that the proposed CA-based PRNG has achieved improved figures compared with other earlier works proposed in [10–15]. Since chaotic maps have been used widely for generating pseudo-random sequences; this proposed work has been compared with chaotic PRNGs in terms of hardware utilization and throughput and NIST 800 – 22 tests.

4 Conclusion

This work aims at generation of Pseudo random keys using five different CA rules such as R30, R90, R105, R150 and R165 and corresponding hardware and randomness analyses. Each rule exhibits an unique characteristic of randomness, which has further been tested through standard metrics and statistical tests. The proposed hardware architecture was implemented on Altera Cyclone II EP2C20F484C7 FPGA and the parameters such as resource utilization, power dissipation and throughputs have been reported. For generating 1024 numbers of 128-bit keys, 461 LUTs and 398 registers were utilized. The PRNG produces random numbers at a throughput of 51.603 Mbps and the power dissipated by the design was 72.26 mW. Future work will be on analysing the CA structure with asynchronous rule model and extend this PRNG for image encryption applications.

Acknowledgement. The authors wish to thank SASTRA Deemed University for providing infrastructure through the Research & Modernization Fund (Ref. No: R&M/0026/SEEE-010/2012-13) to carry out the research work.

References

1. Bakiri, M., Guyeux, C., Couchot, J.-F., Oudjida, A.K.: Survey on hardware implementation of random number generators on FPGA: theory and experimental analyses. Comput. Sci. Rev. **27**, 135–153 (2018)
2. Sivaraman, R., Rajagopalan, S., Sridevi, A., Rayappan, J.B.B., Annamalai, M.P.V., Rengarajan, A.: Metastability-induced TRNG architecture on FPGA. Iran. J. Sci. Technol. Trans. Electr. Eng (2019). https://doi.org/10.1007/s40998-019-00234-2
3. Thesen, A.: Chapter IX - random number generators. In: Thesen, A. (ed.) Computer Methods in Operations Research, pp. 194–213. Academic Press (1978)
4. Sehwag, V., Member, S., Prasad, N., Member, S., Sngs, A.E.: A parallel stochastic number generator with bit permutation networks. IEEE Trans. Circuits Syst. II **65**(2), 231–235 (2018)
5. Deckhakka, M.P., Babitha, P.K., Thushara, T.: FPGA based N-Bit LFSR to generate random sequence number. Int. J. Eng. Gen. Sci. **3**(3), 6–10 (2015)
6. Lee, J.-H., Jeon, M.-J., Kim, S.C.: Uniform random number generator using leap-ahead LFSR architecture. In: Kim, T.-h., Ramos, C., Kim, H.-k., Kiumi, A., Mohammed, S., Ślęzak, D. (eds.) ASEA 2012. CCIS, vol. 340, pp. 264–271. Springer, Heidelberg (2012). https://doi.org/10.1007/978-3-642-35267-6_34
7. Zhang, H., Wang, Y., Wang, B., Wu, X.: Evolutionary random sequence generators based on LFSR. Wuhan Univ. J. Nat. Sci. **12**(1), 75–78 (2007)
8. Fang, X., Wang, Q., Guyeux, C., Bahi, J.M.: FPGA acceleration of a pseudorandom number generator based on chaotic iterations. J. Inf. Secur. Appl. **19**(1), 78–87 (2014)
9. François, M., Grosges, T., Barchiesi, D., Erra, R.: Pseudo-random number generator based on mixing of three chaotic maps. Commun. Nonlinear Sci. Numer. Simul. **19**(4), 887–895 (2014)
10. Dabal, P., Pawel, R.: FPGA implementation of chaotic pseudo-random bit generators. In: MIXDES 2012 (2012)

11. Pande, A., Zambreno, J.: A chaotic encryption scheme for real-time embedded systems: design and implementation. Telecommun. Syst. **52**(2), 551–561 (2013)

12. Azzaz, M.S., et al.: Real-time FPGA implementation of Lorenz's chaotic generator for ciphering telecommunications. In: Joint IEEE North-East Workshop on Circuits Systems and TAISA Conference, pp. 1–4 (2009)

13. de la Fraga, L.G., Torres-Pérez, E., Tlelo-Cuautle, E., Mancillas-López, C.: Hardware implementation of pseudo-random number generators based on chaotic maps. Nonlinear Dyn. **90**(3), 1661–1670 (2017)

14. Garcia-Bosque, M., Pérez-Resa, A., Sánchez-Azqueta, C.: Chaos-based bitwise dynamical pseudorandom number generator on FPGA. IEEE Trans. Instrum. Meas. 1–4 (2018)

15. Hua, Z., Zhou, B., Zhou, Y., Member, S.: Sine chaotification model for enhancing chaos and its hardware implementation. IEEE Trans. Ind. Electron. **66**(2), 1273–1284 (2019)

16. Bakiri, M., Guyeux, C., Galatolo, S., Marangio, L.: A hardware and secure pseudorandom generator for constrained devices. IEEE Trans. Ind. Informatics **14**(8), 3754–3765 (2018)

17. Beatriz, A., López, O., Encinas, L.H., Muñoz, A.M., Vitini, F.M.: A lightweight pseudorandom number generator for securing the Internet of Things. IEEE Access **5** (2017)

18. Anghelescu, P., Sofron, E., Ionita, S., Ionescu, L.: FPGA implementations of cellular automata for pseudo random number generation. In: IEEE Conference, no. 1, pp. 371–374 (2006)

19. Hortensius, P.D., Mcleod, R.D., Card, H.C.: Parallel random number generation for VLSI systems using cellular automata. IEEE Trans. Comput. **38**(40), 185–191 (1989). Commun. ACM Commun. ACM AFIPS

20. Hortensius, P.D., Mcleod, R.D., Pries, W., Miller, D.M., Card, H.C.: Cellular Automata-Based Pseudorandom Number Generators for Built-in Self-Test. IEEE Trans. Comput. Aided Des. **8**(8), 842–859 (1989)

21. Petrica, L.: FPGA optimized cellular automaton random number generator. J. Parallel Distrib. Comput. **111**, 251–259 (2018)

22. Tomassini, M., Perrenoud, M.: Cryptography with cellular automata. Appl. Soft Comput. **1**(2), 151–160 (2001)

23. Abdo, A.A., Lian, S., Ismail, I.A., Amin, M., Diab, H.: A cryptosystem based on elementary cellular automata. Commun. Nonlinear Sci. Numer. Simul. **18**(1), 136–147 (2013)

24. Sundararaman, R., Upadhyay, H.N., Rayappan, J.B.B., Amirtharajan, R.: Logic elements consumption analysis of cellular automata based image encryption in FPGA. Res. J. Inf. Technol. **6**(4), 291–307 (2014)

25. Rajagopalan, S., Upadhyay, H.N., Rayappan, J.B.B., Amirtharajan, R.: Dual cellular automata on FPGA: an image encryptors chip. Res. J. Inf. Technol. **6**(3), 223–236 (2014)

26. Wolfram, S.: Random sequence generation by cellular automata. Adv. Appl. Math. **7**, 127–169 (1986)

27. Bassham, L.E., et al.: A statistical test suite for random and pseudorandom number generators for cryptographic applications. National Institute of Standards & Technology, Gaithersburg, MD, USA, Technical report, no., April 2010

Hardware Trojan on SIMON Architecture for Key Retrieval

Sivappriya Manivannan[1]([⊠])(iD) and K. K. Soundra Pandian[1,2]([⊠])(iD)

[1] Department of Electronics and Communication Engineering,
PDPM-Indian Institute of Information Technology, Design and Manufacturing,
Jabalpur, Madhya Pradesh 482005, India
msivappriya@gmail.com
[2] Controller of Certifying Authorities, Ministry of Electronics and Information
Technology, Government of India, New Delhi 110003, India
soundra.pandian@cca.gov.in

Abstract. The need of an hour is the research on design and impacts of Hardware Trojan Horse in a crypto module to serve the purpose of secret key recovery. SIMON is a light weight block cipher that indulges to optimally work with hardware environment. Few papers have come up with the fault attack on SIMON cipher. In this paper, two bit toggle fault attack on 29th round of the SIMON by intruding Hardware Trojan Horse is realized. The structural design of Hardware Trojan includes activation of two payloads with a single trigger. In consequence, the round key of SIMON cipher is retrieved by executing Differential Fault Analysis, using the fault free and completely faulty ciphertext. The power consumption of the SIMON design for both with and without Hardware Trojan is estimated using Simulation Activity Information File (.saif) on ZYNQ 7000 SoC family FPGA board and observed that there is minimal overhead of 1.32%. Provided, almost negligible difference of one LUT in area utilization is discerned. This infers that the insertion of designed HTH in the SIMON module have created an imperceptible impact and bypasses the testing process.

Keywords: Hardware Trojan Horse · Block cipher · SIMON cipher · Fault attack · Differential Fault Analysis

1   Introduction

SIMON is a Feistel structured block cipher which is designed for the resource constrained device to provide an optimal performance. The SIMON family indulges to optimally work with hardware environments. To provide implementation on multiple device, SIMON cipher supports five block sizes viz., 32,48,64,96 and

Interdisciplinary Cyber Physical Systems (ICPS) project, Department of Science and Technology (DST) for funding this research work under Project Number: DST/ICPS/CPS-Individual/2018/819.

© Springer Nature Singapore Pte Ltd. 2019
V. S. Shankar Sriram et al. (Eds.): ATIS 2019, CCIS 1116, pp. 243–253, 2019.
https://doi.org/10.1007/978-981-15-0871-4_19

128 bits and up to three key sizes for each block size. The US National Security Agency (NSA) first introduced SIMON in the year of 2013 exclusively for IoT applications [1], but the assessments on the security perspective is not been made. Hence it is important for any ciphers to analyze based on the security and ensure it's resistance towards vulnerability that exploits Denial of Service (DoS) attack, side-channel attack that leads to leakage of information, fault attack which is the most predominant, practical and efficient attacks that may even lead to self-destruction of the circuit.

Amongst the proposed work mainly focus on the fault attack through Hardware Trojan Horse. The research about Hardware Trojans and it's impact is an avant-garde for this research era. There are only very few plants who fabricate their own chip and this predicament is a triumph for the adversary. The hardware Trojans can be inserted using two techniques one is Functional Trojans that are built using logic gates which intrudes fault and does the action of maliciousness and the other is Parametric Trojan that varies the parameters viz., temperature, delay, EM, power and optics (laser beam) of the circuit which does the malicious actions. A Hardware Trojan structure is with a Trigger and a Payload, Where the Trigger logic Triggers the Trojan to do the action of maliciousness through the payload.

The need of an hour is to identify the presence of Hardware Trojan Horse (HTH) in the circuit. Because the witty adversary intrudes the HTH in a circuit in such a way that the infected circuit passes through the testing process and the fault becomes redundant. This research era is more concentrated on building a HTH in a crypto system for the secret key retrieval [2,3]. Differential Fault Analysis (DFA) is used to retrieve the key from any crypto system provided with a fault free (original) ciphertext and a completely faulty ciphertext which is the analyzis technique suggested by Piret *et al.* [4,5]. DFA on AES [6] and the families of SIMON and SPECK was realized for the secret key leakage by incorporating bit flip attack between the rounds which is cited in the papers [7,8]. Then the fault attack is made in the key scheduling module of the crypto system in order to reveal the key through DFA [9,10]. As an improvement, a fault attack for random byte is made [11] in the sixth round of the SIMON and applied differential propagation properties to determine the fault injection position. The authors could recover the last round key and also the round keys. A mathematical explanation is included to calculate the average number of fault injection for a random byte fault with an analysis of data complexity. In the paper [12], they have proposed a one byte toggle or fault attack in the ninth round of AES and recovered the round key using DFA.

Contribution

In the proposed work, we present the first Hardware Trojan attack on SIMON cipher. It is proved that the SIMON cipher is insecure to the Trojan attack, where when the Hardware Trojan is inserted between the Feistel structured algorithms could do the action of bits toggling to generate erroneous ciphertexts. In consequence, the adversary can retrieve the round key of the SIMON cipher by introducing the Hardware Trojan which does the action of bit flips. Here in the proposed work two bits are flipped by constructing a multiple payload Hardware Trojan with a single Trigger at the 29th round of the SIMON encryption Fiestel structure. Further, a Differential Fault Analysis is been executed in order to reveal the round key using the original fault-free ciphertext and entirely faulty ciphertext.

2   The SIMON Light Weight Block Cipher

SIMON is designed for exploring an optimized performance in hardware implementation and its sister algorithm is SPECK which optimizes the performance in software implementations. SIMON is a symmetric structured feistel network cipher used in the block cipher constructions. SIMON is a balanced feistel cipher, capable of encrypting blocks of data from 32 bit to 128 bit in a single execution. The SIMON has n bit word with 2n as block length. The key length of the SIMON is multiple of n by 2, 3 or 4 which is denoted as the m value. And hence the denotation of this block cipher is SIMON 2n/nm. SIMON is a collection of three different circuits, (i) Key expander, (ii) Message encryptor and (iii) Message decryptor. There are ten different messages and key bit lengths. For encryption, a segment of the key is given to encryption circuit along with the message, where the key expander circuit will produce new keys for each round. The following is to put the details of the SIMON block cipher in a nut shell,

- Structure: Balanced Feistel Network
- Sizes of Block (2n): 32, 48, 64, 96 or 128 bits
- Sizes of Key (nm): 64, 72, 96, 128, 144, 192 or 256 bits
- Rounds: 32, 36, 42, 44, 52, 54, 68, 69 or 72 (Depending on block and key size).

The figure depicted in Fig. 1 is the encryption module of SIMON cipher in feistel structure where, R is the total number of rounds in the SIMON. $\{A^{r+1}, B^{r+1}\}$ is 2n bit output of the rth round cipher, where $r \in \{0, \ldots, R-1\}$. And the pain text input of the cipher is $\{A^0, B^0\}$. $\{A^{r+1}, B^{r+1}\}^*$ is 2n bit output of the rth round Trojan infected faulty cipher text, where $r \in \{0, \ldots, R-1\}$. k^r is the n bit round key in r^{th} round of cipher, where $r \in \{0, \ldots, R-1\}$. For a SIMON 32/64, the size of the data or plain text is 32 bit and the size of the Key (K_r) is 64 bit. The A and B denoted in Fig. 1 is the concatenation of 32 bit data i.e., $\{A, B\}$. Where A is [31:16]data and B is [15:0]data each of 16 bits respectively. The notation <<N means left circular shift where N is number of places to shift left. The symbol '&' denotes the logic AND operation.

A case study for encryption on SIMON feistel network is as follows,
For SIMON 32/64,
Key = 1918 1110 0908 0100
Plain text = 6565 6877
A = 6565 and B = 6877. Where $k_3 = 1918$, $k_2 = 1110$, $k_1 = 0908$, $k_0 = 0100$

Step 1: Left circular shift the message segment A (0110010101100101) once and also for 8 places followed by executing logic AND.

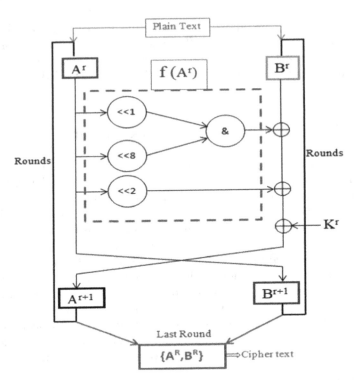

Fig. 1. SIMON feistel encryption network structure

<<1 (A) = 1100101011001010
<<8 (A) = 0110010101100101
<<1(A) & <<8(A) = 1100101011001010 & 0110010101100101
= 0100000001000000

Step 2: EXOR the result of step 1 (0100000001000000) with B (0110100-001110111) 0100000001000000 ⊕ 0110100001110111 = 0010100000110111

Step 3: EXOR the result of step 2 (0010100000110111) with two left circular shift value of A
0010100000110111 ⊕ 1001010110010101 = 1011110110100010

Step 4: EXOR the result of the step 3 (1011110110100010) with round key value. Let us assume that the key value here is K_3 (0000000100000000)
1011110110100010 ⊕ 0000000100000000 = 1011110010100010
The left half of the first round value is 1011110010100010.
Hence the cipher text of first round encryption is 1011110010100010 0110010101100101 (bca2 6565)
    The ciphertext after 32 rounds for the above plaintext and key is c69b e9bb.

3 Proposed Hardware Trojan Design, Insertion, Activation and Action on SIMON

In forthcoming subsections the Hardware Trojan design is clearly depicted and explained. The main intention of HT design is to inject fault inorder to obtain the secret key. Followed with the HT design, the insertion of the designed HT in the appropriate round of the SIMON is made in such a way that the realization of HT's presence is least possible. Then the inserted HT is activated and as an action the completely faulty ciphertext is obtained for further key recovery analysis.

3.1 HTH Design

The Hardware Trojan is inserted in the 29th round of SIMON where the activation of Trojan if triggered takes place after the XORation of 29th round key as clearly shown in Fig. 2.

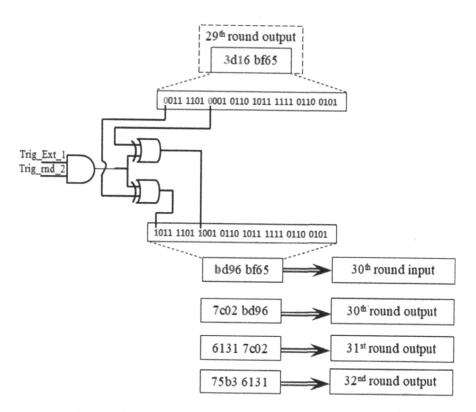

Fig. 2. Multiple payload with single triggered HTH designs.

In the fault attack proposed, a combinational Trojans is designed as illustrated in Fig. 2 with a single AND logic trigger and two XOR logic payloads. The trigger and payloads of the Hardware Trojan designed does the action of fault injection in the parallel way. Once the trigger is activated, the Trojan toggles 2 bits out of 32 bits at 29th round of SIMON after the EXORation of the round key. The effect and propagation of faults from 30th to 32nd round of SIMON 32/64 is shown in Fig. 2, it is ultimately to obtain all 32 bit faulty cipher text. Note: Trig_Ext_1 is the external activation switch and Trig_rnd_2 is the round count of 29.

3.2   Hardware Trojan Insertion and Activation on SIMON

The inserted HTH in SIMON feistel structure as shown in Fig. 3, aids the adversary to precede with fault compliant by applying the Differential Fault Analysis technique. The HTH proposed for two bit fault injection in SIMON involves two activation trigger conditions: one is sliding ON/OFF of an external DIP switch whose activation depends upon the adversary and it's optional too; The other is when the round counter counts 29 then the trigger input gets ON or rise to '1'. During the 29th round the payload gets activated and so the action of fault injection hits to flip the two bits of the 29th round cipher. In consequence to the HT action, the fault propagates and scatters throughout in order to obtain the entire 32 bit ciphertext as faulty one. Using this completely flawed ciphertext the entire 64 bit last round key can be extracted.

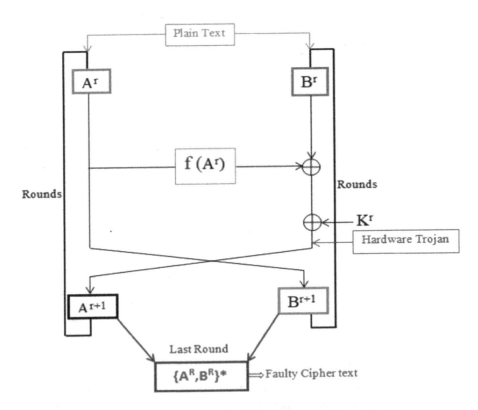

Fig. 3. HTH insertion on SIMON feistel encryption network

The principle of Hardware Trojan based fault injection is tantamount to intentional leakage of confidential informations or blocks for Side Channel Analysis (SCA). For an adversary it is also possible to attack the device or even any crypto system remotely and retrieve the private key.

3.3 The Action of Designed HTH

The following is the trigger condition for the payload action of Hardware Trojan:

A combinational HTH is designed and intruded in the 29th round of the feistel encryption structure after EXORation of the round key. The trigger logic of the designed HTH is a single AND gate whose activation input condition is round count of 29 by the round counter and the external activation switch. When the trigger logic is triggered, the payloads of two XOR gate gets activated and does fault injection action (two bit toggling). This action of payloads reflects in the resulting 29th round ciphertext and those fault propagates and scattered throughout until 32nd round final ciphertext. The propagation of two bit toggling fault, it's position and action are clearly depicted in the Fig. 4.

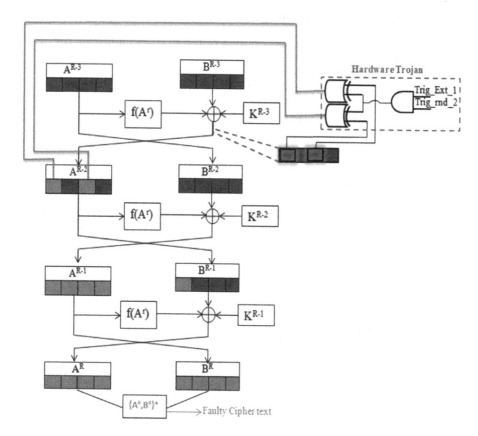

Fig. 4. Fault injection and propagation due to Hardware Trojan in SIMON

The method followed to extract the resulting faulty and fault free ciphertext is explained in the following subscription.

The key extraction is taken place using the technique called Differential Fault Analysis (DFA) for which the faulty free $\{A^R, B^R\}$ and all 32 bit faulty ciphertext 'A^R, B^R*' is required. Hence by computing the SIMON with it's appropriate plaintext $\{A^r, B^r\}$ and the key $\{K^r\}$, fault free and the faulty ciphertext are obtained. Acquiring this uncorrupted and corrupted ciphertext pair $\{\{A^R, B^R\}, \{A^R, B^R\}*\}$, the escalation of DFA attack is ensued. This process results in retrieving the all 64 bit round key successfully from the SIMON encryption module.

4   An Attack Through Fault Injection on SIMON

The characteristic that confers to mount the fault attack is the round function of the SIMON. Hence the round function of the SIMON is discussed in the forth coming subsection followed by the description of fault attack.

4.1   SIMON Round Function

Figure 1 uncloaks the round transformation of the SIMON cipher for the given input plaintext and the key.

One round of SIMON is a function,

f_k: $GF(2^n)$ X $GF(2^n)$ → $GF(2^n)$ X $GF(2^n)$ is defined as:

$$f_{k^r}(A^r, B^r) = (A^{r+1}, A^{r+1})$$
$$= (B^r) \oplus f(A^r) \oplus k^r, A^r \tag{1}$$

where r ∈ $\{0, \ldots, R-1\}$. And, $f(A^r) = (<<1(A^r) \, \& \, <<8(A^r)) \oplus << 2(A^r)$. Using this equation four bits of the rear round key matches in one encryption of fault-free and faulty ciphertext pair.

The fault attack using Hardware Trojan that is described, feat the information leaked through the HT action worn in the round function computation. And also the paper shows that the confidentiality of the key completely relies on the penultimate round of left half input.

4.2   Equations for Last Round Key Retrieval

The final ciphertext of the SIMON is expressed as $\{A^R, B^R\}$, where R is the total number of rounds to be computed.

$$A^R = B^{R-1} \oplus f(A^{R-1}) \oplus k^{R-1}$$
$$B^R = A^{R-1} \tag{2}$$

Hence, the last round key k^{R-1} can be expressed as,

$$k^{R-1} = B^{R-1} \oplus f(A^{R-1}) \oplus A^R \tag{3}$$

As $B^R = A^{R-1}$ and $B^{R-1} = A^{R-2}$,

$$k^{R-1} = A^{R-2} \oplus f(B^R) \oplus A^R \tag{4}$$

The retrieval of last round key k^{R-1} can be successfully done using the above equation, if the A^{R-2} value is known. As per the observation the injected faulty input reveals the fault value information but deny providing any information about A^{R-2}. Withal, if A^{R-2} is targeted, the value of fault induced and A^{R-2} bits can be inferred as well. The fault attack that is been targeted and the retrieval of A^{R-2} in order to recover k^{R-1} are described.

4.3   Analyzing the Position of the Fault and Value

Here the fault e is introduced in the intermediate Feistel encryption structure A^{R-3}. And let the faulty ciphertext denoted as A^R, B^{R*}.

Since $B^{r+1} = A^r$, $r \in \{0, \ldots, R-1\}$, we can derive the following equations. The fault-free and faulty ciphertext,

$$
\begin{aligned}
A^R \oplus A^{R*} &= B^{R-1} \oplus f(A^{R-1}) \oplus B^{R-1*} \oplus f(A^{R-1*}) \\
&= B^{R-1} \oplus f(B^R) \oplus B^{R-1*} \oplus f(B^{R*}) \\
&= A^{R-2} \oplus f(B^R) \oplus A^{R-2*} \oplus f(B^{R*}) \\
&= A^{R-2} \oplus f(B^R) \oplus A^{R-2} \oplus I \oplus f(B^{R*}) \\
&= f(B^R) \oplus e \oplus f(B^{R*}) \\
Therefore, \quad e &= A^R \oplus A^{R*} \oplus f(B^R) \oplus f(B^{R*}) \tag{5}
\end{aligned}
$$

The output of with and without fault computation deduce the position and value of the fault e injected in A^{R-2} and so the bit flips in A^{R-2} are determined.

5   Estimation of Power and Area Overhead of SIMON on ZYNQ 7000 SoC Family

The simulation results of with and without HTH in SIMON is made to facilitate the Piret's Differential Fault Analysis. The Hardware Trojan gets activated when the trigger is ON and two bits are flipped. It is an instantiation of the multiple payload with single trigger HTH that is been inserted in the SIMON depicted in Fig. 2, where the HTH design and the generation of faulty cipher text when the HT is triggered is clearly shown in Fig. 3. The propagation of the fault due to HTH action is clearly depicted in Fig. 4 with the parameter of 32/64 (Size of plain text (2n)/key size(nm)). The design is tested on ZYNQ 7000 SoC family FPGA board.

Table 1 evince the simulation results and comparisons of power consumed by the SIMON module with and without HTH. The estimation of power is done using Simulation Activity Information File (.saif) in XILINX Vivado 2016.4 version. The power difference is realized as only 1.32% which is minimal and almost negligible.

Table 1. Estimation of power for with and without HTH

Design	Total on-chip power (W)	Dynamic power (W)	Device static power (W)
SIMON 32/64 without HTH	2.111	1.874	0.238
SIMON 32/64 with HTH	2.139	1.901	0.238

Table 2. Utilization of area for with and without HTH

Design	Slice LUTs	Slice registers	BRAM	Bounded IOB
SIMON 32/64 without HTH	27 LUT5 - 33	37	0	81
SIMON 32/64 with HTH	27 LUT5 - 32	37	0	81

Table 2 compares the performance of the HTH that is described in the previous sections and the HTH gets activated when trigger is ON. The Hardware Trojan modeled and inserted is very small with only one LUT difference and so it did not create much impact over speed degradation. Provided, this particular configuration made the implementation of DFA attack easy. As a reminiscence, the activation trigger condition of the AND logic inputs are rised to 1'd1, the payload action of the HTH takes place. Thus a fault free and the faulty ciphertext can be obtained for the further DFA analysis to retrieve the key.

6   Conclusion

The design and impacts of Hardware Trojan Horse in a crypto module to serve the purpose of secret key recovery is one of the research highlights. Two bit flip fault attack on 29th round of the SIMON by intruding Hardware Trojan Horse is successfully made. The structural design of Hardware Trojan includes activation of two payloads with a single trigger. In consequence, the round key of SIMON cipher is retrieved by executing Differential Fault Analysis, using the fault free and completely faulty ciphertext. The power consumption for both with and without Hardware Trojan of the SIMON design is estimated and observed that there is minimal overhead of 1.32% using Simulation Activity Information File (.saif) on ZYNQ 7000 SoC family FPGA board. Provided, almost negligible difference of one LUT in area utilization is discerned.

Acknowledgment. Its an immense pleasure for the authors to show their gratitude towards Interdisciplinary Cyber Physical Systems (ICPS) project, Department of Science and Technology (DST) for funding this research work under Project number: DST/ICPS/CPS-Individual/2018/819.

References

1. Beaulieu, R., Shors, D., Smith, J., Treatman-Clark, S., Weeks, B., Wingers, L.: The SIMON and SPECK families of lightweight block ciphers. Cryptology ePrint Archive, Report 2013/404 (2013). https://eprint.iacr.org/2013/404
2. Manivannan, S., Nalla Anandakumar, N., Nirmala Devi, M.: Key retrieval from AES architecture through hardware trojan horse. In: Thampi, S.M., Madria, S., Wang, G., Rawat, D.B., Alcaraz Calero, J.M. (eds.) SSCC 2018. CCIS, vol. 969, pp. 483–494. Springer, Singapore (2019). https://doi.org/10.1007/978-981-13-5826-5_37
3. Takahashi, J., Fukunaga, T., Yamakoshi, K.: DFA mechanism on the AES key schedule. In: Workshop on Fault Diagnosis and Tolerance in Cryptography (FDTC 2007), pp. 62–74, September 2007
4. Piret, G., Quisquater, J.-J.: A differential fault attack technique against SPN structures, with application to the AES and KHAZAD. In: Walter, C.D., Koç, Ç.K., Paar, C. (eds.) CHES 2003. LNCS, vol. 2779, pp. 77–88. Springer, Heidelberg (2003). https://doi.org/10.1007/978-3-540-45238-6_7
5. Giraud, C., Thillard, A.: Piret and quisquater's DFA on AES revisited (2010). http://eprint.iacr.org/2010/440. c.giraud@oberthur.com 14834 received 13 August 2010
6. Ali, S.S., Mukhopadhyay, D., Tunstall, M.: Differential fault analysis of AES: towards reaching its limits. J. Cryptographic Eng. **3**(2), 73–97 (2013). https://doi.org/10.1007/s13389-012-0046-y
7. Tupsamudre, H., Bisht, S., Mukhopadhyay, D.: Differential fault analysis on the families of SIMON and SPECK ciphers. In: Workshop on Fault Diagnosis and Tolerance in Cryptography, pp. 40–48, September 2014
8. Vasquez, J.d.C.G., Borges, F., Portugal, R., Lara, P.: An efficient one-bit model for differential fault analysis on SIMON family. In: Workshop on Fault Diagnosis and Tolerance in Cryptography (FDTC), pp. 61–70, September 2015
9. Kim, C.H.: Improved differential fault analysis on AES key schedule. IEEE Trans. Inf. Forensics Secur. **7**(1), 41–50 (2012)
10. Zhang, J., Wu, N., Zhou, F., Yahya, M., Li, J.: A novel differential fault is on the key schedule of SIMON family. Electronics **8**, 93 (2019)
11. Chen, H., Feng, J., Rijmen, V., Liu, Y., Fan, L., Li, W.: Improved fault analysis on SIMON block cipher family. In: Workshop on Fault Diagnosis and Tolerance in Cryptography (FDTC), pp. 16–24, August 2016
12. Krautter, J., Gnad, D., Tahoori, M.: FPGAhammer: remote voltage fault attacks on shared FPGAs, suitable for DFA on AES. IACR Trans. Cryptographic Hardware Embedded Syst. **2018**(3), 44–68 (2018). https://tches.iacr.org/index.php/TCHES/article/view/7268

Privacy-Preserving Authentication Scheme Using Reduced-Advanced Encryption Standard for Vehicular Ad Hoc Network

S. Sharon[1], T. Suriya Praba[2], R. Anushiadevi[2],
and Veeramuthu Venkatesh[2(✉)]

[1] Department of Electronic and Communication Engineering,
E G S Pillay Polytechnic College, Nagapattinam, India
[2] School of Computing, SASTRA Deemed University, Thanjavur 613401, India
thambivv@gmail.com

Abstract. Vehicular Ad hoc Network (VANET) is a developing technology that provides traffic safety management and makes travelling convenient. The basic goal is to broadcast traffic-related information from one vehicle to other vehicle or from vehicle to Road Side Units (RSU) for offering safety in driving and prevent from road accidents. Security and privacy are required for transmitting the data. These data have to be prevented from various attacks on privacy and misuse of private data. In this paper, the proper mechanism for validating the data and eliminating the illegitimate user from the network is done using a symmetric cryptographic algorithm. The proposed method is an efficient privacy-preserving encryption scheme using Reduced Advanced Encryption Standard (R-AES). It reduces the time taken for encryption, computational complexity, energy consumption and memory requirement for storing keys. It is suitable for hardware implementation and secured against a brute force attack. Thus, the method attains data confidentiality, data privacy, authentication and data integrity. It is effective in terms of meting out time and attains maximum throughput. Finally, it is compared with an existing cryptographic algorithm.

Keywords: Vehicular Ad Hoc Networks · Privacy · Attacks · Authentication · Security

1 Introduction

Vehicular Ad hoc Network (VANET) [1–4] has been attracted in recent decades towards extensive research and development to increase traffic safety and to provide convenience in driving. Every year in the world, hundreds of thousands of lives are lost and or injured due to road accidents. By monitoring and sending traffic-related information as well as alert messages will save many lives from accidents. The network of vehicles that are moving at high speed is made to communicate with each other for a different purpose, particularly for road safety. VANET network consists of vehicles that have an inbuilt On board Unit (OBU) and infrastructure fixed on the road side called as Road Side Unit (RSU). They communicate wirelessly with each other for exchanging the data about traffic and driving status. The data that are to be transmitted are traffic

© Springer Nature Singapore Pte Ltd. 2019
V. S. Shankar Sriram et al. (Eds.): ATIS 2019, CCIS 1116, pp. 254–265, 2019.
https://doi.org/10.1007/978-981-15-0871-4_20

signal, lane change warning, location, vehicle identification number, dangerous road features, crash alert and incidents occurred such as accident, road block etc. Based on this information, another vehicle can change its routes for travelling and avoid the congestion of traffic, which is shown in the Fig. 1. VANET framework model.

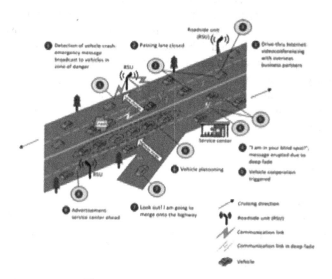

Fig. 1. VANET framework model

VANET framework that shows the communication between V2V and V2R. Initially, vehicle registration is done, and then, data transmission can be done. In V2V communication, data is transmitted from one vehicle to many vehicles. For V2R communication, data transmission occurs between vehicle and road side unit (RSU). Exchange of data happens wirelessly using Dedicated Short-Range Communication (DSCR) with communication with the range of 100–300 ms. VANET predicts the chances of accidents and sends warning notification to the driver of the vehicle and so accidents can be avoided. In case of road block or accident occurred, and the information is transmitted to the driver they can take an alternate travelling route which in turn will save time, avoid traffic jam, and it will save fuel. Transmitting the information about an emergency vehicle travelling on heavy traffic road will notify all other vehicles to provide a way for the emergency vehicle. Attacks, alerts can be predicted, and accidents can be avoided by sending alert messages. Integrity and confidentiality of the message should be preserved for secured data transmission. Security requirements for VANET [5–7] can be classified into two types that are inherited from Mobile Ad Hoc Networks and the other due to cooperative vehicular communication. In VANET, security is the most important for the exchange of data. The performance requirement for VANET in a security system is crucial. Two major reasons are high mobility speed of the vehicle and real-time analysis of data. Purpose of the attack is to create a problem for users to access some information.

There are a variety of attacks such as Replay attack, Forgery attack, Impersonation Attack, Masquerade and Denial of service attacks etc. [8]. In Replay attacks, the transmission of data is repeated or delayed. Forgery attack is sending of false data. Impersonate attack is the one identity of the legitimate user are assumed by the adversary. Masquerading is defined as unauthorized access to the data. In denial of service attack, the attackers prevent the legal users of the system from accessing the service. Since highly sensitive data are transmitted in VANET, it must be secure. Invalid or unauthorized user should be identified initially and blocked. The proper mechanism is required for authenticating the data. This can be done using an encryption-decryption scheme.

The paper is structured as: Sect. 2 describes the literature survey. The proposed scheme is described in Sect. 3. Result, and output is discussed in Sect. 5. Section 6 is about the conclusion and future enhancements.

2 Related Works

Numerous authentication schemes that address the security and privacy challenges are discussed. These schemes can be categorized as 1. Anonymous pseudonym-based authentication 2. Identity based authentication. Using public key infrastructure (PKI) are used for the implementation of pseudonym-based scheme.

In [9] proposed the authentication that uses the anonymous certificate. The real identity of the user is hidden by using certificates. Authentication and integrity are achieved by adopting public key infrastructure. Multiple pairs of the public key along with its certificate, are stored by each vehicle. Different keys are used for signing the message to maintain anonymity. Cost for the verification of the message is high, and the vehicle should be equipped with large storage for key storage. While detecting malicious message it searches to find the real identity of the key that is compromised. In [10] group-based signature was proposed. Vehicle stores the group public key and group private key. This same group key is utilized all the vehicles and signatures are authenticated using the key. This scheme reduced the overhead of storing the anonymous key in the vehicle. But it has computation overhead, the length of the signature is larger, and the cost of computation is high. In [11], low communication overhead with the hashing-based message authentication code was proposed. All the schemes based on PKI have a disadvantage for the storage of the keys. Problems created by the certificate are overcome by Identity-based batch verification. In [12] proposed the scheme that provides low communication cost and anonymity for the users. The vehicle uses a signing key for the signing of the messages. After that, they are sent for verification; all the messages are verified by RSU in the batch process. And the notification messages are sent to the vehicle. The secret key is created and directed to all the members for verification. But disadvantage of the scheme it can be affected by impersonating attacks. In [13] proposed the scheme provides security to the random oracle model. This scheme reduces delay in computation and transmission overhead. It requires constant no pairing and point of multiplication.

Multiple messages are verified at the same time. Messages are signed using the key, and they are broadcasted. RSU receives the messages, and multiple messages are verified. The disadvantage is that the unauthorized signature cannot be identified in batch verification. In [14] proposed the lightweight authentication scheme that provides privacy preservation that makes use of decentralized certificate authority (CA) and biological password-based two-factor authentications it may be fingerprint or iris identification. It achieves conditional privacy and non-repudiation. This also provides a scheme for updating the key when they are leaked. Information about vehicle and driver can be revealed during dispute time. The disadvantage of the scheme is it fully dependent on CA and Keys.

3 Proposed Secured Data Communication System

Data about the traffic events and alert messages are transmitted between vehicles and RSU for safe travelling, which has become our data to day routine [15]. Every vehicle has an inbuilt on-board unit (OBU) which acts as a communication module that wirelessly communicates with the RSU. Whenever a vehicle enters into the road side unit coverage area, it should send the vehicle identification number along with the time for storage. After registration, communication can be established based on the requirement. The data transmitted are traffic events such as traffic signal, location,

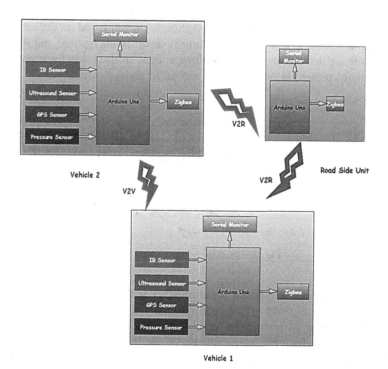

Fig. 2. Secured data communication VANET using Arduino UNO

accident occurred, lane change warning and crash alert etc. These data can be revealed during the dispute period such as an accident etc. This scheme provides resource-constrained implementation of hardware using Arduino Uno, ZigBee and sensors shown in Fig. 2.

3.1 Data Security in VANET Using AES Algorithm

AES is the standard algorithm that utilizes the key size of 128 bits and 10 rounds of operation. For each round four operations are performed, they are

- Sub byte
- Shift row
- Mix column
- Add round key

In Sub byte/Inverse sub-byte is the initial transformation process done using substitution (S-box) table it can operate on each byte of the state independently, and it is a nonlinear type of byte substitution. The inverse of the multiplicative group for Galois field with the finite field is taken. Affine transformation is done to perform the sub-byte operation. For inverse, sub-byte is performed using inverse affine transformation. In this process, values for s-box are calculated every time, which increases the computation complexity.

Shift row/inverse shift row is the transformation that operates within rows of state, which performs cyclic shift by left. The first row remains unchanged, and the last three rows are shifted one, two and three-byte position to the left based on the row location for shifting as shown in Fig. 3. This shifting is done for encryption, and the inverse process is for the decryption process. Shifting is done in right side for inverse operation. Four bytes present in one column is moved to various columns.

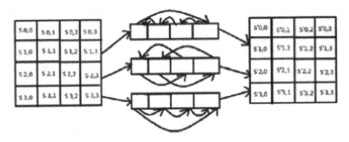

Fig. 3. Transformation of shift rows

Mix column/Inverse mix column transformation is the substitution process that is done with the help of Galois field multiplication and works independently to each column. It is similar to performing matrix multiplication for every column. Fixed matrix is used for multiplying with a column vector. Every byte present in the column is replaced with the new value as the function of 4 bytes within the column present, as shown in Fig. 4. This works on the column of the state, where each column of the state is considered as polynomial four terms. The inverse process is done for decryption. In Add round key is transformation where bitwise XOR operation is performed between the present state and 128 bits round key.

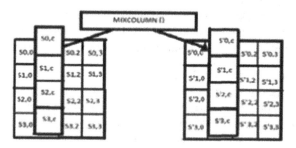

Fig. 4. Transformation of Mix column

4 System Implementation

This proposed work establishes secure communication between three devices, as shown in Fig. 2. Arduino interfaced with sensor and connected with ZigBee acts as the module for vehicle and Arduino connected with ZigBee acts as the road side unit. This shows data transmission between V2V and V2R. Arduino Uno board is the micro-controllers that were programmed to receive data from multiple sensors, and the received data were encrypted using R-AES algorithm and transmitted through ZigBee, which acts as a wireless communication module. Sensors interfaced with Arduino board are IR sensor, ultrasound sensor, pressure sensor and GPS sensor. IR sensor is involved in the detection of the vehicle identification number along with the time stamp. These data are stored in the file by running the program in processing three software, and these data can be referred to when they are required. Ultrasound sensor detects crash alert by measuring the distance less than 20 cms. Accidents are detected by using a pressure sensor on applying pressure. Global Positioning System (GPS sensor) is involved in tracking the vehicle in terms of latitude and longitude where location can be obtained from google map. ZigBee CC2500 was configured using X-CTU software, and Arduino was programmed using Arduino IDE. The output is obtained in the serial monitor separately for 3 devices. Whenever data is detected, they are encrypted, and at the receiver, they are decrypted. Data are securely transmitted by incorporation of R-AES in VANET.

4.1 Reduced AES Algorithm

R-AES algorithm is the modified version of standard AES algorithm that is designed in a resource-constrained way with the key size of 128 bits and the number of rounds as reduces as 7 rounds that decreases the overall processing time and computational complexity. It takes the input of 128 bits plain text and converts it into the output of 128 bits cipher text. It is an iterative algorithm where the same keys are used for both encryption and decryption process, and all the four operations are performed 7 times. During initial operation, plaint text enters into Add round key stage as shown in Fig. 3 and output from that stage goes through 6 main rounds before entering into the 7th round that is the final round. Mix-column is eliminated in the last round. Figure 5 explains the flow of R-AES. Finally, cipher text is obtained as a result of encryption. For decryption cipher text is converted to plain text and it is the inverse process of decryption. Among the four operations of AES shift-rows and mix, the column remains the same for R-AES. Sub byte and add round key transformation are modified

Sub byte/Inverse sub-byte for R-AES values from the s-box is substituted to the corresponding values in the rows and column, as shown in Fig. 6. Multiplication of Galois field is the complicated process; calculated values are substituted to the S-box by the benefit of look up the table instead of calculating values during transformation. This process is carried out in parallel to decrease the latency and computational complexity.

Shift row/inverse shift row is the transformation was shifting the rows of state are similar to AES by performing a cyclic shift in the left side.

Mix column/Inverse mix column transformation is the substitution process that is done similar to AES.

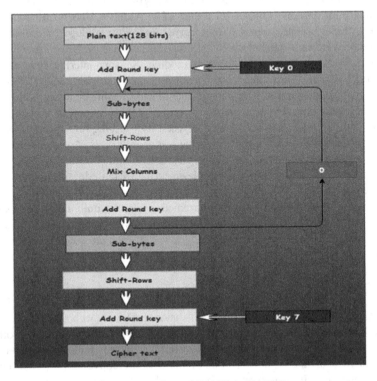

Fig. 5. Data flow of R-AES in VANET

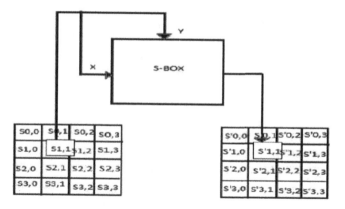

Fig. 6. Transformation of Sub byte

In Add round key transformation between the state key and round key simple XOR operation is performed. Key scheduling is performed to extract the round key from the cipher key. Same sized state key and round key with 128 bits are used. XOR operation is performed for each element to obtain the next state.

Generation of a key in AES

Key generation process in AES is also called as Key expansion that makes use of 4 words, i.e. 16-byte input and produces an output of 44 words, i.e. 156 bytes. Keys are usually generated earlier and stored. Keys for performing round transformation can be taken from the storage when required. In this scheme, keys are generated for each round such that it decreases the storage required for storing keys.

5 Results and Discussion

Every vehicle has to transmit its vehicle identification number and time stamp to the RSU to undergo a verification process. These data are stored in the file and can be revealed when required. By running processing 3 software, the collected data from Arduino can be stored automatically in the notepad. Figure 7 shows information about each vehicle registration.

Figure 8 shows the encrypted data obtained from OBU in vehicle2 about lane change warning and crash alert are transmitted to vehicle 1, and they are decrypted Fig. 9 shows the encrypted data about the location of the accident obtained from RSU. Figure 10 shows the data received from the vehicle about car ID Data detected by the sensors are encrypted and transmitted to the other device and at receiver device they are decrypted. The output is obtained in the serial monitor.

Fig. 7. Vehicle registration information   **Fig. 8.** Encrypted data obtained from OBU

Fig. 9. Encrypted data about the location of the accident   **Fig. 10.** Data received from the vehicle through RSU

From Table 1, it is clear that for sending data with a packet of 128 bytes proposed reduced AES algorithm takes lesser time and fast in encryption/decryption process. Based on the inferences from the table results are plotted. Figure 11a and b shows the comparison based on several rounds for DES, RSA, Lightweight AES, and PRESENT algorithm with R-AES. The no of rounds is very less in PRESENT, but it takes more time for encryption, which causes a delay in the communication. For the present block size and key size are lesser, but encryption time is larger.

Table 1. Comparison factors for the different encryption methods

Algorithm	Key size (bits)	Block size (bits)	Packet size (bytes)	Encryption/Decryption time (ms)	No of rounds
DES	56	64	128	1.2	16
RSA	1024	688	128	5.4	1
Lightweight AES	128	128	128	1.05	10
Lightweight PRESENT	80	64	128	3.3	3
Proposed R-AES	128	128	128	0.7	7

(a)

(b)

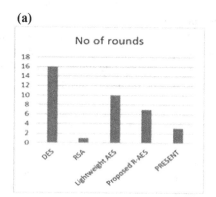

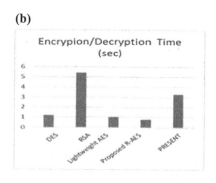

Fig. 11. (a) No of rounds vs Encryption techniques (b) Encryption/Decryption time vs techniques

(a)

(b)

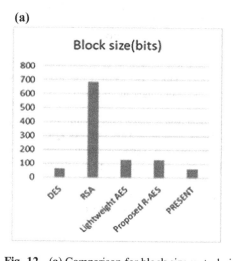

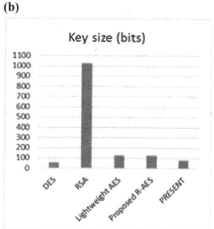

Fig. 12. (a) Comparison for block size vs techniques (b) Comparison for key size vs techniques

Comparison based on key size, block size, Encryption/Decryption time and number of rounds are done for different algorithm shown in Fig. 12a and b. From the graph R-AES algorithm is efficient and provides the encryption time of 0.7 ms as compared to other algorithms, it provides the fastest communication. Since it takes less time for the maximum encryption number of messages can be transmitted within second as compared to other algorithms. Hence it achieves maximum throughput as compared to other algorithms, and it is secure and efficient.

6 Conclusion

Vehicular Ad hoc Network has become the most interesting field for intelligent transportation systems because of the transmission of safety-related information. Security and privacy are important for establishing communication between vehicles and RSU. An efficient privacy-preserving authentication frame for VANET using R-AES algorithm is proposed. It takes less encryption time, and so achieves maximum throughput, reduced energy consumption and storage space for keys. It is efficient in terms of providing fast encryption and secures against attacks. The future scope will be based on introducing a fault-tolerant technique to reduce the delay further.

References

1. Balaji, N.A., Sukumar, R., Parvathy, M.: Enhanced dual authentication and key management scheme for data authentication in vehicular ad hoc network. Comput. Electr. Eng. **76**, 94–110 (2019)
2. Vijayakumar, P., Azees, M., Kannan, A., Deborah, L.J.: Dual authentication and key management techniques for secure data transmission in vehicular ad hoc networks. IEEE Trans. Intell. Transp. Syst. **17**, 1015–1028 (2015)
3. Xie, Y., Wu, L., Zhang, Y., Shen, J.: Efficient and secure authentication scheme with conditional privacy-preserving for VANETs. Chin. J. Electron. **25**, 950–956 (2016)
4. He, D., Zeadally, S., Xu, B., Huang, X.: An efficient identity-based conditional privacy-preserving authentication scheme for vehicular ad hoc networks. IEEE Trans. Inf. Forensics Secur. **10**, 2681–2691 (2015)
5. Tay, J.J., Wong, M.M., Hijazin, I.: Compact and low power AES block cipher using lightweight key expansion mechanism and optimal number of S-Boxes. In: International Symposium on Intelligent Signal Processing and Communication Systems (ISPACS), pp 108–114 (2014)
6. Kang, Q., Liu, X., Yao, Y., et al.: Efficient authentication and access control of message dissemination over vehicular ad hoc network. Neurocomputing **181**, 132–138 (2016)
7. Horng, S.-J., Tzeng, S.-F., Pan, Y., et al.: b-SPECS+: batch verification for secure pseudonymous authentication in VANET. IEEE Trans. Inf. Forensics Secur. **8**, 1860–1875 (2013)
8. Deeksha, A.K., Bansal, M.: A review on VANET security attacks and their countermeasure. In: 4th International Conference on Signal Processing, Computing and Control (ISPCC), pp. 580–585 (2017)

9. Raya, M., Hubaux, J.-P.: Securing vehicular ad hoc networks. J. Comput. Secur. **15**, 39–68 (2007)
10. Lin, X., Sun, X., Ho, P.-H., Shen, X.: GSIS: a secure and privacy-preserving protocol for vehicular communications. IEEE Trans. Veh. Technol. **56**, 3442–3456 (2007)
11. Zhang, C., Ho, P.-H., Tapolcai, J.: On batch verification with group testing for vehicular communications. Wirel. Netw. **17**, 1851–1865 (2011)
12. Chim, T.W., Yiu, S.-M., Hui, L.C.K., Li, V.O.K.: SPECS: secure and privacy enhancing communications schemes for VANETs. Ad Hoc Netw. **9**, 189–203 (2011)
13. Tzeng, S.-F., Horng, S.-J., Li, T., et al.: Enhancing security and privacy for identity-based batch verification scheme in VANETs. IEEE Trans. Veh. Technol. **66**, 3235–3248 (2015)
14. Wang, F., Xu, Y., Zhang, H., et al.: 2FLIP: a two-factor lightweight privacy-preserving authentication scheme for VANET. IEEE Trans. Veh. Technol. **65**, 896–911 (2015)
15. Zuo, C., Liang, K., Jiang, Z.L., et al.: Cost-effective privacy-preserving vehicular urban sensing system. Pers. Ubiquitous Comput. **21**, 893–901 (2017)

On the Security of the Double-Block-Length Hash Function NCASH

Tapadyoti Banerjee[⊠] and Dipanwita Roy Chowdhury

Crypto Research Lab, Department of Computer Science and Engineering,
IIT Kharagpur, Kharagpur, India
tapadyoti@gmail.com, drc@cse.iitkgp.ac.in

Abstract. In this work, we study the security analysis of a newly proposed Non-linear Cellular Automata-based Hash function, NCASH. The uncomplicated structure of this double-block-length hash function instigates us to scrutinize its construction by analyzing the security of the design. Here, we have performed a security analysis with respect to the standard model of concrete security. In addition, structural security has also been investigated by performing the correlation analysis. We have examined the security bound of this scheme by using the random oracle model. The Preimage or Second Preimage Resistance and Collision Resistance of NCASH-256 are 2^{256} and 2^{128} respectively. According to the best of our knowledge, these bounds provide better security comparing with most of the other acclaimed existing schemes.

Keywords: Cellular automata · Double-block-length hash ·
Correlation analysis · Random oracle model

1 Introduction

The one-way hash function produces a compressed and fixed sized output from a variable-length message input. The elementary component of this operation is compression function. Some of the popular modern hash constructions are Sponge construction [7], Merkle Damgård [10], Wide pipe construction [25], etc. Many keyed and unkeyed[1] cryptographic hash functions, such as HMAC [5], Message Digest algorithm [29], Secure Hash Algorithm (SHA) [12], etc. have been proposed based on these constructions. After this first wave, SHA-3 [11] competition has started due to the extensive demand for an efficient and low computational overhead hash function. Here Keccak [6] wins and becomes the hash standard. In the SHA-3, mainly the efficiency of hash designs had been stressed by NIST. In the light of security and from the implementation perspective, it is conspicuous that highly secure designs may not be cost-efficient.

---

[1] Keyed hash functions accept the secret key and the message to produce the hash value whereas, unkeyed hash functions accept only the message.

© Springer Nature Singapore Pte Ltd. 2019
V. S. Shankar Sriram et al. (Eds.): ATIS 2019, CCIS 1116, pp. 266–278, 2019.
https://doi.org/10.1007/978-981-15-0871-4_21

This leads researchers towards the classical trade-off situation, where one can negotiate some of the security aspects to build up optimal architectures. As a result, hitherto, a bit of research has been done to explore Cellular Automata (CA) as a hash-primitive. Recently, a double-block-length hash function, NCASH (Non-linear Cellular Automata-based Hash function) [2] has been suggested, which is constructed only with uncomplicated and elegant CA-structure. In our work, we have done the security analysis of NCASH based on the standard model of concrete security and prove that this scheme provides better security bound in compare with most of the other existing schemes.

The idea of analyzing the CA as a hash-primitive was first proposed by Damgård [10], which was successfully attacked by Daemen et al. [9], and Cellhash has been proposed as a secure hash function. Later, a hash function has suggested by Mihaljevic et al. [26] where linear CA have been used over GF(q). Thenceforth ample research has been done [3,13,21] to explore the CA as a hash-primitive. Although they have explored the CA, some complex design architectures have also been used to make the function secure. Alongside the researchers were also aware of increasing the security bound of the hash functions. In 1992, Xucjia Lai and James L. Massey has proposed 2n-bit hash round functions, Abreast DM and Tandem DM, whose block cipher length is n-bit whereas key length is 2n-bit [22]. This invention leads to another direction of research with a motivation of how to increase collision security. A hash function is considered as a highly secure one if the required number of queries will be $\Omega(2^{n/2})$ for the best collision attack, i.e., the equal complexity of the birthday attack[2]. Thus, one can increase the level of security by introducing 2n-bit hash functions, which is acquainted as double-length hash functions. Hirose has proposed the black-box design of double-block-length hash functions [17], which is later redefined in [18]. Thereafter so many research has been done [14,27] to construct this. Most of these are using a 2n-bit size key with block cipher size n-bit, which seems quite expensive. In the case of NCASH, they have used an n-bit key instead of 2n-bit. Our work addresses this issue and hence determine to examine the strength of this scheme and try to find whether it gives more or an equal level of security.

In our work, we examine the structural security of NCASH. We have shown that the intermediate results of the hash function show almost no correlation. Here, the security values are determined by using the random oracle model [8]. Finally, a comparison has also been done which affirms that this scheme provides the higher security bound against most of the other well-known schemes.

Our Contributions:

- NCASH has been analyzed and it has been shown that the intermediate hash values posses no correlation and thus avoids the correlation attacks.
- Preimage or Second Preimage and Collision Security have been determined with respect to random oracle model.

---

[2] With respect to probability theory, the wellknown birthday problem (sometime defined as birthday paradox) finds the probability of getting the same birthday from a set of N number of people that are chosen haphazardly.

- Finally, it has also been analyze that it contributes better security bound than most of the other existing renouned double-block-length hash functions.

The residuum is arranged in the following way. At the beginning, the basics of Cellular Automata and the newly proposed scheme NCASH has been discussed in Sect. 2. There after Sect. 3 describes the correlation analysis of this scheme. Section 4 determines the security bound of NCASH by using the random oracle model and claims that it is secure over most of the other renouned double-block-length hash functions. Finally, our work has been concluded in Sect. 5.

2   Background and Preliminaries

Very recently, Banerjee and Roy Chowdhury have provided a new one-way double-block-length keyed hash function, NCASH [2]. It is constructed with uncomplicated and elegant Cellular Automata (CA) based structure and uses only bitwise operations. Before presenting the security analysis of NCASH, this section briefly describes the principle of CA [28] and the design structure of NCASH [2].

2.1   Cellular Automata

CA are a discrete trellis of cells placed in a special pattern. They consist of memory element (i.e., flip-flop) with combinational logic function [28]. The cells are updated simultaneously at each clock pulse by using the rule or transition function. The rule is defined by the decimal equivalent of the truth table provided by that function. To update the value of a particular cell, CA take the present values of the cell itself with the neighborhood cells and perform some logical operations. For a one-dimensional three-neighborhood cellular automata, the next status of the ith cell is as follows:

$$S_i^{t+1} = f(S_{i-1}^t, S_i^t, S_{i+1}^t), \text{ where the } i^{th} \text{ state at time stamp } t \text{ is } S_i^t \qquad (1)$$

In the construction of NCASH [2], maximum length hybrid cellular automata are used with rule 90 ($S_i^{t+1} = S_{i-1}^t \oplus S_{i+1}^t$) and rule 150 ($S_i^{t+1} = S_{i-1}^t \oplus S_i^t \oplus S_{i+1}^t$). Where maximum length CA produce all the states except only the one state, all 0's. For hybrid CA, the cells evolve with rules, both linear and non-linear generating Linear Hybrid CA (LHCA) and Non-Linear Hybrid CA (NHCA). In the case of linear CA, only linear operations such as EXOR are used whereas, Non-linear CA are comprised by linear rules along with some non-linear ones such as AND/OR. The linear CA can be converted into non-linear one by injecting the non-linear function at one/more cells [16]. The conversion is described with Fig. 1, which shows a single round null-boundary LHCA. Null-boundary refers that the most and least significant CA-cells consider the state of the boundary neighbors are null or zero. It is converted into NHCA in Fig. 2. The non-linearity inject position is the cell with D_2 flip-flop and the non-linear function is $Q_0 \& Q_4$ where '&' denotes the logical AND operation.

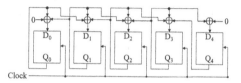

Fig. 1. 5-cell maximum length LHCA with rule $\langle 150, 150, 150, 150, 90 \rangle$

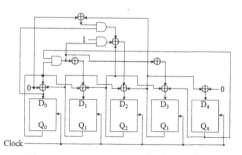

Fig. 2. 5-cell maximum length NHCA with rule $\langle 150, 150, 150, 150, 90 \rangle$

2.2 NCASH: Non-linear Cellular Automata Based Hash

For the shake of clarity, the basic architecture of NCASH [2] has been discussed here. It has been constructed using the LHCA and NHCA. Figure 3 depicts the intricate design of this scheme for l-bit hashtag, where $l = 2b$ and b is the block-length. Here a case with only two blocks of the message is shown. In the message padding stage, the message length len($\mathcal{M}$) is padded with the original message such that the block length should be 'b'. Atfirst the initial 'b'-bits of the private key, $\mathcal{K}$ is inserted into the NHCA and LHCA as the initialization vector (IV).

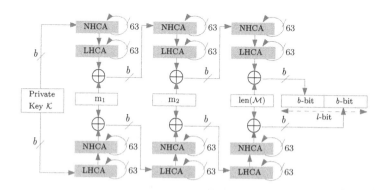

Fig. 3. Design structure of NCASH-l [2]

Then these CA are evolved, and their outputs are fed into the next LHCA and NHCA respectively. The outputs of the CA-chain are EXORed with the message block to produce the ultimate outputs of the compression function. They are considered as the inputs of the next compression function, and so on to generate the ultimate output.

Message Padding: Consider the message is $\mathcal{M} = m_1 m_2 m_3 \cdots m_n$ where each m_i ($i \in 1, \cdots n$) is the ith message block of length 'b'. If $|m_n| < b$, then $m_n = m_n \| 10^*$ ('$\|$' denotes concatenation of two bit strings). Therefore, the size of the $\mathcal{M}$ is padded with the modified message where it may be padded with the zero-string to create the length of the block 'b'.

Compression Function: This is illustrated in the Fig. 4. It is implemented by using a combination of linear and non-linear hybrid CA. In this figure only the ith stage of the function is shown. At the upper half of the compression function, one of the output of the $i-1^{th}$ stage is inserted into the NHCA and 63 number of pulses are applied. Now this output becomes the input of the next LHCA of the CA-chain. Henceforth, to get one of the outputs of this i^{th} stage, the ith message-block (denoted by 'm_i') is XORed with the output generated by the LHCA and it becomes one of the inputs of the $i+1^{th}$ stage. The structure of the lower half is exactly the reverse of the upper half, i.e., the sequence of NHCA and LHCA has changed. The lower half produces the other input for the $i+1^{th}$ stage.

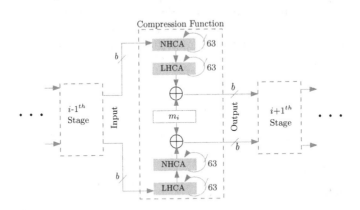

Fig. 4. i^{th} stage of the compression function of NCASH [2]

Tag Generation: The hashtag is produced by the $n+1^{th}$ round of the compression function. The output of the NHCA-LHCA chain is simply concatenated with the output of the LHCA-NHCA chain to construct the l-bit tag, where $l = 2b$.

Design Analysis of NCASH: In case of NCASH, there has a strong theoretical background for choosing the operations and parameters.

- **Importance of LHCA**: CA is a good random number generator [19]. Moreover, LHCA makes the correlation of the intermediate values complex and intricate.
- **Importance of NHCA**: In case of NHCA, finding the previous state is computationally infeasible. Which leads an extensive need of the NHCA to build a one-way function.
- **Use of 63 number of clock pulse**: Several analyses show that the minimum value of the clock pulse to produce a better diffusion is 63.
- **Randomized Value Generation**: The randomness of the hash tags generated by NCASH has successfully passed the NIST Statistical Test Suite for Random and Pseudorandom Number Generators (NIST SP 800-22) [30].
- **Exhaustive Key Search**: Exhaustive key search (i.e., also called brute-force search) for this scheme requires 2^{128} possible entities for NCASH-256.

Design of NCASH is proposed in [2], where the strength of this hash function has been shown against some of the preliminary attacks. In addition, the preimage or second preimage security and collision security of NCASH are only stated without any proof. For the symmetric structure of NCASH and the repeated uses of linear and non-linear functions, the correlation analysis may become the most threatening attack against this design. We have performed the correlation analysis of NCASH, which is described in the following section.

3 Correlation Analysis

NCASH uses two different CA-chains to generate the hash tag. One is the NHCA-LHCA chain belongs to the upper half of the compression function and the other is the LHCA-NHCA chain at the lower half (consider Fig. 4). Here, maximum length linear and non-linear cellular automata are used in each stage to generate the output after XOR-ing with the message. The uses of same LHCA and NHCA in different order has motivated us to perform the correlation analysis of the ith stage of the compression function.

Claim. The reverse executions of the linear hybrid CA and the non-linear hybrid CA show almost no correlation between their final outputs.

Proof. Consider Fig. 5 which breaks the Fig. 4 in two partial halves. Fig. 5(a) describes the upper half and Fig. 5(b) describes the lower half of the compression function. Let us assume that for Fig. 5(a), $\mathcal{W}_{i-1} = \Psi_i$ and $f(\Psi_i) = \tau_i$,

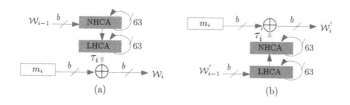

Fig. 5. Compression function in partial form

where $f(\Psi_i) = LHCA(NHCA(\Psi_i))$. Similarly, for Fig. 5(b), let $\mathcal{W}'_{i-1} = \Psi'_i$ and $f(\Psi'_i) = \tau'_i$, where $f(\Psi'_i) = NHCA(LHCA(\Psi'_i))$. Now,

$$\mathcal{W}_i = \tau_i \oplus m_i \tag{2}$$
$$\mathcal{W}'_i = \tau'_i \oplus m_i \tag{3}$$

Combining Eqs. 2 and 3, we get,

$$\mathcal{W}_i \oplus \mathcal{W}'_i = \tau_i \oplus \tau'_i \tag{4}$$

Therefore, we need to check the correlation between τ_i and τ'_i only to determine the correlation between the final output of the reverse CA-chain. Again, consider Fig. 3, here at the initial stage the private key, $\mathcal{K}$ is inserted into the both halves. Hence in this case, $f(\Psi_1) = \tau_1$ and $f(\Psi'_1) = \tau'_1$, where $\Psi_1 = \Psi'_1 = \mathcal{K}$. And for the rest of the cases $f(\Psi_i) = \tau_i$ and $f(\Psi'_i) = \tau'_i$, where $\Psi_1 \neq \Psi'_1$ for $i = 2, 3, \ldots, n$. So, we need to verify both of the cases to check the correlations.

For each of the cases we vary the Ψ (and/or) Ψ' and calculate the difference between τ and τ'. As an experiment we have calculate this for 1 lac different test cases for each of the cases. We have found that there do not exist a single case where the corelation holds. The reason behind this result is that the CA is a good random number generator [19]. Figure 6 shows a sample of the resultant graph of this analysis for 100 test cases. Here the values are plotted for NCASH-256.

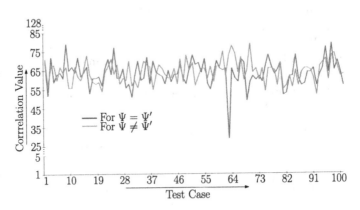

Fig. 6. Correlation analysis for both $\Psi = \Psi'$ and $\Psi \neq \Psi'$

The number of test cases are plotted in the horizontal axis and the correlation values are plotted in the verticle axis. For verticle axis, the scaling of 25 to 85 is proper. Here, 1 and 128 denote only the lower and upper bounds. It is clearly visible that for each 128-bit τ and τ', the correlation values are scattered in the range of 50 to 80, i.e., atleast half of the bits are different.

3.1 Autocorrelation

Autocorrelation is the correlation of a signal with respect to a delayed copy of that signal itself. In the design of NCASH, we need to verify the autocorrelation both for τ and τ' separately. Here, we compare the τ_i (or τ_i') with delayed τ_i (or delayed τ_i'). In this case, we make the delay by introducing a circular shift. We have done this experiment both for τ and τ'. And calculate the values both for $\Psi = \Psi'$ and $\Psi \neq \Psi'$ for each of the cases. Figure 7 presents a specimen of the resultant graph of this analysis for 100 test cases. Here the values are plotted for 128-bit τ and τ'. The delays are plotted in the horizontal axis and the autocorrelation values are plotted in the verticle axis. As per the previous graph, for verticle axis, the scaling of 25 to 85 is proper, and 1 and 128 denote only the lower and upper bounds. It is also clearly visible that for each 128-bit τ and τ', atleast half of the bits are different.

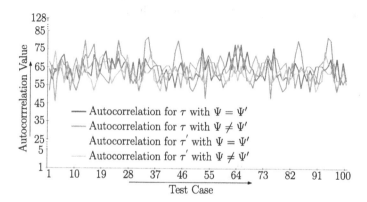

Fig. 7. Autocorrelation analysis for τ and τ' for both $\Psi = \Psi'$ and $\Psi \neq \Psi'$

3.2 Cross-correlation

With respect to signal processing, cross-correlation indicates a measure of the correlation of two signals as a function of the translocation of one relative to the other. In the design of NCASH, we need to verify the cross-correlation of τ with respect to τ'. Here, we compare the τ_i with delayed τ_i'. We consider both of the cases $\Psi = \Psi'$ and $\Psi \neq \Psi'$. And also in this case, we make the delay by introducing a circular shift. Figure 8 shows a sample of the resultant graph of this analysis for 100 test cases. Here the values are plotted for 128-bit τ and τ'. The delays are plotted in the horizontal axis and the cross-correlation values are plotted in the verticle axis. The scaling procedure for verticle axis is same as Fig. 6. It is also clearly visible that for each 128-bit τ and τ', atleast half of the bits are different.

4   Security Analysis with Random Oracle Model

We learn the security properties of the CA-based compression-function (consider Fig. 4) of NCASH against the random oracle model [8,20] $\mathcal{O}$. Suppose, the proposed hash function is $\mathcal{H}$ and the attack algorithm is $\mathcal{A}$. Hence, several adaptive queries can be asked by the adversary to make a list $\mathcal{Q}$ for those query-response pairs. Based on $\mathcal{Q}$, finally a message or might be a pair of messages will be produced by the adversary as the output, and which should be based on the characteristics of the attack. The entire list of the query-response pairs $\mathcal{Q}$ can be defined as the *view* of the adversary. It can be noted that, any output presented by the adversary must be decided only with respect to the *view*. Furthermore, if the adversary will be capable to get collisions for $\mathcal{H}$ and will produce a pair of distinguished mesages $\mathcal{M}$ & $\mathcal{M}'$ as outputs, where $\mathcal{M} \neq \mathcal{M}'$ then the two hash values for $\mathcal{M}$ & $\mathcal{M}'$ (i.e., $\mathcal{H}(\mathcal{M})$ and $\mathcal{H}(\mathcal{M}')$) should be determined only with respect to the *view*. We delineate the complexity of $\mathcal{A}$ with respect to the *view*-size which is to be required to get non-negligible probability of success [4].

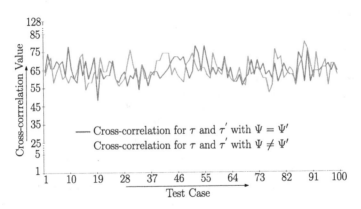

Fig. 8. Cross-correlation analysis of τ and τ' for both $\Psi = \Psi'$ and $\Psi \neq \Psi'$

4.1   Preimage or Second Preimage and Collision Security

Here we are going to analyze the preimage or second preimage and collision security with respect to this model $\mathcal{O}$, described above.

Lemma 1. *Let us assume a random function described as $f : \mathcal{D} \to \mathcal{R}$ whereas, $\{\mathcal{X}, \mathcal{Y}\}$ denotes the subset of f. Then $\Pr[f(\mathcal{X}) = \mathcal{Y}]$ should be equals to $1/|\mathcal{R}|$.*

Proof. According to the definition, f is a random function. Hence $\mathcal{X} \neq \mathcal{Y}$. It implies that $f(\mathcal{X})$ is uniformly distributed on the elements of the set $\mathcal{R}$ and hence $\Pr[f(\mathcal{X}) = \mathcal{Y}] = 1/|\mathcal{R}|$.

Claim. (**Preimage or Second Preimage Security**): If the two sets of the message-tag pairs are $(\mathcal{X}_1, \mathcal{Y}_1)$ and $(\mathcal{X}_2, \mathcal{Y}_2)$, such that $\mathcal{X}_1 \neq \mathcal{X}_2$ with $\mathcal{Y}_1 = \mathcal{Y}_2$ and the hash-tag length is determined by n, then the number of queries are needed to check $\mathcal{H}(\mathcal{X}_1) = \mathcal{H}(\mathcal{X}_2)$ is $O(2^n)$.

Proof. If the adversary can able to place at most q number of queries to the oracle $\mathcal{O}$ then she has atmost q many messages and q number of message-tag pairs, $(\mathcal{X}, \mathcal{Y})$. Therefore, the probability which denotes the ability of the adversary to find $\mathcal{X}_1 \neq \mathcal{X}_2$ with $\mathcal{Y}_1 = \mathcal{Y}_2$, i.e., $\mathcal{H}(\mathcal{X}_1) = \mathcal{H}(\mathcal{X}_2)$ is atmost $q/2^n$ (by using Lemma 1). Thus, the value of q should be equals to $\Omega(2^n)$ to have a important success probability.

Remark 1. The preimage or second preimage security of NCASH-256 is 2^{256}.

Claim. (**Collision Security**): If $(\mathcal{M}, \mathcal{M}')$ is a message-pair, such that $\mathcal{M} \neq \mathcal{M}'$ and the hash-tag length is determinrd by n, then we need $O(2^{n/2})$ many queries to check that $\mathcal{H}(\mathcal{M})$ and $\mathcal{H}(\mathcal{M}')$ gives the same value.

Proof. The reason behind the above attacks is that the number of values of the hash function $\mathcal{H}$ is quite high. Recall the structure of NCASH, (Fig. 5). We consider the output of the upper NHCA-LHCA chain as $\mathcal{W}$ and the lower LHCA-NHCA chain as $\mathcal{W}'$. So, the hash value of a message $\mathcal{X}$ will be $\mathcal{H}(\mathcal{X}) = \{\mathcal{W} \| \mathcal{W}' : |\mathcal{W}| = |\mathcal{W}'| = b, 2b = l\}$. We write $\mathcal{H}_{cf}$ for the set of all outputs of the compression function. In this design $\mathcal{H}_{cf} = \{0, 1\}^l$ and $|\mathcal{H}_{cf}| = 2^n - 1$, by considering $l = n$. As n-bit maximum length CA can evolve all the $2^n - 1$ states, except the all-0 state. Thus, to search a collision on the hash function $\mathcal{H}$, the birthday attack can be applied with respect to the output set $\mathcal{H}_{cf}$. Hence, by the birthday attack, if $(\mathcal{M}, \mathcal{M}')$ is a message-pair, such that $\mathcal{M}$ and $\mathcal{M}'$ are different, we need $O(2^{n/2})$ many queries to check that $\mathcal{H}(\mathcal{M})$ and $\mathcal{H}(\mathcal{M}')$ hold the same value.

Remark 2. The collision sequrity of NCASH-256 is 2^{128}.

4.2 Security Comparison with the Exsisting Schemes

We claim that NCASH gives better security results with respect to most of the other renowned double-length hash functions. The security parameters have been analyzed in Sect. 4.1. Table 1 gives a comparison for NCASH-256 with other existing renowned schemes. It is clearly visible that NCASH gives better result than others. The most notable thing is that NCASH uses an n-bit key to produce a 2n-bit hash-tag. Whereas most of the other hash functions described in Table 1 use a 2n-bit length key to produce a 2n-bit hash-tag.

Table 1. Security comparison result for the double-length compression functions

Compression function	Preimage security	Collision security
Abreast-DM [22]	2^{246} [1]	$2^{124.42}$ [15, 23]
Tandem-DM [22]	2^{246} [1]	$2^{120.87}$ [24]
Hirose-DM [18]	2^{251} [1]	$2^{124.55}$ [18]
Weimar-DM [14]	$2^{252.5}$ [14]	$2^{126.23}$ [14]
MR-MMO [27]	$2^{252.5}$ [27]	$2^{126.70}$ [27]
NCASH-256	2^{256}	2^{128}

5 Conclusion

In this work, we scrutinize the security of NCASH, the cellular automata-based double-block-length hash function. The correlation analyses of this scheme assure that it holds almost no correlation between the intermediate states. We have also performed the security analysis with the Random Oracle Model. It has also been determined that the preimage or second preimage resistance and collision resistance of NCASH-256 are 2^{256} and 2^{128}, which are better than most of the other existing related works.

References

1. Armknecht, F., Fleischmann, E., Krause, M., Lee, J., Stam, M., Steinberger, J.: The preimage security of double-block-length compression functions. In: Lee, D.H., Wang, X. (eds.) ASIACRYPT 2011. LNCS, vol. 7073, pp. 233–251. Springer, Heidelberg (2011). https://doi.org/10.1007/978-3-642-25385-0_13
2. Banerjee, T., Roy Chowdhury, D.: NCASH: non-linear cellular automata based hash function. In: The 5th International Conference on Mathematics and Computing (ICMC 2019), (Presented) (2019)
3. Belfedhal, A.E., Faraoun, K.M.: Building secure and fast cryptographic hash functions using programmable cellular automata. J. Comput. Inf. Technol. **23**(4), 317–328 (2015)
4. Bellare, M.: A note on negligible functions. J. Cryptol. **15**(4) (2002). https://link.springer.com/content/pdf/10.1007
5. Bellare, M., Canetti, R., Krawczyk, H.: Keying hash functions for message authentication. In: Koblitz, N. (ed.) CRYPTO 1996. LNCS, vol. 1109, pp. 1–15. Springer, Heidelberg (1996). https://doi.org/10.1007/3-540-68697-5_1
6. Bertoni, G., Daemen, J., Peeters, M., Van Assche, G.: Keccak sponge function family main document. Submission to NIST (Round 2), **3**(30) (2009)
7. Bertoni, G., Daemen, J., Peeters, M., Van Assche, G.: Duplexing the sponge: single-pass authenticated encryption and other applications. In: Miri, A., Vaudenay, S. (eds.) SAC 2011. LNCS, vol. 7118, pp. 320–337. Springer, Heidelberg (2012). https://doi.org/10.1007/978-3-642-28496-0_19
8. Canetti, R., Goldreich, O., Halevi, S.: The random oracle methodology, revisited. J. ACM (JACM) **51**(4), 557–594 (2004)

9. Daemen, J., Govaerts, R., Vandewalle, J.: A framework for the design of one-way hash functions including cryptanalysis of Damgård's one-way function based on a cellular automaton. In: Imai, H., Rivest, R.L., Matsumoto, T. (eds.) ASIACRYPT 1991. LNCS, vol. 739, pp. 82–96. Springer, Heidelberg (1993). https://doi.org/10.1007/3-540-57332-1_7

10. Damgård, I.B.: A design principle for hash functions. In: Brassard, G. (ed.) CRYPTO 1989. LNCS, vol. 435, pp. 416–427. Springer, New York (1990). https://doi.org/10.1007/0-387-34805-0_39

11. Dworkin, M.J.: SHA-3 standard: Permutation-based hash and extendable-output functions. Technical report (2015). https://ws680.nist.gov/publication/get_pdf.cfm?pub_id=919061

12. Eastlake, D., Jones, P.: Us Secure Hash Algorithm 1 (SHA1). Technical report (2001). https://tools.ietf.org/html/rfc3174?ref=driverlayer.com

13. Echandouri, B., Hanin, C., Omary, F., Elbernoussi, S.: Keyed-CAHASH: a new fast keyed hash function based on cellular automata for authentication. Int. J. Comput. Sci. Appl. **14**(2), 64–180 (2017)

14. Fleischmann, E., Forler, C., Lucks, S., Wenzel, J.: Weimar-DM: a highly secure double-length compression function. In: Susilo, W., Mu, Y., Seberry, J. (eds.) ACISP 2012. LNCS, vol. 7372, pp. 152–165. Springer, Heidelberg (2012). https://doi.org/10.1007/978-3-642-31448-3_12

15. Fleischmann, E., Gorski, M., Lucks, S.: Security of cyclic double block length hash functions. In: Parker, M.G. (ed.) IMACC 2009. LNCS, vol. 5921, pp. 153–175. Springer, Heidelberg (2009). https://doi.org/10.1007/978-3-642-10868-6_10

16. Ghosh, S., Sengupta, A., Saha, D., Chowdhury, D.R.: A scalable method for constructing non-linear cellular automata with period 2^n-1. In: Wąs, J., Sirakoulis, G.C., Bandini, S. (eds.) ACRI 2014. LNCS, vol. 8751, pp. 65–74. Springer, Cham (2014). https://doi.org/10.1007/978-3-319-11520-7_8

17. Hirose, S.: Provably secure double-block-length hash functions in a black-box model. In: Park, C., Chee, S. (eds.) ICISC 2004. LNCS, vol. 3506, pp. 330–342. Springer, Heidelberg (2005). https://doi.org/10.1007/11496618_24

18. Hirose, S.: Some plausible constructions of double-block-length hash functions. In: Robshaw, M. (ed.) FSE 2006. LNCS, vol. 4047, pp. 210–225. Springer, Heidelberg (2006). https://doi.org/10.1007/11799313_14

19. Hortensius, P.D., McLeod, R.D., Pries, W., Miller, D.M., Card, H.C.: Cellular automata-based pseudorandom number generators for built-in self-test. IEEE Trans. Comput. Aided Des. Integr. Circuits Syst. **8**(8), 842–859 (1989)

20. Koblitz, N., Menezes, A.J.: The random oracle model: a twenty-year retrospective. Des. Codes Cryptogr. **77**(2), 587–610 (2015)

21. Kuila, S., Saha, D., Pal, M., Chowdhury, D.R.: CASH: cellular automata based parameterized hash. In: Chakraborty, R.S., Matyas, V., Schaumont, P. (eds.) SPACE 2014. LNCS, vol. 8804, pp. 59–75. Springer, Cham (2014). https://doi.org/10.1007/978-3-319-12060-7_5

22. Lai, X., Massey, J.L.: Hash functions based on block ciphers. In: Rueppel, R.A. (ed.) EUROCRYPT 1992. LNCS, vol. 658, pp. 55–70. Springer, Heidelberg (1993). https://doi.org/10.1007/3-540-47555-9_5

23. Lee, J., Kwon, D.: The security of abreast-DM in the ideal cipher model. IEICE Trans. Fund. Electron. Commun. Comput. Sci. **94**(1), 104–109 (2011)

24. Lee, J., Stam, M., Steinberger, J.: The collision security of tandem-DM in the ideal cipher model. In: Rogaway, P. (ed.) CRYPTO 2011. LNCS, vol. 6841, pp. 561–577. Springer, Heidelberg (2011). https://doi.org/10.1007/978-3-642-22792-9_32

25. Lucks, S.: Design principles for iterated hash functions. IACR Cryptol. ePrint Arch. **2004**, 253 (2004)
26. Mihaljevic, M., Zheng, Y., Imai, H.: A fast cryptographic hash function basedon linear cellular automata over GF(q). (1998). http://citeseerx.ist.psu.edu/viewdoc/download?doi=10.1.1.112.8559&rep=rep1&type=pdf
27. Miyaji, A., Rashed, M.: A new (n, 2n) double block length hash function based on single key scheduling. In: 2015 IEEE 29th International Conference on Advanced Information Networking and Applications, pp. 564–570. IEEE (2015)
28. Pal Chaudhuri, P., Roy Chowdhury, D., Nandi, S., Chattopadhyay, S.: Additive Cellular Automata: Theory and Applications, vol. 1. John Wiley & Sons, Chichester (1997)
29. Rivest, R.: The MD5 Message-Digest algorithm. Technical report (1992). https://tools.ietf.org/pdf/rfc1321.pdf
30. Rukhin, A., Soto, J., Nechvatal, J., Smid, M., Barker, E.: A Statistical Test Suite for Random and Pseudorandom Number Generators for Cryptographic Applications, NIST Special Publication 800–22. Technical report, Booz-Allen and Hamilton Inc Mclean Va (2001)

Security Centric Applications

Tele-Transmission of Secured Prefrontal Cortex Information Records for Remote Health Care

Monish Ram K$^{(\boxtimes)}$, Ananya Sairaj, Ramya Lakshmi Srinivasan, Raajan N R,
and Girish Ganesan R

SASTRA Deemed University, Thanjavur, India
monish.ram16@gmail.com, ananya.sairaj@gmail.com,
ramyasrinivasan18@gmail.com, nrraajan@ece.sastra.edu,
girish.ganesan90@gmail.com

Abstract. Brain waves provide a measure of mental health. Recently, the techniques involved in the measurement of brain waves are a lucrative research area. Diseases related to the brain are variegated and are difficult to diagnose and study. This increases the importance of accurate and reliable measurement of brain waves. Conventionally prefrontal cortex information is used to determine the general brain electrical activity (e.g., to assess trauma, drug poisoning, or magnitude of brain damage in comatose patients). This data is mandated to be confidential and is susceptible to cyber attacks. This work presents a secure transmission methodology which embeds the EEG signal in a high frequency plane using Discrete Rajan Transform (DRT) and Discrete Wavelet Transform (DWT).

Keywords: EEG · Discrete Rajan Transform · Discrete Wavelet Transform

1 Introduction

All signals from an organism that are measured and controlled are referred to as electrical bio signals. These electrical bio signals are produced due to the electrical activities in the organism. Electroencephalography (EEG) signal is one such signal which measures the brain's electrical activity. This 40-year-old psycho-physical research by Berger, has become a topic of research from the early 1890s. Hans Berger started to record the EEG of human from the mid-1920s [1]. Several EEG studies have continued with fresh techniques since then.

An electroencephalogram (EEG) is a test for brain electrical activity associated issues. The variation in voltage among the neurons becomes the cause of EEG activity and this reflects the neuronal synchronous activity with comparable spatial orientation [2]. An EEG device monitors and records patterns of brain waves as shown in Fig. 1. Small metal disks with thin cables (electrodes) are put

© Springer Nature Singapore Pte Ltd. 2019
V. S. Shankar Sriram et al. (Eds.): ATIS 2019, CCIS 1116, pp. 281–289, 2019.
https://doi.org/10.1007/978-981-15-0871-4_22

on the scalp and the outcomes are recorded by sending signals to a computer. These patterns or values can be analyzed by the doctors and can be used for observation.

Several kinds of brain disorders are evaluated using EEG. Seizure activity appears on the EEG as fast spiking waves when epilepsy is present. People with brain lesions which results from tumours or stroke, a depending on the size and place of the lesion, may possess EEG waves which are exceptionally slow. This test is also used to analyse other brain activities which are characteristic of illnesses such as Alzheimer's disease, dementia, narcolepsy and epilepsy [3].

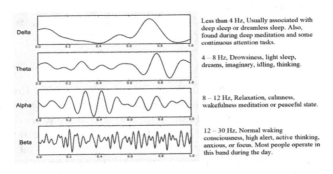

Fig. 1. EEG signal during different activities.

In this work EEG signal is obtained with the help of NeuroSky MindWave device, a product of NeuroSky Inc. It is powerful tool which gives an accurate measurement of EEG signals. Its simple headphone-like structure, Bluetooth connectivity and the fact that it is powered by AAA batteries provides a hassle-free mobile environment. The in-built modules of the MindWave device allow the device to be interfaced with Lab-VIEW to obtain the EEG signals which are of the order of micro-volts. This data can be then processed for further applications.

Once the EEG signals are obtained accurately they might need to be sent anywhere in the world for doctors to consult or may even be uploaded to a database or a server for safe keeping and data collection. In any of the above cases the EEG signal which has been obtained is susceptible to corruption or illegal acquisition. Medical data in general needs to be very private as it might contain important information about the patients' medical history. Hence encryption needs to be done to secure the data which cannot afford to be corrupted.

To provide this encryption and enhance the overall safety of the transmission, different kinds of algorithms can be used. In this scenario we have used the discrete wavelet transformation [4] for encryption and the inverse is used in the receiver side for decryption. A discrete wavelet transformation in numerical analysis and functional analysis is any wavelet transformation where wavelets are sampled discretely. Comparing with other wavelet transforms, it captures both the frequency and place data which is an advantage over the Fourier transform. We also use the discrete Rajan transform to further increase the safety of the transmission. Rajan transform [5] is a coding technique where a sequence of numbers of duration equal to any exponent of two (integer, rational, real or complicated) is converted into a strongly correlated series of numbers. The inverse Rajan transform is done in the receiver side to decrypt the signal. Hence having these two levels of transforms on the data can make the entire process highly secure from any dangers it might face during communication.

2   Review of Literature

The measurement of the brain's electrical activity using the method of Electroencephalography (EEG) has always been an fascinating research area since Hans Berger's experiment. There are many applications with regard to EEG. Research in cognitive science (study of mind and its working) extensively uses EEG [6]. Abnormal conditions in epileptic patients can be analysed [7]. Other disorders related to mental health like Schizophrenia [8] and Alzheimer's disease [9] can also be examined. Gaming industries are trying to revolutionize entertainment with neuro-gaming and one such example is "Throw Trucks with Your Mind". Thus there are many ways for collection and analysis of EEG data and they are vulnerable. The availability of such data is exploding and it increases the data mining opportunities which in turn multiplies the privacy risks.

To prevent the misuse of EEG data, the transmission has to be secure. The process in which information is embedded with digital content is called data hiding. Some techniques used for this are steganography, water marking, cryptography. The practice of concealing information within another non-secret text or image or video is steganography. An algorithm proposed by Warkentin et al. used the audio-visual documents to hide the data [10]. Another algorithm by El-Emam proposed hiding data in colour bitmap. Here the sequentially selected pixels are used for replacement in the filtered image [11]. This work uses Discrete Rajan Transform and Discrete Wavelet Transform to increase the confidentiality, integrity and authenticity of the transmitted EEG data.

3   DRT and DWT

3.1   Discrete Rajan Transform

Discrete Rajan Transform is an algorithm created in line with the DIF-FFT algorithm (Decimation-In-Frequency and Fast Fourier Transform), although being different. Any sequence a(n) having numbers of length N is split equally into two sections containing (N/2) points which holds the subsequent expressions true.

$$x(j) = a(i) + a(i + \frac{N}{2}); \ 0 \leq j \leq \frac{N}{2} \ ; \ 0 \leq i \leq \frac{N}{2} \tag{1}$$

$$y(j) = |a(i) - a(i - \frac{N}{2})|; \ \ 0 \leq j \leq \frac{N}{2} \ ; \ \frac{N}{2} \leq i \leq N \tag{2}$$

The above half will now be further split equally, containing (N/4) points which holds the subsequent expressions true.

$$x_1(k) = x(j) + x(j + \frac{N}{4}); \ 0 \leq k \leq \frac{N}{4}; 0 \leq j \leq \frac{N}{4} \qquad (3)$$

$$x_2(k) = |x(j) - x(j - \frac{N}{4})|; \ 0 \leq k \leq \frac{N}{4}; \frac{N}{4} \leq j \leq \frac{N}{2} \qquad (4)$$

$$y_1(k) = y(j) + y(j + \frac{N}{4}) \ ; \ 0 \leq k \leq \frac{N}{4} \ ; \ 0 \leq j \leq \frac{N}{4} \qquad (5)$$

$$y_2(k) = |y(j) - y(j - \frac{N}{4})| \ ; \ 0 \leq k \leq \frac{N}{4} \ ; \ \frac{N}{4} \leq j \leq \frac{N}{2} \qquad (6)$$

The above procedure has to be carried out until the last division value becomes one. It turns out that the complete amount of phases is log2N. Rajan Transform [12] can be denoted by A(k) when a(n) is of length N = 2k; $k > 0$. Isomorphism is induced by the transform for any number of applicable sequence. Simply, a domain set consisting of cyclic and dyadic sequence permutations is mapped to the range set consisting of A(k)D(r) sequences where A(k) is the permutation invariant RT and the code for encryption for each elements in the domain set is D(r). This is a one-to-one map and there is also an inverse map.

3.2   Inverse Rajan Transform

Data is retrieved using the Inverse Rajan Transform (IRT) [13]. For IRT computations the basic requirements are the encryption values (k values) of the RT coefficients by the function for encryption during RT computation. Inverse Rajan transform (IRT), an iterative algorithm, will transform a long N(1+m) code A(k)D(r) into one of its original sequences which belongs to its permutation class based on the code for encryption D(r) where N = 2m (m represents the stage count). The inverse transform calculation is performed as follows. First, the input sequence is split into two-point sections each.

$$x(2j + 1) = (A(2k) + A(2k + 1))/2 \qquad (7)$$

$$x(2j) = max(A(2k), A(2k + 1)) - x(2j + 1) \qquad (8)$$

if $D_1(2r) = 0$ and $D_1(2r + 1) = 0; 0 \leq j < N; 0 \leq k \leq N; 0 \leq r \leq N$

or

$$x(2j) = (A(2k) + A(2k + 1))/2 \qquad (9)$$

$$x(2j + 1) = max(A(2k), A(2k + 1)) - x(2j) \qquad (10)$$

if $D_1(2r) = 1$ or $D_1(2r + 1) = 1; 0 \leq j \leq N; 0 \leq k \leq N; 0 \leq r \leq N$

The resultant sequences are each split into four-point sections. Each section of 4 points is synthesized according to the operation described in Eqs. (7)–(10). The resulting sequence is further split into eight-point sections and the same operation is repeated. This process is proceeded until no further division is possible.

3.3   Discrete Wavelet Transform

Discrete Wavelet Transform (DWT) [14] is used to decompose a signal into a set of mutually orthogonal wavelet basis functions. This function is different from the sinusoidal based functions since they are localized spatially. The inverse property is used to recover the original signal.

The one dimensional (1-D) discrete wavelet transform as shown in Fig. 2 operates on vectors containing real-values of length 2n where n is greater than 1 and outcomes are transformed into a vector having length equal to that of input vector. Initially the input vector is filtered by the low-pass filter (LPF) L at intervals of two, and the results are saved in the output vector's first eight places. Now, the input vector is again filtered by the high-pass filter (HPF) H at intervals of two, and the results are saved in the output vector's last eight places.

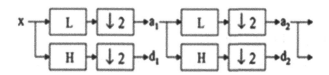

Fig. 2. Discrete Wavelet Transform Tree.

a_j components are used for scaling and d_j components, known as wavelet coefficients, are used for determining the transform output. H[n] and L[n] are coefficients of high and low-pass filter.

$$a_{j+1}[p] = \Sigma_{n=-\infty}^{+\infty} l[n - 2p]a_j[n] \tag{11}$$

$$d_{j+1}[p] = \Sigma_{n=-\infty}^{+\infty} h[n - 2p]a_j[n] \tag{12}$$

The DWT algorithm is computed for images by repeating the process of one dimensional Discrete Wavelet Transform as shown in Fig. 3. Initially, 1-D DWT is applied through the image's rows. Next, it is applied through the columns. The results from the above computations has four different bands - LL, LH, HL and HH. Low-pass filter (LPF) is denoted by L, and High-pass filter (HPF) is denoted by H. LL band is a decimated form of the input image. LH band preserves the localized horizontal features and HL band preserves localized vertical features in the input image. HH band isolates localized high-frequency point features. The below figure represents the 2D wavelet transform where G_1 is the HPF and G_0 is the LPF.

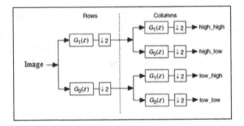

Fig. 3. Two Dimensional Discrete Wavelet Transform.

In our work, G-plane of a colour picture is selected for performing DWT. The basic and oldest wavelet system is Harr wavelet [15], a group of square waves with a range of 1 in the interval [0,1). It is used in numerous applications such as cardiovascular bio-signal's signal-to-noise ratio estimation, in different convergence theorems, etc. The higher frequency component plane is combined with DRT coefficients. IDWT is performed on this modified plane. The original image's red and blue planes are combined with this plane to form the image to be transmitted.

4   Methodology

4.1   The Embedding Process

The embedding process is explained below along with the flowchart in Fig. 4.

1. EEG signal is acquired using the NeuroSky MindWave device.
2. DRT is done on the EEG signal.
3. DWT is done on the G-plane of any image.
4. The DRT values and the HH part of the DWT are multiplied.
5. The multiplied values are made the new HH part and Inverse DWT is done.
6. The original R and B planes are added to the new G-plane.

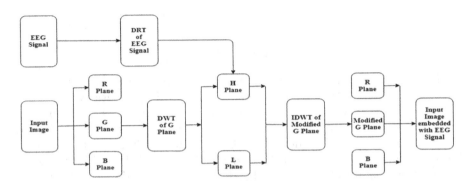

Fig. 4. Flowchart for embedding EEG signal to image.

4.2   The Extracting Process

The extracting process is explained below along with the flowchart in Fig. 5.

1. The G-plane is extracted from the received image and DWT is done.
2. The received G-plane values are divided by the DWT values of the green plane of the original image.
3. The EEG is now obtained by performing Inverse DRT on the values obtained from division.

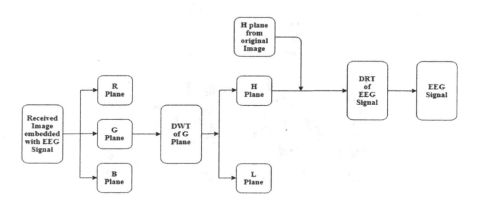

Fig. 5. Flowchart for extracting EEG signal from image.

5   Results and Discussions

The images in Figs. 6 and 7 were obtained during the embedding and extracting of EEG data. Figure 6: Image A is the input image in which the EEG signal will be embedded. This image will be available both with the transmitter and receiver. Figure 6: Image B contains the embedded EEG data obtained from the NeuroSky MindWave device. Figure 6: Image C shows the DWT of the input image's green plane. Any other plane (R or B) can also be used for the transmission of the data. Figure 6: Image D shows the G plane extract of the original image. Figure 6: Image E shows the G plane of the image containing EEG data. The EEG data first undergoes Discrete Rajan Transform and then it is embedded with the high frequency (HH) part. Figure 7: Image F is the input EEG signal which has to be transmitted. Figure 7: Image G is the retrieved EEG signal at the receiver side. The signal is retrieved by following the extracting process. It is seen that the signal on the receiver side is identical to the transmitted image. The transmission of the image becomes more secure by using the Discrete Rajan Transform and Discrete Wavelet Transform. The robustness of this seamless method is tested and the simulation results established a secure transmission approach for the EEG data.

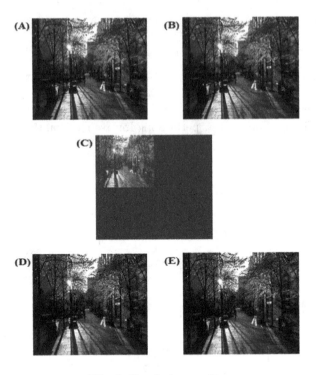

Fig. 6. Simulation results

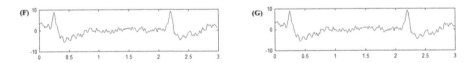

Fig. 7. EEG signal before and after transmission

6   Conclusion

The EEG is an important tool in clinical diagnosis and medical research and reveals significant data about the test subject. This data has to be protected during transmission to ensure safety of the patient or research. DWT and DRT used to encrypt the prefrontal cortex signals in tele transmission is presented. The prefrontal cortex EEG signals were measured using NeuroSky Mindwave Device. Subsequently, Lab-VIEW was used to eliminate noise. Discrete Rajan Transform was applied to this signal and encrypted using DWT and transmitted as stenographic data. Results of frequency and time domain analysis proves the security of the encrypted data. When the data is received, the encryption is reverted to obtain the original signal. A correlation of 0.9988 was observed on the receiving end.

References

1. Millet, D.: Hans berger: from psychic energy to the EEG. Perspect. Biol. Med. **44**(4), 522–542 (2001)
2. Benbadis, S.R., Husain, A.M., Kaplan, P.W., Tatum, W.O.: Handbook of EEG Interpretation. Demos Medical Publishing (2007)
3. Hauk, O.: Introduction to EEG and MEG. MRC Cognition and Brain Sciences Unit (2013)
4. Sai Malathi Anandini, V., Hemanth Gopalakrishna, Y., Raajan, N.R.: Secure electrocardiograph communication through discrete wavelet transform. In: Suresh, L.P., Panigrahi, B.K. (eds.) Proceedings of the International Conference on Soft Computing Systems. AISC, vol. 397, pp. 463–470. Springer, New Delhi (2016). https://doi.org/10.1007/978-81-322-2671-0_44
5. Rajan, E.G., Mandalapu, E.N.: Rajan transform and its uses in pattern recognition. Informatica Int. J. Comput. Inform. **33**, 213–220 (2009)
6. Srinivasan, N.: Cognitive neuroscience of creativity: EEG based approaches. Methods **42**(1), 109–116 (2007)
7. Seong-Hyeon, C., Chung, Y.G., Kim, S.-P.: Statistical spectral feature extraction for classification of epileptic EEG signals. In: International Conference on Machine Learning and Cybernetics (ICMLC), vol. 6 (2010)
8. Azlan, W.A.W., Low, Y.F.: Feature extraction of electroencephalogram (EEG) signal-a review. In: Conference on Biomedical Engineering and Sciences (IECBES) (2014)
9. Ghorbanian, P.: Discrete wavelet transform EEG features of Alzheimer's disease in activated states. In: Engineering in Medicine and Biology Society (EMBC) (2012)
10. Warkentin, M., Schmidt, M.B., Bekkering, E.: Steganography and Steganalysis. Premier reference Source—Intellectual Property Protection for Multimedia Information technology, pp. 374–380 (2008). Chapter XIX
11. El-Emam, N.N.: Hiding a large amount of data with high security using steganography algorithm. J. Comput. Sci. **3**(4), 223–232 (2007)
12. Rajan, E.G.: On the notion of generalized rapid transformation. In: World Multi Conference on Systemics, Cybernetics and Informatics, Caracas, Venezuela, 7–11 July 1997
13. Venugopal, S.: Pattern Recognition for Intelligent Manufacturing Systems using Rajan Transform, MS Thesis, Jawaharlal Nehru Technological University, Hyderabad (1999)
14. Arab, F., Daud, S.M., Hashim, S.Z.: Discrete wavelet transform domain techniques. In: Informatics and Creative Multimedia (ICICM) (2013). ISBN 978-0-7695-5133-3
15. Porwik, P., Lisowska, A.: The haar-wavelet transform in digital image processing: its status and achievements. Mach. Graph. Vis. **13**(1/2), 79–98 (2004)

Encryption by Heart (EbH) for Secured Data Transmission and CNN Based EKG Signal Classification of Arrhythmia with Normal Data

Tarun Kumar D$^{(\boxtimes)}$, Ramya Lakshmi Srinivasan, and Raajan N R

School of EEE, SASTRA Deemed to be University, Thanjavur, India
tarunkumar17398@gmail.com, ramyasrinivasan18@gmail.com,
nrraajan@ece.sastra.edu

Abstract. Remote healthcare monitoring systems are commonly used to manage patient diagnostic data. These systems are subjected to data privacy and security, reliability, etc. A new technique is introduced in this paper to solve privacy and security issues. Using Discrete Wavelet Transforms (DWT), EKG steganography technique is implemented in the proposed method. This method is based on the techniques of encryption and decryption. Encryption is used to hide the EKG signal within an image and to extract the EKG signal from the encrypted image, decryption is used. Subsequently, a prominent amount of raw EKG time series signal information is given as inputs for convolution neural networks (CNN). The representative and key characteristics used to classify the module autonomously are learned. Thus, the features are learned directly from the prominent time domain EKG signals by using a CNN. Trained characteristics can efficiently substitute the hand-crafted characteristics of the time-consuming user and traditional ad hoc characteristics. Using GoogLeNet CNN we have achieved an accuracy of 0.90625.

Keywords: EKG · DWT · CNN

1 Introduction

Cardiovascular disease (CVD), which was mentioned as the underlying cause of death, accounted for roughly 1 in 3 fatalities in the US in 2016. Between 2013 and 2016, there was some type of cardiovascular disease among 121.5 million American adults. Between 2014 and 2015 there were 351.2 billion dollars in direct and indirect expenses (Direct costs of 213.8 billion dollars and lost productivity/mortality of 137.4 billion dollars) [1] for complete cardiovascular diseases and stroke. On an average, for every forty seconds, an American is said to have a heart attack.

Cardiovascular disease is plaque build-up that causes blockages within the body's major blood vessels. These blood vessels may include heart arteries (coronary heart disease), brain (cerebrovascular disease) and legs (arterial peripheral

© Springer Nature Singapore Pte Ltd. 2019
V. S. Shankar Sriram et al. (Eds.): ATIS 2019, CCIS 1116, pp. 290–299, 2019.
https://doi.org/10.1007/978-981-15-0871-4_23

disease). Cardiovascular disease can be responsible for heart attacks, strokes and death (Fig. 1).

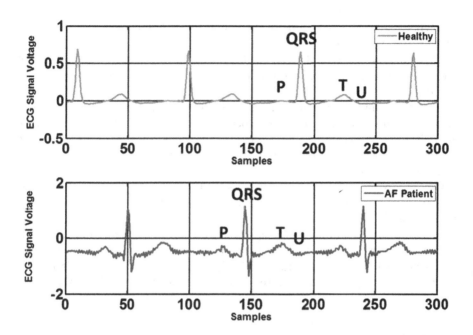

Fig. 1. A healthy (top) and unhealthy (bottom) person's EKG signal.

An electrocardiogram (EKG) is a test that uses detectors that are positioned over the chest on the skin to detect electrical activity in the core. These test scans are conducted during rest or exercise and can detect a variety of heart problems, particularly when conducted during exercise, including coronary heart disease.

Electrocardiographs uses electrodes to record the cardiac activity on the skin as small voltages of the order of one millivolt (mV). The variations in voltage vary with variation of heart activity. The twelve leads provide a clear view of the electrical activity of the heart as EKG wave forms which vary in amplitude and polarity of the P waves, QRS complex, and T waves.

Image encryption is commonly used in open internet works to secure data transmission. Before it is transferred or stored, we need to encrypt the information in order to secure the same from different attacks and for data integrity [2]. Governments, armies, economic institutions, hospitals and private companies deal with confidential pictures of their patients, geographies, enemies, products and economic statuses. Most of this data is now being gathered and stored on electronic computers and transferred to another computer through the network.

Keeping images protected is primarily intended to preserve confidentiality, integrity and authenticity. Cryptography is the study of secret messages from one party to another being transmitted safely [3]. It plays an significant role in ensuring data confidentiality while transferring information through the internet in particular. Confidentiality, authentication, integrity and non-repudiation are some particular safety requirements in the context of any application-to-application communication.

Cryptography is a technique of defending image-based secrets with a computation free process of decoding. In many applications such as: medical picture, confidential video conferencing, defence database, mobile computing, private communication, etc. The safety of digital pictures has become extremely crucial.

Recently, convolutional neural networks (CNNs) have gained considerable interest in multidimensional signal processing issues due to their impregnable capabilities and functionality for various applications, such as image and video recognition, object detection, computer vision classification, and data analysis of time series data.

One of CNN's applications is the classification of time series challenges. It deals in particular with a prominent quantity of information used in various applications in health care systems, bioinformatics, activity recognition, etc. Conventional methods for classifying time series data are highly dependent on the features extracted, but to capture the inherent characteristics of time series data is hard to obtain all the fundamental, proper and key characteristics. We encrypt and decrypt the data securely and predict the type of EKG using Layer based CNN.

2   Methodology

The research aims to develop safe EKG system transmission to safeguard the acquisition, diagnosis, visualization and storage of EKG. The system is user-friendly so that it can be readily used by medical practitioners and scientists and will assist them in further research and diagnosis.

EKG signals were acquired from the 360 Hz sampling frequency MIT-BIH Arrhythmia database. The system will be able to perform EKG signal diagnosis after processing the raw EKG signal and then display the outcome on the screen. The system will alert the scientist or medical practitioner to further diagnosis if the outcome is critical.

Since patient information plays a crucial role in medical diagnosis and therapy, each patient has private medical information at the same moment. Data authentication is essential to guarantee that the patient is not handled incorrectly owing to inaccurate medical information. By using this technique, the EKG signal will be encrypted and decrypted so that only the medical practitioner can comprehend the outcome.

2.1   Discrete Wavelet Transformation (DWT)

The Discrete Wavelet Transformation (DWT) is a linear transformation operating with an integer power of 2 on data vectors, and transforms it into the same length of a numerically distinct vector. It divides information into different frequency parts and matches each element based on the scale. The Fig. 2 below represents filtering cascade, followed by a sub sampling factor of 2 [4] (Fig. 3).

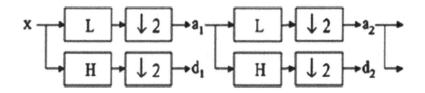

Fig. 2. DWT tree.

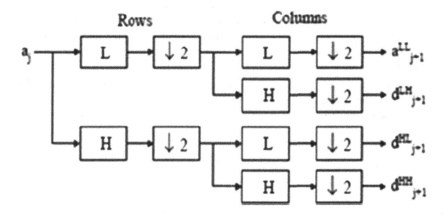

Fig. 3. DWT for two-dimensional images.

Low frequency filtering activities and High frequency filtering activities are referred to as L and H, respectively, down sampled by the factor of 2 which is denoted by 2. Equations (1) and (2) represents outcomes of the filters.

a_k components are used for scaling and d_k components, known as wavelet coefficients, are used for determining the transform output. H[n] is high pass filter coefficient and L[n] is low pass filter coefficient. On scale k+1 the number of 'a' and 'd' elements on scale k is only half.

$$a_{k+1}[B] = \sum_{A=-\infty}^{\infty} l[A - 2B]a_k[n] \tag{1}$$

$$d_{k+1}[B] = \sum_{A=-\infty}^{\infty} h[A - 2B]a_k[n] \tag{2}$$

The DWT algorithm is comparable for two-dimensional images. For all Image rows, the DWT is executed first and then all the columns [4].

First, signal in the wavelet transformation is decomposed by a low pass filter (LPF) and followed by high pass filter (HPF) filter. Half the components of the frequency were filtered out at the input of the filter and can therefore be sampled down [5]. The original input signal is then rebuilt by the inverse procedure of this decomposition [6].

DWT has an impact on day-to-day processing of image, such as enhancing quality of fingerprint [7], Optimizing watermarking of gray- scale image [8], etc. DWT is used in our present implementation to highlight the different frequency planes in the pictures [9].

2.2   Encrypting EKG Using Discrete Wavelet Transformation (DWT)

In our work, G-plane of a colour picture was selected for performing DWT. The basic and oldest wavelet system is Harr wavelet, A square wave group with an interval range of 1[0,1). It is used in many applications, such as the estimation of the SNR of cardiovascular bio-signal, in various theorems of convergence, etc. The higher frequency component hHH plane was divided and the peaks of EKG information were extracted and combined with coefficients in the same plane. This modified hHH plane was used to perform IDWT operation and a modified G-plane was produced. In the original image, this plane was replaced and the

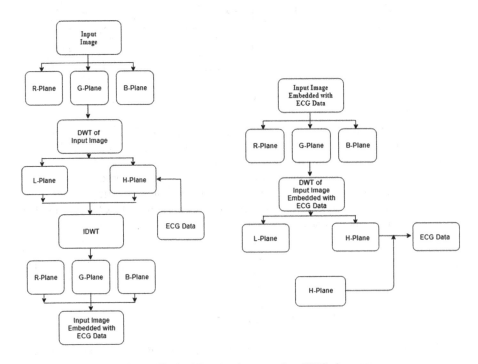

Fig. 4. Embedding and extracting EKG data.

colour image containing the Peaks of EKG information was generated. Block diagram to embed the EKG information peaks is shown below. (Fig. 4).

The colour picture obtained was divided while recovering and the G-plane was divided. On this plane, DWT was conducted and the modified higher frequency component hHH plane was removed. Peaks of EKG information are retrieved by dividing the modified G-plane's coefficients by the original values of hHH. Block diagram below represents the recovery of the Peaks of EKG information (Fig. 4).

2.3 Convolutional Neural Networks(CNNs)

Create EKG signals with time-frequency depictions. These representations are known as scalograms. The absolute value of a signal's CWT coefficients is a scalogram.

Pre-calculate a CWT filter bank for creating the scalograms. The preferred method for obtaining the CWT of many signals using the same parameters is to precompute the CWT filter bank [10]. Load the scalogram images as an image data store. Split the images into two groups at random, one for training and the other for validation. Use 80% of the images for training, and the rest for validation. For reproducibility purposes, we set the default value to the random seed [11].

Load the neuralnetwork pre-trainedby GoogLeNet. Extract the network layer graph and plot the layer graph [12]. Each layer in the network architecture can be considered a filter. The previous layers recognize more prevalent image characteristics like blobs, edges, and colors. In order to distinguish categories, the subsequent layers concentrate on more particular characteristics.

Replace the last four layers of the network to retrain GoogLeNet to our EKG classification problem. pool5-drop 7×7 s1' is a dropout layer, the first of the four layers [12]. With a specified probability, a dropout layer randomly sets input components to zero. To assist avoid over fitting, the dropout layer is used. The default likelihood is 0.5.

Add four new layers to the layer graph: a dropout layer with a 60% dropout probability, a fully connected layer, a softmax layer, and an output classification layer. Set the final fully connected layer to the same size as the new data set's number of classes. In order to learn more quickly in the new layers than in the layers transferred, the learning rate factors of the fully connected layer increase. Store image dimensions of GoogLeNet in inputSize.

Neural network training is an iterative process involving minimizing a loss function. A gradient descent algorithm is used to minimize the loss function. The gradient of the loss function is assessed in each iteration and the weights of the downward algorithm are updated.

Use validation data to evaluate the network. The accuracy is the same as that recorded on the training visualization figure for validation precision. The scalograms were divided into collections for training and validation. To train GoogLeNet, training collections is used. The perfect way to assess the training outcome is to have the information classified by the network that it has not seen. We considered the accuracy of computed validation as the accuracy of the network.

3   Simulation and Results

The EKG data have been embedded in the hHH plane and the image results are as follows.

Scalograms are created using wavelet-based time-frequency representation model of EKG signals. RGB images are produced from the scalograms. Using the images, the profound CNNs are achieved. There was also exploration of activations of distinct network layers. We have divided the image database into two groups, one for training and another one for validation. 80% of the database

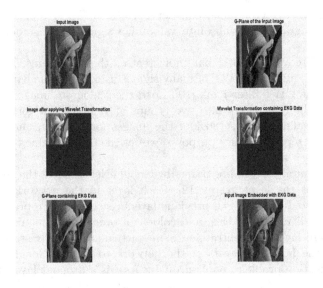

Fig. 5. Encryption of EKG data

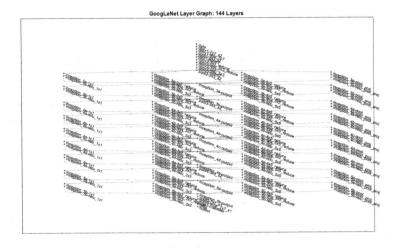

Fig. 6. GoogLeNet layer graph:144 layers

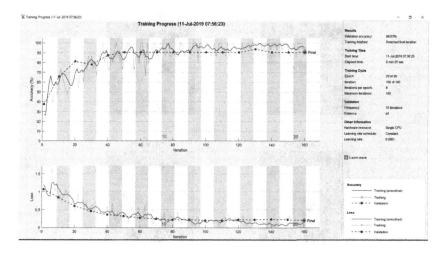

Fig. 7. Training process results

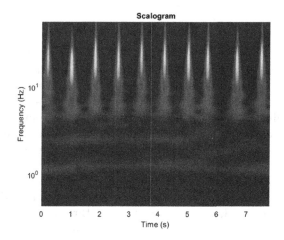

Fig. 8. Scalogram

has been used for training, and the remainder for validation i.e. 130 images for training and 32 images for validation (Figs. 5, 6, 7, 8, 9).

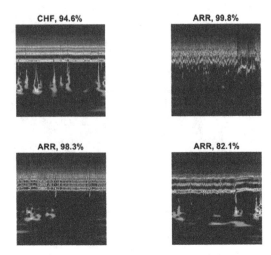

Fig. 9. Sample validation images with expected labels and expected image probabilities.

4   Conclusion

A method of data encryption of EKG signals using wavelet transform is presented. The data for the EKG signal is obtained from physio-net. The wavelet packet decomposition is suggested to decompose the image. The encryption method is introduced to conceal personal information from the patient. Private patient information is integrated within the Image. Encrypted EKG signal is therefore generated by decomposition of the inverse wavelet. The extraction method that distinguishes the image and the EKG signal is then implemented.

The architecture of Deep CNN is then suggested as a methodology for learning features. The proposed CNN network is able to use raw EKG time series signals to acquire and scale down sample features through input vector convolutions with their related weights as well as to determine optimal outputs among nearby neurons.

References

1. https://healthmetrics.heart.org/at-a-glance-heart-disease-and-stroke-statistics-2019/
2. Ibrahim, R., Kuan, TS.: PRIS: image processing tool for dealing with criminal cases using steganography technique. In: 2011 Sixth International Conference on Digital Information Management (ICDIM), pp. 193–198, 26–28 September 2011
3. Liu, T., Pang, C.: Eye-gaze tracking research based on image processing. In: Congress on Image and Signal Processing, CISP 2008, vol. 4, pp. 176–180, 27–30 May 2008

4. Ye, Z., Mohamadian, H., Ye, Y.: Quantitative effects of discrete wavelet transforms and wavelet packets on aerial digital image denoising. In: 2009 6th International Conference on Electrical Engineering, Computing Science and Automatic Control, CCE, pp. 1–5, 10–13 January 2009

5. Hasan, M.M., Singh, S.S.: PAPR analysis of FFT and wavelet based OFDM systems for wireless communications. UITS, Dhaka January 2009

6. Moholkar. S.V., Deshmukh. A.: PAPR analysis of FFT and wavelet based OFDM systems. Int. J. Electron. Commun. Comput. Eng. $5(4)$ (2014). Technovision. ISSN 2249–071X

7. Wang, J.-W., Le, N.T., Wang, C.-C., Lee, J.-S.: Enhanced ridge structure for improving fingerprint image quality based on a wavelet domain. IEEE Signal Process. Lett. $22(4)$, 390–394 (2015)

8. Ali, M., Wook, A.: Comments on optimized gray-scale image watermarking using DWT-SVD and Firefly algorithm. Short Commun. Expert Syst. Appl. 42, 2392–2394 (2015)

9. Tang, H., Tong, D., Dong, B., Dillenseger, J.: A new stationary gridline artifact suppression method based on the 2D discrete wavelet transform. Med. Phys. 42, 1721 (2015). https://doi.org/10.1118/1.4914861

10. Li, T., Zhou, M.: ECG classification using wavelet packet entropy and random forests. Entropy. $18(8)$, 285 (2016)

11. Maharaj, E., Alonso, A.: Discriminant analysis of multivariate time series: application to diagnosis based on ECG signals. Comput. Stat. Data Anal. 70, 67–87 (2014)

12. Russakovsky, O., Deng, J.: Imagenet large scale visual recognition challenge. Int. J. Comput. Vis. $115(3)$, 211–252 (2015)

Ripping the Fabric: Attacks and Mitigations on Hyperledger Fabric

Ahaan Dabholkar[1] and Vishal Saraswat[2]([✉]) [iD]

[1] Department of Computer Science and Engineering, Indian Institute of Technology,
Bhilai, Raipur, India
ahaandabholkar@gmail.com
[2] Robert Bosch Engineering & Business Solutions Pvt. Ltd. (RBEI/ESY),
Bangalore, India
vishal.saraswat@gmail.com

Abstract. In this paper, we take a closer look at the attack surface of permissioned blockchains by focusing on Hyperledger Fabric and present scenarios where the assumptions of trust could lead to possible attacks on an organization's ledger. We systematically examine each participant and treating it as a malicious entity look at the attacks possible on the system as a whole. With the global shift in adopting blockchains as vehicles of trust, a collection of such scenarios would be useful to organizations using Fabric to implement their own Distributed Ledger Technologies (DLT), as it would highlight the possible misuse cases of the platform. It would also help fellow researchers by presenting a primitive idea of the possible attacks and promote further research in preventing them.

Keywords: Blockchain · Hyperledger Fabric · Attacks · Mitigation · Security

1 Prologue: Hyperledger

Hyperledger [8] was announced in December 2015 with the aim of creating an umbrella project to advance cross-industry enterprise-level blockchain technologies. It is an open source global collaborative effort, hosted by The Linux Foundation [17], including leaders in finance, banking, Internet Of Things, supply chains, manufacturing and technology.

In early 2016, it started accepting proposals for incubation of codebases and other technologies as core elements. One of the first accepted proposals was the combined work of Digital Asset [10], Blockstream's libconsensus [6] and IBM's OpenBlockchain [3]. This was later named as *Hyperledger Fabric*. In May 2016, Intel's distributed ledger named Sawtooth [9] was also incubated. In July 2017, the organization announced the release of production ready Hyperledger

The first author carried would like to thank Robert Bosch Engineering & Business Solutions Pvt. Ltd. (RBEI/ESY), Bangalore, where he was a summer intern when this work was carried out.

V. S. Shankar Sriram et al. (Eds.): ATIS 2019, CCIS 1116, pp. 300–311, 2019.
https://doi.org/10.1007/978-981-15-0871-4_24

Fabric 1.0 [4] and the production version of Sawtooth was released in January 2018. Today, Hyperledger Fabric is the most widely used permissioned blockchain platform.

1.1 Attacking Hyperledger Fabric

According to Forbes Blockchain 50 [7], more than 24 of the billion dollar plus companies are building on the Hyperledger Fabric. The Central Bank of Iran has undertaken an ambitious project to revamp its banking system and transform into a digital economy using Fabric [5]. One can cite numerous other such examples, which illustrate the depth to which Fabric has penetrated technology today. And so it is blatantly obvious that the security infrastructure of Fabric has huge consequences that cannot be taken lightly.

In this paper, we analyze and construct attack scenarios for Fabric. We undertake a systematic study of hypothetical attacks on Fabric networks. These attack models take into account the possibility of members of the network getting compromised and describe the extent to which a malicious service can penetrate and harm the network.

Fabric relies on some trusted parties and centralized services to provide a generalized platform for building permissioned blockchains. However, these can be exploited by malicious parties and can lead to attacks that are impractical on a traditional blockchain network. The modular architecture of Hyperledger promotes the use of self serving protocols, however systems built on top of those protocols are then only as secure as the protocols themselves. However this modularity also presents a problem to the attacker as different combinations of protocols need to be exploited in different ways.

1.2 Outline of the Paper

In the following sections, we categorize and describe various attacks and their mitigations on the Fabric.

2 Membership Service Provider Is Compromised

This case deals with the scenario when the Membership Service Provider (MSP) is malicious/is compromised because of a security breach. Since the MSP is the sole authority that is responsible for ID management, a malicious MSP can cause catastrophic damage to the network.

2.1 Sybil Attack

In a *Sybil* attack [2], the attacker subverts the reputation system of a peer-to-peer network by creating a large number of pseudonymous identities and uses them to gain a disproportionately large influence. As the MSP is compromised, an attacker could flood the network with fake identities and use the majority to his advantage.

Consider Org_1's network. Org_1 is a business with a small network infrastructure that has deployed fabric to keep track of their accounts. It enforces a MAJORITY policy for endorsement of transactions. Suppose an attacker A is able to breach security and obtain control of the MSP-admin M.

A then keeps spawning multiple nodes and joins them to the network. He uses M to create trusted certificates for those nodes. He keeps adding nodes to the network until he has a majority and is then able to satisfy the endorsement policy for fraudulent transactions as well.

2.2 Invalid ID Attack

The MSP of an organization identifies the Certificate Authority which issues trusted X.509 certificates to the member nodes. The certificates contain an organizational unit (OU) field that is assigned by the MSP. In case different organizations use the same chain of trust, the OU field is used to identify the members of an organization. Another use of the OU field is to grant channel access.

Suppose Org_1's network has 2 channels C_1 and C_2. And A wants channel access to C_2. A through M easily creates a certificate with the OU set to C_2 and assigns it to a malicious node. A through this node is able to view the ledger and state on C_2, thereby breaking the privacy guarantee of a channel. Some other possible attacks are -

1. Generation of Fraudulent Certificates for genuine peers/competing organizations
2. Invalidating Existing IDs of genuine peers/competing organizations

2.3 Boycott Attacks

Suppose two organizations Org_1 and Org_2 were under the same MSP. If A gained control of MSP-admin M, then he could modify the existing policies and refuse to provide certificates to members of Org_2, hence not letting them connect to the network.

2.4 Blacklisting Attacks

In case of default implementation of the MSP, certain parameters are specified to allow for identity validation. One of these parameters is a list of Certificate Revocation Lists (CRLs), each corresponding to one of the listed MSP Certificate Authorities. These CRLs identify the nodes whose rights to the network have been revoked (including other members of the MSP).

Suppose that the MSP of Org_1 includes two intermediate CAs C_1 and C_2. Attacker A gains access to the MSP, and adds the certificate of C_2 to the CRL. This causes the authority of C_2 to be revoked. A could also configure the MSP to remove the certificate of C_2 from the trusted list of Intermediate CA certificates. This would also have a similar effect.

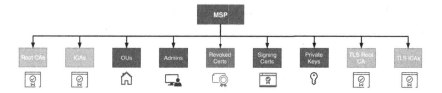

Fig. 1. Local MSP structure

3 Malicious Ordering Service

The Ordering Service of a Fabric network is solely responsible for consensus on generated blocks in the blockchain. Unlike Bitcoin and Ethereum which rely on probabilistic consensus protocols, Fabric's consensus protocol is deterministic. The direct implication of using such protocols is that the blocks generated by the OS are guaranteed to be **final and correct**.

3.1 Sabotage Attacks

Ordering Service Nodes (OSN) are responsible for collecting transactions and consolidating them into blocks. Suppose the OSN, O wants to cause damage to organization Org_a. Suppose P_i^a are the nodes belonging to Org_a. During block consolidation, O does not include transactions from P_i^a. This would effectively incapacitate Org_a.

3.2 Intentional Fork Attacks

The Ordering Service creates a block by consolidating transactions which is considered to be final and correct. But a malicious Ordering Service O could send out different versions of the blocks in response to the broadcast and deliver requests thus corrupting the network. Suppose O is connected to two peers (leaders) P_1 and P_2. P_1 and P_2 both request blocks from O. O creates two blocks B_1 and B_2 and delivers them to P_1 and P_2 respectively. During Gossip, members having B_1 would reject the others blocks and vice versa.

3.3 Block Size Attack

The Ordering Service is also responsible for setting the Channel Configurations. The configurations are stored on the ledger in a `config-block`. Each time the configuration changes, a new `config-block` must be published to the ledger. The latest `config-block` is pulled and kept in memory for fast and efficient operations. Suppose O is a malicious OS-admin. O changes the value of Batch Size to an extremely small/extremely large value. Batch Size defines the number of transactions to include before cutting the block. If the value is very large, then the block will never get published as the number of transactions required is very high. If it is too low then, there would be an impractical number of blocks in the blockchain. Both the attacks would decrease the efficiency of the network. Also since O is an OS-admin, his signature is sufficient for the transaction to be accepted.

3.4 Batch Time Attack

A similar attack can be mounted on the *Batch Timeout* which is the amount of time to wait after the first transaction arrives for additional transactions before cutting a block. Decreasing this value will improve latency, but decreasing it too much may decrease throughput by not allowing the block to fill to its maximum capacity.

O can decrease the timeout to harm the throughput of the network. O can also set this to an extremely large number, so that for future blocks the OS keeps waiting for an infinite amount of time before cutting the block.

3.5 Block Withholding Attacks

Orderers could withhold blocks and manipulate the release of certain blocks which would favour them. This would seem like perfectly normal behaviour and the rest of the network would be ignorant to the intent of the node.

3.6 Transaction Reordering Attack

The OS is responsible for ordering the transactions into blocks. The order in which the transactions are included is considered final and hence is not verified again. Suppose the network was playing a game, where a poorly written chaincode promised to pay the node who solved a puzzle first. In time P_1 solves the puzzle and after some time so does P_2. Both submit their transactions to the ordered O, the orderer however sympathizes with P_2 and hence puts his transactions before P_1's transaction. O then broadcasts the block for validation. The validating peers accept P_2 as the winner and validate his transaction. P_1's transaction is marked as a double spend, invalid.

4 Malicious Validating Nodes

It is the job of the validating nodes to finally validate the transactions according to the Validating System Chaincode, and then after some additional tests update the ledger and the state. A possible attack would be -

4.1 Double Spend Attack

Validating Nodes check the version numbers of the *readset* fields and the current fields for equality. If they are different then, it is equivalent to a double spend. Malicious Validating nodes could thus authorise double spends and append them to the ledger thus breaking its integrity.

4.2 DDoS Attack

DDoS (Distributed Denial of Service) is an attack where the attacker tries to make a common-service unavailable to users by making malicious queries from multiple machines such that the server (which is hosting the service) is over-whelmed by the number of requests and is unable to process them. Blockchain networks are inherently DDoS tolerant as they are distributed. That is, they have built in redundancy. By centralizing the Ordering Service, Fabric becomes somewhat prone to DDoS attacks. To mitigate this issue to a certain degree, OS uses CFT protocols such as Kafka, Raft etc.

A Possible DDoS attack is described below - Validating peers can call the `fetch` function to fetch blocks from the OS. If the blockchain network has a large number of peers, there is a possibility of overwhelming the OS through constant fetch requests.

5 External Attacks

One of blockchains biggest strengths was that it was purely decentralized. How-ever in Fabric, introducing certain amount of centralization was necessary to provide a generalized platform. This re-injection of points of control, and thus points of vulnerability, into blockchains, for example, through 'permissioning' nullifies their main benefits, which come from removing points of vulnerabil-ity [13].

Focusing on the attacks, the MSP admins, the OSNs are all centralized ser-vices on a decentralized platform and are hence vulnerable to -

1. DoS attacks
2. Crash Faults
3. Man in the Middle Attacks

5.1 Collusion

If some of the participating entities in the network collude, they could effec-tively launch an *alternative history attack* which would enable them to rewrite the ledger in their favour. Since in a permissioned blockchain, not everyone is authorized to join and the number of participating nodes is very small compared to permissionless blockchains, collusion is easier and a much more realiztic sce-nario, than in, say Bitcoin.

5.2 Interface Attacks

Each DApp will have a client side interface to receive input data and to enable clients to invoke transactions on the fabric. Web applications being cross-platform compatible are generally used for this purpose. Keeping in mind that blockchains are platforms to generate trust among mutually untrustworthy peers, transactions generally involve confidential data being passed as input. Carelessly built interfaces can leak data. In case of web-apps let's consider an example -

SSL Stripping. SSL Stripping [12] is a MITM attack in which the attacker dupes the client into communicating over an insecure HTTP protocol thereby intercepting all data as plaintext. The attack works as follows -

1. An attacker A intercepts the traffic between the client C and the server S.
2. C wants to login to his bank account which is being hosted on S. So he sends an HTTPS (encrypted) request to S asking for the certificate and supplies his own certificate.
3. A intercepts this request and replaces C's certificate with his own.
4. A intercepts the response from S and relays the certificate to C but makes a small change. He replaces the HTTPS content with HTTP content signalling to C that he will communicate over HTTP only.
5. Thus C now communicates the login information with A in cleartext. On getting the packets, A opens them and inspects their contents after which he encrypts and forwards them to S.
6. The response is similarly decrypted and provided to C.

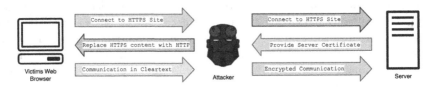

Fig. 2. SSL stripping [15]

5.3 Malicious Clients

Client nodes submit endorsed transactions to the OS for block creation. The OS O by default does not cross-check the transactions against the endorsement policy of that chaincode. (That is a job for the Validation peers). A malicious client C could use this fact to his advantage. C initiates the attack by keeps sending a constant stream of unendorsed transactions to O. O receives the transactions and performs channel access level checks. Since C has write access to the ledger, O packs the invalid transactions into blocks and sends them to the validating nodes. Even though the validating nodes mark the transactions as invalid, they are still included into the blockchain. This pollutes the blockchain and can increases it's size by a large amount.

6 Protocol Based Attacks

One of the unique features about Hyperledger Fabric is the ability to plug and play consensus protocols, depending upon the application. Each protocol has its own advantages and flaws.

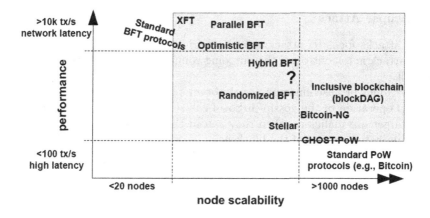

Fig. 3. Protocol comparison graph [18]

6.1   CFT v/s BFT v/s PoW Protocols [18]

CFT (Crash Fault Tolerant) protocols are highly efficient protocols for creating consensus among the ordering nodes. They are crash tolerant, that is, if the leader node crashes, the system can recover and function just as efficiently without data loss.

Fabric offers CFT protocols such as Kafka (based on Zookeeper), Raft, etc. as consensus protocols for the OS. However, CFT protocols (mentioned above) are vulnerable to Byzantine nodes. Even a single malicious node can effectively prevent the network from reaching a consensus.

BFT (Byzantine Fault Tolerant) protocols on the other hand can handle Byzantine nodes to a certain degree (generally 33%). These protocols are required when the members of the network are untrustworthy. However, these protocols do not scale very well and as the number of nodes increase, the throughput decreases dramatically. They are energy efficient, perform well when the number of clients in large, and satisfy consensus finality.

PoW (Proof of Work) is the consensus protocol that is used by Bitcoin and Ethereum in their networks. This protocol is highly scalable with thousands of competing peers and is completely decentralized. The drawbacks of PoW are that it does not guarantee consensus finality, has very high power consumption and has very low throughput.

6.2   Gossip Protocol

Gossip protocol comes into the picture when the orderer delivers the blocks to the peers. Instead of broadcasting the block to several peers, the OS sends the new blocks to only the "leader peers" of the organization. The leader peer then spreads the block to other peers using *gossip*. This system is vulnerable to an eclipse attack.

6.3   Eclipse Attack

Eclipse attacks focus on attacking an individual node in the network. The aim of this attack is to control all the outgoing connections of the target in order to isolate it.

New Nodes or Disconnected nodes obtain an updated copy of the ledger by using an operation of the gossip protocol called pull. If all the connected nodes of the target are malicious, then they can in theory dupe the target by giving him a fabricated version of the blockchain.

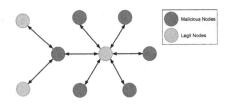

Fig. 4. Eclipse attack

7   Chaincode Vulnerabilities

Fabric was built with the vision of not being constrained to a platform specific language like Bitcoin's Script or Ethereum's Solidity, but to be able to deploy smart contracts written in general purpose languages. As a result fabric contracts called "chaincodes" can be written in languages like Go, NodeJS etc. With such languages that can induce side-effects in the system, improper partitioning of the network and lax access-control can lead to crippling attacks. Possible Vulnerabilities are

1. Unrestricted Chaincode Containers
2. Non-deterministic Chaincodes can cause consensus to fail
3. Halting problem
4. Low level access could be used to corrupt the stack
5. Lack of Input validation

Chaincode invocations are generally requested by clients through web interfaces or the front-end. However by directly executing commands on the Fabric, an attacker can bypass the authorisation controls implemented in the application's interface [14]. These attacks are possible because chaincodes have no inherent access controls built in. Authorisation has to be explicitly coded, which is often overlooked as there is too much reliance on the interfaces authorisation controls.

Since chaincodes often need private data to take as input, unauthorised execution could lead to leaks of personal data, which is catastrophic.

8   Implementation/Architectural Attacks

Since Fabric makes use of other open-source software to provide its services (Docker, gRPC, Apache Kafka), it inherits their flaws and vulnerabilities as well. Thus developers need to keep that in mind while developing their Apps as well. Further, Fabric gives an organization the flexibility to define its own Access-Control, Membership, Validation, Consensus policies. Properly defined policies are a huge deterrent to external attacks. However, more often than not substandard implementations become victims of basic attacks etc. Most developers copy-paste previously written example-code from GitHub, StackOverflow, Company Codebases etc. to save time and effort [11]. Even though this practice increases their efficiency, it propagates errors in the exisiting code leaving the system wide open to a variety of attacks.

We describe two attacks to illustrate each point of failure. The TOCTOU bug attack Sect. 8.1 is an architectural attack while the CouchDB attack Sect. 8.2 is a consequence of using default Access Control settings.

8.1   Docker TOCTOU Bug

Chaincodes are executed in secure docker containers on the peer systems that they are installed on. Chaincodes are instantiated on a particular channel. Since each channel is logically a private subnet, the instantiated chaincode is localised to that channel only.

The docker TOCTOU bug in docker could give an attacker `read/write` access as root to the host system with a cleverly written chaincode and access to `docker cp` command. The **TOCTOU** (Time of Check to Time of Use) attack [19] on Docker containers takes advantage of the fact that the path resolution while using `docker cp` is not atomic in nature. That is, there is a small window between the time the target path is resolved and the time that it is used. If an attacker can add a symlink component to the path after the resolution but before it is operated on, then the system could end up navigating to the host as root [16].

So, if a host system is running `docker cp` command with a compromised docker container then an attacker A can copy protected private-key files on the host and even mount a write attack on the peer to overwrite `config` files and private key files. Essentially, A could corrupt the whole system.

8.2   CouchDB Vulnerability

As with most software implementations, many implementations rely on default codebases and improperly configured access controls. Fabric networks are no different and hence many attack scenarios, including the following which was demonstrated on an example code from IBM Code Patterns at Defcon [14], are highly possible.

Each peer in the Fabric Network contains a summary of the current state of the blockchain (called the "world state") stored in a database management system (LevelDB or CouchDB) as a **Key-Value Store**. The peers use this store for validation and to track the actual state of the blockchain. So if an attacker can modify the database without invoking a chaincode, he can change the peer's view of the blockchain anonymously.

Apache CouchDB [1] is a database management system which follows a schema free document storage model that is optimised for modularisation and scalability. It is used extensively in Fabric based projects because it speaks JSON natively and supports binary data storage securely. CouchDB provides a convenient web-interface to access the database which by default is **not** password protected. So if an attacker A connects to a peer P, he can access and change P's state from the web-interface itself.

9 Conclusion

Fabric is the most popular permissioned blockchain platform today. With heavy investment worth more than a 100 million dollars, from the major tech companies such as Intel, Cisco, IBM etc. as well as major financial organizations like JP Morgan, Deutsche Bank etc., it is clear that this technology is garnering a lot of attention both good and bad. Whether this technology is here to stay or whether it is a passing fad like the Intranet is yet unclear, but permissioned blockchains are a reality atleast for the time being. At the time of writing this paper not much published research has been done in the area of finding architectural flaws in the platform and the possible attack scenarios, hence by bringing it to light we hope to inspire more focused research into the attack scenarios discussed above.

References

1. Apache CouchDB. http://couchdb.apache.org/
2. Sybil Attack. https://en.wikipedia.org/wiki/Sybil_attack
3. Open Blockchain (2016). https://developer.ibm.com/open/projects/open-blockchain/
4. Androulaki, E., et al.: Hyperledger fabric: a distributed operating system for permissioned blockchains. In: EuroSys, pp. 30:1–30:15. ACM (2018)
5. Avan-Nomayo, O.: Iran developing national blockchain platform on hyperledger fabric (2019). https://cointelegraph.com/news/iran-developing-national-blockchain-platform-on-ibm-hyperledger-fabric
6. Back, A.: Blockstream (2014). https://blockstream.com/
7. del Castillo, M.: Blockchain 50: billion dollar babies (2019). https://www.forbes.com/sites/michaeldelcastillo/2019/04/16/blockchain-50-billion-dollar-babies/#39a73cc657cc
8. Hyperledger: Hyperledger.org. https://www.hyperledger.org/
9. Intel: Sawtooth (2016). https://www.hyperledger.org/projects/sawtooth
10. Kfir, S., Rooz, Y., Saraniecki, E.: Digital asset (2014). https://digitalasset.com/
11. Li, Z., Lu, S., Myagmar, S., Zhou, Y.: CP-Miner: finding copy-paste and related bugs in large-scale software code. IEEE Trans. Softw. Eng. **32**(3), 176–192 (2006)
12. Marlinspike, M.: sslstrip. https://moxie.org/software/sslstrip/

13. Potter, J.: The unfortunate rise of permissioned blockchains (2018). https://blog.xtrabytes.global/technology/the-unfortunate-rise-of-permission-blockchains/
14. Riedesel, S., Hakimian, P., Buyens, K., Biehn, T.: Tineola: taking a bite out of enterprise blockchain (2018). https://github.com/tineola/tineola/raw/master/docs/TineolaWhitepaper.pdf
15. Sanders, C.: SSL stripping. http://techgenix.com/understanding-man-in-the-middle-attacks-arp-part4/
16. Sarai, A.: Bugzilla bug report: CVE-2018-15664. https://bugzilla.redhat.com/show_bug.cgi?id=1714722 (2019)
17. Torvalds, L.: The Linux foundation. https://www.linuxfoundation.org/
18. Vukolić, M.: The quest for scalable blockchain fabric: proof-of-work vs. BFT replication. In: Camenisch, J., Kesdoğan, D. (eds.) iNetSec 2015. LNCS, vol. 9591, pp. 112–125. Springer, Cham (2016). https://doi.org/10.1007/978-3-319-39028-4_9
19. Wei, J., Pu, C.: TOCTTOU vulnerabilities in UNIX-style file systems: an anatomical study. In: FAST. USENIX (2005)

Author Index

Printed in the United States
By Bookmasters